101 Things For Kids™ in Las Vegas

A Complete Family Guide

Written by Carol Stout

Cover by Ed Robinson

101 Things Publishing
Indianapolis, Indiana

acknowledgments

ISBN # 1-886161-20-8
Library of Congress Catalog Card # 99-90069
First Edition
Manufactured in the USA

101 Things For Kids™
in
Las Vegas
A Complete Family Guide

Address changes or corrections for future editions, as well as inquiries regarding purchase and discounts for bulk purchases, should be addressed to:

Journey Publications
2920 Kingman Street, Suite 202
Metairie, Louisiana 70006
504-454-7702

Publisher/Author	Carol Anne Stout
Contributing Writers	Kathy Foley, Annie K. Wood
Photography	Dana Wright
Cover Illustration	Ed Robinson
Distribution / Marketing	Journey Publications
Layout and Design	Shelly Wells
Book Manufacturing	Diversified Business Systems
Public Relations	Christa Dickey, Avatar Communications
Great Kid Models	Dustin Sprague, Andrew Sprague, Jeremy Sprague and Whitney and Shelby Damron

Find us on-line at http://www.101thingsforkids.com

contents

2 Acknowledgments

5 Contacts

6 Introduction
- 6   About Las Vegas
- 7   Highway Map
- 8   Important City Phone Numbers

6 Chapter One
Getting Around
- 10   Las Vegas Street Map
- 11   Airlines & Charter Services
- 11   Amtrak & Greyhound
- 13   McCarran International Airport
- 14   Car Rental Companies
- 18   Limousine Services
- 19   Taxicab Companies
- 20   CAT Information

23 Chapter Two
Culture
- 24   Performing Arts, Dance, Music and Theater
- 26   Museums
- 43   Art Museums and Galleries

44 Chapter Three
Things to Do and See
- 45   Things to Do
- 88   Entertainment, Magic, Shows & Theaters
- 96   Book Stores & Libraries
- 99   Sports & Recreation
- 115   Parks & Playgrounds
- 124   Shopping

127 Chapter Four
Outdoor Adventure
- 128   State & National Parks
- 132   Hiking & Rock Climbing
- 136   Horseback Riding
- 137   Water Activities
- 139   Tours and Excursions

contents

141 Chapter Five
Restaurants and Hotels

136   Hotels Offering Kid's Deals
142   Kid Friendly Restaurants
152   Area Kid Friendly Hotels
170   Campgrounds & RV Parks

172 Chapter Six
Parents Survival Guide

173   Places for Kid Parties
175   Party Performers

178 Chapter Seven
Medical Guide

179   First Aid Tips
180   Emergency Clinics
181   Area Hospitals

183 Chapter Eight
**Complete Directory
from A to Z**

184   Directory
231   Index
238   Order Forms

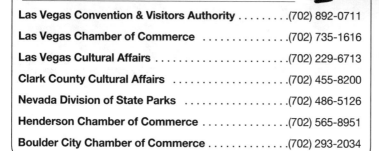

For additional information and schedules for events, fairs and festivals call:

Las Vegas Convention & Visitors Authority . . . .(702) 892-0711

Las Vegas Chamber of Commerce . . . .(702) 735-1616

Las Vegas Cultural Affairs . . . .(702) 229-6713

Clark County Cultural Affairs . . . .(702) 455-8200

Nevada Division of State Parks . . . .(702) 486-5126

Henderson Chamber of Commerce . . . .(702) 565-8951

Boulder City Chamber of Commerce . . . .(702) 293-2034

Las Vegas Websites:

There are literally thousands of websites for Las Vegas. Here are some of the more complete sites.

- www.lasvegas.com
- www.pcap.com/lasvegas.htm
- **Tourist Bureau of Las Vegas Home Page**
  golasvegas.cc
- www.vacationweb.com/lasvegas
- www.lvol.com
- www.vegas.com
- **City of Las Vegas Home Page**
  www.ci.las-vegas-nv.us
- www.ilv.com
- www.lvindex.com
- **Las Vegas Convention & Visitors Authority Home Page**
  www.lasvegas24hours.com

Nevada means "snow capped" in Spanish. Nevada is 110,540 square miles, 485 miles long, 315 miles wide and is the seventh largest state in the US. Las Vegas was founded in 1905. The name Las Vegas means "the meadows" in Spanish. Las Vegas covers a little over 84 square miles. It is the fastest growing city in the United States, will soon become the largest convention city in the world with over 100,000 hotel rooms available, and is simultaneously becoming a prominent family vacation destination.

Las Vegas Curfew Laws

Children under eighteen years of age are barred from Las Vegas area arcades between 10:00 p.m. and 5:00 a.m. weekdays and from midnight to 5:00 a.m. on weekends. The law also requires that security guards be posted in arcades that have a minimum of 20¢-operated machines, and that other security measures, such as surveillance cameras, be used to monitor areas with fewer machines. The new law also establishes guidelines for training guards on how to spot potential pedophiles and child stalkers.

Weather

An average of 310 sunny days allows for year-round use of most Las Vegas swimming pools. While the water can be quite chilly during the winter months, sunbathing around the beautifully landscaped pools is possible almost every day.

With an average rainfall of 4.19 inches, Las Vegas has a dry climate. Umbrellas are rarely needed, but there is an occasional flash flood.

Although the temperature can soar to well over 100° during the summer months, the average annual temperature is 66.3°. At a 2,174-ft. elevation, Las Vegas' nights are comfortably cooler, even after the hottest days, with a pleasant, dry climate during the winter, and the average temperature at 47.5°.

Average Highs & Lows	
January - March	63° to 39°
April - June	89° to 60°
July - September	101° to 72°
October - December	71° to 44°

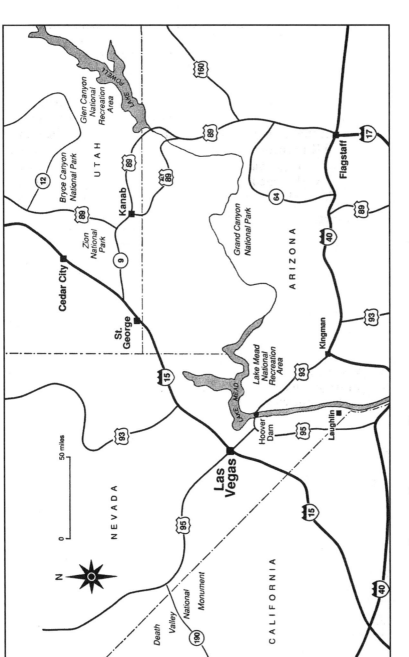

highway map

Important City Phone Numbers

(All Numbers are in the 702 Area Code)

Emergency 911
Clark County Switchboard . . . .(702) 455-4011
Air Ambulance America (airport) . . . .(800) 262-8526
Ambulance Emergency . . . . (702) 384-3400
Desert Rescue . . . .(702) 641-3749
Respiratory Support . . . .(702) 733-7370
Poison Information Center . . . .(702) 732-4989
Highway Patrol . . . .(702) 385-0311
Road Condition . . . .(702) 486-3116
Tourist Information . . . .(702) 892-7575
Weather . . . .(702) 736-3854
Mayor's office . . . .(702) 229-6241
Clark County Sheriff's Office (non emergency) . . . .(702) 229-3394
Metro (non emergency) . . . .(702) 795-3111
Fire Department . . . .(702) 383-2888
Parks & Leisure Activities . . . .(702) 229-6297
Cooperative Extension, 4-H youth programs . . . .(702) 731-3130

Local Connection - Las Vegas

Hot Lines
Suicide Prevention Center of Clark Country . . . .(702) 731-2990
Rape Crisis Center Hot Line . . . .(702) 366-1640
TDD . . . .(702) 385-2952
Domestic Crisis Shelter . . . .(702) 646-4981
Information and Referral HELP of Southern Nevada . . . . . . (702) 369-4357
Juvenile Court Services Abuse and Neglect Hot Line . . . . . (702) 399-0081
Crisis Mental Health Unit . . . .(702) 486-8020
Youth Runaway Emergency Shelter . . . .(702) 385-3330

Utility Companies

Central Telephone Co. . . . . (702) 244-7400
Nevada Power Co. . . . . (702) 367-5555
Southwest Gas Corporation . . . . (702) 365-1555
Las Vegas Valley Water District . . . .(702) 870-4194
Silver State Disposal Service . . . . (702) 735-5151
Henderson Water Department . . . . (702) 565-2110
Prime Cable of Las Vegas . . . . (702) 383-4000

Government and Community Agencies

Department of Motor Vehicles . . . . (702) 486-4368
Las Vegas City Hall . . . . (702) 229-6011
Clark County - main switchboard . . . . (702) 455-4011
Clark County School District . . . . (702) 799-5011

Getting
Around

chapter one

- Las Vegas Street Map
- Amtrak and Greyhound
- Airlines & Charter Services
- McCarran International
- Airport Map
- Car Rental Companies
- Limousine Services
- Taxicab Companies
- CAT Information
- Hotel Shuttle Service

getting there

Street Map: The Strip

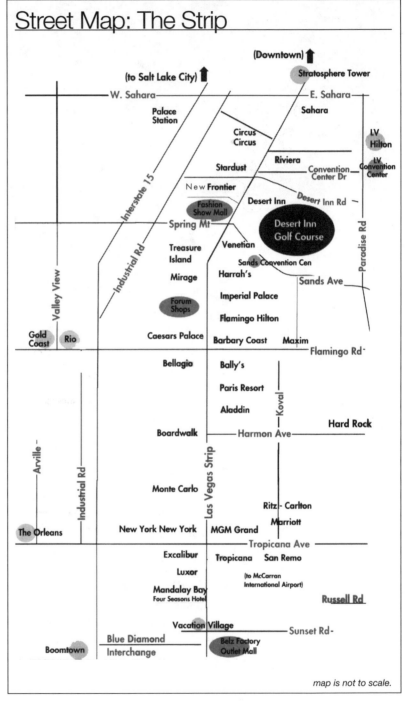

(Downtown) ↑

Stratosphere Tower

(to Salt Lake City) ↑

W. Sahara — E. Sahara

Palace Station

Sahara

LV Hilton

Circus Circus

Riviera

LV Convention Center

Stardust

Convention Center Dr

New Frontier

Desert Inn

Desert Inn Rd

Fashion Show Mall

Spring Mt

Desert Inn Golf Course

Interstate 15

Industrial Rd

Venetian

Treasure Island

Sands Convention Cen

Mirage

Harrah's

Sands Ave

Paradise Rd

Forum Shops

Imperial Palace

Valley View

Flamingo Hilton

Gold Coast

Rio

Caesars Palace

Barbary Coast

Maxim

Flamingo Rd

Bellagio

Bally's

Paris Resort

Aladdin

Koval

Boardwalk

Harmon Ave

Hard Rock

Arville

Industrial Rd

Monte Carlo

Las Vegas Strip

Ritz - Carlton

Marriott

The Orleans

New York New York

MGM Grand

Tropicana Ave

Excalibur

Tropicana

San Remo

Luxor

(to McCarran International Airport)

Mandalay Bay
Four Seasons Hotel

Russell Rd

Vacation Village

Sunset Rd

Blue Diamond

Belz Factory Outlet Mall

Boomtown

Interchange

map is not to scale.

By Train

Amtrak
The train makes two stops a day on its "Desert Wind" run between Los Angeles and Salt Lake City. The depot is adjacent to the Union Plaza Hotel downtown.

1 Main Street Las Vegas

(800) 872-7245

By Bus

Greyhound Bus Lines
The Bus Terminal is adjacent to the Union Plaza Hotel downtown.

200 S. Main St. Las Vegas

(800) 231-2222

By Plane

Major Airlines

Aerolineas Argentinas	(800) 333-0276
Air Canada	(800) 776-3000
Alaska Airlines	(800) 426-0333
American Airlines	(800) 433-7300
American Trans Air	(800) 435-9282
American West Airlines	(800) 235-9292
British Airways	(800) 247-9297
Canada 3000	(800) 998-7958
Canadian Airlines	(800) 426-7000
China Airlines	(800) 227-5118
Condor German Airlines	(800) 524-6975
Continental Airlines	(800) 523-3273
Delta Airlines	(800) 221-1212
Finnnair	(800) 950-5000
Frontier Airlines	(800) 432-1359
Hawaiian Airlines	(800) 367-5320
Japan Airlines	(800) 525-3663
KLM Airlines	(800) 374-7747
Korean Air	(800) 438-5000
Lacasa Airlines	(800) 225-2272
Lufthansa	(800) 645-3880
Mexicana Airlines	(800) 531-7921
Midway Airlines	(800) 650-7844
Midwest Express	(800) 452-2022
Northwest Airlines	(800) 225-2525
Quantas Airways	(800) 227-4500
Reno Air	(800) RENO-AIR
Scenic Airlines	(800) 634-6801
Singapore Airlines	(800) 742-3333

continued on page 12

getting there

Skywest-Delta Connection . . . .(800) 453-9417
Southwest Airlines . . . . (800) 435-9792
Taca Airlines . . . .(800) 535-8780
Trans World Airlines . . . .(800) 892-1976
USAir . . . .(800) 428-4322
United Airlines . . . . (800) 241-6522
Western Pacific Airlines . . . .(800) 930-3030

Charter Services
A Lake Mead Air . . . .(702) 293-1848
Aeroexo . . . .(702) 261-3214
Air Nevada . . . .(702) 736-8900
Eagle Canyon Airlines . . . .(800) 293-2453
Grand Canyon Flights . . . .(702) 293-1848
Kanyon Air . . . .(702) 294-7708
King Air . . . .(702) 361-7811
Lake Powell Air Service . . . .(702) 739-5774
Las Vegas Airlines . . . .(702) 647-3056
Pacific State . . . .(702) 261-3546
Tristar Airlines . . . .(702) 732-8400

McCarran International Airport
Wayne Newton Boulevard
Las Vegas, NV 89119

General Information . . . .(702) 261-5743
Paging . . . .(702) 261-5733
TDD . . . .(702) 261-3111
Administration . . . .(702) 261-5211
Parking Information . . . .(702) 261-5121
McCarran Construction Hotline . . . .(702) 261-5555

Airport Map

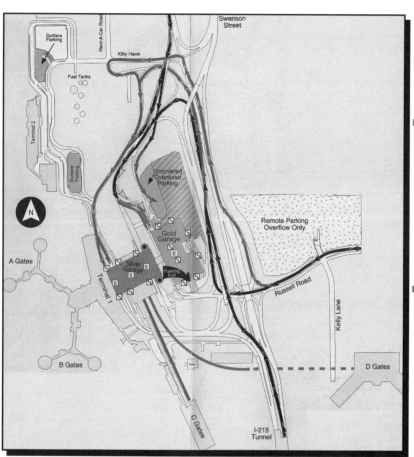

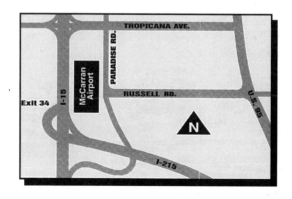

By Car

Car Rental Companies

A B S Rent-A-Car
3100 W. Sahara Ave. #110 Las Vegas . . . .(702) 368-4061

A-Fairway Rent-A-Car
2915 Industrial Rd., Las Vegas . . . .(702) 369-7216

AA Auto Rentals
Las Vegas . . . .(702) 893-1333

Abck Latino Rent-A-Car
Las Vegas . . . .(702) 649-5501

Abbey Rent-A-Car
4990 Paradise Rd., Las Vegas . . . .(702) 736-4988

Advantage Rent-A-Car
Las Vegas . . . .(702) 386-5775
Agency Car Rental Las Vegas . . . .(702) 457-9538

Airport Rent-A-Car . . . .(800) 631-8909
3769 Las Vegas Blvd. S., Las Vegas . . . .(702) 795-0800
3325 Las Vegas Blvd. S., Las Vegas . . . .(702) 732-4232
4990 Paradise Rd., Las Vegas . . . .(702) 795-0800

Airways Rent-A-Car
Las Vegas . . . .(702) 798-6100

Alamo Rent-A-Car . . . .(800) 327-9633
Las Vegas . . . .(702) 263-3030

Allstate Car Rental . . . .(800) 634-6186
5175 Rent-A-Car Lane, Las Vegas . . . .(702) 736-6147
1835 E. Sahara Ave., Las Vegas . . . .(702) 792-9200

Union Plaza Hotel	(702) 382-2918
Avis Rent-A-Car	(800) 831-2847
5164 Rent A Car Lane, Las Vegas	(702) 261-5595
4760 W. Sahara Ave, Suite 26 Las Vegas	(702) 258-3400
3123 N Rainbow Blvd., Las Vegas	(702) 396-7785
East Las Vegas	(702) 641-7220
Bally's Hotel	(702) 736-1935
Caesar's Palace	(702) 731-7790
Las Vegas Hilton	(702) 734-8011
Brooks Rent-A-Car	(800) 634-6721
Las Vegas	(702) 735-3344
Budget Rent-A-Car	(800) 527-0770
5188 Paradise Rd., Las Vegas	(702) 736-1212
TDD	(800) 826-5510
Four Queens Hotel	(702) 474-6060
2830 Las Vegas Blvd S., Las Vegas	(702) 731-6776
2000 Las Vegas Blvd S., Las Vegas	(702) 383-5307
2955 Las Vegas Blvd S., Las Vegas	(702) 737-0295
3267 Las Vegas Blvd S., Las Vegas	(702) 796-6107
3235 Las Vegas Blvd S., Las Vegas	(702) 732-9108
3743 Las Vegas Blvd S., Las Vegas	(702) 796-6107
3712 Las Vegas Blvd S., Las Vegas	(702) 262-2221
4475 W. Tropicana Ave., Las Vegas	(702) 736-1212
Budget Truck Rental	
4475 W. Tropicana Ave., Las Vegas	(702) 362-8668
Car Rental of Vegas	(800) 882-6811
Classic Car Rentals	
5021 Swenson Ave., Las Vegas	(702) 736-2592
Classy Chassis Motor Co.	
3720 S. Valley View Blvd., Las Vegas	(702) 736-2592
Corvette Rentals	
5021 Swenson Ave., Las Vegas	(702) 736-2592
Convertible Rentals	(702) 731-3600
Desert Rent-A-Car	
6005 Las Vegas Blvd. S., Las Vegas	(702) 739-1121
Dollar Rent-A-Car	(800) 800-4000
5301 Rent A Car Rd., Las Vegas	(702) 739-8408
Circus Circus	(702) 369-9302
Monte Carlo	(702) 730-7974
Flamingo Hilton	(702) 732-4180
Excalibur	(702) 736-1369
Luxor	(702) 730-5988
MGM Grand	(702) 891-3012

continued on page 16

getting there

Mirage	.(702) 791-7425
New York, New York	.(702) 740-6415
Treasure Island	.(702) 737-1081
Golden Nugget	.(702) 383-8552
3555 Las Vegas Blvd. S., Las Vegas	.(702) 732-4180
\3801 Las Vegas Blvd. S., Las Vegas	.(702) 739-0196
Enterprise Rent-A-Car	.(800) 736-8222
5032 Palo Verde Dr., Las Vegas	.(702) 795-8842
2333 S. Decatur Blvd., Las Vegas	.(702) 362-2053
5800 W. Sahara Ave., Las Vegas	.(702) 368-6972
3200 S. Rancho Dr., Las Vegas	.(702) 365-6662
5185 W. Sahara Ave., Las Vegas	.(702) 873-5470
2580 S. Duneville #108, Las Vegas	.(702) 368-3772
Holiday Inn Boardwalk	.(702) 734-3977
4950 Alta Dr., Las Vegas	.(702) 870-4144
2575 E. Sahara Ave., Las Vegas	.(702) 641-1078
2121 E. Sahara Ave., Las Vegas	.(702) 735-2124
2711 E. Sahara Ave., Las Vegas	.(702) 431-0884
3470 Boulder Hwy. Las Vegas	.(702) 457-0990
3421 Boulder Hwy, Suite D, Las Vegas	.(702) 457-0066
6900 W. Sahara Ave., Las Vegas	.(702) 242-3277
4645 W. Tropicana, Las Vegas	.(702) 597-2515
280 N. Gibson Rd., Las Vegas	.(702) 558-4160
660 N. Decatur, Las Vegas	.(702) 564-8217
3024 E. Fremont, Las Vegas	.(702) 457-3288
4435 Las Vegas Blvd. N., Las Vegas	.(702) 643-3605
Express Rent-A-Car	
3200 S. Rancho Dr., Las Vegas	.(702) 795-4008
Hertz Rent-A-Car	.(800) 654-3131
TDD	.(800) 654-2280
McCarran Airport	.(702) 736-4900
Desert Inn	.(702) 735-4597
Ladki Car Rental	.(800) 245-2354
795 E. Tropicana Ave., Las Vegas	.(702) 597-1100
North Strip Area	.(702) 362-8993
Downtown Office	.(702) 387-2004
Mesquite Office	.(702) 346-5232
Lloyd's	.(800) 654-7037
3951 Las Vegas Blvd. S., Las Vegas	.(702) 736-2663
Luxury Classic & Sports Car Rental	
3939 Las Vegas Blvd. S., Las Vegas	.(702) 736-2610
Motorcycle Rentals	.(702) 798-7774
National Car Rental	.(800) 227-7368
5233 Rent-A-Car Rd., Las Vegas	.(702) 261-5391

Practical Rent-A-Car	(800) 722-7029
3765 Las Vegas Blvd. S., Las Vegas	(702) 798-5253
Preferred Rent-A-Car	(800) 627-4654
700 E. Naples Dr., Suite 101, Las Vegas	(702) 894-9936
Rebel Rent-A-Car	
5021 Swenson St., Las Vegas	(702) 597-0427
Reddicar Corp.	
5301 Rent A Car Rd., Las Vegas	(702) 739-8408
Rent-A-Vette	
5021 Swenson St., Las Vegas	(702) 736-2592
Rent-A-Wreck	
2310 Las Vegas Blvd. S., Las Vegas	(702) 474-0037
Resort Rent-A-Car	(800) 289-5343
5080 Paradise Rd., Las Vegas	(702) 795-3800
Sav-More Rent-A-Car	
5101 Rent Car Rd., Las Vegas	(702) 736-1234
Sears Car and Truck Rental	(800) 527-0770
4475 W. Tropicana Ave., Las Vegas	(702) 362-8668
3105 E. Sahara Ave.	(702) 457-2277
Snappy Car Rental	
6135 W. Sahara Ave., Las Vegas	(702) 367-4999
Sunbelt Car Rental	
3317 Las Vegas Blvd. S., Las Vegas	(702) 731-3600
Thrifty Car Rental	(800) 367-2277
376 E. Warm Springs Rd., Las Vegas	(702) 896-7600
5750 W. Sahara Ave., Las Vegas	(702) 362-0315
U S Rent-A-Car	(800) 777-9377
4700 Paradise Rd., Las Vegas	(702) 798-6100
Unique Movie Cars	
641 Middlegate Rd., Las Vegas	(702) 566-6193
Value Rent-A-Car	(800) 468-2583
4480 Paradise Rd., Las Vegas	(702) 733-8886
3025 Las Vegas Blvd, S., # 116, Las Vegas	(702) 735-3758
Fitzgerald's	(702) 388-2142
X-Press International Rent-A-Car	(800) 795-2277
3767 Las Vegas Blvd. S., Las Vegas,	(702) 795-4008
3941 Las Vegas Blvd, S., # 15, Las Vegas	(702) 891-0807
4920 Paradise Rd., Las Vegas	(702) 891-0807

By Limousine

The average price for a basic limousine with driver is $33.00 to $42.00 per hour. A stretch limo averages $40.00 to $48.00 per hour, and a super-stretch limo averages $60.00 to $80.00 per hour.

Limousine service between McCarran Airport and Strip hotels costs about $3.50 per person. Between the airport and Downtown, expect to pay around $4.75 per person.

A Limousine Service . . . .(702) 739-6265

A Luxury Limo Referral Service . . . .(800) 780-4373

Arrive In Style . . . .(702) 740-4432

Bell Trans . . . .(702) 385-5466

CLS Of Las Vegas . . . .(702) 740-4545

Elite Limousine By Tecopa . . . .(702) 791-3548

Executive Security . . . .(702) 263-3810

Executive Services . . . .(702) 656-4200

Gray Line Tours . . . .(702) 739-5700

Jade Falcon Limousine . . . .(702) 396-4404

Las Vegas Limousines . . . .(702) 739-8414

On Demand Sedan . . . .(702) 876-2222

Pete's Fleet . . . .(702) 259-7484

Players Universal Security . . . .(702) 631-6222

Presidential Limousine . . . .(702) 731-5577

Rancho Limousine Service . . . .(702) 645-7634

Rent-A-Limo . . . .(702) 791-6466

Stardust Limousine Service . . . .(800) 446-4805

Tecopa Limousines . . . .(702) 233-8579

By Taxi

The following fares represent the most direct route from the airport to the hotel. Taxi drivers are not permitted to take lengthier routes, even if they might save time, without getting approval from the passenger. In most cases, the most direct route will result in the lowest fare.

Cab Fares

Basic taxi fare is $2.20 for the first mile, $1.50 each additional mile plus $.44 cents a minute while sitting at red lights with a five-person maximum. *All fares are governed by the Nevada Taxicab Authority and should be the same for every company.*

Fares from McCarran Airport to different parts of the Strip and Downtown are as follows:

MGM Grand, Tropicana and Luxor area $6.00 to $7.50	**Stardust area** $10.00
Harrah's, Imperial Palace, Bally's and Caesar's Palace area $7.50 to $9.00	**Stratosphere area** $11.00
Desert Inn, Fashion Show Mall and Frontier Hotel area $8.00 to $9.50	**Downtown area** $12.00 to $14.00

Major cab companies

A-North Las Vegas Cab . . . .(702) 643-1041

ABC . . . .(702) 736-8444

Ace . . . .(702) 736-8383

A Vegas Western Cab . . . .(702) 736-6121

Checker . . . .(702) 873-2000

Desert . . . .(702) 386-9102

Henderson . . . .(702) 384-2322

Nell's Cab . . . .(702) 252-0201

Star . . . .(702) 873-2000

Western Cab . . . .(702) 736-8000

Whittlesea . . . .(702) 384-6111

Yellow . . . .(702) 873-2000

Note: *A green light blinking on top of a taxi means the driver is "in distress," possibly being robbed, and the public is asked to phone 911 immediately.*

Strip Trolley

From the Stratosphere Hotel to the Luxor Hotel, with stops at the front door of each major hotel including the Las Vegas Hilton.

9:30 a.m. to 2:00 a.m. daily.
(Trolley runs approximately every 15 minutes.)

$1.40 (exact change)

For more information, call (702) 382-1404

CAT: Citizens Area Transit

CAT operates 39 scheduled routes with service in Laughlin and Mesquite. Route 301 serves downtown Las Vegas and the Las Vegas Strip 24 hours-a-day. CAT operating hours for residential routes are between 5:30 a.m. and 1:30 a.m., 7 days-a-week. Buses run approximately every 10 minutes.

Fares

Pay your fare immediately upon boarding with exact change, tokens, or show one of CAT's convenient passes. Coach operators do not carry change. Fares or overpayments are non-refundable.

Adults (18 + years)	$1.50 one way
Senior Citizens (62 + years)	$ .50 one way
Youths (5 - 17 years)	$ .50 one way
Persons with disabilities	$ .50 one way
Children under 5	Free

(702) 228-7433 (CAT-RIDE)

Airport Shuttle Companies

Bell Transport . . . .(702) 739-7990
Grey Line . . . . (702) 739-5700

Hotel Shuttles

Bally's to Sam's Town	Runs hourly on the quarter-hour 9:15 a.m. to 10:15 p.m.
Belz Mall to Sunset Station	12:30 p.m., 2:30 p.m., 5:00 p.m., 7:00 p.m., 8:30 p.m. (except Sun)
Boulder Station to Fashion Show Mall	9:30 a.m., 11:00 a.m., 2:55 p.m., 6:55 p.m., 10:10 p.m.
Boulder Station to Palace Station	2:00 p.m., 6:00 p.m., and 8:25 p.m.
Boulder Station to Sunset Station	10:20 a.m., 3:50 p.m., 7:45 p.m., 9:30 p.m.
Downtown Las Vegas to Sam's Town	Runs hourly on the half-hour 8:30 a.m. to 11:30 p.m.
Fashion Show Mall to Boulder Station	9:55 a.m., 3:20 p.m., 7:20 p.m., and 9:05 p.m.
Fashion Show Mall to Palace Station	11:25 a.m., 10:35 p.m.
Fashion Show Mall to Palace Station	Runs every half-hour from 9:00 a.m. to 12:30 a.m.
Fashion Show Mall to Texas Station	10:30 a.m., 3:05 p.m., 7:15 p.m., and 9:40 p.m.
Fremont Experience to Texas Station	9:45 a.m., 2:05 p.m., and 6:30 p.m.
MGM to Sam's Town	Runs hourly on the three-quarter hour 9:45 a.m. to 10:45 p.m.
Palace Station to Boulder Station	11:40 a.m., 2:25 p.m., and 6:30 p.m.
Palace Station to Fashion Show Mall	8:50 p.m.
Palace Station to Fashion Show Mall	2:50 p.m., 9:25 p.m.
Palace Station to Texas Station	9:00 a.m., 11:25 a.m., and 5:45 p.m.
Palace Station to Tropicana	Run every half-hour from 8:30 a.m. to midnight
Rio to Strip: Rio Visitors Center located on the Strip & Harmon St.	Runs continuously, Monday - Thursday from 9:00 a.m. to Midnight, Friday and Saturday from 9:00 a.m. to 2:00 a.m.

continued on page 22.

getting there

Sam's Town to Stardust	Runs hourly on the half-hour 9:30 a.m. to 10:30 p.m.
Sam's Town to MGM	Runs hourly on the quarter-hour 9:15 a.m. to 10:15 p.m.
Sam's Town to Bally's	Runs hourly on the three-quarter hour 9:45 a.m. to 10:45 p.m.
Sam's Town to Downtown Las Vegas	Runs hourly on the hour 8:00 a.m. to 11:00 p.m.
Stardust to Sam's Town	Runs hourly on the hour 9:00 a.m. to 10:00 p.m.
Sunset Station to Boulder Station	10:40 a.m., 4:10 p.m., 8:05 p.m., 9:50 p.m.
Sunset Station to Belz Mall	Noon, 2:00 p.m., 4:30 p.m., 6:30 p.m., 8:00 p.m. (except Sun)
Sunset Station to Tropicana	8:30 a.m., 9:30 a.m., 1:00 p.m., 5:30 p.m., 9:00 p.m., 10:00 p.m., 11:00 p.m.
Tropicana to Fashion Show Mall	Runs every half-hour from 8:45 a.m. to 12:45 a.m.
Texas Station to Fashion Show Mall	10:05 a.m., 6:50 p.m.
Texas Station to Fremont Experience	9:25 a.m., 1:45 p.m., 6:10 p.m., 10:05 p.m.
Texas Station to Palace Station	8:35 a.m., 11:00 a.m., 2:25 p.m., 5:00 p.m., 9:00 p.m., 11:30 p.m.
Tropicana to Sunset Station	9:00 a.m., 10:00 a.m., 1:30 p.m., 6:00 p.m., 9:30 p.m., 10:30 p.m.

chapter two

performing arts

Aside from the night life, newcomers are pleasantly surprised to discover the many other pastimes and diverse entertainment Southern Nevada has to offer.

- ■ Dance
- ■ Music
- ■ Theater
- ■ Museums
- ■ Art Museums & Galleries

Dance

American Dance Company

Comprised of dancers age 15 years and up, the company's productions are based on events, educating the audience through dance.

2188 E. Desert Inn Rd. Suite 10
Las Vegas, NV 89109
(702) 735-9181

Nevada Dance Theatre

Nevada's only professional Ballet Company presenting both classical and contemporary ballet performances. All performances are held at the UNLV Performing Arts Center.

Admission: Varies
Hours: Thursday and Friday 8:00 p.m., Saturday 2:00 p.m. and 8:00 p.m., Sunday 2:00 p.m. and 7:00 p.m.

Las Vegas Civic Ballet

The Las Vegas City Cultural and Community Affairs division provides young Las Vegas dancers between the ages of 10 and 23 years of age with a program designed to bridge the gap between dance auditions and concerts. Performances are held twice a year at the Reed Whipple Cultural Center.

Admission: $5.00 Adults, $3.00 Students and Seniors $2.00 Children
821 Las Vegas Blvd. N.
Las Vegas, NV 89101
(702) 229-6211

Music

Brown Bag Concerts

Concerts every Monday at the Debbie Reynolds Celebrity Café with luncheon. Concert at Sun City once a month, residents and invited guests.

Admission: Varies
Hours: Vary

The Performing Arts Society of Nevada
6301 Machalite Bay Ave
Las Vegas, NV 89130
(702) 658-6741

Charles Vanda Master Series

The organization brings classical and performing artists from all over the world to Las Vegas. All performances in the Artemus S. Ham Concert Hall.

Hours: 8:00 p.m.
UNLV Performing Arts Center
405 S. Maryland Pkwy
Las Vegas, NV 89154
(702) 895-3535

Henderson Civic Symphony

Sponsored by the Henderson Parks and Recreation Department, the Henderson Civic Symphony is a 50-member orchestra in its 12th season.

Valley View Recreation Center
500 Harris Street
Henderson, NV
(702) 565-2121

Las Vegas Youth Orchestra

85 member youth orchestra performs four or five times a year. The orchestra is sponsored by the City of Las Vegas Cultural and Community Affairs Division.

Admission: Adults $4.00, Students & Seniors $3.00
Las Vegas Youth Orchestra
2832 E. Flamingo Rd.
Las Vegas, NV 89121
(702) 385-8948

Nevada Chamber Symphony

Featuring both instrumental and vocal soloists, the symphony performs an indoor season October through May, and an outdoor season June through August. Concerts are held at the Clark County Library and Henderson Civic Center.

performing arts

Admission: Free
Hours: Sunday 3:00 p.m.
2229 Marlboro Dr.
Henderson, NV 89104
(702) 433-9280

Nevada School of the Arts

Provides instruction in fine music arts to all ages and abilities. The local not-for-profit organization is supported by a grant from the Nevada State Council on the Arts and the National Endowment for the Arts. Nevada School of the Arts will reach nearly 800 students per year from age three to adult. Nevada School of the Arts offers both private and class instruction.
315 S. 7th Street
Las Vegas, NV 89101
(702) 386-2787

Nevada Symphony Orchestra

Nevada Symphony Orchestra, in its 19th season, is a 100 member symphony with concerts held at Artemus W. Ham Concert Hall at UNLV. Outdoor pop concerts are held at Hills Park, Summerlin.
Admission: $15.00 general, $45.00 reserved cabaret seat with buffet.
(702) 792-4337

Sierra Winds

The group is one of the nation's top chamber music ensembles.
Admission: $30.00 Adults, $22.00 Seniors, Students and Military
UNLV
4505 S. Maryland Pkwy
Las Vegas, NV 89154
(702) 895-3332

Southern Nevada Community Concert Association

Works with Columbia Artists to bring a diversity of outstanding talent to Las Vegas. All performances take place at UNLV's Artemus Ham Hall
Hours: 8:00 p.m.
Admission: $40.00 Adults, $15.00 Students
1620 Stonehaven Dr.
Las Vegas, NV 89108
(702) 895-3801

Southern Nevada Musical Arts Society

A non-profit organization encompassing the Musical Arts Orchestra, The Musical Arts Chorus and the Musical Arts Singers. These groups perform at the Artemus Ham Hall at UNLV and also the CCSN, Reed Whipple Cultural Center and the Clark County Flamingo Library.
Admission: $10.00 Adults, $7.00 Seniors, Students, Military.
3950 Springhill Ave
Las Vegas, NV 89121
(702) 451-6672

Theater

Actors Repertory Theatre

Great Theatre from Shakespeare to *A Christmas Carol* produced at the new Summerlin Library and Performing Arts Center.
Admission: $15.00 Adults, $12.50 Children for matinee, $20.00 Adults, $15.00 Children for Saturday performance
Hours: Friday 8:00 p.m., Saturday 2:00 p.m. and 8:00 p.m., Sunday 2:00 p.m.
1824 Palo Alto Circle
Las Vegas, NV 89108
(702) 647-7469

performing arts

Las Vegas Little Theatre

Performances of five comedies from September through May.
Performances are held at the Spring Valley Library.

> **Admission:** $10.00 Adults, $9.00 Students and Seniors for production, $12.00 Adults, $10.00 Students and Seniors for musicals.
> 4280 S. Jones Blvd.
> Las Vegas, NV 89103
> **(702) 362-7996**

New West Theatre

Comedies, dramas and musicals are performed at the Charleston Heights Arts Center throughout the year.

> **Admission:** $12.50 Adults, $9.00 Students, Seniors, Children under 5 not permitted
> 800 S. Brush Street
> Las Vegas, NV
> **(702) 258-8022**

Rainbow Company Theatre

Children's Theater Group for ages seven to 17, sponsored by the City of Las Vegas Department of Parks and Leisure Activities.

> **Admission:** $5.00 Adults, $3.00 Seniors, $2.00 Children
> 821 Las Vegas Blvd N
> Las Vegas, NV 89101
> **(702) 229-6553**

Super Summer Theatre

Broadway musicals and Shakespeare production are presented throughout the summer.

> **Admission:** $5.00 Adults Wednesday and Thursday, $3.00 Seniors and Students, $7.00 Adults, Friday and Saturday, $4.00 Seniors and Students, Children under 6 free
> **Hours:** Mid-June through the end of August, Wednesday through Saturday. Gates open at 6:00 p.m.

Spring Mountain State Park
(702) 594-PLAY

Museums & Historical Sites

African American Museum & Research Center

A non-profit institution, founded by Gwendolyn and Juanita Walker, the museum strives to preserve and promote the history of people of African decent. It offers a 10,000 piece collection of memorabilia, consisting of ethnic dolls, art, artifacts, figurines, posters, prints, books, and personal items of renown African-Americans. There is a museum gift shop that offers an array of gifts, fashion and accessories.

> **Admission:** Free
> **Hours:** By appointment only
> The Walker Foundation
> 705 W. Van Buren Ave.
> Las Vegas, NV
> **(702) 647-2242**
> **(702) 599-8130** for reservations

Boulder City/Hoover Dam Museum

Established for the preservation of historical artifacts relating to the workers and construction of Hoover Dam, it is one of the seven man-made wonders of the world. Displays of memorabilia and important historical items that impacted the construction also are seen. Free movie screenings of "The Construction of Hoover Dam."

> **Admission:** $1.00 donation
> **Hours:** 10:00 a.m. to 4:00 p.m. daily. Year-round except major holidays
> 444 Hotel Plaza
> Boulder City
> **(702) 294-1988**

Hoover Dam and Lake Mead

Hoover Dam literally changed the face of the American West. It is a part of the Bureau of Reclamations' multipurpose projects on the Colorado River. These projects control floods; they store water for irrigation, municipal, and industrial use; and they provide generation of hydroelectric power, recreation, and fish and wildlife habitat.

The 1,400-mile-long Colorado River, fed by Rocky Mountain snowfields, ran wild for countless centuries as it carved the mighty Grand Canyon in its race west to the Gulf of California. Spring and summer runoff produced by a heavy snowpack caused a rampaging flow that flooded farm lands. It eroded millions of tons of valuable top-soil, causing ruin for farmers and ranchers along its banks.

In drier years, its flow shriveled. Crops withered and cattle died for lack of adequate water. The federal government commissioned a series of studies after the turn of the century to harness the Colorado's erratic rampages. The U.S. Congress passed the Boulder Canyon Project Act in 1928, authorizing construction of Hoover Dam. The 726-foot-high dam was dedicated by President Franklin Roosevelt on Sept. 30, 1935.

The Hoover Dam Power Plant has 17 large generators and has a rated capacity of more then 2,000 megawatts, which is enough power to supply a half million homes for one year. Its power is marketed in Arizona, California and Nevada, and the Bureau of Reclamation has been able to return to the Federal Treasury the cost of it's operations on the Colorado River.

At the peak of construction, more than 5,000 people were employed on the gigantic project in Black Canyon. Ninety-six workers died on the project. The actual cost of Hoover Dam, the All-American Canal, the town of Boulder City, highways, railroads and various other works was $165 million. The dam itself had a price tag of nearly $60 million.

More than 700,000 tourists tour the interior of the dam each year. A guided, 35-minute tour of Hoover Dam take visitors deep inside the monolith for a complete explanation of its history, purpose and inner workings. Tours leave from the visitor center every few minutes. A special "Hard Hat Tour" is also available.

Visitor Center Hours: Daily 8:30 a.m. to 5:45 p.m.

Visitor Center Admission: $6.00 Adults; $2.00 Juniors and $5.00 Seniors; Children under 6 Free.

US 93 (Boulder Hwy) about 35 minutes from the strip

Boulder City, NV

(702) 294-3522

museums

museums

Bruno's Indian & Turquoise Museum

Bruno's Indian Museum promotes and educates the public about the Native American artists of the Southwest, of which 2,000 are represented in the fine art gallery and jewelry store. Dedicated to educating the public about mineralogy and the history of Native American people, this is a unique museum which offers historic detailing regarding mining and jewelry making. You can learn about the Paiute and Anasazi Indians: How they lived, hunted and farmed in the desert. A trading post and gallery are also on site. Featuring collections of earrings, paintings, bronze sculptures and the largest collection of turquoise stones in the country. Two movies are shown throughout the day, one featuring a tour of the Southwest and the other portraits displaying Indian dancing, arts and crafts.

Admission: $2.00

Hours: 10:00 a.m. to 5:00 p.m. daily, year-round

1306 Nevada Highway, Boulder City, NV

(702) 293-4865   (800) 292-3233

Clark County Heritage Museum

Clark County Heritage Museum gives families a chance to explore the rich and colorful history of Southern Nevada, from prehistoric times to the near present. At the 8,000 square foot exhibit center, there are lots of interactive displays kids can touch, including exhibits of old mining and farming equipment. They can see what a mine would have looked like and put their fingers in holes made to hold dynamite sticks. An early Las Vegas tent-house display comes complete with a talking "pioneer" telling about life in the old days. Kids can also see an old Indian dwelling, a model of a giant prehistoric wolf and a desert scene where they are invited to find camouflaged animals in their natural habitat. A section devoted to casino/gaming history contains interesting old photos and relics as well as antique slot machines. The exhibit hall plays host throughout the year to temporary and traveling displays from around the country, on topics ranging from "Schoolhouse on the Prairie" to Native American arts to gem and mineral fairs.

The 25-acre museum complex contains many structures which were salvaged from ghost towns around the state, as well as old Las Vegas houses rescued from the wrecking ball during downtown renovations. The ghost town features a miner's cabin, jail, general store and other unrestored old buildings. Kids can go inside some of the buildings, but others are too fragile. Rusted mining equipment and old vehicles provide an authentic ghost town look. You can visit a restored railroad station, moved to this site from Boulder City, explore the inside of a real 1944 caboose and view a 1922 boxcar and an old Union Pacific steam engine. Heritage Street is a unique collection of historic homes, each restored to show what life was like in Southern Nevada during a particular era. One home was built in 1905 in the mining town of Goldfield, others illustrate life in the early 1900's to 1940's in Las Vegas. You can tour the homes and try to imagine how families lived in the days before air conditioning, television and microwave ovens. Kids will enjoy the old newspaper print shop, complete with authentic press machinery and copies of early newspapers.

Group tours are available, and there is an outdoor picnic area. While visiting the museum, keep a lookout for real desert creatures — cottontail bunnies especially seem to like its relatively remote location. ■

Clark County Heritage Museum Info

1830 S. Boulder Highway

Directions: Take I-95 to Henderson and exit at Horizon Drive. Go left to Boulder Highway and turn right. Or go out Boulder Highway to the far edge of Henderson.

(702) 455-7955

Hours: 9:00 a.m. to 4:30 p.m. daily

Admission: Adults $1.50
Seniors and Children $1.00

Facilities: All indoor and most outdoor displays are wheelchair accessible.

Desert Demonstration Gardens
A collection of water-efficient landscape experiments. The themed gardens offer more than 150 species of vegetation that are designed to be compatible with the desert.
> **Hours:** Weekdays, 8:00 a.m. to 6:00 p.m. and Saturday, 8:00 a.m. to noon.
> 3701 W. Alta Drive
> Las Vegas, NV
> **(702) 258-3205**

Gallery of History
Historical documents can be seen and purchased at this gallery. In addition, letters, manuscripts and photographs of famous people are framed as elegant works of art. These pieces are original historical documents.
> **Hours:** Monday through Friday 8:00 a.m. to 5:00 p.m.
> 3601 W. Sahara Ave.
> Las Vegas, NV
> **(702) 731-2300**

museums

Guinness World of Records Museum

Have you ever wanted to see the world's most tattooed woman, the smallest working bicycle or the person with the longest fingernails? You'll find them all among the 5,200 square feet of exhibits at the Guinness World of Records Museum. Kids can stand next to a model of the world's tallest man or step on a family-sized scale to compare their weight to the world's heaviest man (1,069 pounds). Several categories of world records are featured, including amazing humans, the animal world, sports records, entertainment and space. Many of the interactive displays allow kids to touch a computer screen or push a button to find information about their favorite subjects. A small viewing area allows you to see videos of people setting records, like "Most dominoes toppled at one time." This would be a great way to spend a rainy afternoon with school-age kids, especially if they have a particular interest or hobby that may be featured in the museum. ■

Guinness Museum Information

Days/Hours: 9:00 a.m. to 6:00 p.m. daily (September through May), 9:00 a.m. to 8:00 p.m. (June through August)

Admission: Adults $4.95, Seniors, Students and military $3.95, Children 5 to 12, $2.95, Children under 5 admitted free. Call for group rates.

2780 Las Vegas Blvd. South
Las Vegas, NV
(702) 792-3766

Directions: On the Strip between the Sahara Hotel and Circus Circus

Facilities: Wheelchair accessible

Hard Rock Cafe

Nestled beneath a 100 ft. neon replica of an electric guitar, this restaurant/gift shop/bar classifies as a museum in its own right. The walls are draped with memorabilia from every pop and rock legend of the 50's through the 90's.

Admission: Free

Hours: 11:00 a.m. - 11:30 p.m. weekdays, 12:00 a.m. weekends

4475 Paradise Rd Las Vegas

(702) 733-8400

Imperial Palace Auto Collection

Over 200 antique, classic and special-interest vehicles are on display at the Imperial Palace Auto Collection, which features vehicles once owned by famous people, as well as some of the most rare and historically important cars ever produced. While passenger cars are the stars of the collection, they are complemented by an interesting supporting cast of military vehicles, motorcycles, trucks, tractors and fire engines. The collection actually includes more than 800 vehicles which rotate between this museum, a storage facility and nation-

Continued on page 32.

Imperial Palace Auto Collection Info

Facilities: Wheelchair accessible, restrooms located in the Duesenberg Bar area

Days/Hours: 9:30 a.m. to 11:30 p.m. daily

Admission: Adults $6.95, Seniors and Children 3-12, $3.00, Children under three are admitted free

Location: Imperial Palace
Address: 3535 Las Vegas Blvd. South Las Vegas
(702) 731-3311

Directions: On the Strip. The auto collection is housed on the top floor of the parking garage. Park in the garage and take the elevator.

museums

wide tours, so there is usually something new for repeat visitors. Although most of the exhibits are strictly "hands-off", visitors are allowed to take pictures of the cars and you can sit in a 1913 Model T Ford to have your picture taken. Kids can get close enough to an automatic piano player to see how it works. There is also a Factory Display Chassis showing the frame of a car with its engine. Kids can press a button to make the engine fan turn with a satisfying roaring noise.

The gift shop is sure to please everyone in the family, with model cars, posters, coffee mugs, T-shirts and all sorts of books about cars. Bringing kids through the museum is a good way to feel your age, because they don't recognize the celebrities who used to own some of the famous cars. Hint: explain that Marilyn Monroe was kind of like Madonna. (You're on your own explaining Liberace). ∎

Judes Ranch

A collection of auto memorabilia, replicas and models.

Hours: Monday through Sunday
10:00 a.m. to 6:00 p.m.
Admission: By donation
101 St. Jude's St.
Boulder City, NV
(702) 294-7172

King Tutankhamun's Tomb And Museum

A full-scale replication of King Tut's Tomb, as found by Howard Carter in 1922. This exact is a great attraction for history buffs. The tomb has been built to exacting detail by an Egyptologist, re-created from methods used over 3,000 years ago. You'll see over 500 pieces, including guardian statues, chariots, vases, statuary, beds, pottery, jewelry, lamps, shrines and boxes. The measurements of each room are exact, the same as the original tomb. A 20 minute guided tour takes you through the carved rock walls and artifacts.

Admission: $4.00
Hours: Monday through
Sunday, 9:00 a.m. to 11:00 p.m.
Luxor Hotel
3900 S. Las Vegas Blvd
Las Vegas, NV
(702) 262-4000

Kyle Ranch

Once part of a large ranch, the remains are acknowledged as the oldest standing building in Las Vegas. The unassuming stone and wood ranch house and nearby white shed date back to the mid 1850's, when the entire valley was little more than a railroad stop, and ranching predominated gambling. If you visit the site, please respect all nearby areas marked "private property" and "no trespassing".

Admission: Free
Located just off Losee Road
on the northeast corner of Carey
Ave and Commerce Street in
North Las Vegas.

Las Vegas Natural History Museum

The Las Vegas Natural History Museum can provide a whole day's entertainment and learning for children at a pace that won't exhaust their parents. It's full of kids' favorite animals (dinosaurs, sharks and creepy crawly things) as well as opportunities to touch and explore the natural world. In the Marine Life Room, kids can stand at the edge of a 3,000 gallon tank containing small live sharks. Boys of all ages seem sorely tempted to dabble their fingers as the miniature predators circle by. This room also contains various models of sea life including a 14-foot great white shark. Smaller tanks contain other colorful and interesting underwater creatures. For some real excitement, ask a museum assistant about feeding times for the piranha or sharks. The International Wildlife Room contains many species of mounted animals, including a 16-foot giraffe, bison, antelope, monkeys, a zebra being attacked by lions and a caribou fighting off wolves. The Wild Nevada Room features the sights and sounds of the Mojave Desert's unique life forms. Kids can push a button to hear an elk bugle, feel a piece of mounted fur or hide, and squat down to look through the glass and see tunnels where burrowing animals hide.

The most popular room in the museum is the Prehistoric Room, containing five robotic dinosaurs including a 35-foot-long Tyrannosaurus Rex. The dinos are fitted with sensors which activate them when people come near, making them move and roar. A diorama shows a mother plant-eating dinosaur guarding her nest from invading predators. Ask the kids to name all these creatures - you'll be surprised how many of the tongue-twisting names they know. There are various large and small fossils in the Prehistoric Room, including skulls of a four-tusked elephant and a giant crocodile, as well as fossilized dung (a big hit with the smaller set). Be sure to visit the Young Scientists' Center, a hands-on interactive room where kids dig in the sand to uncover fossils, compare animal tracks with "Whose Foot is It?" and sniff out plants and animals at "Scents Sense." Museum assistants are friendly and helpful and may allow youngsters to pet a hedgehog, hold a snake or let a millipede crawl on their hands. The gift shop is full of great educational toys and books about animals, fish and the natural world. Call the museum for information about seasonal programs, summer day camps and the Young Scientists' Club. ■

Las Vegas Natural History Museum Info

Facilities: Wheelchair accessible

Days/Hours: Open daily 9:00 a.m.-4:00 p.m. every day except Thanksgiving and Christmas

Admission: Adults $4.00, Students, Military & Seniors, $4.00, Children 4 to 12, $2.50. Children under 4 free.

Address: 900 Las Vegas Blvd. North Las Vegas

(702) 384-3466

Directions: Just north of downtown on Las Vegas Blvd, across from the Lied Children's Museum and next to Cashman Field

Liberace Museum

The museum features "Mr. Showmanship's" dazzling jewelry, priceless antiques, million-dollar wardrobe, rare and historical pianos and his unique, one-of-a-kind car collection.

Admission: Donations to the museum are $6.95 for Adults and $4.95 for Seniors and Students. Admission for children under 12 is free. Donations go to the Liberace Foundation for the Performing and Creative Arts, funding scholarships and grants to aspiring musicians across the country.

Hours: Daily 10:00 a.m. to 5:00 p.m., Sunday from 1:00 p.m. to 5:00 p.m.

1775 E Tropicana, Las Vegas, NV

(702) 798-5595   (800) 626-2625

www.liberace.org/museum.html

Magic and Movie Hall of Fame

The Magic and Movie Hall of Fame bills itself as "The Best Hidden Secret in Las Vegas". Many locals don't know about it, although it's one of the few places on the Strip where you can take the family for a G-rated show. Valentine Vox, a performer with over 30 years experience as a magician and ventriloquist, founded the museum in 1992 and serves as its general manager and artistic director. The 20,000 square foot Hall of Fame houses a 4.5 million dollar collection of memorabilia on magic, ventriloquism, clockwork toys and movie costumes. It's a favorite place for school field trips, hosting around 2,000 local children each year.

The Hall of Fame is actually four museums in one. You first pass through the Magic Museum containing exhibits about famous magicians from the earliest known performers to modern stars like David Copperfield and Siegfried and Roy.

Continued on page 36.

Magic and Movie Hall of Fame Info

Location: O'Shea's Casino

Address: 3555 Las Vegas Blvd. South Las Vegas

Directions: On the Strip across from Caesars Palace. Use the parking garage and take the elevator to the second floor.

Phone: (702) 737-1343

Days/Hours: 10:00 a.m. to 6:00 p.m. daily, magic show at 4:30 p.m. During peak times, the magic show may run 2 or 3 times a day. Call first to find out.

Admission: Adults $9.95, Children 12 and under, $3.00. Admission includes a magic show, and adult admission includes a drink in O'Shea's Casino downstairs from the museum. Two-for-one admission coupons are available in many tourist guidebooks.

Facilities: Wheelchair accessible

Kids will enjoy seeing Houdini's trunk and other famous magic props. Video displays at some of the stations explain the scene and show the tricks as they were performed. Dim lighting in this section makes for an appropriately spooky atmosphere. The Magic in Motion collection displays a wonderful assortment of antique clockwork toys and carnival arcade machines. Be sure to see the giant Robot Band from Germany. The Magic Voices museum explains the history of ventriloquism from biblical times to the present, and contains tributes to famous performers like Shari Lewis and Senor Wences as well as hundreds of valuable antique dummies. A model of a ventriloquist dummy's head allows kids to move levers to operate the eyes, mouth, etc. The movie costume exhibit will impress adults more than kids, who probably have no idea who Vivian Leigh or Erroll Flynn were. The costumes are beautiful and tell their own story about the glory days of Hollywood.

Valentine Vox and a small cast perform daily in the Houdini Theater with an entertaining blend of magic tricks, comedy and ventriloquism. Be sure to time your visit so you can see the show either before or after your museum tour. There's also a well-stocked gift shop where you can purchase magic tricks, puppets and books about magic and ventriloquism. The antique arcade machines at the gift shop are not the 3-D, computerized motion simulators you see in modern arcades. They're just honest-to-goodness, old-fashioned mechanical toys which you and the kids should enjoy. ∎

Lied Discovery Children's Museum

Curious children who are constantly hearing, "Don't touch!" will love the Lied Museum. There, they are free to touch and explore over 100 exhibits designed just for kids. They can crawl and slide through the Toddler Towers, be stars on the Performing Arts stage, pilot the Space Shuttle, create color computer prints or tap out a tune on the Musical Pathway. Science Tower exhibits allow kids to bend sound waves in Echo Tubes, check out local weather at the Weather Station and create interesting sights and sounds at the neon and fiber optic display. The museum's exhibits and programs encourage children and adults to share a special learning experience and allow adults to re-live the joy of discovery that we sometimes take for granted as we get older.

For Little Learners, age 5 and younger, drop-in workshops and activities are offered daily from 10:30 to noon. Workshops for kids 6 and older are offered from 1:30 p.m. to 3:30 p.m. on weekends. Recent topics include Icy Activities, Shoes Around the World, Flower Power, Silly Putty Fun, Paper Bag Puppets, Magnet Magic and Sand Painting. Do these sound like fun or what?

Celebrate your child's birthday at the museum's Birthday Party Room. The Classic Party ($100 for the first 10 Children plus $5 for every additional child) is two hours long. During the first hour, your party animals will visit the museum and the second hour is spent in the decorated party room enjoying cake, ice cream and punch. For an extra charge, your party can include a supervised activity like Slime Time, Crazy Kaleidoscope, Body Tracing or Stage Games. The party package includes invitations for you to mail, a museum T-shirt for the birthday child, party favor bags and (best of all) somebody else cleans up the slime.

The Fletcher Jones Cultural Gallery features traveling exhibits designed for the whole family to enjoy. 1999 exhibits will include "Take Another Look," an interactive exhibit which challenges people to look at everyday objects in new ways and "Wade in the Water," tracing the development of African American sacred music traditions. Las Vegas newspaper readers voted the Lied Discovery Children's Museum Las Vegas' #1 museum for eight years in a row. Take the kids and find out for yourself. ∎

museums

Lied Discovery Children's Museum Info

Address: 833 Las Vegas Blvd. North
Directions: Just north of downtown on Las Vegas Blvd. near Cashman Field
Phone: (702) 382-3445
Days/Hours: Tuesday through Sunday, 10:00 a.m. to 5:00 p.m. Closed Mondays except on most school holidays (Call first).

Admission: Adults $5.00, Children 2 and older, Seniors and military $4.00, Children under two and museum members are admitted free. If you plan on going often, an annual membership is a good deal.
Restrictions: Children under 12 must be accompanied by an adult.
Facilities: Wheelchair access, wheelchair rental, diaper changing stations

Lost City Museum of Archaeology

Built in 1935 by the National Park Service to exhibit artifacts that were being excavated from Pueblo Grande de Nevada. These Anasazi Indian sites were being threatened by the waters of Lake Mead as it backed up behind the newly built Hoover Dam. This is one of the most complete collections of early Pueblo Indian artifacts in the southwest, including a full scale reconstruction of an Indian pueblo structure. This museum is a history buff's paradise. You'll see exhibits which cover the human occupation of Nevada from 12,000 years in the past up through when white settlers made Nevada home.

Admission: Adults $2.00, 18 and under free
Hours: Daily 8:30 a.m. to 4:30 p.m.
721 S. Hwy. 169 S. Moapa Valley Blvd., Overton, NV **(702) 397-2193**
60 miles north of Las Vegas

museums

McCarran Aviation Heritage Museum

The Museum shows the history of aviation in Southern Nevada, from the first flight in 1920 through the introduction of jets. The museum focuses on the history of commercial and general aviation. For those who like to watch the operations at the airport, a parking area is available south of the airport on Sunset Road, with a transceiver to listen to the tower's communications with the aircraft landing and taking off. Just tune your AM radio to 1610, and you can follow the conversation.

Admission: Admission is free.

Hours: 24 hours

McCarran International Airport, Las Vegas

The museum's main exhibit is located above baggage claim on level two, with an additional exhibit in the general and corporate aviation terminal operated by Signature Flight Support.

www.co.clark.nv.us/PARKREC/aviation.htm

Marjorie Barrick Museum of Natural History

The Marjorie Barrick Museum of Natural History on the UNLV campus contains a permanent collection of educational exhibits your family may want to check out, as well as a gallery area which hosts art shows and other temporary exhibits. In the lobby, "Mojave Desert Alive" features wildlife native to the Southern Nevada desert. Kids can see lizards, snakes, desert tortoises and other animals close up. The Main Exhibit Hall has a large collection of Native American crafts, including baskets, pottery, jewelry and textiles. The museum contains several mounted animals the kids may like, including a giant standing polar bear, two smaller bears and lots of birds. Unlike the Lied Museum, children aren't allowed to touch anything here, so younger kids may get frustrated. School age children should do fine, however, and it doesn't take long to see all the exhibits.

Marjorie Barrick Museum Info

Location: University of Nevada, Las Vegas

Address: 4505 S. Maryland Parkway

Directions: Enter UNLV on Harmon Avenue on the west end of the campus. Metered visitor parking available. If you don't know your way around UNLV, it's best to check a campus map first.

Phone: (702) 895-3381

Days/Hours: Monday through Friday 8:00 am-4:45 pm Saturday 10:00 am-2:00 pm. Closed on state and national holidays.

Admission: Free

Facilities: Wheelchair accessible

The gift shop contains educational books as well as stuffed animals, T-shirts and toys. Outside, the Xeriscape Demonstration Garden features drought tolerant plants from major deserts of the world. It's a small but pretty garden which shows the desert can grow more than just cacti. UNLV has a beautiful campus, so your family might plan to walk around and see some of the other campus sights after visiting the museum. ■

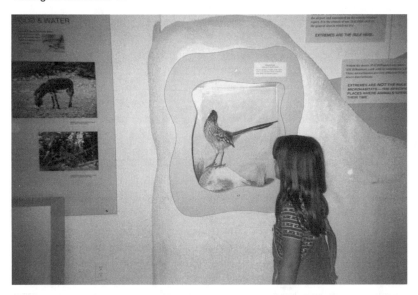

Nevada State Museum and Historical Society

There are lots of things for kids to enjoy at Lorenzi Park: swings and slides, a lake where they can fish and feed ducks, and acres of grass to run around on. The park is also home to a great museum many people don't even know about, and kids under 18 are admitted free. The Nevada State Museum at the south end of the park is a perfect place to learn about the history of Southern Nevada from the ice age to the near-present time. You'll see exhibits of desert animals like the fox, roadrunner and rattlesnake, as well as animals native to the cooler climates in

museums

Nevada State Museum Info

Location: Lorenzi Park

Address: 700 Twin Lakes Drive

Directions: Exit I-95 at Valley View and go north one block to Bonanza Road. Turn right on Bonanza and left on Twin Lakes Drive.

Phone: (702) 486-5205

Days/Hours: The museum is open 9:00 a.m. to 5:00 p.m. seven days a week. The library of historical documents is open 9:00 a.m. to 5:00 p.m. weekdays.

Admission: $2.00 Adults 18 and over. Children under 18 admitted free.

Facilities: Wheelchair access, wheelchair loan, baby changing station, gift shop.

Groups: Guided tours for groups of ten or more are available with advance reservations. The auditorium and gallery areas may also be rented for meetings or private parties.

the surrounding mountains. Be sure to let your children push the button to hear the mountain lion roar. It's scary! There's a nice display of mounted bighorn sheep, and collections of plants, butterflies and insects. Although most of the exhibits are not made to be touched, kids can still get close enough to get a good look. Another exhibit has skeletons of ice age animals that used to live here, including a huge mammoth and a sloth. Kids can feel the ridges on a mammoth's tooth and see a display explaining how packrat burrows contain valuable archeological evidence.

The Regional History room contains all sorts of artifacts about Southern Nevada history, from stone tools used by the earliest residents to Native American baskets and houses, from mining and railroad displays to a reproduction of Bugsy Siegel's hotel suite. There are exhibits showing Southern Nevada's role in World War II, when it was home to the Las Vegas Army Gunnery School (now Nellis Air Force Base), and the plants in Henderson which processed magnesium for the war effort. A model of Woodrow Wilson, the first black man to serve in the Nevada legislature, speaks about living and working in early Las Vegas. It's very educational as well as entertaining.

The museum store offers a wide variety of books and publications about Nevada. For serious researchers, the museum also contains a library of old newspapers, books and photos which give a wonderfully complete look into the way people lived in days gone by. Be sure to pick up a free Nevada map from the front desk before you leave to explore the rest of the park. If the weather is nice, bring a picnic lunch (don't forget food for the ducks) and you could spend the whole day here. ■

Old Las Vegas Fort

A remnant of the first Anglo settlement in the Las Vegas valley dating back to 1855.

Admission: Free
Hours: Daily 8:30 a.m.
to 3:30 p.m.
908 N. Las Vegas Blvd.
Las Vegas
(702) 486-3511
Located on Las Vegas Boulevard and Washington Avenue near Cashman Field

Sports Hall-of-Fame

Largest personal collection of sports memorabilia in the country. Includes card collectables, autographed balls, gloves, bats, photographs.

Admission: Free
Hours: Daily
Las Vegas Club Hotel & Casino
18 Fremont St, Las Vegas, NV
(702) 385-1664

World of Clowns

See how clown and animation sculptures are created. A half hour self guided tour with clown escort takes you from design to casting to the finishing process. World of Clowns is the home of "Hobo Joe" and a production facility for other popular Disney and Warner Brothers characters including Popeye, Betty Boop, E.T. and Rocky and Bullwinkle. Watch craftsmen make clown sculptures in their workroom. Visit "Lara" a live clown, the merry-go-round gallery museum containing clown memorabilia, statues & animated cartoon figures. Clown statues are sold along with shirts, mugs and lots of other items emblazoned with clowns in the gift shop. There is also a cafe with a luncheon style menu on-site.

Hours: Monday through Friday
8:00 a.m. to 5:00 p.m., Saturday and Sunday 9:00 a.m. to
6:00 p.m., Reservations Required,

330 Carousel Pkwy.
Henderson, NV
(702) 434-1700
(off I-95 near Warm Springs
Between Gibson & Stephanie)

Art Galleries and Museums

Art Galleries

Thousands of art pieces to choose from, including collectible autographed sports or celebrity memorabilia, animated art cells, oils, serigraphs, watercolors, posters and mirrors.

Hours: Monday through Friday
9:00 a.m. to 5:30 p.m.
3871 South Valley View, Suite 9
Las Vegas, NV
(702) 368-7888

Art Encounter

Nevada's largest fine art gallery offers quality, selection, and competitive pricing for every art appetite. Conveniently located a short distance from "the strip," this magnificent 8000 square foot gallery features originals by over 100 local and national artists.

Hours: Tuesday to Friday
10:00 a.m. to 6:00 p.m.
Saturday and Monday noon to
5:00 p.m.
3979 Spring Mountain Road
Las Vegas, NV
(702) 227-0220   (800) 395-2996

Boulder City Art Gallery

Boulder Dam Hotel
Original fine arts and local artists are featured.

Hours: Monday through Saturday
10:00 a.m. to 5:00 p.m., Sunday noon to 5:00 p.m.
1305 Arizona Street
Boulder City, NV
(702) 293-6284

museums

Carrara Galleries

The museum quality of Carrara Galleries exhibits a diverse range of original and limited edition artwork featuring 20th century and 60 contemporary artists as well as local artisans. The gallery offers originals, mixed-medium, limited edition signed/numbered prints, as well as sculptures in bronze, marble and alabaster.

Hours: Monday through Saturday 10:00 a.m. to 6:00 p.m., Sunday 10:00 a.m. to 4:00 p.m. or by appt.
1236 Rainbow Blvd.
Las Vegas, NV
(702) 877-4299

Charleston Heights Arts Center

Hours: Monday and Thursday 1:00 p.m. to 9:00 p.m.; Tuesday and Wednesday 10:00 a.m. to 9:00 p.m.; Friday 10:00 a.m. to 6:00 p.m.; Saturday and Sunday 1:00 p.m. to 5:00 p.m.
800 S. Brush St.
Las Vegas, NV
(702) 229-6383

Contemporary Arts Collective

Hours: Friday through Sunday noon to 4:00 p.m., Wednesday and Thursday 6:00 p.m. to 8:00 p.m.
304 E. Charleston Blvd.
Las Vegas, NV
(702) 382-3686

Donna Beam Fine Arts Gallery

Year-round changing exhibitions in all media featuring invited national and regional artists, faculty and students.

Hours: 9:00 a.m. to 5:00 p.m., Monday through Friday
4505 S. Maryland Pkwy
Las Vegas, NV
(702) 895-3893

Glass Artistry

At Glass Artistry, you will find unique one-of-a-kind art in glass. The collection includes sculptures, etched and carved mirrors, fused bowls and platters. The only all-glass gallery in Las Vegas has a wonderful representation of several local artists.

Hours: Monday through Friday 9:00 a.m. to 5:00 p.m.
4200 West Desert Inn Road
Las Vegas, NV
(702) 221-8494

Moonstruck Gallery

International, award-winning gallery and frame design center featuring a wide array of fine crafts including jewelry, pottery, kaleidoscopes, handcrafted musical instruments, desk accessories, hand blown glass, limited edition prints and original works by local and regional artists, Native American flutes, recorded music and books.

Hours: Monday through Saturday 10:00 a.m. to 7:00 p.m.
6322 West Sahara Avenue
Las Vegas, NV
(702) 364-0531   (800) 421-9133

Nevada Institute for Contemporary Art

The 5,000 square foot facility is used to educate elementary school students in the area of art.

Hours: Tuesday, Wednesday and Friday, 10:00 a.m. to 6:00 p.m., Thursday 10:00 a.m. to 8:00 p.m., Saturday and Sunday 10:00 a.m. to 3:00 p.m.
3455 E. Flamingo Rd
Las Vegas, NV
(702) 434-2666

Regal Gallery

Thomas Kinkade fine art is featured in a warm traditional gallery setting. Canvas', lithographs and gift items can be found at this premiere dealer serving East Las Vegas, Green Valley and Henderson.

> **Hours:** Monday through Saturday 9:30 a.m. to 5:30 p.m.
> 3315 East Russell Road, Suite K, Las Vegas, NV
> **(702) 436-4146   (800) 210-8727**

Art Museums

African American Museum & Research Center

For information see page 26.
> The Walker Foundation
> 705 W. Van Buren Ave.
> Las Vegas, NV
> **(702) 647-2242**

Green Valley Sculptures

Life-like bronze statues line Green Valley Pkwy. near Sunset Rd in the Green Valley area of Henderson. Works include permanent and rotating outdoor pieces by J. Seward Johnson, Lita Albuquerque, Lloyd Hamrol, Lee Side. The sculpture museum offers location maps and information on the various outdoor sculptures displayed throughout the Henderson/Green Valley area.

> Green Valley Outdoor Sculpture Museum Information Center
> Green Valley Shopping Plaza on Sunset Rd.
> 2501 N. Green Valley Pkwy.
> Las Vegas, NV
> **(702) 458-8855**

Las Vegas Art Museum

The Art Museum, attached to the West Las Vegas Library, consists of three galleries with displays of national and international painters and sculptures in the main gallery, local artists are displayed in the Nevada Gallery, and the Mini Gallery presents art auctions. The museum occupies two modest one-story buildings. Originally, the structures were part of Twin Lakes Lodge Resort, a popular vacation spot for Hollywood stars in the 1940's. The resort and land was bought by the city of Las Vegas and Lorenzi Park was created. Visiting artists offer special workshops from time to time, and exhibits change monthly. Many contemporary paintings, sculptures and other works, and a growing collection of older famous artists are featured. Numerous temporary traveling exhibits make this a great place to get away for an afternoon of culture. A nice museum gift store offers art and books for the connoisseur. Continuing exhibitions include the Salvador Dali oil painting "Vision of Hell," "Sturman Collection of African Art" and "Desert Sculptors II."

> **Admission:** $3.00 Adults, $2.00 Seniors, $1.00 Students
> **Hours:** Tuesday through Saturday 10:00 a.m. to 5:00 p.m., Sunday 1:00 p.m. to 5:00 p.m., Tours by arrangement.
> 9600 W. Sahara Ave.
> Las Vegas, NV
> **(702) 360-8000**

Veterans Art Museum

Former Nevada Governor, Bob Miller's 50-year collection of western and wildlife art is on display.

> 700 E. Naples Dr.
> Las Vegas, NV
> **(702) 792-8387**

chapter three

things to
do and see

- Entertainment, Magic, Shows & Theaters
- Book Stores & Libraries
- Spectator Sports
- Recreation
- Shopping

Arcades

Atari® Adventure Arcade
Riviera Hotel & Casino
2901 Las Vegas Blvd. South
(702) 734-5110

Cyber Station
Large video arcade and fun center
featuring the latest games.
> **Hours:** Sunday through
> Thursday, 10:00 a.m. to
> 11:00 p.m.
> Forum Shops at Caesars

Gameworks
Featuring more than 250 games of all
types, including the Sega Power
Sled, which features three 8-foot
sleds that riders steer through a
downhill snow course.
> **Hours:** 10:00 a.m. to 4:00 a.m.
> Showcase Mall
> 3785 S Las Vegas Blvd
> **(702) 432-GAME**

Luxor Live
18,000 sq. ft. virtualand arcade. Sega
Virtualand Arcade, Virtual Formula
Race Cars, F-16 Flight simulators,
IMAX Theater shows.
Hours: 9:00 a.m. to midnight
> Luxor Hotel & Casino
> 3900 Las Vegas Blvd. S
> **(702) 262-4000**

Mutiny Bay
Arcade offering video games and
electronically simulated rides.
> **Hours:** 9:00 a.m. to 1:00 a.m.
> Treasure Island
> 3300 Las Vegas Blvd. S
> (702) 894-7111

Pocket Change
70 arcade games.
> **Hours:** Monday through Friday
> 10:00 a.m. to 9:00 p.m.,
> Saturday and Sunday 10:00 a.m.
> to 6:00 p.m.
> Meadows Mall
> 4300 Meadows Lane
> **(702) 878-8776**

MGM Grand

The MGM Grand houses an 11,400-sq.-ft. arcade. There are more than
130 games, including virtual reality and motion simulators.
> **Hours:** 9:00 a.m. to midnight daily.

things to do & see

things to do & see

A. J. Hackett Bungy

Bungy Jumping ... and kids want to this this? This incredible experience is one of a kind. All you can do is stand and watch in horror as your kid jumps off an 18 story platform. Don't let this daring challenge pass you by. Various packages are available with T-shirts and videos too.

> **Admission:** $49.00 for
> the jump only
> 810 Circus Circus Dr.
> Las Vegas, NV
> **(702) 385-4321**

Adventure Canyon Log Flume

You won't want to miss this new and improved adventure for the whole family. You'll race down the swirling waters of a roaring waterfall and enjoy a leisurely ride along Buffalo Bill's "Indoor River" while you test your aim with laser equipped pistols along the way!

> **Admission:** $3.00
> **Hours:** Daily 10:00 a.m. to
> 10:00 p.m. Friday and Saturday
> 10:00 a.m. to 11:00 p.m.
> Buffalo Bill's Resort
> Stateline, NV
> **(800) 367-7383**

Adventuredome At Circus Circus

America's largest indoor theme park, featuring the only indoor double-loop, double corkscrew roller coaster in the world. Over 15 rides for all ages and numerous attractions including midway games, arcade area, clown shows and more. The prehistoric ages are re-created in the Adventuredome at Circus Circus. Kids can try the Fun House Express, roller coasters, a water flume ride and other thrilling attractions.The theme park features water rides, a roller coaster, laser tag, animated dinosaurs, an arcade, gift shop and restaurant. The 5-acre theme park is fully enclosed and climate controlled, boasting a comfortable 72 degrees year-round among sunny skies, picturesque cliffs and lush Southwestern landscaping. The pink glass dome of the theme park is the largest space-frame dome in the United States. Single ride tickets or all-day ride passes are available.

> **Admission:** Park entry is free.
> Ride tickets range from $2.00 to
> $5.00. An unlimited ride pass is
> $11.95 for those 33 to under 48
> inches tall, $15.95 for those 48
> inches tall and over.
> **Hours:** Open Sunday through
> Thursday from 10:00 a.m. to
> 6:00 p.m. and Friday and
> Saturday from 10:00 a.m. to
> midnight.
> Circus Circus
> 2880 Las Vegas Blvd S.
> Las Vegas, NV
> **(702) 794-3939**
> www.circuscircus-lasvegas.com

Atlantis Fountain Show

Recreation of the mythical sinking of Atlantis. Life-like characters of Atlas, Gadrius and Alia and special fire, water, steam and sound effects bring the fall of Atlantis to life. Providing the backdrop for the Lost City of Atlantis Show, a 50,000 gallon marine aquarium.

Hours: Every hour beginning at 11:00 a.m.
Forum Shops At Caesar's Palace
3500 Las Vegas Blvd S.
Las Vegas, NV
(702) 893-4800

Big Shot

Big Shot: "Shoots" 160 feet into the air, experiencing zero-gravity, then free falls back to the launching pad. Located at the Stratosphere Tower. A two-second, 160-foot launch up a tower is startling. Doing it 1,000 feet in the air atop one of the tallest buildings in the world is terrifying. Riders are fully exposed to the vastness of the valley as the machine reverse-bungies riders up and down the mast three times before settling back to the base. Riders experience 4 G's of force from the thrust.

Your thrill ride experiences will never be complete without riding this!

Admission: $6:00, plus $6:00 admission to the Stratosphere Tower, Nevada residents get a reduced rate.
Hours: 10:00 a.m. to midnight weekdays, 10:00 a.m. to 1:00 a.m., weekends
Stratosphere Hotel and Casino
2000 Las Vegas Blvd. S.
Las Vegas, NV
(702) 380-7777

Bonnie & Clyde's "Death Car"

Located in Primm, Nevada, just 35 minutes south of Las Vegas. The Bonnie & Clyde "Death Car" is on display inside Whiskey Pete's. It is the actual Ford that the 1930's robbery team was driving when they were ambushed and killed by the FBI. A letter from Ford Motor Company authenticates the car as Clyde's. And a letter he wrote to Ford Motor Company offering his praises as a fine get-away car is also displayed. Read about the last years of Bonnie and Clyde's turbulent life style, and see the actual blood stained, bullet-holed shirt Clyde was wearing when he was killed. A fascinating piece of American history. Also on display is the restored 1931 Classic Armored Lincoln that was custom built for gangster Dutch Schultz.

Admission: Free
Stateline - about 35 miles south of Las Vegas, NV
(702) 382-1212

Bonnie Springs / Old Nevada

Bonnie Springs Ranch was originally built in 1843 as a stopover for the wagon trains going to California down the Old Spanish Trail. In 1846 General

things to do & see

Fremont, on his way to California, stopped at what is now Bonnie Springs Ranch to gear up for his trip through Death Valley. Since 1952 the ranch has been used as a tourist attraction. Often called "an oasis in the desert," where you can stop for a cool drink of spring water. Today the grounds are a delight for locals and tourists alike. A full scale re-creation of an Old West town with wooden sidewalks and buildings featuring a restaurant, saloon, museum and shops. There are shootouts and hangings hourly in the streets. On Saturdays and Sundays, special children's shows let kids be part of a posse to catch the bad guy. There is a great petting zoo with over 100 animals. A miniature locomotive offers free rides from the parking lot to the entrance. There is a fine dinner house and a quaint cocktail lounge.

Admission: Admission to the zoo is free, admission prices to Old Nevada are $6.50 Adult, $5.50 Seniors and $4.00 Children ages 5 to 11.
Hours: 10:30 a.m. to 5:00 p.m. daily, Cowboy shows daily at 1:30 a.m., noon, 2:00 p.m., 2:30 p.m., 4:40 p.m. and 5:00 p.m.
1 Bonnie Springs Ranch Rd
Old Nevada
(702) 875-4191
Head straight West on Charleston Blvd past Red Rock Canyon, 20 miles.

Buccaneer Bay Sea Battle

Canon fire flares, treasure chests are flung open, powder stores are lost and a ship sinks with all hands on board the pirate ship Hispañiola as it faces the British frigate HMS Britannia in an action-filled performance. The crowds are large, so get there early and plan to spend time on the dock.

Admission: Free
Hours: Nightly 4:00 p.m., 5:30p.m., 7:00 p.m., 8:30 p.m., 10:00 p.m., extra show at 11:30 p.m. on Friday and Saturday.
Treasure Island Hotel front entrance
3300 Las Vegas Blvd. South
Las Vegas
702) 650-7400
www.treasureislandlasvegas.com

Cinema Ride

Cinema Ride boasts the nation's first 3-D motion simulator ride. Four rides, Galactic Flight, Atlantis, Submarine Race, Coaster Crazy and Haunted Graveyard Run, move in 6 degrees of motion.

Admission: Single $8.00, double $12.00, triple $14.00, quad $16.00.
Hours: 10:00 a.m. to 11:00 p.m. daily
Forum Shops at Caesar's
3500 Las Vegas Blvd. S.
Las Vegas, NV
(702) 369-4008

City of Las Vegas Fire Department

Children meet real firemen and paramedics. See real emergency vehicles, equipment, watch a firefighter "suit up" in fire fighting gear. Also see how and where firemen live when they are on duty and see where they learn life saving and emergency information and techniques. Children are encouraged to ask questions and are given information on fire prevention and what to do in an emergency. Schedule the closest firehouse about two weeks in advance.
Las Vegas, NV
(702) 383-2888 - main station

Competition Grand Prix

Features three go-cart tracks, two 18-hole miniature golf courses and an arcade.

Admission: $3.50 for the go-carts and $3.00 for miniature golf
2980 S. Sandhill Road
Las Vegas, NV
(702) 431-7223

Cranberry World

If nagging questions about cranberries have been keeping you awake at night, relax! You'll find out everything you wanted to know about the tart little berries (and then some) at Cranberry World West. In 1995, Ocean Spray Cranberries, Inc. opened a 10,000 square foot visitors' center adjacent to its juice processing and distribution facility, and it's been a favorite school field trip destination ever since. The tour begins in the Cranberry Cinema where you view an eight-minute film hosted by the center's mascot, Carina the Cran Cran Girl (you gotta love it).

Cranberry World Info

Address: 1301 Pacific Drive, Henderson

Directions: Exit I-95 at Lake Mead Drive, go west to Gibson, turn right on Gibson and left on American Pacific.

Phone: (702) 566-7160

Days/Hours: 9:00 a.m. -5:00 p.m. seven days-a-week

Admission: Free

Facilities: Wheelchair accessible, baby changing station, gift shop

www.cranberryworldwest.com

You then go into a museum area where several displays show how the berries are grown and harvested, and a giant berry model shows what they look like inside. If you are going on a self-guided tour, use the buttons on each display to make a recorded message begin. You'll find out lots of interesting facts about cranberries, including how they test for good berries (by seeing how far they bounce). You next go to an observation deck where you can view the giant machines inside the processing plant and get an explanation of how cranberries are turned into sauce, juice, etc. It's fascinating to see how they turn berries into finished products in a matter of minutes. The family will enjoy the popular "Guess the Year" game, in which you watch vintage Ocean Spray television commercials and try to guess what year they were made by looking at the actors' clothes and hair dos.

The tour ends in the demonstration and test kitchen, where you can sample goodies made with cranberry products and belly up to a free juice bar. You and your kids can taste all the different juice blends, including Cranberry-Key Lime, Cran-Blueberry and Cran-Mango. You can go back to the self-service juice bar as often as you want, which is probably one of the reasons kids like it. Be sure to get your free recipe booklet. The gift store sells clothing, Ocean Spray golf balls, cranberry soap and much more in addition to all sorts of food products made with cranberries. Would you believe cranberry salsa, cranberry mustard, or cranberry vinegar? You owe it to yourself to try some of these just to say you did it. The tour is a lot of fun, especially if Carina shows up for photos. ∎

Dansey's Indoor Race Track

The area's only indoor, off-road racetrack for radio-controlled cars.

Admission: Cost is $7.00 all day for those who bring their own cars. Car rentals are $15.00 per hour or $8.00 per half-hour
Hours: 10:00 a.m. to 9:00 p.m. Tuesdays and Fridays and 5:00 p.m. Sunday.
741 N. Nellis Blvd.
Las Vegas, NV
(702) 453-7223

Desert Storm Paintball Games

Must be 10 years of age and older to play. Bring your own paintball gun and save $5.00. Special group rates and field reservations available

Admission: Complete playing packages available for $15. Playing field one mile past asphalt on N. Jones Street
Las Vegas, NV
(702) 595-2555

Discovery Zone

Specially designed indoor padded playground with slides, swings, tunnels and things to climb on and through for children up to age 12. Socks are required for all play participants. Adults can participate free of charge but cannot drop children off. Snack bar, overnight camp-ins available.

Admission: $5.99 per child
Hours: Monday through Thursday 10:00 a.m. to 8:00 p.m., Friday and Saturday 10:00 a.m. to 9:00 p.m., Sunday 11:00 a.m. to 7:00 p.m.
2020 Olympic Ave.
Henderson, NV
(702) 434-9950

Dolphin Habitat

Delightful, dolphins entertain, play and swim in a 1.5 million gallon pool. Educating and fascinating, watch the dolphins play, do flips and being fed.

Admission: $3.00, children under 10 free
Hours: Monday through Friday 11:00 a.m. to 5:30 p.m., Saturday and Sunday 9:00 a.m. to 7:00 p.m.
Mirage Hotel
3400 Las Vegas Blvd.
Las Vegas, NV
(702) 791-7111

Ethel M Chocolate Factory & Cactus Garden

Ethel M's is a great place to go for a field trip - you get credit for teaching your kids valuable lessons while having the perfect excuse to indulge your passion: sweets! Learn about desert ecology, eat chocolate, see how a factory works, eat chocolate, visit a water recycling demonstration, eat chocolate — You get the picture. It's an interesting mix of things to see in one location, not too surprising from a company which has been specializing in "assortments" for so long. In 1911, Forrest Mars' parents started the Mars Candy Company, makers of some of America's favorite goodies, including M&M's and Snickers Bars. When he retired in 1976, Mr. Mars decided to create a line of gourmet chocolates named for his mother, Ethel. The Henderson factory now produces over 60 varieties of high-quality, preservative-free chocolates including cream liqueurs for the grown-ups.

The self-guided tour begins with the kitchen, where the chefs and their assis-

Ethel M's Information

Address: 1 Sunset Way, Henderson

Directions: In Green Valley at the intersection of Mountain Vista and Sunset. Go east from that intersection into the business park and turn left on Cactus Garden Way.

Phone: (702) 433-2500 or (888) 627-0990

Days/Hours: 8:30 a.m. to 7:00 p.m. seven days, but the factory only has a skeleton crew on Sunday, so it's best to go during the week.

Admission: Free

Facilities: Wheelchair access, 2 gift shops

tants whip up centers for lemon butter creams, raspberry, nut, caramel and other yummy candies. The centers are then placed on a chocolate base and move down the assembly line to machines which pours chocolate over them. Kids like to watch the factory through the windows and see how the candies are made. The 20-minute tour ends in the gift shop where Ethel M chocolates and ice cream are sold, and where you get a free sample of candy. You can buy prepackaged assortments of chocolates here or choose your own favorites.

Don't let your chocoholic frenzy make you forget the educational reason for coming here. The three acre cactus garden is really worth seeing. It contains one of America's finest and largest collections of cacti, succulents and other desert plants. It's fun to wander down the winding paths, and if you're quiet, you may surprise a rabbit or a roadrunner in the underbrush. Guided tours are available for groups of ten or more. Be sure to show your kids The Living Machine, a water recycling plant which treats the waste water from the factory. It uses bacteria, snails, fish and plants to remove pollutants from the water. Follow the path of the water as it passes through the various stages of the process, eventually emerging as clean water used for irrigation and other non-drinking uses. After the tour, you can visit the Cactus Garden gift shop and buy a cactus to take home. Or, you could go back to the candy shop for one last truffle. ∎

Favorite Brands International Marshmallow Factory

When you think of marshmallows, you probably remember your childhood, toasting them over a campfire on a lazy summer evening. Or you might recall your marshmallow catching on fire and plopping into the coals as the other kids laughed at you. But one thing you don't think of is Henderson, Nevada, where the puffy little snacks are made. A tour through the Favorite Brands Marshmallow Factory is a good way to find out interesting information about marshmallows and see how factories work. Be sure to call beforehand to find out when the equipment used in the tour will be operating. These machines have actually been replaced by faster, more automated equipment located in another building, but when school groups or tours come through, the company reactivitates the production line so people can see how it works. You first view the cooking kettles, where corn syrup, sugar and other ingredients are blended together and cooked. Then the mixture is puffed with air to make it light and fluffy and squeezed through holes to produce a long roll of marshmallow, which is then sliced into snack-sized bits. At the end of the tour you get a free sample bag of marshmallows in the gift shop, where you can also buy other marshmallow products and souvenirs. Go home and toast some marshmallows in the fireplace with your kids. It's a great way to bring the family together, unless of course your kids laugh when your marshmallow drops into the fire. ■

Favorite Brands International Marshmallow Factory Information

Address: 1180 Marshmallow Lane, Henderson

Directions: Exit I-95 at Lake Mead Drive, go west to Gibson, turn right on Gibson and left on Marycrest. Follow Marycrest to Marshmallow Lane.

Phone: (702) 393-7308

Days/Hours: 9:00 a.m. - 4:30 p.m. Monday through Saturday

Admission: Free

Facilities: Wheelchair accessible, gift shop

Festival Fountains

The Roman statues come to life in an eight-minute battle featuring Bacchus and his entourage in a realistic, animated robotic show that includes lasers, music, fire, steam and sound effects.

Admission: Free

Hours: 11:00 a.m. daily and runs every hour on the hour

Forum Shops at Caesar's Palace

3500 Las Vegas Blvd S., Las Vegas, NV

(702) 893-4800

Flyaway Indoor Skydiving

Have you always wanted to skydive but were afraid you'd end up flat as a possum on a freeway? Relax! Now you can experience the thrill without the danger by skydiving indoors at Flyaway. Flyaway is one of only two commercial wind tunnels in the U.S. designed to simulate the freefall experience of skydiving. You get to fly in a column of air 12 feet across and up to 22 feet high, with vertical airspeeds up to 120 mph. This effect is produced by a giant airplane engine mounted in the floor of the flight chamber. The propeller blows air upwards into the room through a protective screen which forms the floor of the chamber. It makes a great roaring noise which can be heard outside the building.

The price includes a 15 minute training class discussing the fundamentals of flight as well as safety precautions. A cool jumpsuit and helmet and a 15 minute flight, session is shared by a maximum of 5 flyers. Training classes are scheduled every half-hour, and the total experience lasts about an hour. An instructor in the tunnel helps each flyer as they take turns jumping into the air stream. A padded area around the edge allows people to wait their turn out of the air stream and also to land in safety. This can be fun even for novices because the instructor guides you by grabbing onto a hand or onto the baggy jumpsuit and keeps you in the right position so you don't lose control and tumble. An attendant in the control room can vary the speed of the engine according to the skill of the flyer. After a few tries, even a beginner can balance and fly on his own.

Friends and family can watch the action through windows in the observation chamber. It's fun to see experienced flyers somersault and do acrobatics, but its also fun to watch newcomers conquer their fear and learn to balance in mid-air. Observers are encouraged to take pictures and videos to bring home. Those without a video camera can purchase a video of the experience for $15.00.

The 'Learn to Fly' coaching package includes five flights, video services and personalized coaching. This would be a great gift for someone who wants to learn how to skydive. ∎

Flyaway Indoor Skydiving Information

Address: 200 Convention Center Drive

Directions: Between the Stardust Hotel and the Convention Center

Phone: (702) 731-4768

www.gsflyaway@aol.com

Days/Hours: Monday through Saturday 10:00 am-7:00 pm
Sunday 10:00 am-5:00 pm

Admission: *First flight* $35.00; *Double Flight* (twice as long) $55.00; *5 flight book* (for use by one person); $100.00; *Learn to Fly coaching package* $169.00

Restrictions: Height and weight need to be in proportion according to their chart. Minimum weight for Children is 40 pounds. Minors are required to have a parent or guardian present in class.

things to do & see

Formula K Family Fun Park

Two 18 hole miniature golf courses, video arcade, mini go carts for children 5 and up.

Admission: $3.50, Children under 54" ride free with an adult

Hours: Monday through Thursday 3:00 p.m. to 10:00 p.m., Friday 3:00 p.m. to midnight, Saturday noon to midnight, Sunday noon to 10:00 p.m.

2980 South Sandhill Rd

Las Vegas, NV

(702) 431-7223

The Forum Shops

The Forum Shops at Caesars bills itself as 'The Shopping Wonder of the World,' and they have a pretty good claim to the title. It's packed with some of the most exclusive and pricey stores in the world, including Gucci, Louis Vuitton, and Christian Dior, as well as several exclusive and pricey restaurants. But, there are lots of things for your family to see and do here that won't blow your budget. A favorite free attraction is people-watching, as throngs of the rich and famous and not-so-rich and famous from all over the world parade through its streets and plazas. The interior design is a wonder to behold, with Roman arches and columns, fountains, an aquarium where divers swim with tropical fish, and two different shows where animatronic statues move and talk amid jets of water, laser lights and columns of fire. Be sure to watch the ceilings — computer lighting make the artificial sky slowly change from light to dark and back again every hour.

The Race for Atlantis IMAX 3D ride is located in the newest section of the Forum Shops next to the Atlantis Fountain. The entrance to the ride features a 30 foot statue of Neptune battling a sea dragon, and walkways appear suspended over a bed of fog. Inside, strap on your headset and buckle your seat belt for a wild chariot race through Atlantis. The headsets contain liquid crystals and stereo speakers to make images on the giant screen jump out at you as you seem to tear along avoiding obstacles and crashing competitors.

Caesars Garden of Games arcade, located downstairs at the far north end of the mall, contains a good selection of arcade games for kids of all ages. It's also home to the 3D Cinema Ride, a full-motion ride with lots of action and thrills. The Cinema Ride gives you a chance to rocket down ski slopes, race through a haunted graveyard or experience a runaway roller coaster, all in relative safety (as long as your heart can take it). Riders must be 42 inches tall. A single ride is $9 and discounts are available for multiple rides. ■

The Forum Shops Information

Location: Caesars Palace

Address: 3570 Las Vegas Blvd. South

Directions: Located on the Strip at Flamingo Road. Free parking available behind Caesars or valet park at the entrance to the shops.

Phone: (702) 893-4800

Days/Hours: The mall is open 365 days a year, from 10 am to 1 pm Sunday through Thursday and until midnight on Friday and Saturday.

Admission: Free

Facilities: Wheelchair access, wheelchair and stroller rental, guided tours for groups.

Ticket prices: $9.50 Adults, $6.75 kids under twelve, $8.50 Seniors, $8.00 Nevada residents and Students. Riders must be at least 42" tall. Not for expectant moms or those with bad backs.

Fountains Of Bellagio

The fountains span 1,100 feet of the 8-acre lake in front of the Bellagio. The shows are programmed to nine different pieces of music from composers such as Copland and Strauss and vocalists such as Luciano Pavarotti and Frank Sinatra, featuring blasts of water up to 240 feet in the air.

Admission: Free
Hours: every half-hour 2 p.m.-midnight daily
Bellagio
3600 Las Vegas Blvd., Las Vegas, NV
(702) 693-7111

things to do & see

Fremont Street

Fremont Street is where Las Vegas began. At the west end of the street where the Union Plaza now stands, the railroad held an auction of building lots in 1905 to allow private citizens to start constructing homes and businesses in the townsite. Fremont Street was also Las Vegas' first paved street, home to its first traffic light and the first structure designed from the ground up to be a casino (The Golden Nugget). For many years, Fremont Street was the place to go for business, shopping and entertainment in Las Vegas. With the advent of Strip mega-resorts, the development of suburbs and shopping malls, people began drifting away. Downtown casinos and merchants looking for a way to recapture their hearts and dollars hit upon an idea as daring, glitzy and ultimately successful as Las Vegas itself, which they named the Fremont Street Experience.

Fremont Street has been transformed into a covered pedestrian mall with landscaping, patterned paving, benches and a misting system to cool down hot summer temperatures. The real star of the Experience is the huge canopy towering 90 feet above a four-block section of the street. In the light and sound shows presented nightly on the canopy, dazzling, computer-generated images dance to music overhead. There are a variety of themes, including famous Las Vegas entertainers, gigantic slot machine reels and galloping horses, and more shows are constantly being developed. It takes 2.1 million lights, 121 computers and 208 speakers to produce each six minute spectacle. There's plenty to look at in between shows, including live bands, street performers and, of course, other people. A variety of retail carts sell snacks and souvenirs to the rhythm of piped-in music. There are many great restaurants and interesting shops in the hotels lining the street, but if you want to visit them, be sure to keep a tight grip on your child's hand while walking through the casino. Unattended kids in casinos are a big no-no.

Plans for expansion include construction of retail shops at the Parking Plaza and additions to the Neon Museum. The first installment to the outdoor museum is the Hacienda Hotel's horse and rider marquee now located at the intersection of Fremont Street and Las Vegas Boulevard. Of course, there's still plenty of neon at the casinos which line Fremont Street and make it daytime-bright all night long. ■

Fremont Street Experience Information

Address: Fremont Street between Main Street and Las Vegas Blvd. Directions: Exit I-95 at Las Vegas Blvd. and go south (right). Park in the five-story red garage at the corner of Las Vegas Blvd. and Fremont. Or park at one of the hotel parking garages. Parking is free with validation at one of the downtown casinos.

Phone: (702) 678-5777

Days/Hours: Shows run daily after dark

Admission: Free

Fun House Express

Thrilling motion simulator.
Circus Circus
2880 Las Vegas Blvd.
Las Vegas, NV
(702) 794-3939

Gameworks

Gameworks is like a casino for the under-21 crowd: rows of flashing, beeping machines beckon you to spend your money in a huge, windowless room with no clocks. At least here you're not expecting to get your money back, and it's a great place for teenagers to have fun with their friends. Actually, there's something for all ages in the 47,000 square foot basement under the Showcase Mall. Little kids enjoy the simple arcade games, older kids can play more sophisticated games, as well as pool and air hockey, and there's a bar/lounge upstairs for Adults. Funky music, industrial/hi-tech décor and the constant hum of activity make it a happening place on weekend date nights. Gameworks features hundreds of games of all types including the Sega Power Sled, three 8-foot sleds that riders steer through as televised downhill snow course. Nothing works up an appetite like slaying zombies and ninjas, so Gameworks has plenty of places to eat and drink. Besides two snack bars, they have a juice and smoothie station, a Starbucks coffee stand and a full-service restaurant.

Entering Gameworks from the main entrance on the Strip gives you a great

Gameworks Information

Location: Showcase Mall

Address: 3785 Las Vegas Blvd. South

Directions: Located on the Strip just north of the MGM Grand next to the giant Coke bottle.

Phone: (702) 432-4263

Days/Hours: 10:00 a.m. to 1:00 a.m. Sunday through Thursday

10:00 a.m. to 2:00 p.m. Friday and Saturday

Admission: Admission is free. Plastic debit cards for arcade games may be purchased in any dollar amount. Gameworks members receive 10% off all prices.

Facilities: Wheelchair access, diaper-changing station, full-service restaurant and bar, 2 snack bars, gift shop

look at one of its most popular attractions: the world's largest free-standing rock-climbing structure, which rises like the Matterhorn in the center of the building. It's fun to watch climbers struggle up the manmade mountain, and kids who weigh over 40 pounds can sign up to climb it as well. It's all very safe — each climber is harnessed and tethered. A 40 foot climb up the Surge Rock Climbing Experience costs $6.00 and a 75 foot climb to the top of the structure costs $10.00. You may purchase a photo afterwards proving you conquered the rock. ■

Gilcrease Nature Sanctuary

Non-profit safe-haven for exotic game birds and wildlife features the Aviaries and small habitats for birds and animals, all in a beautiful setting filled with trees and flower-lined pathways. The sanctuary is home to The Wild Wing Project, southern Nevada's only non-profit, federally licensed wildlife rehabilitation organization and houses a large collection of game, exotic birds and birds of prey that are being rehabilitated.

> **Admission:** $3.00 Adults, $1.00 Children 6 and older, under 6 Free
> **Hours:** Wednesday through Sunday 11:00 a.m. to 3:00 p.m.
> 8103 Racel Street
> Las Vegas, NV
> **(702) 645-4224**

Hard Rock Café

Nestled beneath a 100 ft. neon replica of an electric guitar, this restaurant/gift shop/bar classifies as a museum in its own right. The walls are draped with memorabillia from every pop and rock legend of the 50's through the 90's. You have a choice of dining among all this rock-n-roll history or you can simply slip into their gift shop and take home a piece of Hard Rock Las Vegas for yourself and friends.

> **Hours:** 9:00 a.m. - 12:00 a.m. weekdays, 9:00 a.m. - 1:30 a.m. Friday and Saturday
> 4475 Paradise Rd, Las Vegas, NV
> **(702) 733-8400**

Henderson Bird Preserve

A 147-acre migratory bird stop and wetlands that encompass basins, lagoons and ponds. Amenities for visitors include boardwalks, trails, trees, benches, blinds, kiosks.

> **Admission:** Free
> **Hours:** 6:00 a.m. to 3:00 p.m. daily
> Henderson Water
> Reclamation Facility
> 3400 Moser St.
> Las Vegas, NV
> **(702) 565-2063**

High Roller

The world's highest roller coaster. Be prepared to make two clockwise rotations, bank sharply at 32-degree angles, and travel at speeds up to 35 miles per hour. Height requirement: Minimum 48 inches for all rides.

> **Hours:** 10:00 a.m. to midnight, Sunday through Thursday, 10:00 a.m. to 1:00 a.m. Friday and Saturday.
> **Admission:** Tower admission plus High Roller $9.00, Tower admission plus 2 rides $14.00, Two-ride pass, $10.00; Tower and ride tickets may be purchased at any ticketing location throughout the casino and on the indoor observation deck (floor 108).
> The Stratesphere
> 2000 Las Vegas Blvd S,
> Las Vegas, NV
> **1-(800) 99-TOWER** or
> **(702) 380-7777**

things to do & see

Lake Mead Fish Hatchery

Tours can be arranged with the hatchery supervisor prior to a visit. Station staff can answer questions about the facility and the operation.

Hours: 8:00 a.m. to 4:00 p.m.
Monday through Friday
245 Lake Shore Rd.
Boulder City, NV
(702) 486-6738

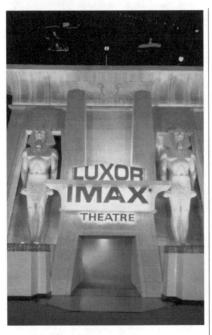

Luxor Imax Theatre

Journey through the past and into the present. State-of-the-art motion simulator ride that will thrill your entire family. Experience Las Vegas' first IMAX Theatre with amazing 2-D and 3-D film technology.

Admission: prices vary
Hours: times vary
Luxor Hotel
3900 Las Vegas Blvd. South
Las Vegas, NV
(702) 262-4555

Lion Habitat

New multi-level, 6,000 sq. ft. habitat is encased with glass skylights and walls giving guests the opportunity to view the lions in the close-to-natural environment with waterfalls, stones, overhangs and trees. Guests can walk through a special glass tunnel that takes you right into the habitat where lions can surround you. The lion cubs have a separate play area, and photo opportunities are available with a cub.

MGM Grand Hotel
3799 Las Vegas Blvd.
Las Vegas, NV
(702) 891-1111

M & M's World

Your tour of M&M's World begins at a gift shop on the ground floor where you can buy Ethel M chocolates, but the real fun is upstairs in the 4-level, 30,000 square foot building. The second floor is a huge gift shop devoted to M&M candies, where you can buy everything from M&M character dolls to pajamas and lunchboxes with the M&M logo. Bins of different colored M&M's are available by the pound for those who want to mix and match colors (there are 21 of them!).

The third floor houses the M&M Academy, where you enter an imaginary university and learn how to become an honorary M&M. This new attraction is loads of fun and very entertaining for adults as well as children. Costumed characters dressed as technicians lead you through a simulated candy factory where you choose whether to be a plain or peanut M&M and go through the process of

being candy-coated, dried and polished in an eerie black light atmosphere. A lab-coated character known as The Professor takes you through an orientation in a computerized control center, complete with a world map showing how the candies are supposedly whisked around the globe through colored pipelines at 400 miles per hour. In order to earn their 'M' and become an 'M-bassador of Fun,' students of M&M Academy must learn its motto in Latin and 'pledge allegiance to the M and the academy for which it stands.' Students don 3-D glasses for a fast-paced movie starring smart-mouthed Red, a plain M&M, and his straight man, Yellow, a peanut candy. The

M & M's World Information

Location: Showcase Mall

Address: 3785 Las Vegas Boulevard South

Directions: Located on the Strip just north of the MGM Grand next to the giant Coke bottle.

Phone: (702) 597-3122

Days/Hours: Sunday through Thursday 10:00 a.m. to midnight, Friday and Saturday 10:00 a.m. to 1:00 a.m.

Admission: $4.00

Facilities: Wheelchair access, diaper changing stations, ATM

movie is funny and exciting, and the 3-D effects have the children grabbing the air in front of them or ducking to avoid 3-D dangers. After the movie, each student receives his M on a sticker and becomes an official graduate.

The fourth floor of the building contains yet another place to buy candy and collectibles. There's even an ATM machine for the weak-willed who've already overspent their souvenir budget. A dessert and coffee bar features ice cream with various candy toppings as well as gourmet coffee and teas. Restrooms are also located on this floor. The entire tour takes less than an hour and is a great way to stretch kids' imaginations. ■

Masquerade Village and Show in the Sky

The Masquerade Show in the Sky is a blending of Mardi Gras, Carnival and Las Vegas, with elaborate floats parading above the casino on tracks in the ceiling. The 12-minute show is presented every two hours and anyone can watch, either from the casino floor or from the balcony above. Performers on the floats do tricks, play music and throw plastic Mardi Gras beads to spectators. After the parade, there are mini-shows at three stages where live performers and animatronic characters sing, dance and perform. For best views of the floats, choose the balconies — the floats are at eye level there. It gets quite crowded, so arrive early if you want your kids to get a good view in front.

For $9.95 you too can be a performer on one of the floats. Purchase tickets from the Play Rio Ticket Sales Counter on the casino level. Everyone dresses in a goofy costume and hat and is handed a musical prop like a tambourine or maracas. Then you get to ride around, make music and throw beads to the people

below. This is good, silly fun if you're not easily embarrassed and if you don't mind heights (13 feet above the floor). After the ride, go downstairs to the Photo Magic shop and see the pictures of your family in costume. For $19.95, you get two photos in a leather album to take home. The Photo Magic shop also does computer morphing of your face with a whole selection of bodies and backgrounds. For a price, you can be a bathing beauty, a biker or a rock star, and they remove wrinkles, fill in bald spots and whiten teeth at no extra charge. If only it transferred over into the real world!

While at the Rio, be sure to visit the shops at the Masquerade Village area. They have everything from fine wines to jewelry to children's clothing. The kids might prefer to check out the small Fun 'n Games arcade upstairs. It's open weekdays from 11:00 a.m. to midnight, Saturday from 10:00 a.m. to 1:00 a.m. and Sunday from 10 :00 a.m. to midnight. Snacks are available on the same level at an ice cream shop and pretzel store. Stop at the Bernard K. Passman Jewelry store, where they have a performer in a Coldstream Guard uniform either marching or standing in the window. See if your kids can make him laugh. He's the only one not having fun. ■

Masquerade Village Information

Location: Rio Suite Hotel & Casino

Address: 3700 W. Flamingo

Directions: Just west of the I-15 freeway

Shortcut: Park on the roof of the parking garage and go across the covered walkway to the Masquerade Village area.

Phone: (702) 252-7777

Days/Hours: 2:00 p.m. to midnight every day except Wednesday

Admission: Viewing is free, $9.95 to ride

Restrictions: Riders on the floats must be 48" tall.

McCarran Airport

Admission: Free tour
Hours: Monday through Friday,
Reservations in advance required
5795 Paradise Rd.
Las Vegas, NV
(702) 261-5153

Menagerie Carousel At The Meadows

An elaborate carousel complete with magical horses and other exotic animals. A relaxing diversion for children and adults alike.

Admission: $.50 admission
Hours: 10:00 a.m. to 9:00 p.m.
Monday through Friday and
10:00 a.m. to 6:00 p.m.
weekends.
The Meadows Mall
4300 Meadow Ln.
Las Vegas, NV
(702) 878-4849

MGM Grand Adventures Theme Park

A fun park for all ages to enjoy. Rides like the bumper cars, flume ride, haunted mine, rapids ride, motion simulator and more. Also see great theatre shows like a Three Stooges presentation, a pirate show, acrobats, etc. Other attractions, fast food and retail shops are also available. The 33-acre MGM Grand Adventures theme park is located in the rear of the MGM Grand.

Admission: Free
Rides $2-$3 or ride all day for $15.
2 people $17.50 ea, 3 people
$12.50 ea. An unlimited rides and shows wristband, excluding the SkyScreamer, is $12, ages 11 and older, $10, ages 2 through 10.
Hours: 10:00 a.m. to 6:00 p.m.
daily
3799 Las Vegas Blvd. South
Las Vegas, NV
(702) 891-7979   (800) 929-1111

Mini Grand Prix

If it's fast-driving, tire-squealing action you want that's just pure fun for all ages, then the Las Vegas Mini Grand Prix is the place for you. The Family Fun Center has Kiddie Karts for youngsters 4 and older, Go Karts for anyone 54 inches or taller and Naskarts for anyone 16 or older. The Naskart track has high banked oval tracks so you can put your foot to the metal and attempt to beat up to 20 cars on the track. The family arcade is air conditioned with a video arcade and snack bar. Test your driving skills on the Adult Grand Prix Track, where you can compare your times with the times of your friends and try to set the track record. Race wheel to wheel on the Super Long Go Kart Track with hairpin turns and fast straight-a-ways.

Admission: $4.00 per ride
Hours: Sunday through Thursday
10:00 a.m. to 11:00 p.m., Friday
and Saturday 10:00 a.m. to
midnight
1401 N. Rainbow Blvd.
Las Vegas, NV
(702) 259-7000
Located about 15 minutes from Strip at exit 82A, Lake Mead East, of US 95.

Motown Café

Collection of Motown memorabilia, including the largest record in the world, which stretches 32-feet across, spinning from the ceiling. The Motown Cafe Moments perform Motown Classics every 20 minutes from noon to 10 p.m. daily

Admission: Free
New York-New York
3790 Las Vegas Blvd. South
Las Vegas, NV
(702) 740-6440

Mountasia

Mountasia is a great place to spend the afternoon with your kids. Indoors, you can skate, play arcade games and have birthday parties. Outdoors, ride go-karts, play miniature golf and ride bumper boats. You can bring your own skates for the indoor rink (remember to bring socks). You can also rent old-fashioned 4-wheeled skates for free or in-line skates for $2.00. Before scheduling anything involving skating, call first to make sure the rink isn't being used for hockey practice. If you want to drive the go-karts, be sure to have the right kind of shoes or you won't be able to ride.

Mountasia is also a great place for birthday parties. They provide everything from invitations to decorations, and from balloons to cleanup. You get the use of a party room with host or hostess for 90 minutes. The Birthday Bash party pack-

Mountasia Information

Address: 2050 Olympic Avenue, Henderson

Directions: Enter off Mountain Vista, one block north of Sunset

Phone: (702) 898-7777

Days/Hours: During the school year, it is open Monday through Thursday 3:00 pm to 9:00 pm, Friday 3:00 pm to 11:00 pm, Saturday 11:00 am to 11:00 pm, Sunday noon to 9:00 pm. Summer hours 10:00 am-10:00 pm weekdays, Friday and Saturday until midnight.

Admission Price: Passport to Fun (all ages) $19.95 includes 1 round of golf, 1 skate session, 3 go-kart rides, 1 bumper boat ride, 10 tokens and one small soft drink. You can also pay separately for golfing ($5.50) or for skating, boats or go-karts ($4.00 each). They also have special golf rates for kids and as well as a family golfing package.

Restrictions: A child must be 54 inches tall to ride alone in a go-karts, and 42" tall to drive with an adult. No shoes or sandals with heel straps may be worn on the go-karts. You must be 44" tall to drive a bumper boat, passengers must be 32" tall.

Facilities: Wheelchair access, family restroom and baby changing station.

things to do & see

age ($8.95 per person) includes pizza and drinks, 12 arcade tokens and choice of one activity. The FunPass Party ($19.95 per person) includes pizza, drinks and tokens plus unlimited activities. Hold your party from Monday through Thursday (excluding holidays) and save $1.00 per person. For other options or reservations, call Mountasia. ■

Mystic Falls Park/Sunset Stampede

Mystic Falls Park is a beautiful and unique 25,000 square foot artificial wilderness containing boulders, waterfalls, trees and lifelike animals that move and make noises. It's fun wandering the pathways of the park, and kids will have fun spotting a woodpecker, squirrel, beaver and other wildlife. The real star of the park is the timber wolf who inhabits a cave on top of the mountain and comes to life during the four daily shows. At 6:00 p.m., 8:00 p.m. and 10:00 p.m., the Sunset Stampede Laser Light and Water Spectacular brings the entire indoor park to life with dancing waters, spectacular laser effects and stirring music. The free show lasts about 15 minutes and is well worth watching. If you stand close to

Mystic Falls Park Information

Location: Sam's Town Hotel and Gambling Hall

Address: 5111 Boulder Highway

Directions: Corner of Boulder Highway and Flamingo Road Park in Parking Barn #2 behind the tallest building

Phone: (702) 456-7777

Days/Hours: Open 24 hours, Shows at 2:00 p.m., 6:00 p.m., 8:00 p.m., and 10:00 p.m.

Admission: Free

Facilities: Wheelchair accessible

the water at the base of the mountain, you get the full effect of the dancing waters and may even get misted. On the other hand, the second-story balcony offers a great view of the entire park and if you arrive early, kids can get a place at the railing where they can see without people standing in front of them. A scaled-down daytime version of the show (without laser lights) plays at 2:00 p.m. Several eating places and shops border the park, including McDonald's and Calamity Jane's Ice Cream Parlor, where they serve great homemade ice cream and milkshakes. ■

Nellis Air Force Base

Guided tours of the Thunderbird Planes lasting about 90 minutes are offered

Admission: Free
Hours: Every Tuesday and Thursday at 2:00 p.m.
Salt Lake Hwy.
Las Vegas, NV
(702) 652-4018

Omnimax Theater

Watch entertaining and educational films on a six-story, 57 foot tall dome-shaped screen. The 368-seat theatre features seats that recline 27 degrees to offer a panoramic view of the specially made 70-millimeter film. The film is ten times the size of ordinary 35-millimeter film. Complementing the visual projection is a sophisticated nine-channel "sensaround" sound system emanating from ten speaker banks. A total of 89 speakers engulf the audience.

Admission: $7:00 for Adults, $5:00 for Children, Seniors, Military personnel, physically challenged and groups of 15 or more ($1.00 discount for Nevada residents)
Hours: Every hour Sunday through Thursday 2:00 p.m. to 10:00 p.m., Friday and Saturday 11:40 a.m. to 11:00 p.m., box office opens 10:00 a.m. to 10:00 p.m.
Caesar's Palace
3570 Las Vegas Blvd.
Las Vegas, NV
(702) 731-7900

things to do & see

Planet Hollywood

This famous restaurant chain offers a huge collection of movie industry memorabilia. Many famous sets, costumes and props from old and recent TV and movies including Emma Peale's boots, James Bond's trick car devices and Theda Barra's headress! Also, you can preview upcoming movies and shows. The gift shop offers T-shirts, hats and more to remember your trip.

> **Admission:** Free to view collection.
> **Hours:** Monday through Sunday 11:00 a.m. to 1:00 a.m.
> Forum Shops
> 3570 S. Las Vegas Blvd
> Las Vegas, NV
> **(702) 791-7827**

Planetarium

Interesting and educational movies with 360 degree screen viewing. The planetarium also offers telescope viewing after last performance, weather permitting. Many astronomical objects can be viewed depending on the time of year and visibility.

> **Admission:** $3.50 general and

$2.25 for senior citizens, community college Students and Children

> **Hours:** Public presentations are Wednesday & Friday 6:00 p.m. and 7:30 p.m. and Saturday 5:30 p.m. and 7:30 p.m.
> Cheyenne campus of the Community College of Southern Nevada Las Vegas
> 3200 E. Cheyenne Ave
> **(702) 651-5059**

Powerhouse Indoor Climbing Center

8,000 square feet of textured climbing terrain that includes roofs, buttresses, dihedrals, bouldering caves and state-of-the-art, dust-free, gymnastic floor padding. Group and individual classes offered. Open to all ages and fitness levels.

> **Admission:** One-day passes are $12.00, equipment rental is $8.00.
> 8201 W. Charleston Blvd
> **(702) 254-5604**

Race for Atlantis

The mythical kingdom of Atlantis is the setting for the world's first giant-screen IMAX 3D motion simulator ride. Must be at least 42 inches tall.

> **Admission:** $9.50 for Adults and $6.75 for Children 12 and under.
> **Hours:** 10:00 a.m. to 11:00 p.m. daily (until midnight Friday-Saturday)
> Forum Shops at Caesar's Palace
> 3570 Las Vegas Blvd S Las Vegas
> **(702) 733-9000**

Rad Trax

Family style slot car racing tacks. The center offers a complete line of cars, performs repairs and rents slot cars, three tracks and video arcade

> **Hours:** Monday through Friday 2:00 p.m. to 10:00 p.m., Saturday and Sunday noon to 11:00 p.m.
> 3650 S Decatur Blvd.
> Las Vegas, NV
> **(702) 253-7568**

Rocks and Ropes

Offers more than 7,000 square feet of sculpted, textured walls for climbing. Forty-five minutes of instruction is included with equipment rental. Also features indoor and outdoor climbing instruction and programs for school age children.

> **Admission:** A one-day pass is $10.00 and equipment rental is $6.00.
> 3065 E Patrick Lane, Suite 4
> Las Vegas, NV
> **(702) 434-3388**

Sahara Speedworld

Sahara Speedworld at the Sahara Hotel is a 35,000 square foot virtual racing center housing two attractions: a 3-D Motion Theater and the Indy Racing Center. The theater is fun for all ages (note the height and weight requirements on page 72). Six people sit in each 'car' mounted on a motion platform and view a 3-D movie of a race while their vehicle keeps up with the fast-paced action on the screen. It's very exciting to have the feeling of racing, jumping over desert dunes, and occasionally crashing. However, this is rather a rough, jolting ride, so if your kids suffer from carsickness or if you have a bad back, this might be a little too realistic for you.

The Indy Racing Center is a hi-tech marvel billed as 'the most technologically advanced virtual reality simulation installment in existence' (Whew!) Twenty-four cars, 1/2 the size of a real Indy car, are mounted on hydraulic platforms, each facing its own 20 foot wrap-around screen projecting a virtual replica of a racetrack. While each car is isolated in its own slot, they all compete against each other in real time on the virtual raceway. After the race, everyone gets a printout showing how they did against the other racers, their average speed, etc. The cars are designed to accurately reproduce the experience of speedway racing, including engine specs, positive steering and a sound system simulating the whoosh of

things to do & see

passing cars, the clatter of tires and the screech and bang of collisions. This is real adrenaline-pumping action, but despite the pre-race instruction video, it's difficult for even experienced drivers to get the feel of the car. Adults and teenagers who are already driving may pick it up quickly, but younger kids are better off at the Motion Theater.

Speedworld has arcade racing games to play for those who are not riding or are waiting for their turn, and you are free to stand behind the race cars and watch the riders go around the course. Speedworld is close to the entrance of the Sahara buffet, but there are two good reasons not to indulge in the buffet before you enter Speedworld: both the Motion Theater and the race cars are realistic enough to make you a little queasy, and the seats in both would be uncomfortable for large people (note the 300 pound weight limit). Better to race now, eat later. ■

Sahara Speedworld Information

Location: Sahara Hotel and Casino

Address: 2535 S. Las Vegas Blvd.

Directions: Corner of The Strip and Sahara Ave. Note: Speedworld is located in the northeast corner of the building. Park across Paradise Road from the hotel and cross on the elevated walkway.

Phone: (702) 737-2750

Days/Hours: Sunday through Thursday 10:00 a.m. - 10:00 p.m. Friday and Saturday 10 a.m. - 11 p.m.

Admission: 3-D Motion Theater $3.00, Race Cars $8.00, Military,

Seniors and Nevada residents with ID receive a $1.00 discount.

Restrictions: No one under age 10 admitted without a responsible adult 18 or over. Minimum height for the 3-D theater 42 inches, for the race cars 48 inches. Weight limit for both attractions 300 pounds. No pregnant ladies, no persons with back or heart problems, etc.

Facilities: Wheelchair accessible, but for the theater each person must have the upper body strength to lift him/herself into the theater seat for the ride. The race cars require use of the foot pedals as in a regular car.

Saturn of West Sahara
The largest collection of space shuttle pictures in the world. Airplane pictures, pilot licenses.

Admission: Free, 5 years and older
Hours: Reservations required
5325 W. Sahara Ave
Las Vegas, NV
(702) 362-0733

Scandia Family Fun Center

Scandia is kid heaven, especially in good weather, and most especially if parents are willing to supply the kids with unlimited tokens on demand. There are three miniature golf courses with the unique mini-golf architecture America has come to love (windmills, castles, lighthouses, etc.). But most kids prefer their fun a little more lively, such as speeding around in miniature race cars at the L'il Indy Raceway. The bumper boats, which operate year round, let seagoing funseekers

Scandia Family Fun Center Info

Address: 2900 Sirius Ave.

Directions: Located just west of I-15 freeway south of Sahara Avenue

Phone: 364-0070

Days/Hours: Sunday through Thursday 10:00 a.m. to 11:00 p.m. Open 24 hours Saturday and Sunday

Admission Price: Supersaver admission $10.95 (all ages) entitles you to 18 holes of miniature golf, one race car ride, one ride on the bumper boats and 5 tokens for the arcade or batting cages. Unlimited admission wristband $15.95 (all ages) entitles you to golf, race and

boat all day long and includes 10 tokens. You can also pay separately for golfing ($5.95) or for boats or race cars ($3.95 each). Batting cages may be rented by the hour, and discounts are available for ball teams. Children five and under golf free with a paying partner.

Restrictions: A child must be 54" tall to ride alone in a race car and 46" tall to pilot a boat by himself. Passengers under height restrictions ride free with a paying adult (must be at least three years old).

Facilities: Wheelchair access, Diaper changing

bump other boats and squirt each other with water cannons. No one gets away without getting soaked, but it's usually hot and dry enough to recover quickly. Several baseball and softball batting cages are available, operated either by tokens or by hourly rental for the serious player. Inside fun includes an arcade with simple games like bowling and a mini-carousel for little kids as well as more sophisticated arcade games for teens. "More tokens, Mom!" A snack bar dispenses all the foods kids like, so don't plan on serving them a healthy dinner right afterwards.

Scandia is a great place for birthday parties, and they offer several packages for groups of five or more. For $7.95 per child, you can choose either the Golf Party (one round of golf and 10 tokens) or the Ride Party (a ride on the cars and the boats plus 10 tokens). The Supersaver Party ($10.95) entitles each child to a round of golf, one race car ride, one boat ride and 10 tokens. For an all-day party, choose the Wristband Party ($16.95) for unlimited use of the attractions. A party room complete with pizza, drinks, balloons and a host/hostess is provided for one hour. And, there's no mess to clean up. You may bring your own birthday cake or pay a little extra for Scandia to provide one. Each party guest receives a coupon good for free tokens on his next visit. ■

Secret Garden of Siegfried & Roy

The Secret Garden of Siegfried & Roy features some of the world's rarest and most exotic animals, including the Royal White Tigers of Nevada and the White Lions of Timbavati. This $15 million, 2.5 acre natural habitat allows the general public a chance to get a closer look at many of the rare breeds of animals which Seigfried and Roy use in their nightly production shows. This unique jungle setting provides maximum comfort and security for the animals while allowing you to view them. Next door, and included in the admission is the Dolphin Habitat.

Admission: $10.00, Children under 10 Free
Hours: 11:00 a.m. to 5:30 p.m. daily, Saturday and Sunday 10:00 a.m. to 5:30 p.m.
Mirage Hotel.
3400 Las Vegas Blvd S.
Las Vegas, NV
(702) 791-7111

Showcase Mall

A specialty retail and entertainment complex on the Las Vegas Strip. Its tenants include M&M's World, GameWorks, United Artists Showcase 8 Cinemas, the World of Coca-Cola and the Official All Star Cafe.
3785 Las Vegas Blvd S.
Las Vegas, NV
(702) 597-3122

Slot Car City

18 lanes on two high-speed tracks and drag strip

Hours: Daily 3:00 p.m. to 11:00 p.m., Wednesday 6:00 p.m. to 11:00 p.m.
4430 E. Charleston Blvd.
Las Vegas, NV
(702) 438-1760

Skyscreamer

The World's Tallest Skycoaster. Soar through the air at speeds up to 70 miles per hour. SkyScreamer combines the sensations of skydiving and hang-gliding from 250 feet. The 33-acre MGM Grand Adventures theme park is located in the rear of the MGM Grand.

Admission: Free into the park. The SkyScreamer is $22.50 for a single flyer, $17.50 each for double flyers, and $12.50 each for triple flyers.
Hours: 10:00 a.m. to 6:00 p.m. daily
MGM Grand Hotel
3799 Las Vegas Blvd South
Las Vegas, NV
(702) 891-7979 (800) 929-1111

Southern Nevada Zoological-Botanical Park

Don't expect to find elephants, giraffes and hippos at the Southern Nevada Zoo, but it can still provide an entertaining and informative field trip for a family or school group. The small zoo houses about 150 different plant and animal species in a 2 1/2 acre area. Exhibits include a Bengal tiger, a cougar named Cougie, a chimpanzee, flamingoes, eagles, emus and wallabies as well as many varieties of reptiles. An important attraction is a family of endangered and rare Barbary Apes, the last family of its kind in the United States. If you are new to Southern Nevada and want to see what some of the desert wildlife looks like, come to the zoo and see the lizards, sidewinders, desert tortoises and coyotes. Kids can see an eight-foot, 300 pound ostrich up close and may feed it if they are brave enough. The 'Botanical' part of the park's name comes from displays of endangered cycads and rare bamboos, although most children will need a little education to tell them from ordinary greenery.

The zoo does not receive any city, county or state funding, and the non-profit group which runs it depends on donations, admission fees and concessions to keep the doors open and the animals fed. Its purpose is to educate children and the general public about endangered species and habitat protection. The zoo is constantly expanding as donations are received, and plans more habitats in the near future including an alligator-wetlands exhibit and an addition to the reptile house. Its Adopt-an-Animal Program allows individuals and groups a chance to contribute to the upkeep and health care of a specific animal. For an annual fee of only $35, your child could be the proud parent of a King Vulture, and for only $100 you can add a Barbary ape to your household. (Warning: this could make sibling rivalry a little more complicated.)

The zoo also offers Desert Eco-Tours via jeep, year round. Tours are available for small groups (2-7 people) or for large groups, who travel by bus. Favorite destinations include gemstone collecting areas, ghost towns, a historic mining district, and the ever-popular Area 51 tour (the zoo foundation cannot be held responsible in case of alien abduction). ■

S. Nevada Zoological-Botanical Park Info

Address: 1775 N. Rancho Drive

Directions: North of the I-95 freeway on Rancho

Phone: (702) 647-4685

Days/Hours: Open daily 9:00 a.m. to 5:00 p.m.

Admission: General Admission $5.95, Seniors (61+) and Children 2-12 $3.95, Children under 2 admitted free

Facilities: Wheelchair access, concession stand, gift shop

Star Trek: The Experience

Star Trek: The Experience is a must for science fiction buffs, Star Trek fanatics and all those who like to exercise their imaginations. It starts with The History of the Future, a self-guided exhibit featuring displays of more than 200 Star Trek costumes, weapons and props used in the television series and motion pictures. Did you know that the medical scanner used by Dr. McCoy was actually a salt shaker? You'll find this and other interesting trivia in the History of the Future, as well as a diagram linking stories from all the Star Trek series, movies and books into one illustrated timeline. The huge model spaceships mounted overhead, as well as all the sets used in the 65,000 square foot Experience are exact replicas of those used in the Star Trek series and films. You can easily see why this attraction cost $70 million to build.

After examining The History of the Future, your family is invited by costumed aliens to enter The Voyage Through Space, where you are beamed to the transporter room aboard the USS Enterprise. On the bridge, you'll find you've become part of a Star Trek adventure which eventually leads to the shuttlecraft bay. The 27-seat shuttlecraft takes off for a full motion simulator ride, rocketing you through time and space and ending with a hair-raising aerial tour of the Las Vegas Strip. It's very realistic and great fun unless you have a bad back or other medical condition.

The shuttlecraft eventually docks at a full-scale recreation of the promenade from Deep Space Nine, featuring lots of places to buy souvenirs and memorabilia. Many beautiful and very expensive collectible items are sold here, but you can also buy keychains, action figures, posters and other items designed for an earth family on a budget. At Quark's Bar and Restaurant, kids' favorites include Hamborger, Glop on a Stick and Tribble Tenders (tastes just like chicken!). The prices are a little more than at your neighborhood fast food eatery, but, consider the cost of shipping food across all those light-years.

The total Star Trek Experience takes about half an hour, including the four minute motion ride. But you can easily spend several hours here if you're a real Trek fan, examining all the details, inspecting the merchandise and collectibles and enjoying a meal in Quark's. If you want to visit the Promenade shops or Quark's Bar and Restaurant without going on the rest of the adventure, you can do so at no charge. ■

STAR TREK
THE EXPERIENCE™
LAS VEGAS HILTON

Star Trek: The Experience Information

Location: Las Vegas Hilton (north tower)

Address: 3000 Paradise Road

Directions: Two blocks east of the Strip, just south of Sahara. Park on the north side of the building.

Phone: (702) 697-8700 or (888) GO BOLDLY

Days/Hours: Open daily 11:00 a.m. to 11:00 p.m.

Admission: $14.95 for all ages (Nevada residents $1.00 discount). Admission to shops and Quark's bar and Restaurant is free.

Restrictions: Guests must be 42" tall for the motion ride

Facilities: Wheelchair accessible

Stratosphere Attractions

For a fabulous view of Las Vegas as well as heart-stopping thrill rides, be sure to visit the Stratosphere Tower. It's twice as tall as any other building in Las Vegas at 1,149 feet (112 stories). The 12 story pod atop the tower features indoor and outdoor observation decks, the High Roller, the world's highest roller coaster, the Big Shot, the world's highest thrill ride, the Top of the World revolving restaurant and a 220 seat cocktail lounge. Your trip to the top begins at The Tower Shops at Stratosphere, a collection of shops and eating places just above the casino level where you will find an arcade as well as a candy shop, ice cream shop and McDonald's. After purchasing tickets, you enter the high-speed elevator which shoots you to the top in only 30 seconds. Be sure to open your mouth — the quick change in pressure can hurt your ears.

At the top, thrillseekers are separated from the more reasonable people who prefer to look out at the beautiful views of the city, either indoors through floor to ceiling windows, or outdoors on the observation deck. Coin-operated telescopes enable you to get a close-up view of the city and surrounding areas. Those brave enough to try the rides go up another level to either the High Roller or the Big Shot. The High Roller would be a pretty tame roller coaster if it were on ground level: no sharp curves, loops or steep plunges. But, consider the fact that you're hanging on the edge of a building over 100 stories tall, connected by only a few strips of metal, and the effect is hair-raising.

Riding the Big Shot is proof of either extreme courage or an excess of male hormones, possibly both. The Big Shot thrusts 16 passengers at a time straight up to the top of the 160 foot spire at the top of the tower. You face outward to get the full terrifying effect of how high you are, as your legs dangle helplessly below. The feeling on lift-off is indescribable. Just when you're praying you don't shoot up all the way into outer space, you drop suddenly and are plunging towards earth at a sickening speed. Brochures say you experience G forces of up to four and fewer than zero (negative G). Whatever the scientific terms, this is definitely a thrill you'll remember. If you are brave enough to do this, be sure to buy a T-shirt advertising the fact so mere mortals can admire you. ∎

Stratosphere Information

Location: Stratosphere Las Vegas

Address: 2000 Las Vegas Blvd. S.

Directions: On the Strip, just north of Sahara Avenue. Easy to find — it's the tallest building west of the Mississippi River.

Phone: (702) 383-4790

Days/Hours: Sunday through Thursday 10:00 a.m. to 1:00 a.m. Friday, Saturday and holidays 10:00 a.m. to 2:00 a.m.

Admission: Elevator to the top of the tower: Adults $6.00, Children 4-12, Seniors and Nevada residents $3.00, Children under 4 free. High Roller $5.00, Big Shot $6.00, Tower admission plus High Roller is $9.00, or plus Big Shot $10.00, Tower Admission plus both rides $14.00

Restrictions: Minimum height 48 inches for both rides

Facilities: Viewing areas are wheel-chair accessible

things to do & see

Sunrise Children's Hospital
General tour of the hospital including the emergency room, kitchen, neonatal unit and nursery. Children 4-7 may also visit the hospital where they learn all about doctors and nurses and how they help children. Each child receives a coloring book.
> **Admission:** Free
> **Hours:** Monday through Friday 10:00 a.m. to 3:00 p.m. 25 minute tour, Children 7 years or older, reservations required
> 3186 S. Maryland Pkwy
> Las Vegas, NV
> **(702) 731-8000**

Sunset Stampede
(see Mystic Falls)
Sam's Town's Sunset Stampede — Visit the 25,000-square-foot indoor Mystic Falls Park. A spectacular laser, light and water show is offered daily.
> **Admission:** Free
> **Hours:** Daily at 2:00 p.m., 6:00 p.m., 8:00 p.m. & 10:00 p.m.
> Sam's Town's Las Vegas
> **(702) 456-7777**

Tiger Habitat
Designed with water sprayers and an air circulation system to maintain a temperature of 78 degrees, the Tiger Habitat was built to house the magnificent tigers that "co-star" with illusionary magician, Rick Thomas.
> Tropicana
> 3801 Las Vegas Blvd. S.
> Las Vegas, NV
> **(702) 739-2222**

Turbo Drop
What goes up must come down. And at 45 miles per hour, the new Turbo Drop thrill ride doesn't leave you hanging! Kids will love the slower, tamer version called the "Rodeo Rider." Both are located in Buffalo Bill's Ghost Town area.
> Buffalo Bill's Resort
> Primm, NV
> **(702) 679-7433**

Thrill Rides

Sky Screamer
Riders are hoisted up a 220-foot launch tower. One of the brave riders pulls the ripcord and riders free-fall 100 feet toward earth. When they hit the end of their rope, so to speak, they then swing from a cable through a 250-foot steel arch flying back and forth by momentum. The giant swing gets riders moving at 70 mph — faster if there are multiple riders per flight.
> **Admission:** Entrance to the park is free, but rides cost money. For all rides (except the Sky Screamer) there is a $12.00 unlimited ride wristband. Children's wristbands are $10.00 each. To ride the Sky Screamer, participants must pay $25.00 per person for each flight ($20.00 per person for doubles, $15.00 per person for triples).
> **Hours:** 10:00 a.m. to 10:00 p.m.
> MGM Grand
> 3799 S. Las Vegas Blvd.
> Las Vegas, NV
> **(702) 891-7979**

Lightning Bolt
A low-impact coaster designed more for family rides with big thrills. With its 35 mph top speed, it's the perfect opportunity for parents wanting to introduce their kids into the roller coaster realm.
> **Admission:** Unlimited-ride wristbands are $10.00 for children and $12.00 for adults with $2.00 discounts for holders of a Nevada driver's license and hotel guests.
> **Hours:** 10:00 a.m. to 6:00 p.m. weekdays, 10:00 a.m. to 10:00 p.m. weekends
> MGM Grand
> 3799 S. Las Vegas Blvd.
> Las Vegas, NV
> **(702) 891-7979**

High Roller

980 feet in the air attached to the needle of the stratosphere, this coaster has a speed of 30 mph and a drop of 32 feet.

> **Admission:** $6.00, plus $6.00 admission to the Stratosphere Tower
> **Hours:** 10:00 a.m. to midnight weekdays, 10:00 a.m. to 1:00 a.m., weekends
> Stratosphere Tower
> 2000 S. Las Vegas Blvd.
> **(702) 380-7777**

Big Shot

Traveling 160 feet up the top Stratosphere Tower mast in 2 seconds is a unique experience. Doing it 1,000 feet in the air atop the tallest building west of the Mississippi is downright terrifying. You are suddenly rocketed skyward with incredible force (riders experience 4 G's) only to be stopped at the top for a gut-wrenching free fall drop. Just when you think it is over, it happens again! The Big Shot reverse-bungees riders up and down the mast three times before settling back to the base.

> **Admission:** $6.00, plus $6.00 admission to the Stratosphere Tower, Nevada residents get a reduced rate.
> **Hours:** 10:00 a.m. to midnight weekdays, 10:00 a.m. to 1:00 a.m., weekends
> Stratosphere Tower
> 2000 S. Las Vegas Blvd.
> **(702) 380-7777**

Excalibur Motion Machines

Located in the midway area of the Excalibur, two motion simulators run every few minutes. Your seats are positioned on a platform that is supported by hydraulic actuators. The movements of the seats are synchronized with a film projected before you for a realistic experience. Several different simulations are available.

> **Admission:** $5.00
> Excalibur Hotel, in the midway.
> 3850 Las Vegas Blvd. S.
> **(702) 597-7777**

Canyon Blaster

74- and 72-foot vertical loops followed by a two-inversion corkscrew. The ride concludes with a tight helix that darts in and out of caves in the faux canyon wall at speeds up to 55 mph. A short but intense coaster ride.

> **Admission:** $5.00 per ride or unlimited-ride wristband $11.95 - $15.95.
> **Hours:** Varies
> Adventuredome at Circus Circus
> 2880 S. Las Vegas Blvd.
> **(702) 734-0410**

Rim Runner

The six-across seat boats produce a massive tidal wave upon impact with the water after building speed on a two-tiered 60-foot chute. Perfect for a hot day. The drop is fun and it DOES GET YOU WET! If you don't want to get wet, plastic ponchos are available to protect you from the water.

> **Admission:** $5.00, or ride unlimited rides in the park for $11.95 to $15.95.
> **Hours:**
> Adventuredome at Circus Circus hotel
> 2880 S. Las Vegas Blvd.
> **702) 734-0410**

things to do & see

Manhattan Express

Buy a token and hop in a taxi cab for a great coaster experience. The Express has a taxi-cab motif, bright yellow cars with headlights. This state-of-the-art roller coaster incorporates high velocity and inversions. A 160-foot drop with a 50-degree angle on the second hill gets the train rolling at 67 mph. The two inversions are a vertical loop and a one-of-a-kind heartline twist and dive — a C-shaped track that turns riders upside down with a barrel roll before diving underneath itself. A series of camel-back hills and a 540-degree spiral complete the Strip standout. The ride is built around the exterior and partly through the interior of the New York, New York Hotel.

> **Admission:** $6.00 for a token.
> **Hours:** 10:00 a.m. to 10:30 p.m., weekdays, 10:00 a.m. to midnight, weekends.
> New York - New York
> 3790 S. Las Vegas Blvd.
> **(702) 740-6969**

Desperado

The highest coaster in North America. The 225-foot drop down a 55-degree descent on the first hill then the Desperado rams through a tunnel burrowing into the desert looks like an anthill. At this point, the train is careening at about 80 mph. The second hill, a high-speed helix, takes off from 155 feet — higher than most coasters' first drop. The camel-back hills leading to the front of the property provide riders with plenty of zero-gravity sensation of getting tossed from the car. The ride wraps up with high-speed upward spiral through a man-made mountain.

> **Admission:** $5.00
> **Hours:** 10:00 a.m. to 11:30 p.m., weekdays, 10:00 a.m. to midnight, weekends.
> Buffalo Bill's, Primm, NV
> **(702) 679-7433**

Turbo Drop

Riders are slowly transported up a 180-foot tower. At the summit, they're yanked down at 45 mph and bounced on a cushion of air.

> **Admission:** $5.00
> **Hours:** 10:00 a.m. to 11:30 p.m., weekdays, 10:00 a.m. to midnight, weekends
> Buffalo Bill's
> Primm, NV
> **(702) 679-7433**

Adventure Canyon

A flume ride with a 35-foot, drip-filled drop. But once riders splash down, the fun continues as they float through an electronic shooting gallery. Following the wild west theme of the property, each rider gets use of a pistol. Targets are illuminated along the path of the flume. Shooting bad guys gives you points; shooting good guys deducts them. At the end of the journey, riders determine the best marksman.

> **Admission:** $5.00
> **Hours:** 10:00 a.m. to 11:30 p.m., weekdays, 10:00 a.m. to midnight, weekends
> Buffalo Bill's
> Primm, NV
> **(702) 679-7433**

Ultrazone, The Ultimate Laser Adventure

Offers a 5,000-square-foot, state-of-the-art, interactive laser-game arena. Network video games are featured in the arcade.

> **Admission:** $7.00 for one game, $12.00 for two. Discount memberships available.
> **Hours:** 11:00 a.m. to 11:00 p.m. Mondays through Thursdays (until 1:00 a.m. Friday), 10:00 a.m. to 1:00 a.m. Saturday, and 10:00 a.m. to 11:00 p.m. Sundays
> 2555 S. Maryland Parkway
> Las Vegas, NV
> **(702) 734-1577**

United States Post Office

Main post office tour. See how the mail system works.

> **Admission:** Free
> 1001 E. Sunset Rd
> Las Vegas, NV
> **(702) 361-9242**

Vegas Chip Factory

Watch kettle-cooked Vegas Potato Chips being manufactured and packaged at the factory.

> **Admission:** Free
> **Hours:** Monday through Thursday 10:00 a.m. to 2:00 p.m.
> 2945 N. Martin Luther King Blvd.
> Las Vegas, NV
> **(702) 727-6900**

Volcano

Set amid a tropical lagoon, The Giant, an artificial volcano erupts every few minutes after dark, spewing smoke and fire 100 feet above the water.

> **Admission:** Free
> **Hours:** every 15 minutes from 6:00 p.m. until midnight
> Mirage Hotel
> 3400 Las Vegas Blvd S
> Las Vegas, NV
> **(702) 791-7111**

things to do & see

Wet 'n Wild

Where do you go when it's 112° in the shade, and there's no shade? To Wet 'n Wild, of course, a perennial favorite with local families looking to escape the heat. Wet 'n Wild has everything from thrilling water slides to relaxing activities for toddlers and grandparents. It's 15 acres of the most amazing rides, slides, chutes, floats and flumes under the sun. Bring a picnic lunch and spend the day with the whole family, or let the park worry about the refreshments - there are plenty of places to eat. Forget your swim suit or sunscreen? You can buy or rent whatever you need here.

Little kids will love the Children's Water Playground with places to climb, paddle, splash and squirt in shallow water. The Bubble Up, a large, inflated bubble, was made for kids to climb and bounce on, then slide down into three feet of water. Take toddlers with you on a raft trip around the Lazy River circling the park at a leisurely two miles per hour, or splash with them in the shallow end of the giant Surf Lagoon.

The park's main attractions are perfect for older kids and teens, who love the challenge of rides like Der Stuka, the fastest water chute in the world, which drops almost straight down creating the sensation of free-falling. If that's not scary enough for you, try the Bomb Bay. Stand inside a bomb-like casing perched 76 feet in the air, then it's 'bombs away' as the casing springs open and you fall straight down. Embrace the terror! The Black Hole is a twisting, turning ride through darkness and fog effects on specially designed two-person tubes. The newest attraction is the Royal Flush, which washes you down a towering chute and around a bowl at speeds reaching a heart-stopping 45 mph. And don't worry, thrillseekers, there are lots more rides that haven't been mentioned.

Wet 'n Wild is fully staffed with certified lifeguards who enforce pool safety

things to do & see

rules, but of course it's always best to keep a close eye on your children, espe-cially when the park is crowded. A word of caution for tourists — you may feel like you're at the beach, but remember you're in the middle of the Mojave Desert and take precautions. Be sure to drink plenty of fluids and apply sunscreen through-out the day (don't forget the tops of your feet and Grandpa's bald spot). ■

Wet 'n Wild Information

Address: 2601 Las Vegas Blvd. South

Directions: On the Strip just south of the Sahara Hotel

Phone: (702) 734-0088

Days/Hours: Open 10:00 a.m. daily from May through September. Closing time varies-call for details.

Admission: General Admission (10 years +) $23.95; Children 3-9 $17.95, Children under 3 admitted free; Seniors 1/2 off. Call to ask about group rates and season passes.

Restrictions: Minimum height of 48" for some water rides. Non-swimmers must be accompanied by an adult who can swim.

Facilities: Wheelchair access, baby changing stations, concession stands, gift shops. Rentals available for tubes, towels and life vests. Locker rentals available for storing personal items. You may bring your own rafts, flotation devices and picnic lunches, but no glass bottles or liquor are allowed in the park.

White Tiger Habitat

Featuring Siegfried and Roy's rare and exotic white tigers, plus exact replica of the white tiger's original habitat.

Admission: Free
Hours: 24-hour viewing
The Mirage, 3400 Las Vegas Blvd. S. Las Vegas
(702) 791-7111

Flamingo Hilton Wildlife Habitat

The Flamingo Hilton recently opened a 15 acre park behind the hotel where you can view exotic birds and animals amid tropical foliage and many beautiful waterfalls. Kids will love the cute African penguins and may even get a chance to see them being fed. Koi, channel catfish and turtles swim in the freshwater pools. You will also see black swans, wood ducks, Chilean flamingoes and even a Sacred Ibis from Egypt. If you park in the Flamingo parking garage and enter by the pool area, you can get in and out quickly without going through the casino, but rest rooms and places to eat are inside the building if needed. ■

Flamingo Hilton Wildlife Habitat Info

Location: Flamingo Hilton Hotel

Address: 3555 Las Vegas Blvd. South

Directions: On the Strip just north of Flamingo Road

Phone: (702) 733-3111

Days/Hours: N/A

Admission: Free

Facilities: Wheelchair access

Wildlife Walk

Located on a walkway between the two hotel towers, the Wildlife Walk offers kids an interesting look at several varieties of tropical birds and animals. Handlers carry parrots and other birds close to kids so they can get a good look. Glass cages along the walkway contain frogs, crabs and other small rainforest animals in addition to an alligator-sized water monitor and a few large snakes. Booths sell jungle-themed gifts like T-shirts and stuffed toys. The swimming pool area below the walkway (for hotel guests only) has its own wildlife: flamingoes, ducks and swans enjoy the water in several ponds, and giant koi come close enough to feed. Viewing the animals takes only a few minutes and isn't worth a special trip across town, but if you're in the Tropicana neighborhood, stop by and talk to the animals. ■

Wildlife Walk Information

Location: Tropicana Resort and Casino

Address: 3801 S. Las Vegas Blvd.

Directions: Corner of The Strip and Tropicana Ave.

Phone: (702) 739-2222

Days/Hours: Open 10:00 a.m. to 4:00 p.m. Wednesday-Sunday. Closed Monday and Tuesday.

Admission: Free

Ron Lee's World of Clowns

Ron Lee has been making and selling clown figurines for over twenty years, and in 1995 he decided to open his new Henderson factory to the public so everyone could see how the metal mini-sculptures are made. He also wanted a place to showcase his collection of circus memorabilia. Clown costumes (including oversized shoes and comical hats) occupy glass cases lining the corridors. The self-guided factory tour is quick — you get to look through the windows and watch people molding, soldering or painting the figurines. Video monitors explain the process in case no one is at work at that particular station. The biggest attraction for your kids will be the large antique carousel with its beautiful horses, circus animals and other creatures to ride on. Rides cost $1.00 each. There is a large gift shop selling figurines and collectibles and the Carousel Café serves sandwiches, drinks and snacks to hungry visitors.

Address: 330 Carousel Parkway, Henderson, NV
Directions: Exit I-95 at Sunset, go west to Marks, south on Marks to Warm Springs, left on Warm Springs to Carousel Parkway.
Phone: (702) 434-1700
Days/Hours: 8:00 a.m. to 5:00 p.m. Monday through Friday, 9:00 a.m. to 5:00 p.m. Saturday, closed Sundays.
Admission: Free
Facilities: Wheelchair accessible, baby changing station, café, gift shop

World of Coca-Cola

The 28,000 square foot attraction literally immerses visitors in the tradition, lore and hype that we've come to know from Coca-Cola over the last 111 years. From the 100 ft. glass Coke bottle front, housing two elevators, to the 12,000 sq. ft. store called "Everything Coca-Cola." For a fee, you can go upstairs to sample all the Coke you can gulp, along with 30 varieties from around the world, served from and production of Coke, complete with a 1920's bottling plant, and stroll through the "Time Walk" or take in the interactive storytelling theater.

> **Admission:** Free to shops and downstairs exhibits. Upper floors, $5.00 Adult, $3.00 Children, under 6 Free.
> **Hours:** Sunday through Thursday 10:00 a.m. to midnight and Friday to Saturday 10:00 a.m. to 1:00 a.m.
> ShowCase
> 3785 S. Las Vegas Blvd.
> Las Vegas, NV
> **(800) 720-COKE (702) 270-5953**

Entertainment, Magic, Shows & Theaters

Magic

Caesars Palace

Caesars Magical Empire
For a really special treat, take the family to Caesars Magical Empire for dinner and magic shows. At $75.00 each, its not cheap, but it does last about three hours, and includes a three-course dinner hosted by a wizard as well as admission to two different magic theaters. Each cozy dining chamber, designed to resemble an underground cave, seats 24 people, so the 'wizards' get a chance to interact closely with everyone and perform their tricks, usually with a humorous twist. After dinner, visitors are guided through the catacombs to the Sanctum Secorum, a seven-story high room surrounded by giant statues. Beware the broken bridge and bottomless pit! It's all scary fun. For the adults, there are two lounges offering drinks as well as wise-cracking skeletons and an invisible piano player. Be sure to visit the Secret Pagoda Theater, which presents masters of close-up magic with shows every 25 minutes. The larger Sultan's Palace Theatre offers more elaborate shows every 50 minutes. Magicians at both theaters like to bring audience members into the act, especially children, so it's great fun. Guests must be at least five years old. Children ages five to 10 are admitted at half the adult price. One way to reduce your cost is to go on a free tour, offered every half hour Friday through Tuesday, from 11:00 am to 3:30 pm. Each tour member gets $15.00 off a ticket to the early dinner seating at 4:30 p.m., which brings the child's price down to $22.50.

> **Hours:** Friday through Tuesday from 4:30 p.m. to 10:00 p.m. (closed Wednesday and Thursday).
> **Admission:** $75.00
> Caesars Palace
> 3570 Las Vegas Blvd. South
> Las Vegas, NV
> **(702) 731-7333**

Harrah's Las Vegas
Spellbound

Producers Dick and Lynne Foster and a strong team have long been known for turning out high-quality magic production shows that achieve strong effects without the multimillion-dollar budgets. Featured magician Joaquin Ayala and spouse Lilia put on a funny and flamboyant show.

> **Hours:** 7:30 p.m. and 10:00 p.m. daily, except Sundays
> **Admission:** $34.95
> Harrah's
> Spellbound Theater
> 3475 Las Vegas Blvd. S
> Las Vegas, NV
> **(702) 369-5222**

Holiday Inn Boardwalk
World Of The Unreal Magic Show
Magician Dixie Dooley

> **Hours:** Daily 2:00 p.m., 4:00 p.m. and 5:30 p.m. except Mondays
> **Admission:** $8.95 Adult, $5.00 Children ages 12 and under.
> Holiday Inn Boardwalk
> Lighthouse Showroom
> 3740 Las Vegas Blvd. South
> Las Vegas, NV
> **(702) 730-3194**

Lady Luck
Steve Wyrick, World Class Magician
This "smaller" magic show is staged a few blocks off the Fremont Street Experience. An unforced and home-spun air to a well-paced and specialty-act-free affair.

> **Hours:** 7:30 and 10:30 p.m. daily, except Mondays.
> **Admission:** $27.95
> Lady Luck
> 206 N. Third St.
> Las Vegas, NV
> **(702) 477-3000, ext. 5982**

Maxim Hotel
Comedy Magic

One of the hidden gems amid Las Vegas' clutter of magical options, this bargain-priced afternoon show is a one-man affair starring Nick Lewin, a charming Brit who weaves funny and autobiographical tales with impressive small-scale magical effects.

> **Hours:** Daily 1:00 p.m. and 3:00 p.m., except Sundays
> **Admission:** $9.95, includes one drink. $12.95, includes buffet.
> Maxim Hotel
> Comedy Max Showroom.
> 160 E. Flamingo Road
> Las Vegas, NV
> **(702) 731-4300**

Mirage
Siegfried & Roy

The German-born duo and longtime Las Vegans launched the city's magic boom of the '90s when they unveiled this $50 million-plus magic spectacle featuring the white tigers that have become their trademark. While the show remains unchanged since "S&R" ushered in a brave new era for Vegas production shows in 1990, it remains a wonder to behold.

> **Hours:** 7:30 p.m. and 11:00 p.m. Fridays through Tuesdays
> **Admission:** $89.35, includes tax, gratuity, two drinks and a souvenir program.
> The Mirage
> Siegfried & Roy Theatre
> 3400 Las Vegas Blvd. South
> Las Vegas, NV
> **(702) 792-7777**

things to do & see

San Remo

Lance Burton: Master Magician

The Lance Burton show is a good old-fashioned magic show featuring disappearing doves, floating balls, dancing handkerchiefs and lots of fun for all members of the family. The $27 million Lance Burton Theatre, specially constructed for the show, is a beautiful reproduction of a theater from grandma's time, with plush carpets, red velvet drapes and uniformed ushers leading you to your seat. Be sure to stop in the lobby to watch the "Talking Head Illusion," a real person's head talking to you from a box. The body must be around somewhere, mustn't it?

The show opens with wonderful music from the $1.5 million state-of-the-art sound system, accompanied by scary storm and thunder sound effects. Unlike some performers, Lance Burton doesn't put on airs. He's full of down-home charm straight from Kentucky and seems to really enjoy interacting with the audience. He asks for kids to come up on stage to join him in illusions, and one lucky boy or girl gets to disappear with him in his flying white Corvette. Each young assistant receives a gift and has his/her picture taken with Lance. Seven dancing girls assist the magician. Since this is a Las Vegas show, the girls' costumes are a little skimpy, but nothing kids haven't seen on TV. Between acts, a guest performer appears, usually somebody with a comedy twist to his act like a joking juggler or a comedian doing card tricks. There are a few fabulous Vegas-style illusions for the grown-ups, but the heart of the show is a nostalgic tribute to the old-time magic which first attracted Lance Burton as a young boy in Louisville.

Before or after the show be sure to visit the Lance Burton Magic Shop next door, where you can see live magic demonstrations from noon to 1:00 a.m., Tuesday through Saturday. Lance Burton himself appears here after the late show for autographs and photos. If your kids can't stay up late enough to see him in person, you can get a photo at the Magic Shop where computer wizardry makes it appear that Lance is sawing you in half or holding your head on a platter. Half the profits from the Magic Shop go to children's charities, such as the Shriners' hospitals and the Variety Club. ■

San Remo Information

Location: Monte Carlo Resort & Casino

Address: 3770 Las Vegas Blvd. South, Las Vegas, NV

Directions: On the Strip between Flamingo and Tropicana. Parking garage is located behind the hotel. It's a very long walk from the garage to the theater. If you're traveling with people who have difficulty walking long distances, you may want to drop them off at the front entrance first.

Phone: (702) 730-7000 or (800) 311-8999

Days/Hours: Tuesday through Saturday 7:30 and 10:30 pm. Dark Sunday and Monday.
Magic Shop is open 9:00 a.m. - 1:00 a.m .Tuesday through Saturday and 9:00 a.m. - 10:00 p.m. Sunday and Monday.

Admission: Reserved seating tickets $39.95 for main floor/mezzanine (all ages), $34.95 for balcony seats. To get good seats, it's best to call in advance (up to 2 months ahead of time) and let them know you'll be bringing children and want to sit close to the stage. Rows 5-20 are ideal.

Facilities: Wheelchair access

Tropicana
The Illusionary Magic Of Rick Thomas
Rick Thomas performs with a tiger and provides enjoyable entertainment in his afternoon show.

Hours: Daily 2:00 p.m. and 4:00 p.m., except Fridays
Admission: $12.95
Tropicana
Tiffany Theatre
3801 Las Vegas Blvd. South
Las Vegas, NV
(702) 739-2411

O'Sheas
That's Magic
An extraordinary nightly revue will amaze and astound you. Find 20,000 sq. ft. of exhibits that are a departure from reality, and colorful tributes to those who created the magical illusions of entertainment. You'll see famous ventriloquists' dummies, fascinating stage sets, animated fortune tellers, magic props, and a great magic show.
O'Sheas Casino
Second Floor
3555 Las Vegas Blvd. South
Las Vegas, NV
(702) 737-1343

More Magic
Starring Valentine Vox,
Hours: 11:30 a.m. and 1:30 p.m., 3:00 p.m. and 4:30 p.m. Tuesdays through Saturdays
Admission: $9.95 Adults, $3.00 Children ages 12 and under.
O'Shea's
Houdini Theatre
3555 Las Vegas Blvd. South
Las Vegas, NV
(702) 697-2711

things to do & see

Shows

It is recommended that parents be aware of the suitability of shows that they consider for children. Though some shows may allow children to attend, parents may be surprised to hear a comedian become suggestive or profane on stage. Some shows with topless performers are done in good taste.

Caesars Palace
Children 6 years and older may attend showroom with parental guidance.

Desert Inn
Children over 5 may attend with parents.

Excalibur
King Arthur's Tournament
All ages welcome.
This medieval-styled revue starts with a eat-with-your-hands meal — part of the reason it draws sellout crowds — before the dirt-covered arena is transformed into a bit of Camelot, complete with knights dashing about on horseback. Kids will love it.

> **Hours:** Daily 6:00 p.m. and 8:30 p.m.
> **Admission:** $29.95, includes dinner.
> Excalibur
> King Arthur's Arena
> 3850 Las Vegas Blvd. S
> Las Vegas, NV
> **(702) 597-7600**

Flamingo Hilton
Forever Plaid
Children 5 & over may attend.
A real Broadway-quality play. Creator Stuart Ross' heartwarming '50s musical spoof has been a success in cities across the country and has become a runaway hit here as well. The Plaids are a mediocre white-guy harmony group who return from the dead. Life on Earth has been shortened when they meet a busload of Beatles fans, and their comic quest is to have that one great gig that always eluded them.

> **Hours:** 7:30 p.m. and 10:00 p.m. Tuesdays through Sundays
> **Admission:** $19.95
> Flamingo Hilton
> Bugsy's Celebrity Theater
> 3555 Las Vegas Blvd. South
> Las Vegas, NV
> **(702) 733-3333**

Flamingo Hilton
Children 5 and over may attend The Rockettes

Holiday Inn Boardwalk
The Dream King
Children must be 3 or over.
Starring Elvis stylist Trent Carlini

> **Hours:** 8:30 p.m. daily, except Mondays
> **Admission:** $19.95
> Holiday Inn Boardwalk
> Lighthouse Showroom
> 3740 Las Vegas Blvd. South
> Las Vegas, NV
> **(702) 730-3194**

Imperial Palace
Legends in Concert
No age minimum.
Producer John Stuart's star-impersonator show was the first of its kind, branched out to other cities, and has since it maintains a large stable of rotating look- and sing-alike performers who mimic the likes of Elvis, the Blues Brothers, Elton John, Liberace, Roy Orbison and Sammy Davis Jr., among others. The lineup changes often and the quality sendups are supported by a live band and dancers.

> **Hours:** 7:30 p.m. and 10:30 p.m. daily, except Sundays

Admission: Adults $29.50, includes two drinks, tax and gratuity. $14.75 children 12 and under.
Imperial Palace
Imperial Theater
3535 Las Vegas Blvd. South
Las Vegas, NV
(702) 794-3261

Luxor
Imagine: A Theatrical Odyssey
Children of all ages may attend. The talent-laden show features a progressive live score and some stunning dancing/acrobatics from a solid ensemble, high-flying strap and bungee acts, quality staging and a bit of magic to boot.

> **Hours:** Daily 7:30 p.m. and 10:00 p.m. except Thursdays
> **Admission:** $39.95
> Luxor
> Luxor Theater
> 3900 Las Vegas Blvd. South
> Las Vegas, NV
> **(702) 262-4400**

MGM Grand
EFX
Children must be 5 or older. This revamped and eye-catching spectacle stars Tommy Tune. Tune plays a burned-out busboy, searching for the magic and love missing from his life, and isn't overwhelmed by all the grand-scale effects. Bill Wray and Billy Payne (of Little Feat fame) added some funk to a couple of up-tempo tunes (the pretty ballads remain mostly unchanged) and the show features a talented 72-member cast of dancers, singers-actors and specialty acts.

> **Hours:** 7:30 p.m. and 10:30 p.m. Tuesdays through Saturdays
> **Admission:** $51.50 and $72.00, includes a full-color program, tax and facilities charge.

$37.00, children 5-12.
MGM Grand
Grand Theatre
3799 Las Vegas Blvd. South
Las Vegas, NV
(702) 891-7777

New York-New York
Michael Flatley's Lord of the Dance
All ages welcome.
Irish step-dance show featuring talented young dancers (ages 16-22) and two live violinists. There are some truly rousing ensemble moments in this Celtic tale of good versus evil. The warring clans duel by dance with the entire cast of 40 on stage at once. 90 minute show.

> **Hours:** 7:30 p.m. and 10:30 p.m. Tuesdays, Wednesdays and Saturdays and at 9:00 p.m. Thursdays and Fridays
> **Admission:** $50.00 Tuesday through Thursdays, $60.00 Fridays through and Sunday.
> New York-New York
> Broadway Theater
> 3790 Las Vegas Blvd. South
> Las Vegas, NV
> **(702) 740-6815**

things to do & see

San Remo
Broadway Cabaret
Ages 5 or older.
Featuring songs from some of New York's biggest hit shows.

> **Hours:** 7:30 p.m. and 9:30 p.m. Mondays through Saturdays.
> **Admission:** $24.50, which includes one free drink during the show and one free drink after the show.
> San Remo
> Parisian Cabaret
> 113 E. Tropicana Ave.
> Las Vegas, NV
> **(702) 597-6028**

Stratesphere
American Superstars
Children under the age of 5 will not be admitted and anyone under the age of 21 must be accompanied by an adult. An "impersonator show" that actually pays tribute to the living. Featuring tributes to the likes of Madonna, Charlie Daniels, Gloria Estefan, the Spice Girls and Michael Jackson. The show gets great support from one of the best live bands in town.

> **Hours:** Daily 7:00 p.m. and 10:00 p.m. except Thursdays,
> **Admission:** $22.95, adults. $16.95, children ages 5 to 12
> Stratosphere
> Broadway Showroom
> 2000 Las Vegas Blvd. S
> Las Vegas, NV
> **(702) 380-7711**

Treasure Island
Mystére
All ages welcome.
Simply the most artful and challenging show in Las Vegas, this animal-free nouvelle circus by the Canadian-based Cirque du Soleil is whatever one wants to make of it with its progressive live music, glowing effects and a com-
pelling cast of acrobats, high-wire artists and "bungee birds" who swoop up and down over the crowd. The staging and sound alone in the state-of-the-art theater are reasons enough to experience this wondrous piece of modern theater.

> **Hours:** 7:30 p.m. and 10:30 p.m., Wednesdays through Sundays
> **Admission:** $63.50
> Treasure Island
> Mystere Theatre
> 3300 Las Vegas Blvd.
> Las Vegas , NV
> **(800) 392-1999**

Movie Theaters

Boulder Station Cinemas
Eleven THX sound theaters, late night shows Friday and Saturday.

> **Admission:** $6.50 adults, children under 12 and senior citizens $3.75, matinees $3.75 before 6:00 p.m.
> Boulder Station
> 4111 Boulder Hwy.
> Las Vegas, NV
> **(702) 221-2283**

Boulder Theatre
First run movies in this National Historical Landmark theater.

> 1225 Arizona Street
> Boulder City, NV
> **(702) 293-3145**

Century Desert 16
First run movies.

> 2606 S Lamb Blvd
> Las Vegas, NV
> **(702) 641-2500**

Cinedome 12

Admission: $6.75 Adults,
Children 2-11 and Seniors $4.00,
matinees
$4.00 weekdays before 5:45 p.m.
851 S. Boulder Hwy
Henderson, NV
(702) 566-1570

Cinedome 12

Admission: $6.75 Adults,
Children 2-11 and Seniors $4.00,
matinees
$4.00 before 6:00 p.m.
3200 S Decature Blvd
Las Vegas, NV
(702) 362-2550

Cinema 8

United Artists second-run features.
Admission: $1.00 all shows
3025 E. Desert Inn Rd.
Las Vegas, NV
(702) 734-2124

Green Valley Cinemas

United Artists, 8 screens, THX sound
system, DTS digital sound.
Admission: $6.75 Adults, $5.00
Students, Seniors and children 12
and under $4.00, matinees $4.00
before 6:00 p.m.
4500 E. Sunset Rd.
Henderson, NV
(702) 458-2880

Gold Coast Twin

First run movies.
Admission: $6.75Adults, $4.00
Seniors and children, $4.00
Matinees before 6:00 p.m.
weekdays
Gold Coast Casino
4000 W. Flamingo Rd
Las Vegas, NV
(702) 367-7111

Rainbow Promenade Theater

Admission: $6.75 Adults, $4.00
Seniors and Children under 12,
$4.00 matinees before 6:00 p.m.
2321 N. Rainbow Blvd.
Las Vegas, NV
(702) 225-4828

Rancho-Sante Fe Theater

16 screens
Admission: $6.75 Adults, $4.00
Seniors and Children, $4.00
matinees before 5:45 p.m.
weekdays and 2:00 p.m.
weekends
5101 N. Rancho Dr
Las Vegas, NV
(702) 645-5518

Redrock 11 Theaters

Admission: $6.75 Adults, $4.00
Seniors and Children under 12,
$4.00 matinees before 5:45 p.m.
week days and 2:00 p.m.
weekends and holidays
5201 W. Charleston Blvd
Las Vegas, NV
(702) 878-9255

Showcase Cinema

United Artists Theatres Showcase
eight wall-to-wall screens, state-of-the-
art projection and DTS, SDDS, Dolby
Digital and THX sound systems provide the ultimate movie-going
experience.
Admission: $6.75 Adults, $4.00
Seniors and Children 12 and
under, $4.00 matinee before
6:00 p.m., late night shows.
Showcase Mall
3785 Las Vegas Blvd. S
Las Vegas, NV
(702) 740-2468

Sunrise Dollar 751 Cinema

Seven screens, second-run movies
Admission: $1.00 all movies
751 N. Nellis Blvd

things to do & see

Las Vegas, NV
(702) 438-5321

Sunset Station Cinemas
THX, Dolby Stereo Digital and Sony
Dynamic Digital Sound.
  Admission: $6.50 Adults, $3.75
  Seniors and Children under 12,
  $3.75 Matinees before 6:00 p.m.
  and late night shows Friday and
  Saturday
  1301 W. Sunset Rd
  Henderson, NV
  (702) 221-2283

Texas 12 Cinemas
  Admission: $6.50 Adults, $3.75
  Seniors and Children under 12,
  $3.75 Matinees before 6:00 p.m.
  and late night shows Friday and
  Saturday
  2101 Texas Star Lane
  Las Vegas, NV
  (702) 221-2283

Torrey Pines Discount Cinema
Four screens, first-run movies and
foreign films
  Admission: $.99
  6344 W. Sahara
  Las Vegas, NV
  (702) 876-4334

Vegas 4 Drive-In Theatre
  Admission: $5.50 Adults, children
  under 12 free
  Hours: Sunday through Thursday
  7:00 p.m. and 10:00 p.m., Friday
  and Saturday 6:30 p.m. and
  10:30 p.m., shows start after
  dusk.
  4158 W. Carey Ave
  Las Vegas, NV
  (702) 646-3565

Bookstores

Barnes & Noble
  567 Stephanie Street
  Henderson, NV
  (702) 434-1533
  Hours: Daily 8:00 a.m. to
  11:00 p.m.
  Children's Story Hour: Saturday
  11:00 a.m.

Barnes & Noble
  2191 Rainbow
  Las Vegas, NV
  (702) 631-1775
  Hours: Daily 8:00 a.m. to
  11:00 p.m.
  Children's Story Hour: Friday
  7:00 p.m.

B. Dalton Bookseller
  3680 S. Maryland Pkwy
  Las Vegas, NV
  (702) 735-0008
  Hours: Monday through Friday
  10:00 a.m. to 9:00 p.m., Saturday
  11:00 a.m. to 7:00 p.m., Sunday
  11:00 a.m. to 6:00 p.m.

B. Dalton Bookseller
  4300 Meadows Lane
  Las Vegas, NV
  (702) 878-4405
  Hours: Monday through Friday
  10:00 a.m. to 9:00 p.m., Saturday
  and Sunday 10:00 a.m. to
  6:00 p.m.

B. Dalton Bookseller
  1300 W. Sunset Rd
  Henderson, NV
  (702) 434-1331
  Hours: Monday through Saturday
  10:00 a.m. to 9:00 p.m., Sunday
  11:00 a.m. to 6:00 p.m.

BookStar

3910 S. Maryland Pkwy
Las Vegas, NV
(702) 732-7882
Hours: Daily 8:00 a.m. to
11:00 p.m.

Bookstar

4730 Faircenter Pkwy
Las Vegas, NV
(702) 877-1872
Hours: Daily 9:00 a.m. to
11:00 p.m.

Book Warehouse

9155 Las Vegas Blvd. S
Las Vegas, NV
(702) 896-5344
Hours: Monday through Saturday
10:00 a.m. to 8:00 p.m., Sunday
10:00 a.m. to 6:00 p.m.

Borders Book Shop

2323 S. Decatur Blvd
Las Vegas, NV
(702) 258-0999
Children's Story Hour: Sunday at
2:00 p.m., Wednesday 11:00 a.m.
preschool story time.

Borders Book Shop

2190 N. Rainbow Blvd
Las Vegas, NV
(702) 638-7866
Hours: Monday through Saturday
9:00 a.m. to 11:00 p.m.
Children's Story Hour: Saturday
and Sunday at 12:30 p.m.,
Monday 7:00 p.m.

Borders Book Shop

1445 W. Sunset Rd
Henderson, NV
(702) 433-6222
Hours: Monday through Saturday
9:00 a.m. to 11:00 p.m.
Children's Story Hour: Monday
7:00 p.m.

Waldenbooks

Meadows Mall
4300 Meadows Lane,
Las Vegas, NV
(702) 870-4914
Hours: Monday through Friday
10:00 a.m. to 9:00 p.m., Saturday
and Sunday 10:00 a.m. to
6:00 p.m.

Waldenbooks

Fashion Show Mall
3200 Las Vegas Blvd.
Las Vegas, NV
(702) 733-1049
Hours: Monday through Friday
10:00 a.m. to 9:00 p.m., Saturday
10:00 a.m. to 7:00 p.m., Sunday
noon to 6:00 p.m.

Libraries

City of Las Vegas Public Libraries

Las Vegas Library and District
Headquarters
833 N. Las Vegas Blvd.
(702) 382-3493
Hours: Monday through Thursday
9:00 a.m. to 9:00 p.m., Friday and
Saturday 9:00 a.m. to 5:00 p.m.,
Sunday 1 p.m. to 5:00 p.m.
Literacy Program .... (702) 382-3493
Microcomputer Lab... (702) 382-3493
Young People's Library (702) 382-2003
Young Adult Book line (702) 594-7700

things to do & see

Children 12 years to 18 years can call for a review on a book available at the library. Reviews change each week.

Branches

Blue Diamond Library
50 Cottonwood Dr.
Blue Diamond, NV
(702) 875-4295

Boulder City Library
813 Arizona Street
Boulder City, NV
(702) 293-1281
Hours: Monday through Thursday 9:00 a.m. to 9:00 p.m., Friday and Saturday 9:00 a.m. to 5:00 p.m., Sunday 1:00 p.m. to 4:00 p.m.

Enterprise Library
25 E. Shelbourne Ave
(702) 269-3000
Young People's Library
(702) 269-8027
Hours: Monday through Thursday 9:00 a.m. to 9:00 p.m., Friday and Saturday 9:00 a.m. to 5:00 p.m., Sunday 1:00 p.m. to 5:00 p.m.

Flamingo Branch
1401 E. Flamingo Rd.
Las Vegas, NV
(702) 733-3616
Hours: Monday through Thursday 9:00 a.m. to 9:00 p.m., Friday and Saturday 9:00 a.m. to 5:00 p.m., Sunday 1:00 p.m. to 5:00 p.m.

Green Valley Library
2797 N. Green Valley Parkway
Henderson, NV
(702) 435-1840
Young Peoples Library
(702) 435-2078
Hours: Monday through Thursday 9:00 a.m. to 9:00 p.m., Friday and Saturday 9:00 a.m. to 5:00 p.m., Sunday 1:00 p.m. to 5:00 p.m.

Henderson Library
280 S. Water Street
Henderson, NV
(702) 565-8402
Hours: Monday through Thursday 9:00 a.m. to 9:00 p.m., Friday and Saturday 9:00 a.m. to 5:00 p.m., Sunday noon to 4:00 p.m.

Mt. Charleston Library
1252 Aspen Ave
(702) 872-5585

North Las Vegas Public Library
2300 Civic Center Dr N.
Las Vegas, NV
(702) 633-1070
Hours: Monday 9:00 a.m. to 6:00 p.m., Tuesday through Thursday 9:00 a.m. to 9:00 p.m., Friday and Saturday 9:00 a.m. to 6:00 p.m.

Rainbow Library
3150 N. Buffalo Dr.
Las Vegas, NV
(702) 243-7323
Young People's Library
(702) 243-7307
Hours: Monday through Thursday 9:00 a.m. to 9:00 p.m., Friday and Saturday 9:00 a.m. to 5:00 p.m., Sunday 1:00 p.m. to 5:00 p.m.

Sahara West Library
9002 W. Sahara Ave.
Las Vegas, NV
(702) 228-1940
Young People's Library
(702) 228-3321
Hours: Monday through Thursday 9:00 a.m. to 9:00 p.m., Friday and Saturday 9:00 a.m. to 5:00 p.m., Sunday 1:00 p.m. to 5:00 p.m.

Searchlight Library
200 Michael Wendell Way
Searchlight, NV
(702) 297-1442

Spring Valley Library

4280 S. Jones Blvd.
Las Vegas, NV
(702) 368-4411
Young People's Library
(702) 368-4940
Hours: Monday through Thursday
9:00 a.m. to 9:00 p.m., Friday and
Saturday 9:00 a.m. to 5:00 p.m.,
Sunday 1:00 p.m. to 5:00 p.m.

Summerlin Library and Performing Arts

1771 Inner Circle
Las Vegas, NV
(702) 256-5111
Young People's Library
(702) 256-1414
Hours: Monday through Thursday
9:00 a.m. to 9:00 p.m., Friday and
Saturday 9:00 a.m. to 5:00 p.m.,
Sunday 1:00 p.m. to 5:00 p.m.

Sunrise Library

5400 Harris Ave Las Vegas
(702) 453-1104
Young People's Library
(702) 453-1180
Hours: Monday through Thursday
9:00 a.m. to 9:00 p.m., Friday and
Saturday 9:00 a.m. to 5:00 p.m.,
Sunday 1:00 p.m. to 5:00 p.m.

West Charleston Library

6301 W. Charleston Blvd
Las Vegas, NV
(702) 878-3682
Young People's Library
(702) 878-2606
Hours: Monday through Thursday
9:00 a.m. to 9:00 p.m., Friday and
Saturday 9:00 a.m. to 5:00 p.m.,
Sunday noon to 5:00 p.m.

West Las Vegas Library

951 W. Lake Mead Blvd
Las Vegas, NV
(702) 647-2117

Young People's Library
(702) 647-4857
Hours: Monday through Thursday
9:00 a.m. to 9:00 p.m., Friday and
Saturday 9:00 a.m. to 5:00 p.m.,
Sunday 1:00 p.m. to 5:00 p.m.

Whitney Library

5175 E. Tropicana Ave.
Las Vegas, NV
(702) 454-4575
Young People's Library
(702) 454-4649
Hours: Monday through Thursday
9:00 a.m. to 9:00 p.m., Friday and
Saturday 9:00 a.m. to 5:00 p.m.,
Sunday 1:00 p.m. to 5:00 p.m.

Sports & Recreation

Spectator Sports

Las Vegas Thunder Professional Hockey Team

Members of the Las Vegas Thunder
and their polar bear mascot, Boom
Boom, travel to schools throughout
Clark County to conduct assemblies
about setting goals, saying no to drugs
and staying in school. They are also
involved with the Clark County Public
Education Foundation, which raises
money to supply books to school
libraries. During hockey season, the
team sponsors a Kids' Day, when kids
are admitted free to a Thunder game at
the Thomas and Mack Center. Kids 15
and under can join the Boom Boom
Club for $10. Membership includes six
free tickets to Thunder games and six
coupons good for ice skating at the Ice
Gardens where the Thunder practice. It
also includes a monthly newsletter and
an invitation to a party with the players.
(702) 798-7825

things to do & see

things to do & see

Las Vegas Stars Professional Baseball

The Las Vegas Stars offer discounted game tickets for youth groups like Boy Scouts and Boys and Girls Clubs. They also give kids lots of opportunities to participate in games during baseball season. Little Leaguers can run out to their positions on the field as that position is announced over the loudspeaker, and in the Field of Dreams promotion they get a chance to line up and try to hit a ball over the left field wall. Just being out on a real professional field under the lights is a real thrill for most kids. Membership in the Junior Stars Club includes tickets to Stars games, a picnic with the Stars, and baseball clinics to teach kids the basics of baseball. They also get a chance to win prizes for being the Junior Star of the Month. For information on joining the Junior Stars, call the Stars office at (702) 386-7200.

Las Vegas Dust Devils

Continental Indoor Soccer League, June through September
(702) 739-8856

Las Vegas Flash

Professional Roller Hockey
May through August
(702) 262-9795

Las Vegas Sting

Indoor Arena Football,
May through August
(702) 739-8856

Big West Football and Basketball

September through March
(702) 895-3900

Las Vegas Motor Speedway

Offering 24 racing venues and 15 unique driving schools on its sprawling 1,500-acre property. This complex includes a 1.5 mile super speedway, 2.5 mile road course, .25 mile dirt oval drag strip, go-kart tracks and a variety of motorsports attractions, and a campground/RV park

7000 Las Vegas Blvd. N.
Las Vegas
(702) 644-4444 (800) 644-4444
Race tickets only: **(702) 644-4443**
www.lvms.comn

All-American SportPark

What kind of sports does your family like? Skating, baseball, rock climbing, golf, auto racing? Whatever your sports passion, you can indulge it at the All-American SportPark. Practice batting at the Major League Baseball Slugger Stadium with 16 batting stations and various speeds for all levels of baseball and softball players. The home run wall at the far end is a reproduction of features from famous major league ballparks, so you can imagine you're pounding one out of Wrigley Field or Yankee Stadium. The NASCAR SpeedPark takes up a sizeable piece of the 25-acre SportPark property. It has three separate tracks: the High Performance Road Course for licensed drivers, the Sprint Track and the Challenge Track. At the Challenge family track, the two-seat cars are designed so an adult or older child can drive with a younger child as passenger. At the Sprint Track, even very small kids can ride in a race car by themselves. The cars are 5/8 scale replicas of NASCAR stock cars and the authentic look of the race course

All-American SportPark Information

Address: 121 E. Sunset Road

Directions: Located just east of Las Vegas Blvd. (south end of the Strip) across from the airport runway.

Phone: (702) 798-7777 or (702) 317-7827

Days/Hours: Summer hours: Sunday thru Thursday 10:00 a.m. to midnight, Friday and Saturday 10:00 a.m. to 1:00 a.m. Shorter hours in winter.

Admission: Activities are priced separately, averaging $4-$5 each. A Stars package offers $30 worth of play for $25, and a Stripes package is $20 worth of play for $15. Group rates are also available.

Restrictions: Children under 10 must be accompanied by an adult. To drive at the High Performance Track, you must be a licensed driver. At the Challenge family track, drivers must be 58" tall and riders must be 36" tall.

Facilities: Wheelchair access, ATM

extends to the grandstands, Victory Lane and Winner's Circle.

There's more action indoors at the AllSport Arena, a multi-purpose area which can be converted to roller skating, baseball, indoor pee-wee football or other events. It's equipped with bleachers, a broadcast booth, skybox suites and a 32-foot video screen. The 40-foot Rockreation Sport Climbing Wall is reputed to be one of the best in the city. While grandma is scaling the mountain, dad may want to practice his putting at the 18 hole indoor putting course, complete with water features. This is big-kid golf practice, not miniature golf, and is as authentic as putting can be without having to worry about the weather. Meanwhile, the kids can have a ball at the sports-themed arcade, featuring all the latest games for big and little kids.

If all this activity makes you hungry, there are plenty of places to eat. The Boston Garden Experience is a two-story restaurant (downstairs) and bar (upstairs) offering food, drinks, big screen TV and pool tables in a reproduction of the famed Boston Garden. There are also booths selling pizza, hot dogs and other stadium favorites.

Birthday parties are a blast at the All-American SportPark. All parties include a reserved party area for an hour, a 'party referee' to supervise, soft drinks, arcade tokens and a group photo. You can purchase food from the concession stands at reduced prices. ■

Youth Sports

Pop Warner football, recreational basketball leagues, Little League, junior and senior American Legion, winter league and T-ball baseball programs, volleyball, soccer and Bobby Sox softball are but a few of the sports open to Southern Nevada youngsters. A wide range of equestrian events, from gymkhanas to rodeo teams, are also available.

Clark County Parks & Leisure Activities
(702) 229-6297

Archery

Silver Bowl Sports Complex
Features 32 practice targets ranging in distance from 10 to 70 yards.
Admission: Free
Hours: Daily 7:00 a.m. to 11:00 p.m.
6800 E. Russell Road
Las Vegas, NV
(702) 367-1505
The facility is east of the Sam Boyd Stadium

Sunset Park
Archery targets
2601 Sunset Rd.
Las Vegas, NV

Pacific Archery
Shooting lanes, pro shop, instruction
Hours: Monday through Friday 9:00 a.m. to 9:00 p.m., Saturday 9:00 a.m. to 5:00 p.m.
4084 Schiff Dr.
Las Vegas, NV
(702) 367-1505

Bike Rentals and Tours

Cyclery 'n Cafe´
Bike shop, rentals, scheduled rides, coffee bar
7016 W. Charleston Blvd
Las Vegas, NV
(702) 228-9460

McGhies
Road and mountain bike rentals
4503 West Sahara
Las Vegas, NV
(702) 252-8077

things to do & see

Downhill Bicycle Tours Inc.
18 miles of scenic beauty "all downhill" through three environments.
1209 S. Casino Center Blvd.
Suite 122
Las Vegas, NV
(702) 897-8287

Escape The City Streets Mountain Bike Tours
Rentals, maps, equipment & delivery to your hotel. Daily wilderness tours.
8221 W. Charleston, Ste. 101
Las Vegas, NV
(702) 596-2953   (800) 596-2953

Blue Diamond Bicycles
Bike tours, rentals, maps
14 Cottonwood Drive
Blue Diamond, NV
(702) 875-4500

Bike Trails
Contact the following organizations for information about other cycling trails:

Las Vegas Valley Bicycle Club
(702) 897-7800

Nellis Meadows
20 acre cycling track
4949 East Cheyenne Ave.
Las Vegas, NV
(702) 453-1663

Silver Springs Park
1950 Silver Springs Pkwy
Henderson, NV
(702) 435-3814

Rim Trail System

Floyd Lamb State Park
Bike paths through tree-shaded groves
9200 Tule Spring Rd.
(702) 486-5413

Red Rock Canyon
Bicycles are prohibited from hiking trails and must stay on the designated roads. *Scenic Loop:* 13 mile ride through the canyon's red sandstone cliffs. Start from the visitor's center and follow the one way traffic along the loop.

Bowling Centers

Gold Coast Hotel
72 lanes, pro shop & resident pro
Admission: Monday through Friday $1.90 per game, 16 & under $1.55 per game, Seniors $1.35 per game, Saturdays, Sundays & Holidays, $1.90
Hours: 24 hours
4000 W. flamingo Rd
Las Vegas, NV
(702) 367-4700

Orleans Hotel

70 Lanes, pro shop, snack bar, arcade.
Admission: Adults $2.10, Seniors and Juniors $1.60
Hours: 24 hours
4500 W. Tropicana Ave.
Las Vegas, NV
(702) 365-7111

Primm Valley Resort

Eight lanes
Hours: Sunday through Thursday noon to 10:00 p.m., Friday and Saturday 10:00 a.m. to midnight.
(702) 382-1212

Sam's Town Hotel

56 lanes, automatic scoring, pro shop & resident pro. Youth bowling program for children, parties, tournaments and special events.
Admission: Monday through Friday $1.70 Adults, Seniors and Children $1.30, Saturday, Sunday and Holidays $1.90 for all ages
Hours: 24 hours closed for league bowling Sunday through Friday 5:30 to 11:00 p.m., Saturday 5:30 to 9:00 p.m.
5111 Boulder Hwy.
Las Vegas, NV
(702) 456-7777

Santa Fe Hotel

60 lanes, pro shop, nursery, video arcade, party room, pee-wee bumper bowling league for children 3 to 6 years in the summer.
Admission: Monday through Friday 9:00 a.m. to 5:30 p.m. Adults $8.50 per hour, Seniors and Children 18 and under $7.50 per hour, Monday through Thursday 6:00 p.m. to midnight $10.50 per hour, Friday and Saturday 6:00 p.m. to midnight $12.50 Saturday and Sunday
Hours: 24 hours

4949 N. Rancho Dr.
Las Vegas, NV
(702) 658-4995

Showboat Hotel

106 championship lanes, PBA host, pro shop & resident pro
Admission: Adults $2.50, children 18 & under and Seniors $1.65
Hours: 24 hours
2800 Fremont Street
Las Vegas, NV
(702) 385-9153

Silver Nugget

Cosmic bowling & laser lights
Admission: $1.50 before 6:00 p.m., $2.00 after 6:00 p.m., Jrs. & Srs. $1.50
Hours: 9:00 a.m. to midnight
2140 N. Las Vegas Blvd.
Las Vegas, NV
(702) 657-2750

Sunset Lanes

40 lanes, Alley Gators sportz grille, pro shop.
Admission: $1.50 before 6:00 p.m., $2.10 after 6:00 p.m.
Hours: Sunday through Thursday 8:30 a.m., Friday and Saturday, 24 hours.
4565 E. Sunset Rd.
Green Valley, NV
(702) 736-2695

Terrible's Town Casino & Bowl

16 lanes, bar, snack bar
Admission: Monday through Friday Adults $1.75, Children under 12 $1.25, Saturday & Sunday $1.95 for all
Hours: 24 hours
642 S. Boulder Hwy.
Las Vegas, NV
(702) 564-7118

Area Golf Courses

Angel Park Golf Club

(Public) Designed by Arnold Palmer. Two 18-hole courses, the Palm and the Mountain, plus the Cloud Nine course with replicas of the most famous par 3's in the world. Lighted driving range, a real-grass putting course and clubhouse facilities. Drinks are served on the course and inside the lounge.

Mountain Course: (Public) 18 holes, Par 71, 5,751 yards. Huge desert ravines, wide fairways
Palm Course: (Public) 18 holes, par 70, 5,438 yards. Well bunkered surrounded by desert canyon.

Green Fees: Palm or Mt. $110.00 including cart, $60.00 twilight, Cloud Nine $22.00, club rentals $25.00
100 S. Rampart Blvd.
Las Vegas, NV
(702) 254-4653
www.lasvegasgolf.com

Badlands at Peccole Ranch

(Public) Designed by Johnny Miller. 18 holes, par 72, 6,500 yards. Clubhouse, golf shop and driving range, restaurant & bar. **Green Fees:** Winter $98.00 to $115.00 (Twilight $70.00) Summer $58.00 to $70.00 (Twilight $45.00)
9119 Alta Drive
Las Vegas, NV
(702) 242-4653
www.badlandsgolf.com

Black Mountain Golf & Country Club

(Private/Semi-Private) 18 holes, par 72, 6,541 yards. Driving Range, coffee shop, cocktail lounge and dining room. **Green Fees:** Monday through Thursday $55.00 including cart, Friday through Sunday and holidays $60.00 including cart, Club rental $13.00 Call for tee times.
500 E. Greenway Rd.
Henderson, NV
(702) 565-7933

Boulder City Municipal Golf Course

(Public) 18 holes, par 72, 6,561 yards. Driving range, putting green, four chipping greens, clubhouse, snack bar.
Green Fees: $27.00, $36.00 including cart. Club rental $15.00.
1 Clubhouse Dr.
Boulder City, NV
(702) 293-9236

Callaway Golf Center

(Public) 9 hole, par 3, 1,033 yards, lighted course. Golf training facility. Driving range and practice facility, David Leadbetter Golf Academy, pro shop, performance center and restaurant. **Green Fees:** $35.00, $45.00 including cart, Club rental $25.00.
6730 Las Vegas Blvd. S
Las Vegas, NV
(702) 896-4100

Craig Ranch Golf Course

(Public) 18 holes, par 70, 6,000 yards. Driving range, pro shop, snack bar. **Green Fees:** 9 holes $9.00, $14.00 including cart, 18 holes $15.00, $21.00 including cart.
628 W. Craig Rd., Las Vegas
(702) 642-9700

Desert Inn Golf Club

(Public) 18-hole, par 72, 6,732 yards. Pro shop, driving range, putting green, restaurant, bar. **Green Fees:** Desert Inn guests $150.00 including cart, Non-hotel guests $215.00, Club rental $40.00.

> 3145 Las Vegas Blvd. S.
> Las Vegas, NV
> **(702) 733-4290**

Desert Pines (Municipal) Golf Course

(Public) 18 holes, par 71, 6,450 yards. Two tiered, state-of-the-art, driving range, putting green, restaurant, cocktail lounge, club rentals. **Green Fees:** Monday through Thursday $115.00, $130.00 weekends including cart, Club rentals $50.00.

> 3415 E. Bonanza
> Las Vegas, NV
> **(702) 436-7000 888-397-2499**

Desert Rose Golf Course

(Public) 18 holes, Par 71, regular yardage 6,135, driving range, putting green, restaurant, cocktail lounge, pro instruction. Fees lower in the afternoon. Club rentals. **Green Fees:** Non-residents $50.00, residents $28.00 weekdays, $30.00 weekends.

> 5843 Club House Dr.
> Las Vegas, NV
> **(702) 431-4653**

Desert Willow

(Public) Designed by Billy Casper. 18 holes, par 60, 3,454 yards. Driving range, putting green, restaurant, beverage carts. **Green Fees:** Non-residents $50.00, $60.00 cart included, Residents $35.00, $45.00 including cart.

> 2010 Horizon Ridge Pkwy.
> Las Vegas, NV
> **(702) 263-4653**

Highland Falls Golf Club

(Public) 18 holes, par 72, 6,500 yards. Driving range, chipping greens, pro shop, restaurant and bar.
Green Fees: 9 holes $50.00, 18 holes $95.00, Club rentals $30.00.

> 10201 Sun City Blvd.
> Las Vegas, NV
> **(702) 254-7010**

Las Vegas Golf Club

(Municipal) 18 holes, par 72, 6,337 yards. 72 station driving range, five putting greens, restaurant, cocktail lounge. **Green Fees:** Non-residents $37.00, $46.00 including cart, Resident $19.00, $28.00 including cart, senior rate $7.50

> 4300 W. Washington
> Las Vegas, NV
> **(702) 646-3003**

Las Vegas Hilton Country Club

(formerly Sahara Country Club) (Public) 18 holes, par 71, 6,418 yards. Lighted driving range, pro shop, snack bar and cocktail lounge. **Green Fees:** Monday through Thursday before 1:00 p.m. $120.00, $80 after 1:00 p.m., $45.00 after 3:00 p.m., Friday through Sunday $150.00 before 1:00 p.m., $90.00 after 1:00 p.m., $45.00 after 3:00 p.m., club rentals $25.00.

> 1911 E. Desert Inn Rd.
> Las Vegas, NV
> **(702) 796-0013**

Las Vegas Paiute Golf Course

(Public) Designed by Pete Dye. 36 holes developed on the Paiute reservation. Designed with wide fairways, wide variety of tee lengths and angles. Driving range, pro shop, putting & chipping greens and snack bar. Nu-wav Kaiv course: 18 holes, par 72, 6,035 yards. Tav-Ai Kaiv course: 18 holes, par 72, 6074 yards. **Green Fees:** 9 holes $13.50 including cart, 10 holes $21.00 including cart, Club rentals $5.00 and $8.00.

> 10325 Nu-Way Kaiv Blvd.
> Las Vegas, NV
> **(702) 658-1400 (800) 711-2833**
> www.lvpaiute.com

Legacy Golf Club

(Public) Designed by Arthur Hill. 18 holes, par 72, 6,744 yards. Driving range, pro shop, lounge, restaurant, full practice facility with PGA instruction. **Green Fees:** Monday through Thursday $120.00, Friday through Sunday and holidays $125.00 including cart, club rental $25.00

> 130 Par Excellence Dr.
> Henderson, NV
> **(702) 897-2187**
> www.legacyvegas.com

Mt. Charleston Golf Resort

(Public) 9 holes, par 35, 3,200 yards. Miniature golf, full pro shop, snack bar, club house, chipping and putting greens. **Green Fees:** Non-residents $75.00 including cart, Residents $35.00 Monday through Friday, $49.00 Saturday and Sunday including cart, club rental $25.00

> 1 Kyle Canyon Rd.
> Mt. Charleston, NV
> **(702) 872-4653**
> 30 miles northwest of Las Vegas off State Route 157
> www.mtcharleston.com

North Las Vegas Golf Course

(Public) 9 holes, par 27, 1,158 yards. Lighted for night play, pro shop, putting green and snack bar. **Green Fees:** Monday through Friday $5.00, Seniors $4.00, Students $4.50, Saturday and Sunday $6.50, club rental $10.00.

> 324 E. Brooks Ave.
> N. Las Vegas, NV
> **(702) 633-1833**
> **(702) 649-7171**

Painted Desert Country Club

(Public) Designed by Jay Moorish. 18 holes, par 72, 6,323 yards. Golf shop, driving range, putting green, snack bar, lessons. **Green Fees:** Non residents: Monday through Thursday $100.00, Friday through Sunday $120.00, Residents $50.00, club rental $25.00.

> 5555 Painted Mirage Way
> Las Vegas, NV
> **(702) 645-2568 (702) 645-2570**

Palm Valley Golf Club

(Semi-Private) 18 holes, par 72, 6,341 yards. Driving range, pro shop, putting greens, snack bar & bar. **Green Fees:** $75.00

> 9201 Del Webb Blvd.
> Las Vegas, NV
> **(702) 363-4373**

Primm Valley Golf Course

(Public) Designed by Tom Fazio. Two championship courses, par 71 and par 72. 18-hole putting green, driving range, CompuSport Academy of Golf, clubhouse.

> Primm, Nevada
> **(702) 679-5553 (800) 386-7867**
> just 35 minutes south of
> Las Vegas off I-15
> www.primadonna.com/golf
> course.html

Rhodes Ranch

(Public) Designed by Ted Robinson. 18 holes, par 72, 6,850 yards.
Green Fees: Season rates - January 16th through June 1st 1999

	M-TH	F-SUN
Resort Player	$110.00	$125.00
Resort Twilight	$55.00	$65.00
Local Resident	$65.00	$75.00
Local Twiligh	$40.00	$40.00

All Rates include cart fee per person. Spectator riding fee is $20.00
Rhodes Ranch Country Club does not permit non-playing children under the

things to do & see

age of 16 on the golf course or practice facility, club rental (Titleist or Mizuno) $30.00.

> 9020 Rhodes Ranch Pkwy.
> Las Vegas, NV
> **(702) 740-4114**
> www.rhodesranch.com

Rio Secco Golf Club

(Public) Designed by Rees Jones. 18 holes, par 72, 6,951 yards. Pro shop, putting & chipping greens, driving range, Harmon School of Golf with Tiger Woods' coach, Butch Harmon. **Green Fees:** $190.00 including cart, club rental $40.00.

> 2851 Grand Hills Drive,
> Henderson, NV
> **(702) 889-2400**
> www.playrio.com

Wildhorse Country Club

(Public) 18 holes, par 72, 6,513 yards. Pro shop, driving range, lockers, snack bar, café, full practice facility with instruction. **Green Fees:** Non-residents Monday through Thursday $95.00, Friday through Sunday $110.00 including cart, Residents Monday through Thursday $50.00, club rental $20.00.

> 2100 W. Warm Springs Rd.
> Henderson, NV
> **(702) 434-9009**

Skating

All American Sports Park
(702) 798-7777

Crystal Palace Roller Rink

Snack bar and arcade at each location. Roller Hockey Youth Clinic at all locations.

> **Admission:** Tuesday through Thursday $5.00, Friday & Saturday $6.00, Tuesday is family night for a family of up to four $10.00 including skate rental.
> **Hours:** Tuesday through Thursday 7:00 p.m. 9:30 p.m. Friday & Saturday 7:00 p.m. to 11:00 p.m., Closed Sunday
> 3901 N. Rancho Drive
> Las Vegas, NV
> **(702) 645-4892**

Crystal Palace Roller Rink

Snack bar and arcade at each location. Roller Hockey Youth Clinic at all locations.

> **Admission:** Tuesday through Thursday $5.00, Friday & Saturday $6.00, Tuesday is family night for a family of up to four $10.00 including skate rental.
> **Hours:** Tuesday through Thursday 7:00 p.m. to 9:30 p.m. Friday & Saturday 7:00 p.m. to 11:00 p.m., Sunday & 7:00 p.m. to 10:00 p.m.
> 4680 Boulder Hwy.
> Las Vegas, NV
> **(702) 458-7107**

Crystal Palace Roller Rink

Snack bar and arcade at each location. Roller Hockey Youth Clinic at all locations.

> **Admission:** Tuesday through Thursday $5.00, Friday & Saturday $6.00, Tuesday is family night for a family of up to four $10.00 including skate rental.
> **Hours:** Tuesday through Thursday 7:00 p.m. 9:30 p.m. Friday & Saturday 7:00 p.m. to 11:00 p.m., Closed Sunday
> 9295 W. Flamingo Rd.
> Las Vegas, NV
> **(702) 253-9832**

Crystal Palace Roller Rink

Snack bar and arcade at each location. Roller Hockey Youth Clinic at all locations.

> **Admission:** Tuesday through Thursday $5.00, Friday and

Saturday $6.00, Tuesday is family night for a family of up to four $10.00 including skate rental.
Hours: Tuesday through Thursday 7:00 p.m. to 9:30 p.m. Friday & Saturday 7:00 p.m. to 11:00 p.m., Closed Sunday
1110 E Lake Mead Dr.
Henderson, NV
(702) 564-2790

Las Vegas Ice Gardens
Daily skating, the facility offers learn to skate programs for both figure skating and hockey and youth and adult hockey leagues.
Admission: Daily memberships are $5.00, monthly memberships are $30.00. The adults only Coffee Club meets 10:00 a.m. to noon Tuesdays. Cost is $5.00 per session, free for monthly members.
Hours: Skate sessions are 8:00 a.m. to 10:00 a.m. and 3:00 p.m. to 4:45 p.m. Monday through Friday and 2:00 p.m. to 4:00 p.m. Saturday and Sunday.
3896 Swenson St.
Las Vegas, NV
(702) 731-1062

Mountasia Family Fun Center Roller Rink
Public sessions, birthday parties
Admission: $2.00 in-line skate rental, $4.00 quad skate rental
Hours: Monday through Thursday 3:00 p.m. to 10:00 p.m., Friday 3:00 p.m. to midnight, Saturday noon to midnight, Sunday 11:00 a.m. to 8:00 p.m.
2050 Olympic Ave
Henderson, NV
(702) 898-7777

Sahara Ice Palace
Public skate sessions, classes, clinics and skating programs, broomball and a hockey league. Tuesday night is Gospel Skating to Christian music. Small arcade, restaurant, a birthday party room and private ice available.
Admission: $5.00 Adults, $4.00 Children under 12 and Seniors, skate rentals $2.00
Hours: Daily, noon to 2:00 p.m., Tuesday & Wednesday 5:45 p.m. 7:45 p.m., Friday to Saturday 8:00 p.m. to 10:00 p.m.
800 E. Karen Ave.
Las Vegas, NV
(702) 862-4262

Santa Fe Hotel Ice Arena
17,000 sq. ft. of ice with a 2,500 seat arena.
Admission: $5.00 Adults, $4.00 Children 3 to 12, Children 2 and under free, $1.50 skate rental
Hours: Hours vary. Senior citizens skate Wednesdays noon to 2:00 p.m.
4949 N Rancho Dr.
Las Vegas, NV
(702) 658-4993

Thrillseekers Unlimited
In-line skating tour of the Strip. Lessons for beginners to advanced stunt skating.
3172 N. Rainbow Blvd., Ste 321
Las Vegas, NV
(702) 699-5550

Snow Skiing

Las Vegas Ski & Snowboard Resort
(Formerly Lee Canyon ski area) Approximately one hour northwest of Las Vegas on mount Charleston in the Toiyabe National Forest. The resort has 12 runs and three chairlifts. The base offers a snack bar, cocktail lounge, and ski and snowboard rentals. The ski season generally runs from late November to early April.

things to do & see

If you want to learn to snow ski or snowboard they have great beginner packages: $40.00 ski rental equipment, lift ticket and a 1 hour group lesson or $59.00 snow board rental equipment, lift ticket and a 1 hour group lesson. If you're already a skier, lift prices are $28.00 adults and $21.00 children. 1 hour drive from the strip. - State Highway 156, Mt Charleston, Nv (702) 872-5462 or in town ticket sales (702) 645-2754. Snow info: (702) 593-9500.

Bally's

8 lighted outdoor courts
> Admission: $10.00 per hour for hotel guests, $15.00 for non-guests
> 3645 Las Vegas Blvd. S.
> Las Vegas, NV
> **(702) 739-4598**

Bob Baskin Park

4 lighted courts
> S. Rancho Dr. and W. Oakey Blvd.
> Las Vegas, NV

Tennis

There are more than 200 tennis courts in the greater Las Vegas area, and all area park and recreation departments have tennis courts available for public use.

Parks & Recreation:
Las Vegas . . . . **(702) 229-6297**
Henderson . . . . **(702) 565-4264**
Boulder City . . . . **(702) 293-9256**
Clark County . . . . **(702) 455-8200**

Angel Park

2 lighted courts
> Westcliff Dr. and Durango Dr.
> Las Vegas, NV

Baker Park

4 courts
> 1100 E. St. Louis Ave.
> Las Vegas, NV

Bruce Trent Park

2 lighted courts
> W. Vegas Dr. and Rampart Blvd.
> Las Vegas, NV

Bunker Family Park

2 lighted courts
> W. Vegas Dr. and Rampart Blvd.
> Las Vegas, NV

Cheyenne Sports Complex

5 lighted courts
> 3500 E. Cheyenne Ave. N.
> Las Vegas, NV

Desert Inn (Sheraton)

4 lighted outdoor courts. lessons, rentals, ball machines
> **Admission:** no charge for hotel guests, $10.00 per day for non-guests
> **Hours:** 6:00 a.m. to 10:00 p.m.
> 3145 Las Vegas Blvd. S.
> Las Vegas, NV
> **(702) 733-4577**

Discovery Park

2 lighted courts

2011 Paseo Verde Pkwy.
Henderson, NV

Ethel Pearson Park

2 courts

Washington Ave. and D St.
Las Vegas, NV

Flamingo Hilton Hotel

4 lighted outdoor courts

Admission: $12.00 per hour for
hotel guests, $16.00 per hour for
non-guests
Hours: Monday through Thursday
7:00 a.m. to 8:00 p.m., Friday
through Sunday 7:00 a.m. to
7:00 p.m.
3555 Las Vegas Blvd. S.
Las Vegas, NV
(702) 733-3111

Frontier Hotel

2 lighted outdoor courts

Admission: no fee
Hours: 8:00 a.m. to 11:00 p.m.
3120 Las Vegas Blvd. S.
Las Vegas, NV
(702) 794-8200

Gary Dexter Park

Evergreen and Fulton Place
Las Vegas, NV

Guinn Middle School

4 lighted courts

6480 Fairbanks Rd.
Las Vegas, NV
(702) 455-8200

Hartke Park

3 lighted courts

1638 N. Bruce St.
N. Las Vegas, NV

Hidden Palms

2 lighted courts

8855 Hidden Palms Pkwy.
Las Vegas, NV
(702) 455-8200

Hills Park

2 lighted courts

Hillpoint Dr. and Rampart Blvd.
Summerlin, NV

James A. Gay III Park

2 lighted courts

Morgan and B St.
Las Vegas, NV

Jaycee Park

Lighted courts

St. Louis and Eastern Ave.
Las Vegas, NV

Joe Knelp Park

2 lighted courts

2127 McCarran St.
N. Las Vegas, NV

Las Vegas Hilton Hotel

6 courts, 4 lighted

3000 Paradise Rd.
N. Las Vegas, NV
(702) 732-5111

Las Vegas Racquet Club

3 lighted outdoor courts

Admission: $5.00 per day
Hours: Monday through Thursday
10:00 a.m. to 5:00 p.m.
3333 Raven Ave.
Las Vegas, NV
(702) 361-2202

Las Vegas Sporting House

2 lighted outdoor courts

Admission: $20.00 per
non-member
Hours: 24 hours
3025 Industrial Rd.
Las Vegas, NV
(702) 733-8999

things to do & see

things to do & see

Laurelwood Park
2 lighted courts
    4300 Newcastle Rd.
    Las Vegas, NV
    (702) 455-7573

Lorenzi Park
8 lighted courts, reservations required, fee
    3333 W. Washington Ave.
    Las Vegas, NV
    (702) 229-6297

MGM Grand
4 lighted courts, Private and group lessons, kids tennis camps and guest partner match up, Pro shop, rentals
    Admission: $20.00
    Hours: 24 hours
    3799 Las Vegas Blvd. S.
    Las Vegas, NV
    (702) 891-3085

Morrell Park
2 lighted courts
    500 Harris St.
    Henderson, NV

Mountain View Park
2 lighted courts
    1961 Wigwam Pkwy.
    Henderson, NV

O'Callaghan Park
4 lighted courts
    601 Skyline Rd.
    Henderson, NV

Orr Middle School
4 courts
    1562 E. Katie Ave.
    Las Vegas, NV
    (702) 799-5573

Paradise Park Community Center
2 lighted courts
    4770 S. Harrison Dr.

Las Vegas, NV
(702) 455-7513

Paul Meyer Park
2 lighted courts
    4525 New Forest Dr.
    Las Vegas, NV
    (702) 455-7513

Pecos Legacy park
2 lighted courts
    150 Pecos Rd.
    Henderson, NV

Petitti Park
4 lighted courts
    2505 N. Bruce Street
    Las Vegas, NV

River Mountain Park
2 lighted courts
    1941 Appaloosa Rd.
    Henderson, NV

Riviera
3 lighted outdoor courts
    Admission: no fee to hotel guests, $10.00 non-guests
    Hours: 7:00 a.m. to 7:00 p.m.
    2901 Las Vegas Blvd. S.
    Las Vegas, NV
    (702) 734-5110

Silver Springs Park
2 lighted courts
    1950 Silver Springs Pkwy.
    Henderson, NV

Sunrise Community Center
2 courts
    2240 Linn Lane
    Las Vegas, NV
    (702) 455-7600

Sunset Park
8 lighted courts
    2575 E. Sunset Rd.
    Las Vegas, NV
    (702) 455-8243

Sunset Tennis Club

8 lighted outdoor courts, lessons
$30.00 per hour over 6 years old.
Groups $8.00 per hour

Admission: $3.00 per hour until
7:00 p.m., $5.00 per hour after
7:00 p.m.
Lorenzi Park
2601 E. Sunset Rd.
Las Vegas, NV
(702) 260-9803

Thurman White School Park

4 lighted courts
1661 Galleria Dr.
Henderson, NV

UNLV

Twelve outdoor lighted outdoor courts.
Admission: $5.00 per person, per
day - reservations suggested
Hours: 8:00 a.m. to 10:00 p.m.
4505 S. Maryland Pkwy
Las Vegas, NV
(702) 895-3207

Wells Park

2 lighted courts
1608 Moser Dr.
Henderson, NV

Whitney Community Center

3 lighted courts
5700 Missouri Ave.
Las Vegas, NV
(702) 455-7573

Wildhorse Country Club

2 lighted tennis courts
1 Showboat Country Club Dr.
Henderson, NV
(702) 434-9000

Winchester Community Center

2 lighted courts
3130 S. McLeod Dr.
Las Vegas, NV
(702) 455-7340

Winterwood Park

2 lighted courts
5310 Consul Ave.
Las Vegas, NV
(702) 455-7340

YMCA

Admission: $3.00 per person,
members free, no reservations
necessary
Hours: Monday through Friday
6:00 a.m. to 10:00 p.m., Saturday
8:00 a.m. to 7:00 p.m

Fishing and Hunting

Fishing and Hunting activities are available nearly year-round in Nevada. Fishing in the area is freshwater lake fishing. Any Nevada resident is required to have a basic fishing license. Non-residents must have a basic non-resident fishing license. Licenses can be purchased from most local sporting goods stores, marinas, and also at the Wal-mart and K-Mart outlets. To be eligible for a resident license, a person must be a citizen of the U.S. and has lived in the state of Nevada for at least 6 months. Children under 12 years of age are not required to have a license to fish in Nevada. Short term one-day permits can also be acquired. All resident hunters must have a basic resident season license when hunting game. In addition, a big game permit is required for hunters who hunt deer, antelope, elk, mountain goat and bighorn sheep. Tag applications for these big game animals are distributed in the mail in early March. For complete hunting and fishing regulations, season dates, and archery and trapping information, contact the Nevada Department of Wildlife at 4747 Vegas Drive, Las Vegas, NV 89108 or call (702) 486-5127

Fishing in the Las Vegas Area

Lake Mead
Season is open year round any hour of the day or night except for posted areas. The Lake Mead Hatchery outflow stream to Lake Mead is closed to fishing. Large-mouth bass, striped bass, channel catfish, crappie and sunfish are the most prevalent species found in the lake. Limits are five trout, six large mouth black bass, 25 catfish, 15 crappie and 20 striped bass.

Lorenzi Park Pond
Season is open year round. The pond is stocked with rainbow trout in the winter and channel catfish during the spring and summer. Limit is three game fish.
>   3333 W. Washington Ave
>   Las Vegas, NV

Sunset Park Pond
Season is open year round. The pond is stocked every other week with 300 pounds of rainbow trout in the winter and channel catfish during the spring and summer. Limit is three game fish.
>   2601 Sunset Rd.
>   Las Vegas, NV

Floyd Lamb State Park
Season is open year round. Limit is three game fish.

Fishing Charters and Guides

Anglers Guide Service
30 years experience on Lake Mead
>   161 E. Rancho Dr.
>   Henderson, NV
>   **(702) 564-1558**

Donoho's Guide Service
>   **(702) 451-4004**

Fish, Inc.
>   1500 Palamino Dr.
>   Henderson, NV
>   **(702) 565-8396**

Jr.'s Guide Service
>   **(702) 361-7039**

Karen Jones Fishing Guide
>   1018 Cutter Street
>   Las Vegas, NV
>   **(702) 871-1399**

Las Vegas Area Parks

Alexander Villas Park
Playground, lighted ballfield, basketball courts, exercise course, jogging trails, picnic facilities, volleyball
3620 Lincoln Rd.
Las Vegas, NV

Allegro Park
Tot playground, soccer/football field, picnic area, barbecues and restrooms
1023 Seven Hills Dr.
Henderson, NV

An San Sister City Park
Playground, sand volleyball court, walking paths
Ducharme Ave and Villa Monterey
Las Vegas, NV

Angel park
Playground, tennis court, exercise course, fitness course, jogging path and restrooms
Westcliff Dr. and Durango Dr.
Las Vegas, NV

Arroyo Grande Sports Complex
Playground, little league complex, softball complex, two baseball fields, basketball courts, play stations, trails and restrooms
298 Arroyo Grande Blvd
Henderson, NV

Baker Park
Playground, ball fields, swimming pool, tennis court, football field, exercise course, frisbee golf course
1100 E St. Louis Ave
Las Vegas, NV

Beckley School Park
Playground, ballfield
3223 S. Glenhurst Dr.
Las Vegas, NV

Blue Diamond Park
Playground, ballfield, and picnic area
Blue Diamond, NV

Bob Baskin Park
Playground, picnic & barbecue facilities, swimming pool, tennis court, exercise course, restrooms
S. Rancho Dr. W. Oakey Blvd
Las Vegas, NV

things to do & see

Boris Terrace Park
Playground, picnic area, basketball courts
> 2200 E. Cartier Ave.
> N. Las Vegas, NV

Brooks Tot Lot
Playground
> 1421 Brooks Ave
> N. Las Vegas, NV

Bruce Trent Park
Softball complex, fitness course, jogging track, tennis courts, picnic area with grills, volleyball, horseshoes, restrooms
> W. Vegas Dr. and Rampart Blvd
> Las Vegas, NV

Burkholder Jr. High
Lighted ballfields, soccer field and restrooms
> 645 W. Victory Rd.
> Henderson, NV

Cannon School Park
Lighted ball fields, soccer field
> 5850 Euclid Ave.
> Las Vegas, NV

Cashman School Park
Lighted ballfields, soccer fields, restrooms
> 4622 W. Desert Inn Rd.
> Las Vegas, NV

Charleston Heights Park
Playground, picnic and barbecue facilities, swimming pool, volleyball court, fitness course
> Maverick and Smoke Ranch Rd.
> Las Vegas, NV

Chester Stupak Park
Playground, picnic facilities and basketball courts
> 231 W. Boston Ave.
> Las Vegas, NV

Cheyenne Ridge Park
Playground, walking path, basketball court, sand volleyball, and picnic tables
> 3814 Scott Robinson Dr.
> N. Las Vegas, NV

Cheyenne Sports Complex
Concessions, soccer/football fields, five lighted tennis courts, four lighted softball fields, jogging course
> 3500 N. Cheyenne Ave.
> N. Las Vegas, NV

Children's Memorial Park
Playground, Little League fields, jogging track, fitness area, and restrooms
> Gowan Rd. and Torrey Pines Dr.
> Las Vegas, NV

City of Las Vegas Parks and Leisure
> 749 Veterans Memorial Dr.
> Las Vegas, NV
> **(702) 229-6297**

City View Park
Playground, picnic areas, barbecue area, pond, waterfall, horseshoe pits, fitness stations
> 101 Cheyenne Ave.
> N. Las Vegas, NV

Civic Center Park
> Five acre park with restrooms
> 200 Water Street
> Henderson, NV

Clark County Parks & Recreation
> 2601 E. Sunset Rd.
> Las Vegas, NV

Coleman Park
Playground
> Daybreak Rd. and Carmen Blvd
> Las Vegas, NV

College Park
Playground
 2613 Tonopah Ave.
 N. Las Vegas, NV

Cragin Park
Playground, baseball field, fitness course, tennis, and restrooms.
 900 Hinsen Lane
 Las Vegas, NV

Davis Park
Playground, exercise course, jogging trails, picnic facilities
 2796 Redwood St.
 Las Vegas, NV

Dearing School Park
Ballfield
 3046 S. Ferndale St
 Las Vegas, NV

Desert Breeze
Playground, ballfields, rollerblade courts, picnic tables, basketball courts, jogging and walking path
 8425 Spring Mountain Rd.
 Las Vegas, NV

Desert Inn Park
Playground, ballfield, swimming pool, restrooms
 3570 Vista Del Monte Dr.
 Las Vegas, NV

Dexter Park
Playground, ballfields, picnic and barbecue facilities, restrooms
 Evergreen and Fulton Place
 Las Vegas, NV

Discovery Park
Lighted tennis courts, two lighted sand volleyball courts, lighted basketball court, picnic area, barbecue area, horseshoe pits
 2011 Paseo VeRd.e Pkwy
 Henderson, NV

Doolittle Park
Playground, ballfields, picnic and barbecue facilities, swimming pool, football/soccer field, basketball court, restrooms
 W. Lake Mead Blvd and J Street
 Las Vegas, NV

Ed Fountain Park

Playground, ball fields, picnic and barbecue facilities, football/soccer field,
horseshoe pit, Volleyball court,
restrooms
> Vegas Drive and Decatur
> Las Vegas, NV

Eldorado Park

Playground for tots, picnic area, and
walking path
> 5900 Camino Eldorado Blvd
> N. Las Vegas, NV

Ethel Pearson Park

Playground, barbecue facilities, tennis
court, exercise course
> Washington Ave and D Street
> Las Vegas

Fitzgerald Tot Lot

Playground, shuffleboard
> H Street and Monroe Ave
> Las Vegas, NV

Fox Ridge Park

Playground, playing field, walking path,
picnic and barbecue area, shaded
shelter, restrooms
> 420 Valle Verde Dr.
> Henderson, NV

Freedom Park

Playground, lake, fitness area, ballfields, beach volleyball, picnic and barbecue facilities, football/soccer field,
restrooms
> Mojave and E. Washington Ave
> Las Vegas, NV

Grapevine Springs Park

Playground, volleyball, jogging track,
and picnic area
> 5280 Palm Ave.
> Las Vegas, NV

Green Valley Park

Playground equipment, basketball
court, horseshoe pit, picnic and barbecue area and shelters
> 370 N. Pecos Rd.
> Henderson

Hadland Park

Playground, ballfield, picnic and barbecue facilities, football/soccer field,
pool, restrooms
> 2800 Stewart Ave.
> N. Las Vegas, NV

Hartke Park

Playground, gymnasium, racquetball,
three lighted tennis courts, three softball fields, swimming pool, picnic area
> 1638 N. Bruce St.
> N. Las Vegas, NV

Hebert Memorial Park

Playground, baseball field
> 2701 Basswood Ave.
> N. Las Vegas, NV

Heers Park

Playground, football/soccer field
> Smoke Ranch Rd. and Zorro
> Las Vegas, NV

Hidden Palms Park

Playground, basketball courts, volleyball courts, tennis courts, jogging trail,
picnic area, covered shelter and barbecue area
> 8855 Hidden Palms Pkwy
> Las Vegas, NV

Hills Park

Playground, picnic area with grills, ball
fields, sand volleyball, tennis courts,
volleyball, basketball
> Hillpoint Dr. and Rampart Blvd
> Las Vegas, NV

Huntridge Circle Park

Playground, picnic facilities
Maryland Pkwy and Franklin Ave
    Las Vegas, NV

James A. Gay III Park

Playground, tennis court, basketball courts
    Morgan and B Street
    Las Vegas, NV

Jaycee Park

Playground, ballfields, jogging track, picnic shelters with barbecue facilities, tennis, football/soccer field, volleyball court, horseshoe pits, bocce and shuffleboard courts, exercise course, basketball court, fitness court and restrooms.
    St. Louis and Eastern Ave
    Las Vegas, NV

Joe Kneip Park

Two lighted baseball fields, soccer field, picnic area
    2127 McCarran Street
    N. Las Vegas, NV

Joe Shoong Park

Exercise course, picnic facilities, restrooms
    1503 Wesley Street
    Las Vegas, NV

Laurelwood Park

Playground, lighted ballfield, basketball court, jogging trails, tennis courts, restrooms
    4300 Newcastle Rd.
    Las Vegas, NV

Lewis Family Park

Playground, horseshoes, basketball courts, sand volleyball, jogging and walking paths
    1970 Tree Line Dr.
    Las Vegas, NV

Lorenzi Park

Playground, softball fields, soccer fields, outdoor basketball, fitness course, wheelchair fitness course, shuffleboard, tennis courts, jogging track, picnic and barbecue facilities, large lake, restrooms
    3333 W. Washington Ave
    Las Vegas, NV

Mary Dutton Park

    Charleston Blvd and 10th street
    Las Vegas, NV

Maslow Park and Pool

Playground, lighted ballfield, picnic facilities, soccer field, swimming pool, restrooms
    4902 Lana Ave.
    Las Vegas, NV

Mirabelli Park & Community Center

Playground, ballfield
    6200 Elton Ave.
    Las Vegas, NV

things to do & see

things to do & see

Mojave Ball Fields

Ballfields, tennis court, restrooms
Mojave Rd. and Bonanza Rd.
Las Vegas, NV

Monte Vista Park

Playground, picnic tables, jogging track
4910 Scott Robinson Dr.
N. Las Vegas, NV

Morrell Park

Playground, four lighted tennis courts, lighted basketball court, lighted sand volleyball courts, five ball fields, grass picnic areas with grills, fitness and jogging course and restrooms. Recreation center contains a gym, three racquetball courts, weight room.
500 Harris St
Henderson, NV

Mountain View Park

Playground, lighted basketball court, tennis courts, softball field, sand volleyball, picnic area and restrooms
1961 Wigwam Pkwy
Henderson, NV

Mountain View School Park

Lighted ballfields.
5436 E. Kell Ln
Las Vegas, NV

Nellis Meadows

Playground, picnic facilities, two ballfields, restrooms.
4949 E. Cheyenne Ave.
Las Vegas, NV

Nicholas E. Flores, Jr. Park

Playground, checkerboard tables, exercise stations, picnic area, horseshoe pits, shuffleboard, jogging track.
4133 Allen Ln.
N. Las Vegas, NV

North Las Vegas Parks & Recreation Dept

2200 Civic Center Dr.
N. Las Vegas, NV
(702) 633-1171

O'Callaghan Park

Playgrounds, lighted baseball field, basketball court, handball courts, lighted tennis courts, horseshoe pits, frisbee golf target baskets, picnic area, tot lot, fitness and jogging course and restrooms.
601 Skyline Rd.
Henderson, NV

Overton Town Park

Playground, lighted ballfield, community center, horseshoe pit, picnic facility, tennis court, restrooms.
Overton, NV

Paradise Park

Playground, lighted ballfield, basketball court, community center, exercise course, horseshoe pit, jogging trail, picnic facilities, soccer field, swimming pool, lighted tennis court, volleyball court, restrooms.
4770 S. Harrison Dr.
Las Vegas, NV

Paradise Vista Park

Playground, picnic facilities.
5582 Stirrup Street
Las Vegas, NV

Parkdale Park

Playground, basketball court, community center, picnic facilities, swimming pool, volleyball court, restrooms.
3200 Ferndale Street
Las Vegas, NV

Paul Meyer Park
Playground, lighted ballfield, basketball court, exercise course, jogging trails, picnic facilities, soccer field, volleyball court.
> 4525 New Forest Dr.
> Las Vegas, NV

Pecos Legacy Park
Playground, lighted ballfields, restrooms, softball field, lighted tennis courts, lighted basketball court.
> 150 Pecos Rd.
> Henderson, NV

Petitti Park
Playground, swimming pool, three baseball fields, picnic area, restrooms.
> 2505 N. Bruce Street
> N. Las Vegas, NV

Potosi Park
Two lighted ballfields, volleyball court, restrooms.
> 2790 Potosi St.
> Las Vegas, NV

Prosperity Park
Playground, ballfield, basketball court, exercise course, jogging trail, picnic facilities, restrooms.
> 7101 Parasol Lane
> Las Vegas, NV

Pueblo Park
Playground, jogging path, nature area, bike path, picnic area basketball courts.
> W. Lake Mead Blvd and
> Pueblo Vista Dr.
> Las Vegas, NV

Rainbow Family Park
Playground, ballfields, soccer field, fitness course, walking and jogging path, picnic area with grills and restrooms.
> Oakey Blvd and O'Bannon Dr.
> Las Vegas, NV

Regional Park
Miniature aircraft field, toilets, shelter.
> 4400 Horse Dr.
> N. Las Vegas, NV

Richard Tam Park
Playground, softball field, picnic and barbecue area.
> Donna & Craig Streets
> N. Las Vegas, NV

Richard Walpole Rec. Area
Horseshoes, picnic area, shuffleboard, walking course.
> 1621 Yale Street
> N. Las Vegas, NV

River Mountain Park
Playground, basketball courts, picnic tables, horseshoe pits, restrooms.
> 1941 Appaloosa Rd.
> Henderson, NV

Robert E. Lake School Park
Playground ballfields, picnic facilities.
> 2904 Meteoro St
> Las Vegas, NV

Rotary Park
Playground, picnic and barbecue facilities, swimming pool, horseshoe pit, volleyball pit and restrooms.
> W. Charleston Blvd and Hinson St.
> Las Vegas

Rotary Tot Lot
Playground for tots.
> 2600 Magnet Street
> N. Las Vegas, NV

Shadow Rock Park
Playgrounds, softball field, jogging trail, picnic areas.
> 2650 Los Feliz Street
> Las Vegas, NV

things to do & see

things to do & see

Silver Bowl Sports Complex
Playground, six lighted ballfields, archery, soccer field and restrooms, remote control aircraft field and remote control car track.
>6800 E. Russell Rd.
>Las Vegas, NV

Silver Springs Park
Ballfields, tennis courts, restrooms, pool.
>1950 Silver Springs Pkwy
>Henderson, NV

South Meadows Park
Playground, basketball courts, football, soccer.
>Boston Ave and Fairfield Ave
>Las Vegas, NV

Spring Valley Park
Playground, ballfield, basketball court, picnic facilities, and restrooms.
>4220 S. Ravenwood Dr.
>Las Vegas, NV

Stewart Place Park
Playground, picnic and barbecue facilities.
>Marion Dr. and Chantilly Ave
>Las Vegas, NV

Sunrise Park
Playground, 2 lighted ballfields, basketball court, community center, picnic facilities, soccer field, swimming pool, tennis court, volleyball court and restrooms.
>2240 Linn Lane
>Las Vegas, NV

Sunset Park
Playground, eight lighted ballfields, archery, basketball court, community center, exercise course, frisbee course, horseshoe pit, jogging trail, stocked lake, model boat race area, picnic facility, soccer field, swimming pool, eight lighted tennis courts, volleyball pits, restrooms.
>2601 Sunset Rd.
>Las Vegas, NV

Tate School Park
Playground
>2450 Lincoln Rd.
>Las Vegas, NV

Thomas School Park
Playground, ballfield.
>1560 E. Cherokee Ln.
>Las Vegas, NV

Thurman White Middle School Park
Ballfields, basketball court, volleyball court and tennis courts.
>1661 Galleria Dr.
>Henderson, NV

Titanium Field
Play area, baseball field.
>Lake Mead Dr. and Water Street
>Henderson, NV

Tom Williams Park
Playground, basketball court, picnic area, shade area.
>1844 Belmont St.
>N. Las Vegas, NV

Tonopah Park
Playground, basketball court, frontier village.
>204 E. Tonopah Ave.
>N. Las Vegas, NV

Ullom School Park
Playground, soccer field, ballfield.
>4869 Sun Valley Dr.
>Las Vegas, NV

Valley View Park
Picnic area, basketball courts, softball field.
>2000 Bennett Street
>N. Las Vegas, NV

Vegas Heights Tot Lot
Playground.
> Balzar Ave and Concord Street
> Las Vegas, NV

Walker Park
Picnic area, basketball courts, softball field.
> 2227 W. Evans Ave.
> N. Las Vegas, NV

Walker Park
Playground, swimming pool, picnic area, grills, basketball courts.
> 1509 June Ave
> N. Las Vegas, NV

Warm Springs Softball complex
Lighted ballfields.
> Eastern Ave at Warm Springs Rd.
> Las Vegas, NV

Wayne Bunker Family Park
Playground, jogging track, volleyball, horseshoe pits, picnic shelters, barbecues and restroom .
> Tenaya Way and Alexander Rd.
> Las Vegas, NV

Wells Park
Playground, basketball court, picnic area, lighted adult softball field, lighted

tennis courts and restrooms.
> 1608 Moser Dr.
> Henderson, NV

West Charleston Lion Park
Playground, picnic facilities.
> Essex Dr. and Fulton Place
> Las Vegas, NV

Whitney Park
Playground, ballfield, community center, horseshoe pit, picnic facilities, soccer field, volleyball court, pool, restrooms.
> 5700 E. Missouri Ave.
> Las Vegas, NV

Wildwood Park
Playground, picnic facilities, swimming pool, exercise course.
> Shadow Mountain and Wildwood
> Las Vegas, NV

Winchester Park
Playground, basketball courts, bocce ball court, community center, horseshoe pit, jogging trail, picnic facilities, shuffleboard, tennis court, volleyball court, restrooms
> 3130 S. McLeod Dr.
> Las Vegas, NV

things to do & see

Winterwood Park
Playground, lighted ballfield, exercise course, picnic facilities, soccer field, tennis court, restrooms.
> 5310 Consul Ave.
> Las Vegas, NV

Woofter Family Park
Playground, fitness course, jogging track, spray fountain.
> Vegas Dr. and Rock Springs Dr.
> Las Vegas, NV

Youth Center Park
Play area, lighted basketball court, swimming pool.
> 105 W. Basic Rd.
> Henderson, NV

Shopping

Belz Factory Outlet Mall
The first fully-enclosed, climate-controlled outlet mall that is 145 outlets including 25 clothing stores. Included in the Belz mall are Nike, Carter's childrens wear, G.H. Bass Apparel Store, Oneida, Oshkosh, Danskin, Soss Simon Jewelers, Ducks Unlimited, Adolfo II and Levis. The mall has a permanent state-of-the-art laser show designed by Richard Sandhaus, a nationally-known laser artist.
> **Hours:** Monday through Saturday 10:00 a.m. to 9:00 p.m. and Sunday from 10:00 a.m. to 6:00 p.m.
> 7400 South Las Vegas Blvd.
> Las Vegas, NV
> **(702) 896-5599**

Boulevard Mall
Nevada's largest shopping center with more than 150 fine shops and an elaborate food court. In addition to well-known retailers such as Dillard's, J.C. Penney, Sears and Broadway

Southwest, there are a variety of specialty stores including Nature Company, Sesame Street General Store, Sanrio Surprises, Going to the Game, Charlotte Russe, and Howard and Phil's Western Wear. Wheelchairs are available free of charge, strollers are available for rent. Valet and covered parking are available.
> **Hours:** Monday through Friday from 10:00 a.m. to 9:00 p.m., Saturday from 10:00 a.m. to 8:00 p.m., and Sunday from 11:00 a.m. to 6:00 p.m.
> 3528 Maryland Parkway
> Las Vegas, NV
> **(702) 732-8949**

Fashion Show Mall
There are over 145 shops featuring many top names from California and New York such as Neiman Marcus, Saks Fifth Avenue, Macy's, Dillard's and Robinsons-May Company. Shoppers also may sample the many cafes in the Fashion Show's interna-

tional food court or relax in a fine dining restaurant. Valet parking available, car wash. Wednesday through Saturdays, 10:00 a.m. to 2:00 p.m.. Strollers and wheelchair rental at the concierge desk.

> **Hours:** Monday through Friday 10:00 a.m. to 9:00 p.m., Saturday 10:00 a.m. to 7:00 p.m. and Sunday noon to 6:00 p.m.
> 3200 Las Vegas Blvd. S
> Las Vegas, NV
> **(702) 369-8382**

Forum Shops

The host to more than 100 unique shops and exciting restaurants in an ancient Roman setting. Among the distinguished tenants are Gucci, Louis Vuitton, Ann Taylor, Guess, Escada, Gianni Versace, Versus, Estee Lauder and Christian Dior. Restaurants include Spago, The Palm, Bertolini's, Stage Deli, Planet Hollywood and La Salsa. Valet parking is available via the underground traffic tunnel at Caesers Blvd. (north driveway). Visitors may also self-park in Caesars Palace five- story, free covered parking facility.

> **Hours:** Sunday through Thursday 10:00 a.m. to 11:00 p.m., Friday and Saturday 10:00 a.m. to midnight.

3500 Las Vegas Blvd. S
Las Vegas, NV
(702) 893-4800

Galleria at Sunset

The area's newest mall, featuring two levels with 130 specialty retailers and a 600-seat food court. The major tenants of this 900,000 sq. ft. mall include J C Penney, Robinsons-May and Mervyn's. Other fine specialty stores are Ann Taylor, Cache, Charlotte Russe, Miller's Outpost, and many more.

> **Hours:** Monday through Saturday 10:00 a.m. to 9:00 p.m. and Sunday 11:00 a.m. to 6:00 p.m.
> 1300 Sunset Rd.
> Henderson, NV
> **(702) 434-0202**

Las Vegas Factory Stores of America

A factory direct center with more than 50 stores featuring name brands. The Outlet Lounge, the only sports/casino style bar in an American mall is among the tenants, where lounge patrons can play video poker and slot machines. Famous name outlets lining the mall include Adolfo II, American Tourister, Corning/Revere, Prestige Fragrance and Cosmetics, Book Warehouse, Florsheim Shoes, Mikasa, Geoffrey

Beene, Van Heusen and West Point Pepperell.

Hours: Monday through Saturday 10:00 a.m. to 8:00 p.m., Sunday 10:00 a.m. to 6:00 p.m.
9155 Las Vegas Blvd. S.
Las Vegas, NV
(702) 897-9090

Meadows Mall

Offering more than 144 distinctive shops and department stores and the Menagerie Carousel. The enclosed mall is designed with two levels of specialty stores and five courtyards that wind through an elongated "Z" pattern. Anchor stores include Dillard's, Broadway, J.C. Penney and Sears.

Hours: Monday through Friday 10:00 a.m. to 9:00 p.m., Saturday 10:00 a.m. to 7:00 p.m. and Sunday 10:00 a.m. to 6:00 p.m.
4300 Meadows Lane
Las Vegas, NV
(702) 878-4849

Tower Shops at Stratosphere

A selection of 35 fine shops and 13 retail carts located on the second floor of the Stratosphere. The Tower Shops are located up the escalator from the casino level on the second floor. All visitors that proceed to the Tower will pass through The Tower Shops themed street scene areas of Paris, Hong Kong and New York on their way to the elevators to the top of the Tower. Among the tenants are Aerosoles Footwear, Jitters Freshly brewed gourmet coffees, Antares Women's fashions, Kid Vegas Kid's clothes, toys and more, Ancient Creations Ancient coins in jewelry settings, Magic Masters Show and sell magic tricks, Bath & Body Works bath gels, lotions, shampoos and Marshall Rousso men's and women's apparel.

Hours: Sunday through Thursday 10:00 a.m. to 11:00 p.m.
Stratasphere
Las Vegas, NV
(702) 388-1130

outdoor adventure

chapter four

- State & National Parks
- Hiking & Rock Climbing
- Horseback Riding
- Water Activities
- Tours and Excursions

State and National Parks

Ash Meadows National Wildlife Refuge

A natural oasis in the desert. Located about 90 miles northwest of Las Vegas in Amargosa Valley, it consists of over 22,000 acres of spring-fed wetlands and alkaline desert uplands. Here you can find more than 20 plants and animals found nowhere else in the world, including a few on the endangered list. You can also see environmental extremes from sand dunes, to ash tree groves, to wetlands all in one desert environment.

Hours: Open sunrise to sunset
Las Vegas, NV
(702) 372-5435

Bonnie Springs / Old Nevada

Located in the Red Rock canyon National Conservation Area. Bonnie Springs Ranch was originally built in 1843 as a stopover for the wagon trains going to California down the Old Spanish Trail. In 1846, General Fremont, on his way to California, stopped at what is now Bonnie Springs Ranch to gear up for his trip through Death Valley. Since 1952 the ranch has been used as a tourist attraction.

Hours: 10:30 a.m. to 5:00 p.m.
Admission: $6.50 Adults, $5.50 Children
Las Vegas, NV
(702) 872-5500

Davis Dam/Lake Mohave

Completed in 1953, Davis Dam regulates the flow of water to the lower Colorado River region. Spanning the Colorado River near Laughlin, Davis Dam backs up the river's waters to form Lake Mohave, 67 miles downstream from Hoover Dam. Lake Mohave, behind Davis Dam, is part of Lake Mead National Recreation Area administered by the National Park Service. The area around the lake and along the Colorado River below Davis Dam provides a multitude of recreational opportunities, including fishing, boating, swimming, water skiing, camping, picnicking, exploring, photography and just plain relaxing. Facilities for public use are located at Katherine's Landing in Arizona near Davis Dam and at Cottonwood Cove east of Searchlight, Nevada.

Hours: 8:00 a.m. to 4:00 p.m.
Davis Dam Field Division
Bullhead City, Arizona 86429
(520) 754-3628
95 miles south of Las Vegas, take U.S. 95 south to SR 163.

Death Valley National Monument

Located 135 miles from Las Vegas is Death Valley National Park. Death Valley National Park has more than 3.3 million acres of spectacular desert scenery, interesting and rare desert wildlife, complex geology, undisturbed wilderness, and sites of historical and cultural interest. Bounded on the west by 11,049 foot Telescope Peak and on the east by 5,475 foot Dante's View, Death Valley is the lowest dry point below sea level in the Western Hemisphere (280 feet).

Hours: Visitors Center, 8:00 a.m. to 6:00 p.m.
Admission: $10.00 per vehicle
State Route 190
Death Valley, CA 92328
(760) 852-4524
136 miles north of Las Vegas take U.S. 95 north to Lathrop Wells, take State Route 373 south to Death Valley Junction, State Route 190 to Death Valley.

Floyd Lamb State Park

Originally known as Tule Springs, this park was an early watering stop for Indians. It later became a privately owned working ranch, as well as a guest/dude ranch in the 1950's. Facilities include picnic facilities, fishing lakes, walking/biking path, trapshooting range, horseback riding, ducks and geese roam throughout the park.

Hours: 8:00 a.m. until sunset
Admission: $4.00 per vehicle
9200 Tule Springs Rd.
Las Vegas, NV
(702) 486-5413
10 miles north of Las Vegas take U.S. 95 north to Tule Springs Rd.

Grand Canyon National Park

Visitors here can experience some of the most spectacular views on earth. Named the greatest natural wonder of the world, the Grand Canyon was formed over millions of years by the swift water of the Colorado River, as well as by constant exposure to the wind and sun. The result, miles of formations of rocks and earth, greets the eye in a profusion of striking colors and depths. The Grand Canyon is located 300 miles southeast of Las Vegas, approximately 6 hours by car. The South Rim is open year-round. You can drive along the rim or see it by mule. For those who would rather see the sights by air, several airlines offer regularly scheduled air tours

Hours: 8:00 a.m. to 5:00 p.m. winter, 7:00 a.m. to 9:00 p.m. summer.
Admission: $10.00 per vehicle
Grand Canyon National Park
P.O. Box 129 Grand Canyon, AZ
(520) 638-7888
300 miles southeast of Las Vegas take U.S. 93 southeast to Kingman, take I-40 east to Williams, and take 64 north to the canyon.

Hoover Dam

One of the engineering marvels of the world. The structure and the body of water behind it, Lake Mead, are a must see during any trip to Las Vegas. Hoover Dam is an arch-gravity dam 726 feet high and 660 feet thick at its base. The Hoover Dam project including the dam, the All American Canal, the town of Boulder City, highways, railroads and various other works, cost $165 million to build.

Admission: $8.00 Adults, $7.00 Seniors, Children under 16 $2.00, Includes tour of dam and movie.
Hours: 9:00 a.m. to 4:15 p.m. daily
Box 299
Boulder City, NV
(702) 293-8367
40 miles southeast of Las Vegas take U.S. 93 to dam

Lake Havasu/London Bridge

Brought over stone by stone and reconstructed in 1971, Lake Havasu's London Bridge forms the central focus of a modern "Old English Village" on the shore of the lake. Dozens of gift shops, antique shops and cafes line the shore of this man-made lake north of Parker Dam. Boating, fishing and many other water sports are available.

Hours: 8:00 a.m. until dusk
Lake Havasu Tourist Bureau
(520) 855-2784

outdoor adventure

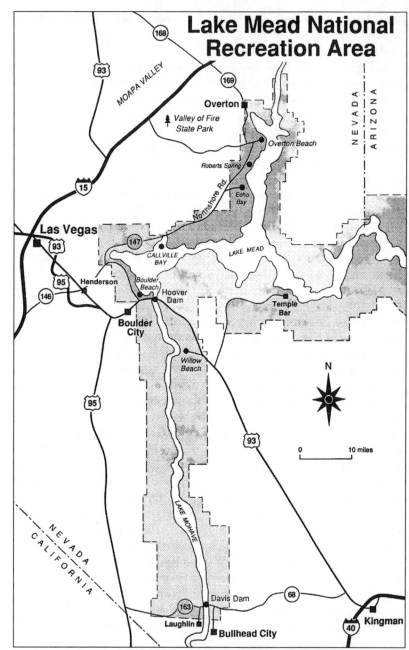

Lake Mead National
Recreation Area

Lake Mead National Recreation Area

Lake Mead National Recreation Area offers a wealth of things to do and places to go year-round. With 1.5 million acres, it is twice the size of Rhode Island. Its huge lakes cater to boaters, swimmers, sunbathers, and fishermen while its desert rewards hikers, wildlife photographers, and roadside sightseers. Three of America's four desert ecosystems — the Mojave, the Great Basin, and the Sonora Deserts — meet in the Lake Mead National Recreation Area. As a result, this seemingly barren area contains a surprising variety of plants and animals, some of

which may be found nowhere else in the world.

Hours: Open year-round, 24 hours, 7 days a week. Visitor center: 8:30 a.m. to 4:30 p.m., and 8:30 a.m. to 5:30 p.m. between Memorial Day and Labor Day.

Admission:
Las Vegas
(702) 293-8906
To get to the Lake Mead National Recreation Area from the Las Vegas area take U.S. 93 or 95 south. Access is also available north on Interstate 15.

Mount Charleston/Toiyabe National Forest

Always an average 30 degrees cooler than downtown Las Vegas and two miles higher in altitude, it's a great place to get away from the heat and the gambling for awhile. There are skiing and sleigh rides in the winter, and horseback riding, wagon rides and hiking in the summer. Full service camping is available from May 1 through Sept. 30, 7 days a week.
The tranquil scenery is a beautiful place to visit all year round.
(702) 872-5462

For snow conditions call (702) 646-3805
45 miles north west of Las Vegas, take Highway 95, turn off onto Highway 157 at Kyle Canyon.

Red Rock Canyon

Once the home of ancient Indian tribes, this magnificent canyon was formed by a thrust fault — a fracture in the earth's crust where one rock plate is thrust horizontally over another. Red Rock Canyon is home to wild horses and burros, as well as various species of wildlife including desert bighorn sheep and antelope. The 13-mile scenic loop drive offers picnic areas and hiking trails and the visitor's center features information about the area and a gallery.

Hours: 8:30 a.m. to 4:30 p.m.
Admission: $5.00 fee to enter the area or a $20.00 fee for an annual pass.
Bureau of Land Management
1000 Scenic Drive, Las Vegas
(702) 363-1921
16 miles west of Las Vegas, take Charleston Boulevard

Spring Mountain Ranch

Situated at the base of the Wilson Cliffs, travelers along the Old Spanish Trail used the area of the ranch as a rest stop in the 1830's because of the spring fed creek running through the ranch. Chester Lauck of the comedy team "Lum & Abner" radio show built the ranch house in 1948 that stands today and is used as a visitors center for the park. German born actress Vera Krupp purchased the ranch in 1955 and raised Herefords and Brahma. Because of health reasons, she sold the ranch to Howard Hughes in 1967. The Nevada Division of State Parks bought the 528 acre ranch in 1974. Facilities in the park include picnic facilities, interpretive trails, play area, stage for theatrical programs and concerts, ranch house.

> **Hours:** Tour of the Main Ranch House and Visitors Center, Monday and Friday 12:00 p.m. to 4:00 p.m., Saturday and Sunday 10:00 a.m. to 4:00 p.m. Closed Tuesday and Thursday.
> Picnic area open every day.
> **Admission:** $5.00 per car
> P.O. Box 124
> Blue Diamond, NV
> **(702) 875-4141**
> 18 miles west of Las Vegas take Charleston Blvd. West to park.

Valley of Fire

Dedicated in 1935, it is Nevada's oldest State Park. It encompasses over 46,000 acres and derives its name from brilliant red sandstone formations that were formed from great shifting sand dunes over 150 million years ago. Complex uplifting and faulting of the region, followed by extensive erosion, have created the present topography. Ancient Indian petroglyphy can be seen at Petroglyphy Canyon. One of the most beautiful features of the desert are the brilliant red rocks that are scattered throughout Valley of Fire. Looking across the barren, hot desert valley it is hard to believe that 600 million years ago the entire area was under water. Animal and plant life was abundant here at that time and as the waters subsided over the next 400 million years the thriving ocean floor became a unique desert valley. The sandstone rocks vary in color from deep reds and purples to tans and whites and their unique formations have been formed by millions of years of erosion, wind and climatic change. Some of the most interesting rock formations are the "Seven Sisters" which are seven unusual rock formations which stand in a row. They are remnants from the harsh erosion which has changed their shape over the years. The visitors center includes an art gallery and maps and information

> **Hours:** Daily 8:30 a.m. to 4:30 p.m.
> **Admission:** $3.00 per vehicle, $7.00 camping fee
> Valley of Fire State Park
> Box 515
> Overton, NV 89040
> **(702) 397-2088**
> 55 miles northwest of Las Vegas take Interstate 15 to State Route 169

Hiking

There several nice hiking trails just outside of downtown Las Vegas. Since this is a 'kids' book, we will just touch on the kid friendly trails and a few tips for keeping everyone happy. Do remember that several of these trails have drop-offs and loose rock.
*Always remember to bring plenty of sunscreen — SPF 25, bring plenty of water, take along some type of first aid

kit and most importantly — tell some-one your plans and where you are going.

Red Rock Canyon
Children's Discovery Trail

A very easy .7 mile loop takes approximately 1 hour. Very informative and educational. Pick up a Children's Discovery Guide from the visitor's center at the entrance of Red Rock Canyon, you will need to ask the personnel at the counter for it. The trail is marked with stopping points where children can refer to the guide, and learn interesting facts about the vegetation and terrain. The hike begins at a well-marked trail head and information board. It starts in the open desert, crosses a large wash, then begins to climb the hillside. After 1/4 mile, the trail will junction with the Willow Spring Loop Trail. After another 1/4 mile, the trail joins the Lost Creek Trail and from that point descends down the hillside to the parking area.

Directions: After entering Red Rock Canyon Park, continue straight from the stop sign about 7.5 miles. The Willow Spring turnoff will be on your right. Park at the pullout on the left.

Lost Creek

Easy 0.6 mile hikes with open desert, streams, vegetation, and seasonal waterfall and rock formations. The hike begins at a clearly marked trail-head and information board. Walk through the open desert following the trail across a large wash and up the hillside. The trail will become narrower with some side trails evident. Lush vegetation followed by large boulders keep the hike twisted and interesting. Along the way there is a small stream on the left, at one point there are park benches near the stream which makes a won-derful resting spot. The trail ends at a box canyon with a waterfall.

Directions: 7.5 miles into the Red Rock canyon park, take the Willow Spring turnoff on your right. Park at a pullout on the left.

Moenkopi

A 2.0 mile hike up and down hills and along small ridges. The hike begins at a marked trail-head. Throughout this hike other trails join and leave from the Moenkopi trail so watch marked posts at each junction. The loop starts southwest of the visitor center and to the crest of the hill on the west side, giving a hiker great views of the Red Rock area. The trail goes in and out of washes, up on ridges from the north to the south and then east, back to the visitor center.

Directions: At the stop sign turn left to the visitor center. The trail begins on the south side of the visitors center.

White Rock Spring

6 mile hike. The trailhead begins on the left side of the dirt turn around. The trail is a closed dirt road that descends to the spring.

Directions: At the stop sign continue into Red Rock Canyon Park for 5.8 miles until you reach the White Rock Spring pull off.

Mount Charleston
Little Falls Spring

A short 1/2 mile hike. The trailhead begins up the embankment at the parking area. Follow the trail to the right until you reach a fork in the trail, stay to the left following the trail as it leads uphill. The canyon will slowly close in, ending at a small waterfall.

Directions: Take U.S. 95 north for 7.5 miles past Craig Road to the Route 157 turn off. Travel West on

outdoor adventure

Route 157 for 20 miles until you reach the parking area.

Valley of Fire

Petroglyph Canyon

An easy 1/2 mile hike. The trail-head is at the east end of the parking area near the restrooms. Follow the red sandstone as it curves through the canyon. Watch for petroglyphs (A carving or line drawing on rock, especially one made by prehistoric people) on the canyon walls. An informative marker about the petroglyphs is near the restrooms. The trail curves to the left, ending at Mouse's tank. The tank is a natural depression in the sandstone which collects rain water.

> **Directions:** Take Interstate 15 north for 22.5 miles past the Speedway exit to Route 169. Turn east on Route 169 and continue to the Valley of Fire State Park. In the park, turn left following the signs to the visitor's center. Just before reaching the center, the road will fork. Take the road to the left to the Petroglyph Canyon turnoff.

Lake Mead

Grapevine Canyon

Easy 0.4 mile hike to the petroglyphs. Moderate hike up the canyon.
Follow the path paralleling a large wash on your right at the end of the parking area. After 0.40 mile large rock formations mark the entrance to Grapevine Canyon. There is an abundance of petroglyphs etched into the boulders. Hiking up the canyon, you will reach the runoff from a spring in the canyon. If you follow the spring further up the canyon, it becomes more difficult with rock scrambling. This spring provides much limited water to the desert attracting all types of wildlife.

> **Directions:** Take 93/95 south out

of town to the 95 turnoff just before Boulder City. Drive south for 55 miles until reaching the 163 turnoff to Laughlin. Head east. Turn left after approximately 14 miles onto a dirt road. After about two miles turn left again, the road dead ends at the parking area.

Historic Railroad Trail

Easy 2.6 mile hike. Take the trail to the east as it follows the path the historic railroad used to bring equipment to construct Hoover Dam. This hike will lead you through a series of four tunnels. Throughout the hike, there are spectacular views of Lake Mead on your left.

> **Directions:** Take 93/95 south out of town to Boulder City, at the stoplight make a left following 93 toward the Hoover Dam. Turn left onto Lakeshore Road towards the Alan Bible Visitor Center. Make the second right into a parking lot. The trail-head is off the south-east end of the parking lot.

Redstone

An easy 0.5 mile loop. Begin your hike at the Redstone Picnic area on east side of the parking lot. You will see an obvious path. Wind your way through red sandstone monoliths and learn about the geology of the area. Interpretive signs are provided along the trail. The path winds around to the right bringing you back to the parking area.

> **Directions:** Take Lake Mead Blvd east over Sunrise Mountain. At the stop sign make a left onto Northshore Scenic Drive. Make a right at mile-marker 27 into the Redstone Picnic Area.

River Mountain Hiking Trail

Five-mile, round-trip restored hiking trail built in 1935 by the civilian conservation corps offering breathtaking views of Lake Mead and Las Vegas valley. Information: 293-2034; fax 293-0574 or c/o Boulder City Chamber of Commerce, 1305 Arizona St., Boulder City 89005.

Guided Hikes

Lake Mead National Recreation Area
Guided hikes and lectures
Alan Bible Visitors Center
Lakeshore Rd. Boulder City
(702) 293-8906

Red Rock Canyon
Planned hikes
Bureau of Land Management
(702) 363-1921

Sierra Club
Recorded listing of weekly hikes
(702) 363-3267

Rock Climbing

Sky's The Limit
The Spring Mountain's unique peaks and canyons feature routes to captivate the beginner and challenge the most accomplished climber. Easy approaches and an accessible location just twenty minutes' drive from Las Vegas make this wild and beautiful eastern slope of the spring mountains — a true climbers' paradise. Certified rock and alpine guide accredited climbers teach an introductory course, "discover climbing".
Admission: discover climbing introductory course: $169.00 1/2 day, $250.00 full day, basic rock craft course: two days of climbing and transportation: $220.00
Hcr 33, Box 1
Las Vegas, NV
(702) 363-4533

Jackson Hole Mountain Guides
Jackson Hole Mountain Guides offers daily rock climbing classes and guided climbs in the Red Rock National Conservation Area. All ages and abilities welcome. No experience necessary.
Hours: 8:00 a.m. to 5:00 p.m.
Admission: basic beginning course $65.00 per person (5 1/2 hours), technical climbing $230.00 per person full day, $120.00 1/2 day
P.O. Box 248
Blue Diamond, NV
(702) 223-2176

Thrillseekers Unlimited
Rock climbing guide.
Admission: $150.00 per day
3172 N. Rainbow Blvd, Ste 321
Las Vegas, NV
(702) 699-5551

outdoor adventure

Horseback Riding and Wagon Adventures

2 R Riding Stables

Guided trail rides in the Eldorado Mountains overlooking Lake Mead

> **Admission:** Call for rates.
> **Hours:** 8:00 a.m. to dusk, daily, year-round.
> 1400 Desert Hills Dr.
> Las Vegas, NV
> **(702) 293-3434**

Bonnie Springs Trail rides

Take a relaxing horseback ride through scenic Red Rock Canyon.

> Hwy. 159 west of Las Vegas
> Las Vegas, NV
> **(702) 875-4191**

Cowboy Trail Rides

Horseback riding in beautiful Red Rock Canyon. Morning, afternoon and sunset rides. Horseback riding, Mustang viewing, campfire music and cowboy poetry. Cowboy trail rides offers a variety of horseback rides at Loval Canyon, Mt. Charleston, Valley of Fire and Red Rock Canyon. Choose hour-long rides to overnight trips, cattle drives, fishing trips, barbecues and more.

> **Admission:** $25.00 an hour, $225 overnight
> **Hours:** 8:00 a.m. to 9:00 p.m., daily, year-round
> 1211 S. Eastern Ave.
> Las Vegas, NV
> **(702) 387-2457**

Mount Charleston Riding Stable

The 3-hour trail ride takes you into Fletcher canyon where beautiful aspen trees and huge evergreens abound. A great activity for watching birds and wildlife. Sleigh rides in the winter when the snow is deep or hayrides in the cool summer evenings. Overnight wilderness rides are available too. A short 38 miles from downtown. Inquire at Mt. Charleston restaurant & lodge.

> **Admission:** Three hour ride is $60.00 prepaid and pre-reserved, the 25 minute rides are $8.00 adults, $6.00 children 3 to 6.
> Las Vegas, NV
> **(702) 872-7009**

Mountain T Ranch

Riding stable offers day and overnight horseback rides plus parties, weddings, and barbecues. 25 minutes from the "strip." The 6-hour ride includes lunch on the trail and a barbecue upon your return to the ranch.

> **Admission:** 1 to 1 1/2 hours $20.00; 2 hours and 20 minutes $30.00; 3 1/2 hours $50.00; 4 1/2 hours $65.00; 6 hours $100.00
> **Hours:** Daylight to dusk daily. Year-round.
> 140 Kyle Canyon Rd.
> Las Vegas, NV
> **(702) 656-8025**

outdoor adventure

Silver State "Old West" Tours

Rides range from an hour-long horse-back tour of the ranch to an all day ride which includes lunch.

Admission: $25.00 per hour or $97.50 all day
Hours: Hourly rides
Spring Mountain Ranch
Las Vegas, NV
(702) 798-6565

Pioneer Territory Wagon Tours

Experience the old west just like the frontiersmen did. Wagon rides out to the Ash Meadows National Wildlife Refuge. An all day ride takes you to the many natural springs located in this protected environment and then on to beautiful Crystal Lake. After the trek, enjoy a traditional camp fire and chuck wagon dinner. For the really adventur-ous, spend a night under the stars at the cow camp. Abundant wildlife and terrific for bird watchers, a place not to be missed.

Hours: Day wagon rides only, $40.00 per person including dinner. Overnight stays at the cow camp including dinner only $75.00 per person. Small groups welcome.
Pahrump
(702) 727-8332

Water Activities

Black Canyon Raft Tour

Take a 12-mile rapid free raft tour through scenic Black Canyon. This three-hour ride goes down the Colorado River from Hoover Dam to Willow Beach. Waterfalls, hot springs, geology and history.

Admission: $79.95 per person - includes lunch, bus return to expedition depot from Willow Beach, and all transfers. Visa, Mastercard & Discover accepted.
Hours: Hotel pick-ups are between 8:00 a.m. and 8:45 a.m., and return you to your hotel at approximately 4:45 p.m. Tours depart daily at 9:30 a.m.
1297 Nevada Hwy
Boulder City, NV
(702) 293-3776   (800) 696-raft

Grand Canyon - Colorado River Rafting Trips

There is no experience in the world that equals the grandeur and history of the Grand Canyon. From towering vis-tas and majestic canyons, you will descend back in time as you traverse the heart of the Colorado River. Trip lengths and prices vary.

Bar 10 Ranch
(801) 628-4010

outdoor adventure

Boulder City Water Sports
Boat rentals
  Las Vegas, NV
  (702) 293-7526

Cottonwood Cove Resort & Marina
Boat rentals
  Las Vegas, NV
  (702) 297-1464

Down River Outfitters
Boat rentals
  Las Vegas, NV
  (702) 293-1190   (800) 748-3702

Action Adventure Watercraft Rentals
Personal, party or fishing watercraft rentals on nearby Lake Mead
  Overton Beach Marina
  Overton, NV
  (800) 553-5452

Advanced Marine Service & Transport
Boat rentals
  Las Vegas, NV
  (701) 565-1005

Boat Doc
Boat rentals
  Las Vegas, NV
  (702) 452-1191

Calvin Bay Marina Lake Mead
Houseboats, fishing boats and deck cruiser rentals
  Box 100 Hcr-30
  Las Vegas, NV
  (702) 565-4813

Callville Bay Resort & Marina
Boat rentals
  Las Vegas, NV
  (702) 565-8958

Desert Princess
Cruise Lake Mead on a unique triple-deck 19th century sternwheeler. Daily excursions year-round to Hoover Dam aboard the "Desert Princess," an authentically designed Mississippi paddlewheel. Breakfast, early dinner and dinner/dance cruises available.
  Admission: Adults $16.00 to $43.00; children under 12, $6.00 to $43.00

Hours: Year-round except Christmas
P.O. Box 62465
Las Vegas, NV
(702) 293-6180
Hwy 95 at Lake Mead
Lakemead@Lakemeadcruises.com

Get It Wet Watercraft

Explore Lake Mead on 3-seater jet skis. Discover hidden beaches, coves and the Hoover Dam. Self-guided tours.

661 W. Lake Mead Dr.
Henderson, NV
(702) 294-7547

Lake Mead Resort Marina

Full resort facilities include motel lodging, restaurant, coffee shop and a "floating lounge." Our complete marina offers ski, fishing and patio boats, as well as personal watercraft rentals, grocery store, snack bar, boat launch, moorage and fuel dock. Take a cruise to Hoover Dam on the magnificent Desert Princess, a 250-passenger Sternwheeler now moored at the marina.

322 Lake Shore Rd.
Boulder City, NV
(702) 293-3484

Tom's Water Sports Charter

Tom's Water Sports Charter & Instruction in Boulder City offers full and half-day trips on Lake Mead, including water skiing, wake-boarding, tubing and other water sport activities. Equipment, instruction, lunch and snacks and beverages provided.

Admission: Prices start at $79.00 per person. Family and group rates available
Las Vegas, NV
(702) 433-3263

Tours & Excursions

Adventure Photo Tours

Enjoy the photo opportunities of a lifetime on a tour through the desert in an off-road vehicle. Tours are offered to Red Rock Canyon, Valley of Fire, ghost mines and other destinations. All major credit cards accepted.

Las Vegas, NV
(702) 889-8687 (888) 363-8687

Cactus Jack's Wild West Tour Company

Bus tours to the Grand Canyon. A variety of Grand Canyon air and ground tours and a Lake Mead Cruise, Hoover Dam and free Laughlin tour.

Las Vegas, NV
(702) 731-2425

Grand Canyon Sightseeing

Choose from one of eight different tours to the Grand Canyon. Hoover Dam, Lake Mead and Laughlin tours are also available. Visa, MC & Amex accepted.

Las Vegas, NV
(702) 471-7155

Grand Canyon Tour Company

Scenic air tours, guided bus tours, helicopter tours, overnight packages and whitewater rafting as well as Hoover Dam and city tours and custom charters.

Las Vegas
(702) 655-6060 (888) 512-0075

Gray Line Tours

Visit Hoover Dam, spend the day in Laughlin, cruise Lake Mead, see the Grand Canyon on a scenic air tour or take a mini-city bus tour or a trip to Red Rock Canyon. Visa, MC, Amex, and Discover accepted.

Las Vegas, NV
(702) 384-1234

outdoor adventure

outdoor adventure

Escape The City Streets! Hiking Tours

Hiking tours of spectacular Red Rock Canyon. Choose from four different half-day hikes of varying skill levels in Scenic Mountain and desert terrain. Includes transportation from your hotel.

> 8221 W. Charleston, Ste. 101
> Las Vegas, NV
> **(702) 596-2953**

Las Vegas Tour & Travel

Tours of the Grand Canyon, Death Valley, Hoover Dam and Lake Mead, Zion and Laughlin by air, bus, boat and raft. Special day and night city tours of Las Vegas are also available. Visa, MC, & Amex accepted. 24-hour reservations.

> Las Vegas, NV
> **(702) 739-8975**

Maverick Helicopter Tours

Check out the Grand Canyon by day or the Las Vegas strip by night from high above the ground in a fun-filled helicopter tour. Visa, MC, & Amex accepted.

> Las Vegas, NV
> **(702) 261-0007   888-261-4414**

Papillon Grand Canyon Helicopters

Daytime tours of the Grand Canyon and nighttime tours of the Las Vegas strip in state-of-the-art, jet-powered helicopters. Visa, MC, & Amex accepted.

> Las Vegas, NV
> **(702) 736-7234   888-635-7272**

Sightseeing Tours Unlimited

Various Grand Canyon tours, from the three-hour scenic air tour to the ten-hour deluxe motor coach tour. Hoover Dam and Laughlin tours too. Visa, MC, & Amex accepted.

> Las Vegas, NV
> **(702) 471-7155**

restaurants
and **hotels**

chapter five

- Kid Friendly Buffets & Restaurants
- Hotels that cater to kids
- MGM Grand Hotel
- Circus Circus
- Excalibur
- Boulder Station
- Luxor
- Caesar's Palace
- Hotel Listing
- Campgrounds & RV parks

restaurants

Buffets

- **Arizona Charlie's**
  Wild West Buffet
  (702) 258-5200
  Hours: 7:00 a.m. to 10:00 p.m.
  Kids under 4 free
  Crab Leg Buffet Monday
  4:00 p.m. to 10:00 p.m.
- **Bally's**
  Big Kitchen Buffet
  (702) 739-4111
  Hours: 7:00 a.m. to 10:00 p.m.
  Children 4 - 7, half price
- **Boulder Station**
  The Feast
  (702) 432-7777
  Hours: 7:00 a.m. to 10:00 p.m.
  Children 4 - 8, half price
  Each night a different specialty
- **Buffalo Bill's**
  Miss Ashley's Buffet
  (702) 386-7867
  Hours: Weekdays 8:00 a.m. to
  8:00 p.m., 8:00 a.m. to 10:00 p.m
  Friday & Saturday
  Children 4-11, half price
  Seafood Buffet Friday & Saturday
- **Caesar's Palace**
  Palatium Buffet
  (702) 731-7110
  Hours: 8:00 a.m. to 10:00 p.m.
  Children under 12, half price,
  under 3 free
  Saturday & Sunday Buffet Brunch
  & Champagne Brunch
- **Circus Circus Hotel**
  Circus Circus Buffet
  (702) 734-0410
  Hours: 6:00 a.m. to 11:00 p.m.
  No children's price
- **Desert Inn Hotel**
  Terrace Point Buffet
  (702) 733-4444
  Hours: 6:00 a.m. to 2:30 p.m.
  (brunch only)
  Children 4 - 12, half price
  Special Sunday Brunch
- **Excalibur Hotel**
  Roundtable Buffet
  (702) 597-7777
  Hours: 6:30 a.m. to 10:00 p.m.
  Children 4 - 10, $1 off regular price
- **Fiesta Hotel**
  Festival Buffet
  (702) 631-7000
  Hours: 7:00 a.m. to 10:00 p.m.

Kids under 3, free
Seafood Buffet Wednesday
- **Fitzgerald Hotel**
  Molly's Buffet
  (702) 382-6111
  Hours: 7:00 a.m. to 10:00 p.m.
  Children 3 - 8, $1 off regular price
- **Flamingo Hilton**
  Paradise Garden Buffet
  (702) 733-3111
  Hours: 6:00 a.m. to 10:00 p.m.
  Children 3 - 12 half price
  Different international specialties
  each night
- **Fremont Hotel**
  Paradise Buffet
  (702) 385-3232
  Hours: 7:00 a.m. to 11:00 p.m.
  Children under 4 ,free
  Seafood fantasy Sunday, Tuesday,
  Friday
- **Frontier Hotel**
  Cattleman's Buffet
  (702) 794-8200
  Hours: 4:00 p.m. to 10:00 p.m.
  Children 4-7 half price
  Seafood Buffet Friday,
  Champagne Buffet Sunday 7:00 a.m.
  to 3:30 p.m.
- **Gold Coast Hotel**
  Gold Coast Buffet
  (702) 367-7111
  Hours: 7:00 a.m. to 10:00 p.m.
  Children 3 and under, free
  Seafood Buffet Wednesday
- **Gold Strike Hotel**
  Gold Strike Buffet
  Hours: 11:00 a.m. to 9:00 p.m.
  (lunch & dinner only)
  Children under 7, free
- **Golden Nugget Hotel**
  Golden Nugget Buffet
  (702) 385-7111
  Hours: 7:00 a.m. to 10:00 p.m.
  Children 10 and under, half price
- **Harrah's Hotel**
  Fresh Market Buffet
  (702) 369-5000
  Hours: 7:00 a.m. to 11:00 p.m.
  Children 4 - 5, half price
- **Holiday Inn Boardwalk**
  Surf Buffet
  (702) 735-2400
  Hours: 6:00 a.m. to 11:00 p.m.
  Children 4 and under, free
  Steak & Eggs Buffet 11:00 p.m. to
  6:00 a.m.

- **Imperial Palace**
  Emperor's Buffet
  (702) 731-3311
  Hours: 7:00 a.m. to 10:00 p.m.
  Children under 10, half price
- **Lady Luck Casino**
  Lady Luck Buffet
  (702) 477-3000
  Hours: 6:00 a.m. to 10:00 p.m.
  Children 6 - 12, half price
  Prime Rib & Seafood every day
- **Las Vegas Hilton**
  Buffet of Champions
  (702) 732-5111
  Hours: 7:00 a.m. to 10:00 p.m.
  Children 3 - 12, half price
- **Luxor Hotel**
  Pharaoh's Feast
  (702) 262-4000
  Hours: 6:30 a.m. to 11:00 p.m.
  Children 4 - 10, half price
- **Main Street Station**
  Garden Club Buffet
  (702) 387-1896
  Hours: 7:00 a.m. to 10:00 p.m.
  Children under 3, free
  T-Bone Steak Tuesday,
  Seafood Friday
- **Maxim Hotel**
  Maxim Buffet
  (702) 731-4300
  Hours: 9:00 a.m. to 10:00 p.m.
  Children under 12, half price
- **MGM Grand Hotel**
  Grand Buffet
  (702) 891-1111
  Hours: 7:00 a.m. to 10:00 p.m.
  Children 4 - 12, $2.99 brunch,
  $4.99 dinner
- **Mirage Resort**
  The Mirage Buffet
  (702) 791-7111
  Hours: 7:00 a.m. to 10:00 p.m.
  Children 4 - 10 get $2.00 to $4.00 off
  adult price
  Champagne Brunch Sunday
- **Monte Carlo**
  Monte Carlo Buffet
  (702) 730-7777
  Hours: 7:00 a.m. to 10:00 p.m.
  Sundays only, children
  4 - 10 half price
  Champagne Brunch Sunday
- **Palace Station**
  The Feast Buffet
  (702) 367-2411
  Hours: 7:00 a.m. to 10:00 p.m.

Children under 3, free
T-Bone Thursday, Seafood Friday,
Lobster Sunday
- **Primadonna Hotel**
  The Greens Buffet
  (800) 386-7867
  Hours: Weekdays 11:00 a.m. to
  8:00 p.m., Weekends till 10:00 p.m.
  Children 4 - 12, $2.95
- **Rio Suites Hotel**
  Carnival World Buffet
  (702) 252-7777
  Hours: 8:00 a.m. to 11:00 p.m.
  Children 3 and under, free
  Saturday & Sunday Brunch
  8:30 a.m. - 3:30 p.m.
- **Riviera Hotel**
  World's Fare Buffet
  (702) 734-5110
  Hours: Breakfast 7:00 a.m. to 10:00
  a.m., Dinner 4:00 p.m. to 10:30 p.m.
  Children under 4, free
  Saturday & Sunday Brunch,
  10:00 a.m. to 3:00 p.m.
- **Sahara Hotel**
  Oasis Buffet
  (702) 737-2111
  Hours: 6:00 a.m. to 10:00 p.m.
  Children under 3, free. Discount for
  Children 4 - 12 at Sunday Brunch
  Saturday & Sunday Champagne
  Brunch 9:00 a.m. to 3:00 p.m.
- **Sam's Town**
  The Great Buffet
  (702) 456-7777
  Hours: 8:00 a.m. to 9:00 p.m.
  Children under 6, half price
  Champagne Brunch Sunday
- **San Remo Hotel**
  Ristorante de Fiori Buffet
  (702) 739-9000
  Hours: 6:30 a.m. to 9:00 p.m.
  Children under 6, free
  Champagne Brunch Saturday &
  Sunday
- **Santa Fe Hotel**
  Lone Mountain Buffet
  (702) 658-4900
  Hours: 7:30 a.m. to 9:00 p.m.
  (10:00 p.m. weekends)
  Children 3 - 8, half price
  Seafood Night Thursday
- **Showboat Hotel**
  Captain's Buffet
  (702) 385-9123
  Hours: 10:00 a.m. to 10:00 p.m.
  Children 3 - 11, $1.00 off adult price

restaurants

Brunch Saturday & Sunday 9:00 a.m. to 3:30 p.m.

■ **Silverton Hotel**
Blue Diamond Buffet
(702) 263-7777
Hours: 7:00 a.m. to 10:00 p.m.
Children under 7, free
Special menu each day

■ **Skyline Casino**
Skyline Buffet
(702) 565-9116
Hours: 11:00 a.m. to 10:00 p.m.
(lunch & dinner)
All prices under $4.00

■ **Stardust Hotel**
Warehouse Buffet
(702) 732-6111
Hours: 7:00 a.m. to 10:00 p.m.
Children 2 and under, free
Sunday Brunch 7:00 a.m.- 3:30 p.m.

■ **Stratosphere Hotel**
Stratosphere Buffet
(702) 380-7777
Hours: 8:00 a.m. to 9:00 p.m.
Children 4 and under, free

■ **Sunset Station**
The Feast Buffet
(702) 547-7777
Hours: 7:00 a.m. to 10:00 p.m.
Children 4 - 8 get $2.00 to $3.00 off adult price
Sunday Brunch 7:00 a.m. - 3:30 p.m.

■ **Texas Station**
Feast Around the World
(702) 631-1000
Hours: 7:00 a.m. to 10:00 p.m.
Children 4 - 8, half price

■ **The Orleans**
French Market Buffet
(702) 365-7111
Hours: 7:00 a.m. to 10:00 p.m.
Children under 3, free
Special cajun dishes daily, Seafood Night Monday, Sunday Champagne Brunch

■ **Treasure Island**
Treasure Island Buffet
(702) 894-7111
Hours: 6:45 a.m. to 10:30 p.m.
Children 4 - 11, half price
Brunch Saturday & Sunday 7:30 a.m. to 3:30 p.m.

■ **Tropicana Hotel**
All You Can Eat Buffet
(702) 739-2222
Hours: 7:30 a.m. to 1:30 p.m. Brunch
5:00 p.m. to 10:00 p.m. Dinner

Children 5 - 10 get $2.00 to $3.00 off adult price

■ **Westward Ho Hotel**
The Buffet
(702) 731-2900
Hours: 7:00 a.m. to 2:00 p.m.
Brunch, 4:00 to 10:00 p.m. dinner
Children under 6 not allowed in buffet

■ **Whiskey Pete's**
Wagon Wheel Buffet
(702) 386-7867
Hours: Weekdays 7:30 a.m. to 8:00 p.m., weekends till 10:00 p.m.
Children 4 - 10, half price

■ **5 n Diner**
1900 N. Buffalo Dr./Lake Mead
(702) 233-5083
6840 W. Sahara Ave./Rainbow
(702) 368-7903
Hours: 6:00 a.m. - 11:00 p.m., 7 days
Kids Menu
Placemat with crayons
Rock n Roll music, 50's decor, paper hats to take home
Highchairs

■ **All Star Cafe**
3785 Las Vegas Blvd. So./Tropicana
(702) 795-8326
Hours: 11:00 a.m. - 11:00 p.m., 7 days
Kids Menu
colors, arcade in restaurant, sports showing continuously on television screens
Highchairs, Diaper Changing

■ **America Cafe**
Inside New York New York, 3790 Las Vegas Blvd. So.
(702) 740-6969
Hours: Open 24 Hours:, 7 days
Kids Menu
Map of U.S. to color
Large map of the U.S. in the middle of the restaurant is interesting
Highchairs, Diaper Changing

■ **Applebee's**
4760 W. Sahara Ave./Decatur
(702) 878-3399
500 N. Nellis Blvd./Stewart
(702) 452-7155
699 Stephanie St./Sundayset
(702) 433-6339
3340 S. Maryland Pkwy./
Desert Inn Rd.
(702) 737-4990
3501 S. Rainbow Blvd./Flamingo Rd.
(702) 220-3070

Hours: 11:00 a.m. to 11:00 p.m. Monday. through Saturday., 11:00 a.m. to 10:00 p.m. Sunday
Kids Menu
Activity book with crayons and stickers. Balloons, some locations have magicians or balloon animals on weekends
Highchairs

■ **Black Angus Restaurant**
5125 W. Sahara/Decatur
(702) 251-9300
651 Mall Ring Circle, Henderson
(702) 451-9300
Hours: 11:00 a.m. to 10:00 p.m. weekdays, 11:00 a.m. to 11:00 p.m. Friday, 3:00 p.m. to 11:00 p.m. Saturday, 12:00 to 10:00 p.m. Sunday
Kids Menu
Placemat with crayons
Buckaroo plastic cup to take home
Highchairs

■ **Blueberry Hill Family Restaurant**
1280 S. Decatur Blvd./Charleston
(702) 877-8867
1723 E Charleston Blvd./Bruce
(702) 382-3330
3790 E. Flamingo Rd./Sandhill
(702) 433-9999
1505 E. Flamingo Rd./Maryland Pkwy.
(702) 696-9666
5000 E. Bonanza Rd./Nellis
(702) 453-5555
Hours: 5:30 a.m. to 10:00 p.m. daily, some locations are open 24 Hours:
Kids Menu plus daily specials
Placemat with crayons
Highchairs

■ **Bonnie Springs Ranch Restaurant**
1 Bonnie Springs Ranch Rd., Blue Diamond
(702) 875-4300
Hours: 8:00 a.m. to 11:00 p.m., 7 days
Kids Menu
Placemat with crayons
Half hour from Las Vegas, Authentic Old West building, petting zoo right outside door
Highchairs

■ **Cadillac Grille**
2801 N. Tenaya Way/Cheyenne
(702) 255-5555
Hours: Sunday through Friday 10:00 a.m. to 11:00 p.m., Saturday 9:00 a.m. to midnight

Kids Menu, crayons & color sheet
Highchairs

■ **Carluccio's Restaurant**
1775 E. Tropicana Ave./Spencer St.
(702) 795-3236
Hours: 4:30 p.m. to 10:00 p.m. daily, closed Mondays
Kids Menu, 1/2 orders available on some menu items
Highchairs

■ **Carrow's Restaurant**
4680 S. Maryland Parkway
(702) 736-6908
3780 Las Vegas Blvd. So./Tropicana
(702) 736-4501
169 E. Tropicana Ave./LV Blvd.
(702) 736-3936
Hours: Open 24 Hours:, breakfast available 24 Hours:
Kids Menu, Placemat with crayons
Highchairs

■ **Chapala Mexican Restaurant**
3335 E. Tropicana Ave./Pecos Rd.
(702) 451-8141
2101 S. Decatur Blvd./Sahara
(702) 871-7805
Hours: 11:00 a.m. to midnight 7 days
Kids Menu, Children's plate
Highchairs

■ **Chevy's Mexican Restaurant**
Galleria Mall, Henderson
(702) 434-8323
4090 S. Eastern Ave./ Flamingo Rd.
(702) 731-6969
6800 W. Sahara Ave./Rainbow Blvd.
(702) 220-4507
Hours: Saturday through Thursday 11:00 a.m. to 10:00 p.m., Friday & Saturday 11:00 a.m. to 11:00 p.m.
Kids Menu, Placemat with crayons
Tortilla dough balls to play with and take home
Highchairs, Diaper Changing

■ **Chili's Bar & Grill**
2011 N. Rainbow Blvd./Lake Mead
(702) 638-1482
2520 S. Decatur Blvd./Sahara
(702) 871-0500
2751 N. Green Valley Pkwy.
(702) 433-3333
Hours: Monday through Thursdays 11:00 a.m. to 10:30, Friday & Saturday 11:00 a.m. to 11:00 p.m, Sunday 11:00 a.m. to 10:00 p.m.
Kids Menu, all $2.99. Menu of 4-6 pages, plus crayons.
Highchairs, Diaper Changing

restaurants

Chuck E. Cheese's Pizza
7381 W. Lake Mead/Tenaya
(702) 243-3222
Hours: Sunday through Thursday
10:00 a.m. to 10:00 p.m., Friday &
Saturday 10:00 a.m. to 11:00 p.m.
Kids Menu, Pizzas for all ages
Games & rides, Chuck E. Cheese
animated show, good birthday party
spot
Highchairs, Diaper Changing

Country Inn
2425 E. Desert Inn Rd./Eastern Ave.
(702) 731-5035
1401 S. Rainbow Blvd./Charleston
Blvd.
(702) 254-0520
1990 W. Sundayset Road/Valle
Verde Dr.
(702) 898-8183
Hours: 7:00 a.m. to 10:00 p.m., 7 days
Kids Menu, placemat with crayons
Highchairs

Coyote Cafe
MGM Grand (Studio Walk)
(702) 891-7349
Hours: 8:30 a.m. to 11:30 p.m., 7
days
Kids Menu
Highchairs
Diaper Changing
Restaurants on Studio Walk share
restroom

Crocodile Cafe
4500 Sundayset Rd./Green Valley
Parkway
(702) 456-7880
Hours: Sunday through Thursdays
11:00 a.m. to 10:00 p.m., Friday &
Saturday
11:00 a.m. to 11:00 p.m.
Kids Menu, Placemat with crayons
Plastic crocodile cup to take home
Highchairs, Diaper Changing

DiMartino's Your Neighborhood Italian Eatery
1000 N. Green Valley
Parkway/Pebble
(702) 269-7144
Hours:4:30 p.m. to 10:00 p.m., 7 days
Kids Menu, all $2.95
Placemat with crayons
Grandpa DiMartino entertains kids
with jokes and drawings, on Sundays
performers create balloon animals
Highchairs

Dive!
Fashion Show Mall, 3200 LV Blvd.
So.
(702) 369-3483
Hours: Sunday through Thursdays
11:30 a.m. to 10:00 p.m., Friday &
Saturday 11:30 to 11:00 p.m.
Kids Menu, Placemat with crayons
The restaurant looks like a submarine,
fun for the imagination
Highchairs

Dona Maria's
910 Las Vegas Blvd.
South/Charleston
(702) 382-6538
Hours: 8:00 a.m. - 10:00 p.m., 7 days
Kids Menu
Authentic Mexican food
Highchairs

The Egg & I
4533 W. Sahara Ave./Decatur
(702) 364-9686
Hours: 6:00 a.m. to 3:00 p.m., 7 days
Kids Menu
Placemat with crayons
Kids pictures are put into a drawing
and one is chosen each Monday to
receive a free bike, which is displayed
on the wall of the restaurant
Highchairs

Freddie G's Deli & Diner
325 Hughes Center Dr.
(Flamingo/Paradise)
(702) 892-9955
Hours: 7:00 a.m. to 10:00 p.m.,
closes Sunday at 3:00 p.m.
Kids Menu
Crayons and color books
Highchairs

Furr's Cafeterias
2985 E. Sahara Ave./McLeod
(702) 457-0166
150 S. Valley View Blvd./Meadows
Mall
(702) 878-0901
Hours: 11:00 a.m. - 8:00 p.m., 7 days
Kids special price for cafeteria style
eating
Highchairs

Gameworks
Showcase Mall (3785 Las Vegas
Blvd./Tropicana)
(702) 432-4263
Hours: Sunday through Thursday
10:00 a.m. to 1:00 a.m., Friday &
Saturday 10:00 a.m. to 2:00 p.m.
2 places to eat inside Gameworks,

surrounded by arcade games of all types, Highchairs, Diaper Changing

- **Gandhi India**
4080 Paradise Rd./Flamingo Rd.
(702) 734-0094
Hours: 11:00 a.m. - 2:30 lunch,
5:00 p.m. - 10:30 p.m. dinner, 7 days
Kids Menu
Highchairs

- **Garlic Cafe**
3650 S. Decatur Blvd./
Spring Mtn. Rd.
(702) 368-4000
Hours: Monday through Saturday
11:00 a.m. to 2:00 p.m. for lunch,
Sunday through Thursday 5:00 p.m.
to 10:00 p.m. for dinner, Friday &
Saturday 5:00 p.m. to 11:00 p.m.
Child's portions of menu items

- **Grape Street Cafe**
7501 W. Lake Mead Blvd./Buffalo
(702) 228-9463
Hours: Weekdays 11:00 a.m. to 10:00
p.m., Friday & Saturday 11:00 a.m. to
11:00 p.m., Closed Mondays
Kids Menu
Family atmosphere, music, retail wine
and cheese shop
Highchairs

- **Green Shack**
2504 E. Fremont
St.(Boulder/Charleston)
(702) 383-0007
Hours: 5:00 p.m. to 11:00 p.m., 6
days (closed Monday)
Kids Menu
Placemat with crayons
Las Vegas' oldest restaurant, historic
place
Highchairs

- **Happy Days Diner**
512 Nevada Highway, Boulder City
(702) 294-2653
Hours: 7:00 a.m. to 8:00 p.m., 7 days
Kids Menu
Kids like authentic 50's jukebox.
Highchairs

- **Hard Rock Cafe**
4475 Paradise Rd./Harmond Ave.
(702) 733-8400
Hours: 11:00 a.m. to midnight 7 days
Kids Menu
Placemat with crayons
Retail booth with Hard Rock T-shirts
& Teddys, rock n' roll music and
memorabilia,
Highchairs, Diaper Changing

- **Hill Top House Supper Club**
3500 N. Rancho Dr.
(702) 645-9904
Hours: 5:00 p.m. to 9:30 p.m., 7 days
Kids Menu, 4 items
Highchairs

- **Hungry Hunter**
2380 S. Rainbow Blvd./Sahara Ave.
(702) 873-0433
Hours: Monday through Friday 11:30
a.m. to 2:30 p.m. for lunch,
Sunday through Thursdays 5:00 p.m.
to 9:00 p.m. for dinner and Friday &
Saturday 5:00 p.m. to 10:00 p.m.
Kids Menu, Placemat with crayons
Highchairs, Diaper Changing

- **The Hush Puppy**
1820 N. Nellis Blvd./Lake Mead Blvd.
(702) 438-0005
7185 W. Charleston Blvd./Buffalo
Hours: 5:00 p.m. to 10:00 p.m., 7
days for dinner
Kids Menu, Features catfish and
other Southern specialties
Highchairs

- **International House of Pancakes
(IHOP)** various locations
Hours: Weekdays 6:00 a.m. to
10:00 p.m., Friday & Saturday
6:00 a.m. to 12:00 p.m.
Kids Menu, includes Funny Face
pancakes, Placemat with crayons
Balloons, Highchairs
Diaper Changing
(also in men's room)

- **Jamm's Restaurant**
1029 S. Rainbow/Charleston
(702) 877-0749
2227 N. Rampart/Lake Mead
Kids Menu
Friendly, neighborhood cafe
Highchairs

- **Jeremiah's Steak House**
171 E. Tropicana/Las Vegas Blvd.
(702) 736-3044
Hours: Sunday through Thursday
4:30 p.m. to 10:00 p.m., Friday &
Saturday, 4:30 p.m. to 11:00 p.m.
Kids Menu, Placemat with crayons
Highchairs, Diaper Changing

- **Joe's Crab Shack**
1991 N. Rainbow/Lake Mead
(702) 646-3996
Hours: Sunday through Thursdays
11:00 a.m. to 10:00 p.m., Friday &
Saturday 11:00 a.m. to 11:00 p.m.
Kids Menu, Placemat with crayons

restaurants

Full playground in front of building
Highchairs
Diaper Changing (also in men's)

■ **Keuken Dutch**
6180 W. Tropicana/Jones
(702) 368-1077
Hours: 24 Hours
Kids Menu
Highchairs

■ **La Barca**
2517 E. Lake Mead Blvd./Civic
Center Dr.
(702) 657-9700
Hours: Monday through Thursday
10:00 a.m. to 10:00 p.m., Friday
through Sunday
10:00 a.m. to midnight
Child's plate, Funhouse mirrors,
balloon animals, Mariachi musicians
Mexican seafood a specialty
Highchairs

■ **La Piazza Food Court**
Caesars Palace, 3570 Las Vegas
Blvd. So.
(702) 731-7110
Hours: Monday through Thursdays
11:00 a.m. to 11:00 p.m., Friday
11:00 to midnight, Saturday &
Sunday 8:30 a.m. to 11:00 p.m.
International food court with every-
thing from pizza to Chinese food to
ice cream
Highchairs

■ **Lindo Michoacan Mexican
Restaurant**
2655 E. Desert Inn Rd./Eastern
(702) 735-6828
Hours: Monday through Wednesday
11:00 a.m. to 10:00 p.m., Thursday &
Friday 11:00 a.m. to 11:00 p.m,
Saturday & Sunday 9:00 a.m. to
11:00 p.m.
Kids Menu, Placemat with crayons
Homestyle Mexican food
Highchairs

■ **Lone Star Steakhouse & Saloon**
1290 E. Flamingo Rd./Maryland
(702) 893-0348
1611 S. Decatur Blvd./Oakey
(702) 259-0105
210 N. Nellis Blvd./Stewart
(702) 453-7827
3131 N. Rainbow Blvd./Cheyenne
(702) 656-7125
Hours: Sunday through Thursday
11:00 a.m. to 10:00 p.m., Friday &
Saturday 11:00 a.m. to 11:00 p.m.

Kids Menu, Placemat with crayons
Highchairs, Diaper Changing

■ **Los Cabos**
2490 E. Freemont/Charleston
(702) 384-7881
Hours: Weekdays 7:00 a.m. to
9:00 p.m., Friday & Saturday
7:00 a.m. to 11:00 p.m.
Kids Menu, Placemat with crayons
Mexican and American dishes
Highchairs

■ **Macayo Vegas**
1741 E. Charleston Blvd./Bruce St.
(702) 382-5605
1375 E. Tropicana Ave./Maryland
Pkwy.
(702) 736-1898
4457 W. Charleston Blvd./Decatur
(702) 878-7347
8245 W. Sahara Ave./Buffalo
(702) 360-8210
Hours: Weekdays 11:00 a.m. to
10:00 p.m., Friday & Saturday
11:00 a.m. to 11:00 p.m.
Kids Menu, Placemat with crayons
Americanized Mexican food kids
usually like
Highchairs

■ **Margarita Grille**
Las Vegas Hilton, 3000 Paradise Rd.
(702) 732-5111
Hours: Weekdays 7:00 a.m. to
10:00 p.m., Friday & Saturday
7:00 a.m. to 11:00 p.m.
Kids Menu, Placemat with crayons
Mexican food, with full bar for adults
Highchairs

■ **Marie Callendar's Restaurant &
Bakery**
4875 W. Flamingo/Decatur
(702) 365-6226
4800 S. Eastern Ave./Tropicana
(702) 458-2127
600 E. Sahara Ave./6th Street
(702) 734-6572
3081 N. Rainbow/Cheyenne
(702) 655-8200
Hours: Weekdays 7:00 a.m. to
11:00 p.m., Friday & Saturday
7:00 a.m. to 10:00 p.m.
Kids Menu, Placemat with crayons
Balloons, Highchairs

■ **Metro Pizza**
4001 S. Decatur/Flamingo Rd.
(702) 362-7896
3870 E. Flamingo Rd./Sandhill
(702) 458-4769

2250 E. Tropicana Ave./Eastern Ave.
(702) 736-1955
Hours: Weekdays 11:00 a.m. to
10:00 p.m., Friday & Saturday 11:00
to 11:00 p.m.
Kids Menu, Placemat with crayons
Highchairs

■ **Olive Garden Italian Restaurant**
1545 E. Flamingo Rd.
(702) 735-0082
1361 S. Decatur Blvd.
(702) 258-3453
6850 W. Cheyenne Ave./I95
(702) 658-2144
80 N. Nellis Blvd.
(702) 438-0082
4400 E. Sunset Rd.
(702) 451-5133
Hours: Sunday through Thursday
11:00 a.m. to 10:00 p.m., Friday &
Saturday 11:00 a.m. to 11:00 p.m.
Kids Menu, Placemat with crayons
Kids get plastic cups they can take
home
Highchairs, Diaper Changing

■ **Omelet House**
2160 W. Charleston Blvd./Rancho
(702) 384-6868
316 N. Boulder Highway, Henderson
(702) 566-7896
Hours: 7:00 a.m. to 3:00 p.m., 7 days
Kids Menu, Kids can pick toys,
books and crayons from a basket
Highchairs

■ **Omelet House & More**
3050 E. Desert Inn Rd.
(702) 737-0377
Hours: 7:00 a.m. to 3:00 p.m., 7 days
daily specials for everyone are
$2.95/$3.95
Placemat with crayons
Highchairs

■ **Original Pancake House**
4833 W. Charleston Blvd./Decatur
(702) 259-7755
Hours: 7:00 a.m. to 3:00 p.m., 7 days
Kids Menu, Highchairs,Diaper
Changing

■ **Outback Steakhouse**
4141 S. Pecos Rd./Flamingo Rd.
(702) 898-3801
1950 N. Rainbow Blvd./Lake Mead
(702) 647-1035
3685 W. Flamingo Rd./
Valley View Blvd.
(702) 253-1020
8671 W. Sahara Ave./Durango

(702) 228-1088
4423 E. Sundayset Road/
Mountain Vista
(702) 451-7808
Hours: Monday through Thursdays
4:00 p.m. to 10:30 p.m., Friday &
Saturday 3:00 p.m. to 11:00 p.m.,
Sunday 1:00 p.m. to 10:00 p.m.
Kids Menu, Activity books with
Australian theme, including puzzles
& coloring. Special toys for babies
Highchairs, Diaper Changing

■ **Panini**
4811 S. Rainbow Blvd./Tropicana
(702) 365-8300
3460 E. Sundayset Rd./Pecos
(702) 436-3100
Hours: Monday through Thursday
11:00 a.m. to 10:30 p.m., Friday
11:00 a.m. to 11:00 p.m., Saturday &
Sunday 5:00 p.m. to 11:00 p.m.
Kids Menu, Placemat with crayons
Italian food and sandwiches
Highchairs

■ **Pasta Mia**
2585 E. Flamingo Rd./Eastern Ave.
(702) 733-0091
4455 W. Flamingo Rd./Arville
(702) 251-8871
Hours: 11:30 a.m. - 9:30 p.m. 7 days
Child portions of most menu items
Activity book with colors and
stickers

■ **Pasta Shop & Ristorante**
2495 E. Tropicana Ave./Eastern
(702) 451-1893
Hours: 11:30 a.m. to 1:30 p.m. daily
for lunch, 5:00 p.m. to 9:00 p.m.
daily for dinner
Kids Menu, Crayons & plain paper
Highchairs

■ **Peking Market**
Flamingo Hilton, 3555 Las Vegas
Blvd. So.
(702) 733-3322
Hours: 5:30 p.m. to 11:00 p.m., 7
days
Meals ordered family style-children
eat at 1/2 price
Highchairs

■ **Peter Piper Pizza**
3665 S. Rainbow/Spring Mountsin
(702) 365-8190
560 S. Decatur/Alta
(702) 877-8873
3430 E. Tropicana/Pecos
(702) 454-6366

350 N. Nellis/Stewart
(702) 459-1200
2401 E. Lake Mead Blvd./Civic
Center
(702) 399-1115
Hours: 10:00 a.m. to 10:00 p.m. 7
days (most locations)
Arcade games, Skeeball, birthday
parties, carousel
Highchairs, Diaper Changing

■ **Pick Up Stix**
4500 E. Sundayset Road/Mountain
Vista
(702) 837-6600
2101 N. Rainbow Blvd./Lake Mead
(702) 636-6600
Hours: Weekdays 11:00 a.m. to
9:00 p.m., Friday & Saturday
11:00 a.m. to 9:30 p.m.
Kids Menu
Chinese food to eat in or take out
Highchairs

■ **Pink Pony Cafe**
Inside Circus Circus Hotel, 2880 Las
Vegas Blvd. So.
(702) 734-0410
Hours: Open 24 Hours, 7 days
Kids Menu
Circus placemat with crayons
Carousel theme decor, with horses
and mirrors
Highchairs, Diaper Changing

■ **Pizza Hut**
various locations
Hours: 11:00 a.m. to 10:30 p.m.
Kids Menu, Placemat with crayons
Highchairs, Diaper Changing

■ **Pizza Palace**
Inside Imperial Palace Hotel, 3535
Las Vegas Blvd. So.
(702) 731-3311
Hours: 11:00 a.m. to midnight, 7 days
Pizza and pasta
Highchairs

■ **Pizzeria Uno**
2540 S. Decatur Blvd./Sahara
(702) 876-8667
Hours: Monday through Thursdays
11:00 a.m. to 11:00 p.m., Friday &
Saturday 11:00 a.m. to midnight,
Sunday 11:00 a.m. to 10:00 p.m.
Kids Menu, Placemat with crayons
Highchairs

■ **Planet Hollywood**
Forum Shops at Caesars Palace,
3500 S. Las Vegas Blvd.
(702) 791-7827

Hours: 11:00 a.m. to midnight,
7 days
Kids Menu, Placemat with crayons
Movie memorabilia decor fascinates
kids & grownups.
Highchairs

■ **Quark's Bar & Restaurant**
Inside Star Trek Eperience, Las
Vegas Hilton, 3000 Paradise Rd.
888-GO-BOLDLY
Hours: 11:00 a.m. to 11:00 p.m.,
7 days
Starfleet Cadet Menu includes
Hamburger, Glop on a Stick (corn-
dog) and Tribble Tenders
Dine in the 24th century with futuris-
tic menu & table settings, role-play-
ing waiters.
Highchairs

■ **Red Lobster**
200 S. Decatur Blvd./Meadows Lane
(702) 877-0212
2325 E. Flamingo Rd./Eastern
(702) 731-0119
Hours: Sunday through Thursdays
11:00 a.m. to 10:00 p.m., Friday &
Saturday 11:00 a.m. to 11:00 p.m.
Kids Menu, Placemat with crayons
Highchairs, Diaper Changing

■ **Red Robin Grill and Spirits**
151 N. Nellis Blvd.
(702) 453-8611
Hours: Sunday through Thursday
11:00 a.m. to 10:00 p.m., Friday &
Saturday 11:00 a.m. to 11:00 p.m.
Kids Menu, Placemat with crayons
Arcade room in restaurant
Highchairs, Diaper Changing

■ **Ricardo's Mexican Restaurant**
2380 E. Tropicana/Eastern
(702) 798-4515
4930 W. Flamingo Rd./Decatur
(702) 871-7119
Inside MGM Grand (Studio Walk)
(702) 736-4970
Hours: Sunday through Thursdays
11:00 a.m. to 10:00 p.m., Friday &
Saturday 11:00 a.m. to 11:00 p.m.
Kids Menu, Placemat with crayons
Highchairs

■ **Roadhouse Grill**
521 Stephanie St./Warm Springs
(702) 456-7405
7341 W. Lake Mead Blvd./Tenaya
(702) 256-2755
Hours: Sunday through Thursdays
11:00 a.m. to 10:00 p.m., Friday &

Saturday 11:00 a.m. to 11:00 p.m.
Kids Menu, Etch-a-sketch
Arcade in restaurant, buckets of
peanuts to shell at your table —
throw the shells on the floor!
Highchairs

- **Romano's Macaroni Grill**
2400 W. Sahara Ave./Rancho
(702) 248-9500
2001 N. Rainbow/Lake Mead
(702) 648-6688
573 Stephanie St., Henderson
(702) 433-2788
Hours: Sunday through Thursday
11:00 a.m. to 10:00 p.m., Friday &
Saturday 11:00 a.m. to 11:00 p.m.
Kids Menu, Placemat with crayons
Highchairs, Diaper Changing

- **Round Table Pizza**
various locations
Hours: Sunday through Thursdays
11:00 a.m. to 10:00 p.m., Friday &
Saturday 11:00 a.m. to 11:00 p.m.
Kids Menu, Placemat with crayons
Arcade room, Highchairs,
Diaper Changing (also in men's)

- **Sizzler**
307 S. Decatur Blvd./Meadows Lane
(702) 878-1223
4901 S. Eastern Ave./Tropicana
(702) 736-3120
3553 S. Rainbow/Sahara
(702) 227-0131
Hours: Sunday through Thursdays
11:00 a.m. to 9:00 p.m., Friday &
Saturday 11:00 a.m to 9:30 p.m.
Kids 3-10 eat for $2.99 except for
steak.
Placemat with crayons. A special hot
and cold salad bar for kids
Highchairs, Diaper Changing

- **Strings Italian Cafe**
2222 E. Tropicana Ave./Eastern
(702) 739-6400
Hours: Tuesday through Saturday
11:00 a.m. to 10:00 p.m., Sunday
11:00 a.m. to 9:30 p.m.
Kids Menu, Placemat with crayons
Highchairs

- **Terrible Mike's**
Inside The Orleans Hotel, 4500 W.
Tropicana
(702) 365-7111
Hours:10:00 a.m. to midnight, 7 days
Serves hamburgers and other fast
food.
Highchairs

- **TGI Friday's**
1800 E. Flamingo/Spencer
(702) 732-9905
4570 W. Sahara/Decatur
(702) 889-1866
Hours: 11:00 a.m. to 2:00 am
Kids Menu
Coloring menu plus crowns to color
and wear. Balloons, Kids Crew Club
— free meal on birthday plus
coupons sent by mail.
Highchairs, Diaper Changing

- **Thirstbusters**
697 N. Valley Verde Dr./Sundayset Rd.
(702) 454-9200
Hours: Open 24 Hours, 7 days
Kids Menu, also Early Bird dinner
specials and breakfast specials
Placemat with crayons
Well-behaved kids can choose a toy
grab bag when they leave
Highchairs, Diaper Changing

- **Tony Roma's**
620 E. Sahara Ave./Sixth St.
(702) 733-9914
Fremont Hotel, 200 E. Fremont St.
(702) 385-6257
Stardust Hotel
3000 Las Vegas Blvd.
(702) 732-6111
2040 N. Rainbow/Lake Mead
(702) 638-2100
555 Stephanie St./Sunset
(702) 436-2227
Hours: Sunday through Thursday
11:00 a.m. to 10:00 p.m., Friday &
Saturday 11:00 a.m. to 11:00 p.m.
Kids Menu, Safety awareness activity books. At non-casino locations,
kids eat free with an adult meal on
Tuesdays. Highchairs

Tuscany Grill (formerly Che Pasta)
4350 E. Sundayset Road/Green
Valley Parkway
(702) 435-0036
Hours: 4:30 p.m. to 11:00 p.m., 7 days
Kids Menu, Placemat with crayons
Italian food, nightly specials
Highchairs

restaurants

hotels

MGM Grand Hotel, Casino & Theme Park

If you're in Las Vegas, you won't want to miss MGM Grand — The City of Entertainment. Encompassing a 114 acre site on the Las Vegas strip, the MGM Grand is comprised of four 30-story, eye popping emerald green "towers", evocative of a modern-day Emerald City. For visitors with families, the MGM Grand provides two attractive features: the MGM Grand Youth activity Center, a child-care facility, and the MGM Grand Adventures outdoor theme park.

MGM Grand Hotel, Casino & Theme Park Info

Address: 3799 Las Vegas Blvd.
Las Vegas, NV 89109

Phone: (702) 891-1111
(888) 646-1203

MGM Grand Youth Activity Center

If you want to experience Las Vegas adult attractions and wish to leave your child in a safe environment for a moderate amount of time, you are invited to use MGM Grand's Youth Activity Center. Located at the end of Studio Walk, the Youth Center is a colorful, friendly four-room facility accommodating children three through twelve years of age. Though each of the rooms is geared for different ages and activities, children can play in any room at any time. This free-flowing format is great for siblings, making it possible for them to stick together in unfamiliar surrounding. The Youth Center is paced with activities, including floor hockey, basketball, dodge-ball, air hockey, foosball, pool, Super Nintendo, children's movies, an arts and crafts room, and a host of toys, puppets, blocks, and games. For an additional charge, meals and snacks are served throughout the day.

Due to licensing restrictions, a child can stay in the Youth Center for a maximum of five hours at a time. Children may be returned after a two hour break. Also, children must be completely toilet trained and out of diapers and training pants.

Prices of MGM Grand's Youth Activity Center vary, ranging between $6.00 and $9.00 per hour, and are on a per child, per hour basis. Hours of operation vary by season. Contact the Youth Activity Center directly at (702) 891-3200 for current information, or to make reservations. Guests of other hotels are allowed to use the Youth Center on a limited basis, but reservations are recommended for summer, holidays, and peak periods.

MGM Grand Adventures

MGM Grand Adventures is a seasonal outdoor entertainment complex designed to provide fun for a wide range of ages. Located behind the hotel/casino, Grand Adventures features theme park rides, live entertainment, shopping and casual dining to make it possible for adults, teens, and children of any age to have a great time.

Each of the park's streets are cleverly named, with an appropriate theme. You enter Grand Adventures at Asian Village and make your way through Canterbury Square, New Orleans Street, Gold Rush Junction, Salem Waterfront and French Street. Rides include Grand Canyon Rapids, the guaranteed-to-get-you-wet Over the Edge, bumper cars, a rollercoaster, bumper and paddle boats, and the legendary SkyScreamer, the world's largest Skycoaster. Visitors of MGM Grand Adventures will find a number of coin-operated games and attractions throughout the park, as well as Super Shots, an arcade located in Gold Rush Junction.

Restaurants are kiddie-proven and include Burger King, Nathan's Famous, Haagen Dazs ice cream, a pizzeria, an oriental restaurant, as well as a selection of snacks and sweets.

There are two indoor theaters which feature live entertainment, a number of retail stores, including the popular Backstage Collectibles. Located on New Orleans Street, Bayou Toys carries a variety of specialty toys, as well as licensed clothing and accessories for children.

For your convenience, Guest Services is located on Canterbury Square. Staffed with upbeat Cast Members who can answer your questions and give you directions. Guest Services also provides a lost and found. You're invited to make use of Canterbury Square's coin operated lockers, as well as the Kodak Photo Center, where visitors can rent wheelchairs and strollers.

Hours of operation vary. The park is generally open during the summer season from 11:00 a.m. to 7:00 p.m. Please call (702) 891-7979 for current pricing information. Tickets to the SkyScreamer must be purchased separately.

Arcades

Studio Walk Arcade: An 11,400 square foot arcade located at the end of Studio Walk. Featuring games of skill, as well as the latest high-tech, virtual reality games. Open year round, 9:00 a.m. to midnight daily.

Super Shots Arcade: Located in Gold Rush Junction in the Grand Adventures Theme Park. Open during theme park hours of operation.

Food

Studio Walk Food Court: McDondald's, Nathan's Famous, Mamma Ilardo's Pizzeria, Haagen Dazs, and more.

Grand Adventures Theme Park: Mamma Ilardos' Pizzeria, Burger King, Nathan's Famous, Trolley Treats, Annie's Ice Cream Parlour and more.

There is a 24-hour Studio Café, as well as the Grand Buffet. Meals are served at various times to children staying in the Youth Center.

Gifts

You won't have trouble picking out a gift at MGM Grand. The Hollywood and Wizard of Oz themed merchandise are tried and true child pleasers. There are a number of gift shops in MGM Grand adventures, including Bayou Toys, Backstage Collectibles (featuring popular cartoon characters) Just Oz, Celebrity Wear, and Screamin' Attitudes, also within Grand Adventures, offers a wide variety of cool clothing and accessories for children.

Hours

MGM Grand's Youth Activity Center: Hours of operation vary by season. Call for information.

MGM Grand Adventures: Hours of operation vary by season. Call for information.

Studio Walk Arcade: Hours of operation vary. Call for information.

Safety

All Grand adventures and Youth activity Center "Cast Members" have undergone nationwide background checks, and are CPR and First Aid certified. For safety's sake, parents and other guardians are not allowed to come into the Youth Center to play with their children. Photo identification is required to pick children up from the Youth Center. Additional safety measures include a First Aid station in the MGM Grand Adventures Theme Park.

Circus Circus Hotel/Casino

Circus Circus Hotel/Casino, was the first Las Vegas resort to make an effort to appeal to families. Circus Circus continues to expand and update its grounds and facilities with the entertainment and safety needs of children in mind.

Circus Circus has two major areas of attraction for kids and families — the Circus Circus Carnival Midway, located on the Las Vegas strip-side of the main casino above the casino floor, and The Adventuredome, America's largest indoor theme park at the opposite end of the property.

Circus Circus Hotel/Casino Information

Address: 2880 Las Vegas Blvd.   **Phone:** 1 (800) 444-CIRCUS
South Las Vegas, NV 89109
(At the center of Las Vegas Blvd. at
Sahara Ave.)

The Adventuredome

The Adventuredome at Circus Circus Las Vegas features the world's only indoor double-loop, double-corkscrew roller coaster, The Canyon Blaster. The Adventuredome packs a tremendous amount of entertainment into its glass-domed five acres.

The Adventuredome is a cool 72 degrees regardless of the weather. Entrance to the park is free, so you may want to duck into The Adventuredome to escape the heat. (In Vegas, summertime temperatures can reach a sizzling 120 degrees!) While entrance into the park is free, one must purchase tickets for most of The Adventuredome's attractions. Individual ride tickets vary according to the size of the ride:

$2.00 - small rides   **$4.00** - large rides   **$5.00** - premium rides

The best value is an All-day Ride Pass, Which allows you to ride most rides as many times as you wish for an entire day. The price of the pass is based on height: Under 33" tall, FREE (but must be accompanied by a paying Adult); 33" to under 48" tall, $12.95; 48" and over, $16.95.

The Adventuredome is designed to resemble the Grand Canyon. Theme park rides share space with caverns, artificial rock walls, and a 90-foot waterfall. As an added bonus, check out the eight, life-sized animatronic dinosaurs. In addition, the Adventuredome also features the Canyon Blaster, and the Rim Runner, a water ride which plunges over a 60-foot waterfall, providing a soak and a scream for adults and children alike.

The Adventuredome also includes amusement park favorites like the ferris wheel, bumper cars, carousel, and carnival games, as well as rides for smaller children. There are a number of free attractions, which are especially suited for young children, like the park's Cliff Hangers, a play area made of tunnels, slides, nets and ball-filled cages.

Older kids, teens, and adults will get a kick out of Hot Shots Laser Tag, a team warfare game set in a well decorated, black-lit, graffiti-covered laser tag arena. The IMAX Ridefilm Fun House Express has similar "virtual" appeal. Featuring three motion simulator machines, the ride promises a hair raising journey full of fun and surprises for all ages.

Circus Circus Carnival Midway

Though Circus Circus Hotel and Theme Park Casino is full of one-of-a-kinds, the resort's signature aspect is the Carnival Midway. Located beneath the pink and white Big Top, the Midway features a tremendous assortment of midway games that can be played for as little as a quarter. These are the classic carnival games you find at most fairs, things like ring tosses, pitching and race games, and skee-ball. Only at Circus Circus, the midway is cleaner and safer, and the prizes are much larger. If you win top prize, you'll walk away from most booths with a life-sized stuffed animal. Even the "small" prizes are worth the change it takes to play the game, assuming that your aim is decent!

The Midway's free circus acts are a longstanding Circus Circus tradition. Acrobats, highwire and balancing artists, trained animal acts, jugglers, comics, and contortionists perform on the Carnival Midway. The current line-up of acts at Circus Circus includes Gregory Popovitch, a native of Russia who was once part of the legendary Moscow circus. Also, the Pavlovics, an acrobatic duo from Lithuania, The Osorio Brothers, three high-wire-walking siblings from Mexico, The Zhaos, a trio from china who perform incredible feats on bicycles, and three daring trapeze troupes: The Flying Vasquez, The Flying Cacares and the Flying Jimenez. Catch an act every half hour on the Midway's center stage, from 11:00 a.m. to midnight, which is complete with flashing lights, live band, and ring master or mistress. There's plenty of centrally-located, comfortable seating, making this a great place for parents to catch their breath while older kids explore the Midway's carnival games. The Midway also has a number of inexpensive rides which even the smallest children can ride, this may be the best way to please a cranky toddler.

Arcades

Sega Gameroom: located on the Carnival Midway, is a real treat for video game lovers. Boasting 192 games, fans of virtual video games will think they have gone to heaven. You (or your kids) can ski, surf, skate, race, battle, and more, without leaving the midway. Circusland RV Park Arcade: has 20 video game and located in the RV park's general store

Food

The Adventuredome: Outpost cafe, snack bar, snack carts. **Midway:** McDonald's. **Other:** Pizzeria in the main casino, sweet shop and Frozen Fusion on the Promenade.

Gifts

Located on the Promenade, Circus Kids has cool clothing, especially appropriate for kids under 10, and great jewelry for kids and teens.

Hours

The Adventuredome Theme Park: The park opens at 10:00 a.m., and closing hours vary throughout the year. Call (702) 794-3939 for more information.

Carnival Midway Acts: Circus acts perform daily from 11:00 a.m. to midnight, appearing every half hour on center stage at the Circus Circus Hotel/Casino Carnival Midway.

Safety

There is a first aid station in the center of The Adventuredome. Circus Circus Hotel/Casino has E.M.T.'s and security officers throughout the property.

Though The Adventuredome is conveniently located near the Promenade, and the Carnival Midway is located above the main casino, these areas do not provide sitter services. For the safety of your children and the benefit of all the resort's guests, young children must be accompanied by an adult at all times. As tempting as it may be to drop the little ones off at The Adventuredome and hit the Promenade for some quick shopping, DON'T DO IT!

Circus Circus Hotel/Casino strictly adheres to Las Vegas's curfew regulations. Sunday through Thursday, children 17 years of age or younger must be accompanied by an adult after 10:00 p.m. On Fridays and Saturdays, the time is extended to midnight. Small children must be accompanied by an adult at all times.

Additional

What circus would be complete without clowns? Circus Circus Hotel/Casino has a free show, "The Clown Revue," which is performed periodically in the Adventuredome. Call (702) 794-3939 for location and details. Become a clown yourself. Kids of all ages can don colorful make-up and bright red noses at The Adventuredome's "Be A Clown" booth. The make-up is water soluble and the round, red nose is a must for Circus Circus enthusiasts.

Excalibur Hotel/Casino

A glowing white castle, complete with towers, parapet, and brightly colored turrets, commands your attention. That is Excalibur! The castle houses the large casino, as well as shopping and dining areas. Most of Excalibur's children's entertainment is part of the Fantasy Faire. The Fantasy Faire is located beneath the main casino and includes the Wizard's Arcade, two motion simulator theaters, King Arthur's Arena, and numerous medieval-themed Midway games.

Excalibur Hotel/Casino Information

Address: 3850 South Las Vegas Blvd., Las Vegas, NV 89193 (At the intersection of Las Vegas Blvd. South and /Tropicana Ave.)

Phone: 1-(800) 937-7777

Midway Games

Fantasy Faire's Midway games have the look and feel of a carnival midway with a medieval twist. Your child can test his or her luck with an electric crossbow, darts, and a host of other pitching and aiming games. Most games can be played for $1.00 per try, and your child has a chance at winning a life-sized stuffed animal. Many animals are popular Disney or Warner Brothers characters.

Merlin's Magic Motion Machines

Merlin's Magic Motion Machines are two motion simulator theaters located on Excalibur's Fantasy Faire level. Each film, or "ride," is an action-packed 3 to 6 minutes in length. Films change every hour. The cost is $3.00 per person per ride, and is well worth it. Merlin's Magic Motion Machines are a safe bet for fast-paced, affordable fun. Because of safety restriction, there is a 42" height requirement.

Fun Fact

Merlin's Magic Motion Machines are said to be the first motion simulator rides in America.

King Arthur's Tournament

Be sure to attend King Arthur's Tournament, the dinner show in King Arthur's Arena. Located on the Fantasy Faire level, King Arthur's Arena is a 900 seat theater-in-the-round. An audience of all ages sits on wooden benches and eats medieval faire, while a tournament, complete with colorful knights, galloping horses, a king, queen, and Merlin (of course), takes place on the sand covered stage below. When the Dark Knight appears, the tournament turns into a well orchestrated battle royale ending in magic, celebration, and spectacle. King Arthur's Tournament is performed twice nightly, with shows starting at 6:00 p.m. and 8:30 p.m. Tickets are $29.95 per person. Though the show is recommended for children ages seven and up (Merlin is a little bawdy at the beginning) children three and under get in free, as long as they sit on an adult's lap (space is limited).

King Arthur's Tournament is a spectacular bargain. The show is full of stunts and surprises. Dinner, though simple enough to please a finicky child, is delicious, and the portions are generous. Tickets can be purchased in advance by visiting one of Excalibur's show ticket desks, or by calling 1-(800) 933-1334

Arcades

Wizard's Arcade: A huge, state-of-the-art arcade located in the Fantasy Faire level. Hours from 9:00 a.m. to 1:00 a.m. daily, varying slightly by season.

Medieval Village Arcade: A smaller arcade located on the Medieval Village level (level two) above the main casino. Hours from 10:00 a.m. to 1:00 a.m. daily, varying slightly by season.

Food

Fantasy Faire: Hansel and Gretel's Snack Bar, Medieval Village (level two) Sherwood Forest Café (24 hours, offing a children's menu) Robin Hood's snack Bar, a sweet shop, and the moderately priced Round Table Buffet.

Additional: A three course meal is served during the performance of King Arthur's Tournament.

Located on the Medieval Village Level, Kids of the Kingdom offers a large assortment of gifts for younger children (about eight and under) including high-quality (but pricey) costumes, as well as small toys, dolls, games, and jewelry.

Check out this unique photo find — if you or your children are really into Medieval life, visit Castle Cameos, an old-time photo studio on the Medieval Village level. Adults and children can be photographed wearing colorful Medieval clothing and other costumes. There is a $5.00 per person dress and shoot fee. Photo packages range from $27.00 to $70.00. Makes a great gift or souvenir.

Hours

Merlin's Magic Motion machines: shows run from 9:00 a.m. to 1:00 a.m. daily, varying slightly by season. Films change approximately every hour. **Fantasy Fare Midway games:** Open from 9:00 a.m. to 1:00 a.m. daily, varying slightly by season.

King Arthur's Tournament: Performed twice nightly in King Arthur's Arena. Shows start at 6:00 p.m. and 8:30 p.m.

Dragon Battle: a battle between Merlin and a gigantic mechanical dragon (fire-breathing, of course!) takes place every evening in the moat at the castle's front entrance, every hour on the hour from dusk until midnight.

The Glockenspiel Fairy Tale: Played out daily over the giant clock at the rear entrance at the top and bottom of each hour, from 10:00 a.m. to 10:00 p.m.

Safety

There is 24 hour video surveillance throughout the Fantasy Faire level and security officers at both arcades, but these areas do not provide sitter services. Young children should not be left unattended. See page 6 for notes on Las Vegas's curfew.

To make your adventure complete

Costumed entertainers wander the Medieval Village level, doing their best to charm, juggle, joke, and stilt-walk a smile on the faces of Excalibur's young guests. Catch a free performance by these entertainers every half hour on the Jester's Stage, also on the Medieval Village level. Performances are approximately ten minutes long.

Boulder Station

If you're not interested in staying on the strip or feel like getting away from it for a bit) Boulder Station is an attractive alternative. The clean, classy casino is decorated in a subtle Old West motif (the hardwood floors and sky-blue ceilings are gorgeous!) and the friendly folks at Boulder Station genuinely care about your kids. Among other things, you'll find a Kids' Quest play facility, special dining arrangements for kids and families, and a strict set of safety standards upheld throughout the hotel/casino. In general, the feel of Boulder Station is mellower than that of the hotel/casinos on the strip. The colors are less jarring, and the buildings are more intimate. Additionally, if you plan on spending most of your vacation in the recreations areas surrounding Las Vegas, you may want to stay at Boulder Station, or one of the other off-strip hotel/casinos, to avoid Vegas traffic.

Boulder Station Information

Address: 4111 Boulder Hwy
Las Vegas, NV

Phone: (702)432-7777
1 (800)683-7777

Kids' Quest

Kids' Quest is a play center where kids ages six weeks to 12 years old can play under staff supervision. Kid's Quest has a free-flow environment, offering children their choice of games and activities. There are eight video game stations (featuring Sega, Sega Saturn, Super Nintendo, and Nintendo 64 games) free arcade games, and interactive computer learning games. Virtual Reality World puts your kids in the game, and is a very simple introduction to virtual reality technology.

The Quest Play Piece is an indoor playground comprised of nets, ball cages, tunnels, and slides. Staff members often climb into the Quest Play Piece to have fun with their tiny guests, making it easy for kids to have a good time. Also in Kid Quest, find Barbie Land, with all the Barbie furniture, dolls, and fashions your kid could ever want, and Lego World, with over 1,000 Legos, a super-sized Lego train, and a Lego house big enough for your kids to walk into and make-believe. One of Kids' Quest most popular attractions is the karaoke stage. Kids can dress up, sing, and dance to their favorite tunes, while watching themselves perform on overhead TV screens. If your kids tire themselves out, they can rest in the movie room, a mini theater with comfy, colorful chairs. Kids' Quest has access to fifty-five movies, many of which are Disney films. Kids are encouraged to request their favorite film, and something appropriate is always playing.

Children ages six weeks to two and a half years old stay in the Kids' Quest toddler room, where they are given diaper changes and feedings as needed. Little ones have a large assortment of Little Tykes toys to choose from, and other activities to keep them occupied. Best of all, toddler room kids are under constant supervision, making their separation from you a little easier and safer.

Kids' Quest's other young guests are given a lunch and dinner they're sure to like — Burger King Kids' Meals, which are served at 11:30 a.m. and 5:30 p.m.. The cost is an additional $2.50 per meal. There is also a counter stocked with candy, snacks, and sodas for children to choose from and eat as they wish. Parents can pre-set a limit (which is advised) or allow kids to run a tab. Meals and snacks are paid for when parents pick up their children.

The current cost for children to stay in Kids' Quest is $5.00 per hour on weekdays, and $6.00 per hour on Fridays and Saturdays. Because Kids' Quest can only take a maximum of 199 kids, reservations are recommended, especially for weekends.

All staff members are CPR and First Aid certified, Kids' Quest is a supervised activity center, not a day care facility. Kids can not be left in Kids' Quest for more than 3 1/2 hours. While children are in Kids' Quest, parents or guardians must stay on Boulder Station's property. Also, parents or guardians must present their child's immunization record before leaving a child in Kids' Quest.

Arcades

Sega Station Arcade: Features many "virtual" games, as well as an air hockey table and a basketball toss.

Kids' Quest: There are free arcade games and video game stations in Kids' Quest which are especially appropriate for kids age twelve and under.

Food

Food Court: Seven food outlets can be found in Boulder Station's food court, including Mexican and Chinese eateries, a pizzeria, Burger King, Pretzel Gourmet, and TCBY.

Iron Horse Cafe´: Featuring the Lil' Engineers Kids' Menu, this is a great place for a relaxed meal. A cut above fast food.

Boulder Station Buffet: Offers discounts to Seniors and children.

Enjoy a traditional, family-style meal at Boulder Station's Guadelajara Restaurant. You can order a main dish and a number of sides for a reasonable price, then serve yourself and your family. Like home, but better. You don't have to cook and clean!

Safety

The folks at Boulder Station are concerned with your children's safety in a number of ways, and do their best to encourage responsible behavior on the part of parents. This is for the benefit and well-being of the families who stay at Boulder Station, as well as the hotel/casino's other guests. For instance, children and minors are allowed to cross the casino floor, but are not allowed to loiter near the machines, even when accompanied by an adult. If a child is found alone on Boulder Station's property, and a parent can not be readily located, officials report the incident to the police, and have the option of pressing charges under the state's child endangerment laws. Additional safety measures are taken in Kids' Quest, including an impressive anti-germ regimen. In fact, the balls in the Quest Play Piece are sanitized daily. For identification and pick-up purposes, children staying in Kids' Quest must wear a computer generated sticker at all times stating their names, the names of their parents, and a valid local phone number (it can be a hotel room extension).

Catch a current movie release in Boulder Station's cinema, complete with eleven oversized screen and high-tech sound. The theater is a great place for teens to spend time, parents to take a break, and entire families to escape the usual vacation induced stressed. Adults pay $6.75 per show, children only $3.75. There are bargain matinee prices as well. ∎

Luxor Las Vegas

The Attractions Level at the Luxor would be fun to visit even if you didn't want to go to the attractions. It's located in the center of the pyramid and has amazing views of Egyptian statues, obelisks and architecture. There's lots to see and do here, and you could easily (and happily) spend half a day doing it. The 312 seat IMAX Theater is a technological wonder which projects lifelike images on a screen seven stories high, accompanied by a booming 15,000 watt sound system whose bass notes vibrate your bones. Each moviegoer dons a headset containing Liquid Crystal Display 3-D glasses as well as its own surround sound system. The films last about half an hour and are very realistic. This is fun for all ages.

"In Search of the Obelisk" is a motion simulator ride about a wild trip through an underground excavation in a flying machine. The motion pod seats about fifteen people, and the whole room seems to move along with the action on the

screen. The story line is totally confusing, but no one seems to care as they swerve, dive and scream along with the full-motion adventure. This is great fun, but can be a little too intense for the very young or those with fragile backs.

The Attractions Level also houses the Tomb and Museum of King Tutankhamun, a full-scale replica of King Tut's tomb containing authentic reproductions of the items found there by Harold Carter in 1922. A 15-minute, self-guided walking tour allows visitors to view the treasures while listening to a description of each room. Kids with an interest in King Tut may find this as fascinating as the Adults, but more action-oriented kids may prefer the arcade next door. The Virtualand Arcade has the usual array of games kids love and is undergoing an expansion to put in even more. The food court on this level has something for everyone: McDonalds, Nathan's Hot Dogs, Swenson's Ice Cream and Little Caesar's Pizza. There's even a coffee bar for the big kids. Restrooms are convenient and clean, and there are a couple of gift shops for the Egyptian souvenirs everybody has to bring home. ■

Luxor Las Vegas Information

Location: Luxor Las Vegas

Address: 3900 Las Vegas Blvd. South

Directions: On the Strip south of Tropicana Ave. Look for the giant pyramid.

Phone: 262-4000

Days/Hours: Open daily 9 am-11 pm. Food Court opens earlier and stays open later.

Admission: IMAX Theater $7.50 (2-D movie) or $8.95 (3-D movie) "In Search of the Obelisk" ride $6.00; Tomb and Museum of King Tut $4.00; Master Pass $20.95 includes Obelisk Ride, entrance to museum, a 2-D movie and a 3-D movie, plus 2-for-1 arcade tickets.

Restrictions: IMAX Theater: no lap sitting. Children must be able to sit alone.

Obelisk ride: Must be 42 inches tall, not pregnant, no back or heart problems. You may request a non-motion ride.

Facilities: Wheelchair access, gift shops, food court

Caesars Palace

There are many things to see and do with kids at Caesars Palace, with prices ranging from free to expensive. The Omnimax Theatre is a good value for your entertainment dollar. Housed in a giant dome on the north side of the hotel, its curved screen (82 feet high and 82 feet wide) gives you a 180 degree panorama of beautiful scenes from nature. Together with the nine-channel "sensaround" sound system, it puts you in the middle of breathtaking scenes like thousands of buffaloes stampeding across the prairie or an eagle's eye view of flying through the Grand Canyon. Movies are screened every hour on the hour seven days a week, from 11:00 a.m. to midnight. Admission charge is $4.00 for Adults and $3.00 for children 12 and under. There is also a small arcade outside the theater entrance where the kids can play while waiting for the show to start.

For a really special treat, take the family to Caesars Magical Empire for dinner and magic shows. At $75 each, its not cheap, but it does last about 3 hours, and includes a three-course dinner hosted by a wizard as well as admission to two different magic theaters. Each cozy dining chamber, designed to resemble an underground cave, seats 24 people, so the "wizards" get a chance to interact closely with everyone and perform their tricks, usually with a humorous twist. After dinner, visitors are guided through the catacombs to the Sanctum Secorum, a seven-story high room surrounded by giant statues. Beware the broken bridge and bottomless pit! It's all scary fun. For the adults, there are two lounges offering drinks as well as wisecracking skeletons and an invisible piano player. Be sure to visit the Secret Pagoda Theater, which presents masters of close-up magic with shows every 25 minutes. The larger Sultan's Palace Theatre offers more elaborate shows every 50 minutes. Magicians at both theaters like to bring audience members into the act, especially children, so it's great fun. Guests must be at least five years old. Children 5-10 are admitted at half the adult price. One way to reduce your cost is to go on a free tour, offered every half hour Friday - Tuesday from 11:00 a.m. to 3:30 p.m. Each tour member gets $15.00 off a ticket to the early dinner seating at 4:30p.m., which brings the child's price down to $22.50. The Magical Empire is open Friday through Tuesday from 4:30 p.m. to 10:00 p.m. (closed Wednesday and Thursday). ■

Caesars Palace Information

Attraction: Omnimax and Caesars Magical Empire

Location: Caesars Palace

Address: 3570 Las Vegas Blvd. South

Directions: Located on the Strip at Flamingo Road. Free parking available behind the hotel.

Phone: (702) 731-7110 (Omnimax) (702) 731-7333 (Magical Empire)

Days/Hours/Admission: see above copy

Area Hotels

hotels

- **Alexis Park**
  3 swimming pools, tennis courts, refrigerators, babysitting
  375 E. Harmon Ave.
  (702) 796-3300
  (800) 582-2228
- **Arizona Charlie's**
  Video arcade, pool
  740 S. Decatur Blvd.
  (702) 258-5200
  (800) 342-2695
  www.azcharlies.com
- **Bally's**
  5 restaurants, large video arcade, Olympic sized swimming pools, 8 lighted tennis courts, basketball courts, babysitting
  3645 Las Vegas Blvd. S.
  (702) 739-4111
  (800) 634-3434
  www.ballyslv.com
- **Barbary Coast**
  No swimming pool, babysitting, McDonald's restaurant
  3595 Las Vegas Blvd. S.
  (702) 737-7111
  (800) 634-6755
- **Best Western Mardi Gras Inn**
  Large rooms, kitchenettes, swimming pool
  3500 Paradise Rd.
  (702) 731-2020
  (800) 634-6501
- **Binion's Horseshoe**
  Swimming pool
  128 Fremont Street
  Las Vegas
  (702) 382-1600
  (800) 937-6537
- **Boulder Station**
  Kid's Quest, swimming pool, video arcade, 11 plex movie theater
  4111 Boulder Hwy.
  Las Vegas
  (702) 432-7777
  (800) 683-7777
  www.boulderstation.com
- **Buffalo Bills**
  http://www.primadonna.com
- **Caesars Palace**
  Adventure Fun Center Video Arcade, 4 swimming pools, tennis courts, Festival Fountain in the Forum Shops, Omnimax Theatre,

babysitting
3570 Las Vegas Blvd.
(702) 731-7222
(800) 634-6661
www.caesars.com
- **California Hotel**
  Swimming pool, video arcade
  12 E Ogden Ave.
  (702) 385-1222
  (800) 634-6255
  www.vegas.com/hotels/cal/
- **Circus Circus Hotel**
  Video arcade, indoor and outdoor swimming pools, monorail, McDonald's, Adventurdome theme park, Circus acts, carnival midway,
  2880 Las Vegas Blvd. S.
  (702) 734-0410
  (800) 634-6255
  www.circuscircus-lasvegas.com
- **Continental**
  Swimming pool
  4100 Paradise Rd.
  (702) 737-5555
  (800) 634-6641
  http://continentalhotel.com
- **Desert Inn Resort**
  Swimming pool, tennis courts, golf course, babysitting
  3145 Las Vegas Blvd. S.
  (702) 734-4444
  (800) 634-6906
- **El Cortez**
  Video arcade, babysitting
  600 E. Fremont Street
  (702) 385-5200
  (800) 634-6703
- **Excalibur Hotel**
  Fantasy Faire — 2 motion simulator theaters, Arcade and midway games, Medieval Village with strolling entertainers, King Arthur's Tournament, Court Jester's stage, 2 swimming pools, water slides, 7 restaurants
  3850 Las Vegas Blvd. S.
  (702) 597-7777
  (800) 937-7777
  www.excalibur-casino.com
- **Fiesta Casino Hotel**
  2400 Rancho Dr.
  (702) 631-7000
  (800) 731-7333
- **Fitgeralds/Holiday Inn**
  301 Fremont Street
  (702) 388-2400
  (800) 274-5825
  www.fitzgeralds.com

Flamingo Hilton Hotel
5 swimming pools, tennis courts, wildlife habitat, video arcade, babysitting
3555 Las Vegas Blvd. S.
(702) 733-3111
(800) 732-2111
www.hilton.com

Four Queens
202 Fremont Street
(702) 385-4011
(800) 634-6045
www.fourqueens.com

Fremont Hotel
Babysitting, small video arcade
200 Fremont Street
Las Vegas
(702) 385-3232
(800) 634-6460

Gold Coast
Video arcade, bowling center, ice cream and soda shop, twin movie theaters, child care facility
4000 W. Flamingo Rd.
Las Vegas
(702) 367-7111
(800) 331-5334
www.goldcoastcasino.com

Golden Nugget Hotel
Olympic sized swimming pool, babysitting
129 Fremont Street
Las Vegas
(702) 385-7111
(800) 634-3454
www.goldennugget.com

Hard Rock Hotel
Sand bottom swimming pool, water slide, arcade, big-screen TV, babysitting
4455 Paradise Rd
(702) 693-5000
(800) 473-7625
www.hardrock.com

Harrah's
Swimming pool, arcade
3475 Las Vegas Blvd. S.
(702) 369-5000
(800) 634-6765
www.harrahslv.com

Holiday Inn - Boardwalk
3750 Las Vegas Blvd. S.
(702) 735-2400
(800) 465-4329
www.hiboardwalk.com

Imperial Palace Hotel
Auto collection, 24 hour medical facility, Olympic-size pool with waterfall, video arcade, babysitting

3535 Las Vegas Blvd. S.
(702) 731-3311
(800) 634-6441
www.imperialpalace.com

Lady Luck Casino & Hotel
Swimming pool
206 N. Third Street
(702) 477-3000
(800) 523-9582
www.lady-luck.com/ladyluck/

Las Vegas Club
Sports hall of fame
18 Fremont Street
(702) 385-1664
(800) 634-6532

Las Vegas Hilton
Video arcade, Star Trek: The Experience tm, Swimming pool, 6 lit tennis courts, 9 hole putting green, table tennis, babysitting
3000 Paradise Rd.
(702) 732-5111
(800) 732-7117
www.hilton.com

Luxor Hotel
Arcade, King Tut's Tomb & Museum, swimming pool, Imax Theater, babysitting, pets allowed
3900 Las Vegas Blvd. S.
(702) 262-4000
(800) 288-1000
www.luxor.com

Main Street Station
200 N. Main Street
(702) 387-1896
(800) 713-8933
www.vegas.com/hotels/stardust/

Maxim Hotel
Swimming pool
160 E. Flamingo Rd.
(702) 731-4300
(800) 634-6987

MGM Grand Hotel
MGM Grand Adventures Theme Park, Youth Activity Center for ages 3-12, Pool with beach, Oz midway and video arcade, tennis courts, monorail, babysitting, pets allowed
3799 Las Vegas Blvd. S.
(702) 891-1111
(800) 929-1111
www.mgmgrand.com

Mirage
swimming pool, erupting volcano, Royal White tiger habitat, dolphin habitat, Secret Garden, Olympic size heated pool, video arcade

hotels

3400 Las Vegas Blvd. S.
(702) 791-7111
(800) 627-6667
www.themirage.com

■ **Monte Carlo**
Pool with Lagoon, kiddie pool, wave pool, Easy River Ride, lighted tennis courts
3770 Las Vegas Blvd. S.
(702) 730-7000
(800) 311-8999
www.monte-carlo.com

■ **Nevada Palace**
5255 Boulder Hwy.
(702) 458-8810
(800) 634-6283

■ **New Frontier Hotel**
Swimming pool, tennis courts, video arcade
3120 Las Vegas Blvd. S.
(702) 794-8200
(800) 634-6966

■ **New York New York**
Coney Island Emporium with carnival rides, laser tag, video arcade, Manhattan Express rollercoaster, swimming pool, magic shop
3790 Las Vegas Blvd. S.
(702) 740-6969
(800) 693-6763
www.nynyhotelcasino.com

■ **Orleans**
Pool, bowling center, child care center, 12 plex movie theater, video arcade
4500 W. Tropicana Ave.
(702) 365-7111
(800) 675-3267
www.orleanscasino.com

■ **Palace Station**
2 swimming pools, video arcade
2411 W. Sahara Ave.
(702) 367-2411
(800) 634-3101
www.stationcasino.com

■ **Plaza Hotel**
Lighted tennis courts, swimming pool, Ice Cream parlor
1 Main Street
(702) 386-2110
(800) 634-6575

■ **Primadonna resorts**
www.primadonna.com

■ **Quality Inn - Key Largo**
Heated swimming pool, wet bars & refrigerators in rooms
377 E. Flamingo Rd.

(702) 733-7777
(800) 634-6617

■ **Reserve Hotel**
Swimming pool, African safari dÈcor with sound system.
777 W. Lake Mead Dr. Henderson
(702) 558-7000
888-899-7770

■ **Rio Suite Hotel**
3 swimming pools, sandy beach, beach volleyball, Pizza Parlor, Ice Cream Shop, Video Arcade, golf, Masqurade Show in the sky
3700 W. Flamingo Rd.
(702) 252-7777
(800) 752-9746
www.playrio.com

■ **Riviera Hotel**
Swimming pool, video arcade, food court, tennis courts
2901 Las Vegas Blvd. S.
(702) 734-5110
(800) 634-6753
www.theriviera.com/

■ **Royal Hotel**
Swimming pool
99 Convention Center Dr.
(702) 735-6117
(800) 634-6118

■ **Sahara Hotel**
Swimming pool, video arcade, Sahara Speedway virtual reality Indy car racing, 3-D theater
2535 Las Vegas Blvd. S.
(702) 737-2111
(800) 634-6666

■ **Sam's Town**
56-lane bowling center, Coca Cola Museum, video arcade, supervised play area for children, swimming pool, volleyball, sunset stampede water show
5111 Boulder Hwy
(702) 456-7777
(800) 634-6371
www.samstownlvnv.com

■ **San Remo**
Video arcade, heated swimming pool
115 E. Tropicana Ave.
(702) 739-9000
(800) 522-7366
www.sanremolasvegas.com/

■ **Santa Fe Hotel**
Bowling center, ice skating, nursery, video arcade
4949 N. Rancho Dr.
Las Vegas

(702) 658-4900
(800) 872-6823

- **Showboat Hotel**
  Video arcade, bowling center, supervised children's play area,
  2800 E. Fremont Street
  (702) 385-9123
  (800) 826-2800
  www.showboat-LV.com

- **Silverton**
  3 heated swimming pools, video arcade
  3333 Blue Diamond Rd.
  (702) 263-7777
  (800) 588-7711

- **Stardust**
  3 swimming pools, video arcade, Ralph's 50's Diner, babysitting
  3000 Las Vegas Blvd. S.
  (702) 732-6111
  (800) 634-6757
  www.vegas.com/hotels/stardust

- **Stratosphere**
  World's highest roller coaster, Big Shot thrill ride, Kid's Quest child care center, light show, video arcade
  2000 Las Vegas Blvd
  (702) 380-7777
  (800) 998-6937
  www.stratlv.com

- **Sunset Station**
  Kid's Quest child care facility, swimming pool, volleyball, Sega GameWorks video arcade, 13-screen movie theater complex
  1301 W. Sunset Rd
  (702) 547-7777
  888-786-7389
  www.stationcasino.com

- **Texas Station**
  Swimming pool, Texas 12 movie theater
  2101 Texas Star Lane
  (702) 631-1000
  (800) 654-8888
  www.stationcasino.com

- **Treasure Island**
  Swimming pool with 200 ft slide, Mutiny Bay video arcade, Cirque du Soleil (circus), Pets allowed
  3300 Las Vegas Blvd. S.
  (702) 894-7111
  (800) 944-7444
  www.treasure islandlasvegas.com

- **Tropicana**
  Arcade, wildlife walk, island pool area with waterslide, babysitting,
  pets allowed
  3801 Las Vegas Blvd. S.
  (702) 739-2222
  (800) 634-4000
  www.tropicana.com

- **Vacation Village**
  Video arcade, 2 swimming pools
  6711 Las Vegas Blvd. S.
  (702) 897-1700
  (800) 338-0608

- **Western Hotel/Casino**
  899 Fremont Street
  (702) 384-4620
  (800) 634-6703

- **Westward Ho**
  2900 Las Vegas Blvd S
  (702) 731-2900
  (800) 634-6651
  www.westwardho.com

- **Whiskey Pete's**
  www.primadonna.com

RV Parks and Campgrounds

■ American Campgrounds
34 camping spaces, full hook-ups, showers; grass area for tents; daily and weekly rates.
Admission: Tent area $7.50
3440 Las Vegas Blvd. N., Las Vegas
(702) 643-1222

■ Bond Trailer Lodge
76 long term spaces, laundry, cable, telephone, storage
284 E. Tropicana Ave., Las Vegas
(702) 736-1550

■ Boulder Lakes RV Resort and Country Club
417 Full hook-ups, showers, pool, Jacuzzi, store, laundry, four tennis courts, cable and telephone service to all sites
Admission: $18.90 daily; $124.20 weekly; $316.60 monthly plus power
6201 Boulder Hwy., Las Vegas
(702) 435-1157

■ Canyon Trail RV Park
Showers, store, recreation hall, laundry
Admission: $17.00 daily; $90/$100 weekly; $270/$280 monthly
1200 Industrial Rd., Las Vegas
(702) 293-1200

■ Circusland RV Park
369 full hood-ups, showers, pool and Jacuzzi, store, laundry, monorail to main casino, fenced pet runs; reservations well in advance are advised
Admission: $16.96 - $30.74 daily
500 Circus Circus Dr., Las Vegas
(702) 794-3757

■ Cottonwood Cove Resort & Marina
P.O. Box 1000
Lake Mohave
(702) 297-1464

■ Desert Sands RV Park and Motel
300 full hook-ups, showers, store, pool and sauna, laundry
Hours: $15 daily; $95 weekly; $240 monthly
1940 N. Boulder Hwy., Las Vegas
(702) 565-1945

■ Good Sam's Hitchin Post Camper Park
Security gates, laundry, showers, pool, drive-thru spaces, phone hook-ups
Admission: $18.00 daily; $108.00 weekly; $295.00 monthly plus power
3640 Las Vegas Blvd North
Las Vegas
(702) 644-1043

■ Holiday Travel Trailer Park
403 full hook-ups, Showers, pool and spa, recreation room, laundry
Admission: $14.00 daily
3890 Nellis Blvd. South, Las Vegas
(702) 451-8005

■ King's Row
3660 Boulder Hwy., Las Vegas
(702) 649-7439

■ KOA Campgrounds
240 hook-ups, Free shuttle to casinos, showers, pool and Jacuzzi, store, daily and monthly rates
4315 Boulder Hwy., Las Vegas
(702) 451-5527

■ Lakeshore Trailer Village
84 full hook-ups, Showers, laundry
Admission: $15.00 daily; $85.00 weekly; $290.00 monthly
268 Lakeshore Rd (Nevada 166)
Las Vegas
(702) 293-2540

■ Mount Charleston RV Site
15 self contained units, no water or toilets
Admission: $55.00 daily
State Rd 157, Las Vegas
(800) 283-2267

■ Nevada Palace VIP Travel Trailer Park
168 full hook-ups, Showers, pool, laundry; pets under 20 pounds
Admission: $15.12 daily; $105.84 weekly
5325 Boulder Hwy., Las Vegas
(702) 451-0232

■ PrimaDonna Hotel RV Park
199 Full-Service Hook-Ups, Swimming Pool, Jacuzzi, Sand Volleyball Court, Recreation Room, children's Playground, Convenience Store, Showers, Satellite TV, 24 Hour Security, Free Shuttle Service to all Casinos
Admission: $12.00 a night per space
Jct 1-15 & 1-15 Bus Rt., Exit 120 E
Las Vegas
(702) 382-1212   1-(800) FUN-ST

campgrounds

- **Riviera Travel Trailer Park**
  136 full hook-ups, pool and spa,
  showers, store, small pets welcome;
  daily, weekly and monthly rates
  Admission: $16.98 daily; $101.74
  weekly; $260 monthly
  2200 Palm Street, Las Vegas
  (702) 457-8700
- **Road Runner RV Park**
  Admission: $14.00 daily; $95.00
  weekly; $315.00 monthly
  4711 Boulder Hwy., Las Vegas
  (702) 456-4711
- **Sam Boyd's California Hotel and RV Park**
  222 spaces, 192 full hookup, 30 with
  water & electric only. Restroom,
  shower, laundry, dog run, swimming
  pool and Jacuzzi, convenience store,
  dump station.
  1st St. and Ogden Ave., Las Vegas
  (702) 388-2602   (800) 634-6255

- **Sam's Town RV Park - Boulder**
  5225 Boulder Hwy., Las Vegas
  (702) 454-8055
- **Sam's Town RV Park - Nellis**
  4040 S. Nellis Blvd., Las Vegas
  (702) 454-8056
- **Silver Nugget Casino and RV Park**
  152 full hook-ups, Pool, Jacuzzi
  Admission: $13.75 - $15.25; $305.00
  - $320.00 monthly
  2236 N. Las Vegas Blvd., Las Vegas
  (702) 649-7439
- **Sunrise RV Park**
  240 hook-ups, shower, laundry,
  pool/spa, convenience store, coffee
  shop, clubhouse, group activities,
  propane, casino shuttle
  4575 Boulder "Strip"
  Las Vegas
  (702) 434-0848
  (800) 362-4040

chapter six

parents
survival guide

- Places For Kids Parties
- Party Performers

Places for Kid's Parties

All American Sports Park

Birthday parties are a blast at the All-American SportPark. All parties include a reserved party area for an hour, a "party referee" to supervise, soft drinks, arcade tokens and a group photo. You can purchase food from the concession stands at reduced prices.

> 121 E. Sunset Road Las Vegas
> **(702) 798-7777 or (702) 317-7827**

Burger King Restaurants

Package includes cake, decorations, kids meals, supervised play time at locations with playgrounds. $32.00 for up to 10 children, $2.00 each additional child.

Celebrate Kids

Magical theme parties. Packages range from $85.00 to $225.00 includes cakes, entertainment, decorations and prizes. Package includes set-up, clean-up, and everything in between.

> **(702) 656-7004**

Crystal Palace

Party package includes admission and skates, pizza or hot dogs, ice cream, soft drinks and use of the party room for up to 30 minutes. Invitations are available. $60.00 for up to 10 children, $6.00 each additional child.

> 4680 Boulder Hwy., Las Vegas
> **(702) 458-7107**
> 4740 S. Decatur Blvd., Las Vegas
> **(702) 564-2790**
> 1110 E. Lake Mead Dr.
> Henderson
> **(702) 564-2790**
> 3901 N. Rancho Dr., Las Vegas
> **(702) 645-4892**

Dansey's Indoor R-C & Hobbies

Design your own party. R/C racing, model building, rocket building

> 741 N. Nellis Blvd., Las Vegas
> **(702) 453-7223**

Discovery Zone

Private birthday room for 45 minutes, one hour of play time, birthday cake. 10 children (minimum) $79.99 to $129.90.

> 2020 Olympic Ave.
> **(702) 434-9575**

GameWorks

Gameworks is a good place to have a birthday party, especially for game-aholics. Their Party Packages for groups of ten or more include: a fully decorated party area for 90 minutes with Gameworks host, birthday cake, a balloon bouquet, pizza or hot dogs and fries, unlimited (!) sodas, and a gift package for the Birthday Person including a Gameworks T-shirt and other goodies. Each guest at the Basic Party ($20) also receives one party favor and a $20 game card. For $30 per person, The Works Party Package allows each guest 2 party favors and

an hour and a half of unlimited game play. Gameworks motto is, 'Life's a game. It's meant to be played.'

> 3785 S. Las Vegas Blvd.
> Las Vegas
> **(702) 432-4263**

Gold Coast Bowling Center

Party package includes two games of bowling, shoe rental, hot dogs or pizza and soda, party favors $5.00 to $6.00 per child.

> 4000 W. Flamingo
> Las Vegas, NV
> **(702) 367-4700**

J R Pony Parties

Complete children's parties at the farm. Pony rides, wagon rides, petting zoo, BBQ.

> **(702) 647-3676**

Lied Discovery children's Museum

Party includes invitations, guided museum tour, souvenir T-shirt, customized cake, party favors and refreshments.

> 833 Las Vegas Blvd N.
> Las Vegas, NV
> **(702) 382-3445**

Marabelli Community Center

Personal birthday party service. Parties are 90 minutes and include a host, games, face painting, piñiata, decorations, punch and invitations. You provide the cake.

> **(702) 229-6359**

McDonald's

$45.00 up to 10 children, $2.50 each additional child. Price includes Happy Meals for each child, host, cake, ice cream, games, gift for birthday child, decorations, and use of party room where available.

Mountasia Family Fun Center

Two 18 hole miniature golf course, roller skating, roller blading, arcade, Go Carts, bumper boats, large clubhouse, McDonalds.

> 2050 Olympic Ave.
> Henderson, NV
> **(702) 898-7777**

My Paint Box

Have fun painting your own ceramics.

> 4500 E. Sunset Rd.
> Henderson, NV
> **(702) 454-8797**

Peter Piper Pizza

Deluxe party package includes cake, ice cream, pizza, drinks, balloons, party favors and game tokens $8.95 per child, 6 child minimum.

> 701 S Decatur Blvd., Las Vegas
> **(702) 877-8873**
> 3430 E. Tropicana Ave.
> Las Vegas, NV
> **(702) 454-6366**
> 350 N. Nellis Blvd.
> Las Vegas, NV
> **(702) 459-1200**
> 2401 E. Lake Mead Blvd N.
> Las Vegas, NV
> **(702) 399-1115**

Santa Fe Hotel Ice Arena

Ice Castle Package includes admission and skates, party room for one hour, $80.00 (10 children). The Stanley Cup package includes party room for one hour, cake, punch, party favors and decorations. Admission and skates included plus a 30 minute skating lesson for the birthday child. $100.00 (10 children) $5.00 charge for each additional child.

> 4949 N. Rancho Dr.
> Las Vegas, NV
> **(702) 658-4991**

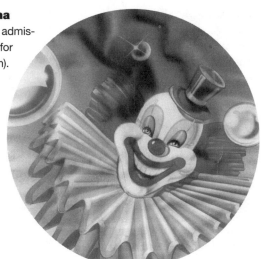

Scandia Family Fun Center

Batting range, miniature golf, bumper boats, lil'l Indy Raceway, Video arcade.

> 2900 Sirius Ave.
> Las Vegas, NV
> **(702) 364-0070**

Spence Tumble Bus

Birthday parties at the gym or the Tumble Bus will come to your party with rope course, climbing wall, obstacle course, cargo net, rings, tumble mats and mini trampoline. $125.00 for up to 15 children.

> 4860 A W. Lone Mountain Rd.
> Las Vegas, NV
> **(702) 658-9003**
> 1000 Stephanie Pl. Henderson
> **(702) 436-7333**

Ultrazone

> 2555 S. Maryland Pkwy
> Las Vegas, NV
> **(702) 734-1585**

Zoological Botanical Park

Facility can be rented for parties for $2.00 per person, with a minimum of 15 people.

> **(702) 647-4685**

Party Performers & Entertainment

All In One Balloons & Entertainment

Willy the Clown, Googie & friends. Clowns, Magicians, face painting, balloon artists, Kid's characters.

> **(702) 871-3174**

Apple Annies

Clowns, magic, face painting, animal balloons.

> **(702) 876-7529**

ABC Fiesta Jumping Balloons

Packages available with tables, chairs & Pinata.

> **(702) 525-5600**

Astro Jump of Las Vegas

Hours of inflatable entertainment. Choose from 15 X 15 ft. air bounce dinosaur, castle, elephant, dragon, lion, trains or space station. Misting system available.

> **(702) 435-5867**

survival guide

survival guide

August Entertainment

Zoo to You. A unique party theme with live snakes, funny monkeys, hedgehogs and more. Photos, giveaways and surprises.

(702) 644-4100

BoBo & Precious the "Silliest" clowns in Las Vegas

Magic, Balloons, face painting, prizes, fun, laughter & general buffoonery for all ages.

(702) 260-6609

Bounces Plus

Castle Jumps, clowns, balloons, face-painting.

(702) 871-9007

Cakes 4 kids

Custom Cakes

(702) 233-3442

Calico Farms Pony Rides

(702) 397-8086

Carnival Of Critters

Fun, safe, educational reptile shows. Free photos and prizes.

(702) 646-7885

Charlie the Clown

Birthday parties for children of all ages. Fire juggling, face painting, stilt walker, magic, unicycle.

(702) 362-3556
www.CharlietheClown.com

Clowns Plus

Balloons, face painting, mimes, magicians, jugglers, air bounces, stiltwalking, costumed characters.

(702) 871-9007

Classic Kids Parties

Signing telegrams, karoke artist, cartoonists, magicians, balloons, face painting.

(702) 376-9746

Cowboy George's

BBQ's, pony rides, hay rides, western prop rentals, air bounce.

(702) 385-7355
www.cowboygeorge.com

Dancing Bear Desserts & Novelties

Let a dancing bear host your child's next party.

(702) 871-4438

Dandy the Clown

Clowning with energy & love. Magic, face painting, stilts, juggling, balloons, caricatures.

(702) 255-0905

Dixie Pony Rides

(702) 459-7146

Entertainment 4 All

Characters, magicians, pony rides, petting zoo, cotton candy, popcorn, snow cone and hot dog machines, Moon Bounces.

(702) 643-5867

Las Vegas Entertainment Productions

Themed parties, clowns, magicians, jugglers, mimes, stiltwalkers, carnival rides, DJ's.

(702) 871-9007

Lords & Ladies

children's dress up tea parties. Juggling, ventriloquism, magic.

(702) 460-6442

Lucky the Clown Show

W.C. Fields show, comedy juggling act, face painting, magic, balloons.

(702) 646-2213

survival guide

Magicians & Clowns & Co.

Featuring Penny Poo the Clown. Birthday party specialists, face painting, balloon animals, dunk tanks.

(702) 873-9382

Marshmallow the Clown & Company

Magic, face painting, balloon animals, live animals, stilt walkers, games, custom made pinatas.

(702) 644-1015

Pony Express

Ponies for your party.

(702) 873-1288

Pony Parties

(702) 565-3098

Pony Path Ranch

Children's Pony Parties.

(702) 645-0531

Steve-N-Kids

Games, dancing, magic, candy and characters.

(702) 433-4649

Streamers

Costume parties for kids. Pow Wow, Hoe Down, Luau, Medieval, 50's, Tea party. Costumes, invitations, cake, props, party bags provided. Completely supervised, full catering available.

(702) 361-5457

Sue-Z-Q-Rides & Expo

We come to your party. Full size carnival with children's rides and games.

(702) 565-1590

chapter seven

medical guide

- First Aid Tips
- 24-Hour Emergency Clinics
- Area Hospitals

First Aid Tips

Information provided by the American Red Cross

Taking a trip with the kids can be one experience after another. If it's not the many trips to the bathroom it's the bumps and bruises to deal with. One of the first things to remember in any situation is not to panic. Many cuts and scraps look much worse than they actually are. Here is a guide to help you while you are waiting for professional assistance if needed:

Sunburn
Cool the Burn, Protect from further damage by staying out of sun or wearing a protective lotion, Protect unbroken blisters with loose bandages and keep broken blisters clean to prevent infection

Electrical Burns
Never go near a victim until the power is turned off. If a power line is down, wait for the fire department. Check breathing and pulse if person is unconscious. Give rescue breathing or CPR if needed. Do not cool burn, Cover burn with dry, sterile dressing.

Chemical Burns
Flush both skin and eyes with large amounts of cool running water until ambulance arrives. Always flush away from the body. Remove clothing and jewelry that may trap chemical against the skin or on which chemicals may have spilled.

Bruises
Apply ice or a cold pack to help control pain and swelling. Place a cloth between source of cold and skin to prevent injury. Elevate injured part to reduce swelling.

Nosebleed
Have person lean slightly forward, pinch the nostrils together for about 10 minutes. Apply an ice pack on the bridge of the nose or apply pressure under upper lip and gum.

24-Hour Emergency Clinics

Fremont Medical Center
520 Fremont Street
Las Vegas, NV
Main Number: **(702) 382-5200**
Location: Near intersection of Fremont
St. and N. Las Vegas Blvd.

Fremont Medical Center
4880 S. Wynn Rd
Las Vegas, NV
Main Number: **(702) 871-5005**
Location: Corner of Tropicana Ave.
and Wynn Rd.

Hogan Clinic
4241 S. Nellis Blvd.
Las Vegas, NV
Main Number: **(702) 898-1405**
Weekdays 6:00 a.m. to 11:00 p.m.
Friday and Saturday 24 hours
Location: Near intersection of
S. Nellis Blvd. and Boulder Hwy.

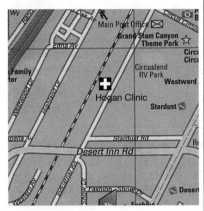

Hogan Clinic
2975 Industrial Rd.
Las Vegas, NV
Main Number: **(702) 735-0010**
Location: *See above map.*

![hospital or medical center icon] **hospital or medical center**

Industrial Medical Group of Las Vegas
3673 Polaris Ave.
Las Vegas, NV
Main Number: **(702) 871-1721**
Location: Near intersection of Polaris
Ave. and W. Twain Ave.

Inn House Doctor
*In your room treatment
Main Number: **(702) 382-9100**

Las Vegas Medical Center
150 E. Harmon St.
Las Vegas, NV
Main Number: **(702) 796-1116**
Location: *See above map.*

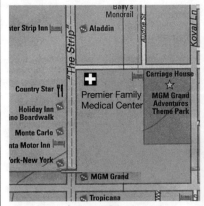

Premier Family Medical Center
111 E. Harmon Ave. (next to MGM)
Las Vegas, NV
Main Number: **(702) 891-8606**
Location: *See above map.*

University Medical Center
Quick Care Center
1769 Russell Rd
Las Vegas, NV
Main Number: **(702) 261-3600**
Location: *See map (left).*

Las Vegas Area Hospitals

Boulder City Hospital
901 Adams Street
Boulder City, NV
Main Number: **(702) 293-4111**
Location: Near intersection of Adams
Street and Buchanan Blvd.

Desert Springs Hospital
2075 E. Flamingo Rd
Las Vegas, NV
Main Number: (702) 733-8800
Emergency: (702) 369-7647
Maternity Center: (702) 894-5656
Location: *See above map.*

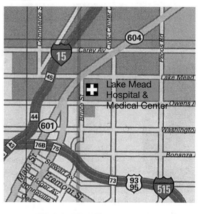

Lake Mead Hospital
Medical Center
1409 E. Lake Mead Blvd.
N. Las Vegas, NV
Main Number: (702) 649-7711
Emergency: (702) 657-5512
www.Tenethealth.com/LakeMead
Location: *See above map.*

Mountainview Hospital
3100 N. Tenaya Way
Las Vegas, NV
Main Number: (702) 255-5000
Emergency: (702) 255-5025
Maternity: (702) 255-5137
www.mountainview -hospital.com
Location: Near intersection of N. Tenaya
Way and W. Cheyenne Ave.

medical guide

Nellis Federal Hospital
4700 Las Vegas Blvd. N.
Las Vegas, NV
Main Number: **(702) 653-2222**
Location: Near intersection of Las Vegas Blvd. N. and **???**

Summerlin Hospital and Medical Center
657 Town Center Dr.
Las Vegas, NV
Main Number: **(702) 233-7000**
Emergency: **(702) 233-7200**
The BirthPlace: **(702) 233-7100**
Location: Near intersection of Town Center Drive and Summerlin Pkwy.

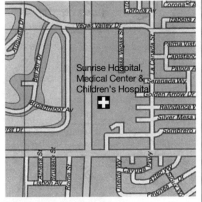

Sunrise Hospital and Medical Center
3186 S. Maryland Parkway
Las Vegas, NV
Main Number: **(702) 731-8000**
Emergency Room: **(702) 731-8080**
Location: *See above map.*

Sunrise Children's Hospital
3186 Maryland Pkwy
Las Vegas, NV
Main Number: **(702) 731-8000**
Pediatric Emergency: **(702) 731-8181**
Kids' Healthcare: **(702) 731-0500**
Parent Advice line: **(702) 731-5437**
Location: *See above map.*

St. Rose Dominican Hospital
102 E. Lake Mead Dr.
Henderson, NV
Main Number: **(702) 564-2622**
Emergency: **(702) 564-4600**
Location: Near intersection of W. Lake Mead Drive and Highway 93

University Medical Center
1800 W. Charleston Blvd.
Las Vegas, NV
Main Number: **(702) 383-2000**
Specialties: Burn care unit, pediatrician staffed ER, trauma center, Cancer Center
Location: *See above map.*

Valley Hospital
620 Shadow Lane
Las Vegas, NV
Main Number: **(702) 388-4000**
Emergency: **(702) 388-4500**
Babies are Beautiful: **(702) 671-8501**
Cradle Corner: **(702) 671-8523**
Location: *See above map.*

 hospital or medical center

chapter eight

- Directory
- Index
- Order Forms

Airlines

Aerolineas Argentinas	800-333-0276
Air Canada	800-776-3000
Alaska Airlines	800-426-0333
American Airlines	800-433-7300
American Trans Air	800-435-9282
American West Airlines	800-235-9292
British Airways	800-247-9297
Canada 3000	800-998-7958
Canadian Airlines	800-426-7000
China Airlines	800-227-5118
Condor German Airlines	800-524-6975
Continental Airlines	800-523-3273
Delta Airlines	800-221-1212
Finnair	800-950-5000
Frontier Airlines	800-432-1359
Hawaiian Airlines	800-525-3663
Japan Airlines	800-525-3663
KLM Airlines	800-374-7747
Korean Air	800-438-5000
Lacasa Airlines	800-225-2525
Lufthansa	800-645-3880
Mexicana Arilines	800-531-7921
Midway Airlines	800-650-7844
Midwest Express	800-452-2022
Northwest Airlines	800-225-2525
Quantas Airways	800-227-4500
Reno Air	800-736-6247
Singapore Airlines	800-742-3333
Skywest-Delta Connection	800-435-9417
Southwest Airlines	800-435-9792
Taca Airlines	800-535-8780
Trans World Airlines	800-892-1976
United Airlines	800-241-6522
USair	800-428-4322
Western Pacific Airlines	800-930-3030

Amusement Places

Akropolis Sports Ctr
3896 Swenson St
Las Vegas .... (702) 735-2000

All American Sport Park Inc
121 E Sunset
Las Vegas .... (702) 796-6338

Arcade Of Pros
3655 S Durango Dr
Las Vegas .... (702) 341-8118

Atari© Adventure Arcade
Riviera Hotel & Casino
2901 Las Vegas Blvd. South
Las Vegas .... (702) 734-5110

Battletech Center
3053 Las Vegas Blvd S
Las Vegas .... (702) 369-3583

Circus Circus Enterprises Inc
2880 Las Vegas Blvd S
Las Vegas .... (702) 734-0410

Club Fun Time USA Pizza
3665 S Rainbow Blvd
Las Vegas .... (702) 222-0300

Cyber Station
Forum Shops
3500 Las Vegas Blvd S
Las Vegas .... (702) 893-3350

Desert Storm Paintball Games
1213 N Tenaya Way
Las Vegas .... (702) 363-4055

Discovery Zone Inc
2020 Olympic Ave
Henderson .... (702) 434-9950

Discovery Zone Inc
3165 N Rainbow Blvd
Las Vegas .... (702) 656-3000

Formula K Family Fun Park
2980 S Sandhill Rd
Las Vegas .... (702) 431-7223

Grand Slam USA
2880 Las Vegas Blvd S
Las Vegas .... (702) 794-3939

Gymboree
918 S Valley View Blvd
Las Vegas .... (702) 877-0074

Luxor Live
Luxor Hotel & Casino
3900 Las Vegas Blvd. S
Las Vegas .... (702) 262-4000

MGM Grand Adventures Park
3799 Las Vegas Blvd S
Las Vegas .... (702) 891-7777

Mountasia Family Funn Ctr
2050 Olympic Ave
Henderson .... (702) 898-7777

Mutiny Bay
Treasure Island
3300 Las Vegas Blvd. S
Las Vegas .... (702) 894-7111

Paintball Games Of Las Vegas
3888 W Sahara Ave
Las Vegas .... (702) 459-3459

Paintball's Adventure Quest
1401 N Decatur Blvd
Las Vegas .... (702) 647-0000

Parque Divertido
1811 S Commerce St
Las Vegas .... (702) 384-7912

Pocket Change
4300 Meadows Ln
Meadows Mall
Las Vegas .... (702) 878-8776

Richard Petty Driving Exprnc
7000 Las Vegas Blvd N
Las Vegas .... (702) 643-4343

Sega© Virtualand Arcade
Luxor Hotel & Casino
3900 Las Vegas Blvd. S
Las Vegas .... (702) 262-4555

Slipgate
2980 S Sandhill Rd
Las Vegas .... (702) 798-7211

Stratosphere Corp
2000 Las Vegas Blvd S
Las Vegas .... (702) 382-4446

Tilt Family Amusement Ctr
1300 W Sunset Rd
Henderson . . . . (702) 451-3688
Treasure Island Corp
3300 Las Vegas Blvd S
Las Vegas . . . . (702) 894-7111
Ultrazone
2555 S Maryland Pkwy
Las Vegas . . . . (702) 734-1577
US Red Rock Visitors Ctr
1000 Scenic Dr
Las Vegas . . . . (702) 363-1921
Vekoma Of The America's
7340 Obannon Dr
Las Vegas . . . . (702) 341-7248
Virtual World Entertainment
3055 S Las Vegas Blvd # 11
Las Vegas . . . . (702) 369-3583
Wet 'N Wild
2601 Las Vegas Blvd S
Las Vegas . . . . (702) 734-0088

Archery

Archery Plus
4001 S Decatur Blvd # 473
Las Vegas . . . . (702) 631-4777
Pacific Archery Sales Equip
4084 Schiff Dr
Las Vegas . . . . (702) 367-1505

Art Galleries

Addi Bally's Galleries
3645 Las Vegas Blvd S
Las Vegas . . . . (702) 737-9795
Addi Galleries Intl
2901 Las Vegas Blvd S
Las Vegas . . . . (702) 796-6552
Alphamega Gallery
5608 Boulder Hwy
Las Vegas . . . . (702) 451-8608
American Collectibles
3871 S Valley View Blvd
Las Vegas . . . . (702) 871-2737
Apple Bryan Studios
3750 S Valley View Blvd
Las Vegas . . . . (702) 221-0462
Art & Gift Shop
600 Jackson Ave
Las Vegas . . . . (702) 648-4949
Art Affair
3871 S Valley View Blvd # 9
Las Vegas . . . . (702) 368-7888
Art At Your Door
2605 S Decatur Blvd
Las Vegas . . . . (702) 365-9127
Art At Your Door
8605 W Sahara Ave
Las Vegas . . . . (702) 256-7278
Art Encounter
3979 Spring Mountain Rd
Las Vegas . . . . (702) 227-0220

Art From The Heart
4020 N Tenaya Way
Las Vegas . . . . (702) 656-8250
Art Group
3119 E Post Rd
Las Vegas . . . . (702) 896-2218
Art Of St Jules
2719 Burton Ave
Las Vegas . . . . (702) 880-1150
Artv Inc
1752 Industrial Rd
Las Vegas . . . . (702) 732-7779
Azariah Art
1717 S Decatur Blvd
Las Vegas . . . . (702) 870-4278
Azariah Art
3455 Boulder Hwy
Las Vegas . . . . (702) 431-3693
Black To Brite
1750 Marion Dr
Las Vegas . . . . (702) 437-4086
Boulder City Art Guild
1305 Arizona Street
Boulder Dam Hotel
Las Vegas . . . . (702) 293-6284
Brent Thomson Art & Framing
1672 Nevada Hwy
Boulder City . . . . (702) 293-4652
Burk Gal'ry
1305 Arizona St
Boulder City . . . . (702) 293-0500
Carrara Galleries
1236 S Rainbow Blvd
Las Vegas . . . . (702) 877-4299
Celebrity Estate
2735 Industrial Rd
Las Vegas . . . . (702) 735-0553
Centaur Sculpture Galleries
3200 Las Vegas Blvd S
Las Vegas . . . . (702) 737-0004
Charleston Heights Arts Center
800 S. Brush St
Las Vegas . . . . (702) 229-6383
Community College Of Southern Nevada Art
3200 E. Cheyenne Ave
Las Vegas . . . . (702) 643-6060
Contemporary Arts Collective
103 E Charleston Blvd # 102
Las Vegas . . . . (702) 382-3886
Contemporary Arts Collective
304 E. Charleston Blvd.
Las Vegas . . . . (702) 382-3686
Crockett Gallery
2800 W Sahara Ave # 7c
Las Vegas . . . . (702) 253-6336
Debora Spanover Fine Art
1775 E Tropicana Ave # 22
Las Vegas . . . . (702) 739-0072
Diva Art Group
6534 Boxwood Ln
Las Vegas . . . . (702) 227-3342
Donna Beam Fine Arts Gallery
4505 S. Maryland Pkwy
Las Vegas . . . .(702) 895-3893

Duncans Framing Gallery
3220 N Rancho Dr
Las Vegas . . . . (702) 656-3403
Entertaining Images
1300 W Sunset Rd
Henderson . . . . (702) 898-6219
Eternal Treasures
1725 South Rainbow Blvd., Suite 5
Las Vegas . . . . (702) 256-9134
Eternal Treasures
3432 N Bruce St
North Las V... . . . . (702) 642-6580
Fine Line Gallery & Frame Work
4301 S Valley View Blvd # 8
Las Vegas . . . . (702) 248-6072
Fire & Water Gallery
Hotel Plz # 555
Boulder City . . . . (702) 294-4177
Gallerie Michelangelo
3520 Las Vegas Blvd S
Las Vegas . . . . (702) 796-5001
Gallery Michelle
2000 Las Vegas Blvd S # 53
Las Vegas . . . . (702) 384-7811
Gallery Of History Inc
3601 W Sahara Ave
Las Vegas . . . . (702) 364-1000
George Sterman Fine Art
114 N 3rd St
Las Vegas . . . . (702) 382-1971
George Sturman Fine Art
3111 Bel Air Dr
Las Vegas . . . . (702) 734-2787
Gideon Gallery Ltd
4011 Industrial Rd
Las Vegas . . . . (702) 791-2777
Glass Artistry
4200 West Desert Inn Road
Las Vegas . . . . (702) 221-8494
Image On Canvas
4300 Meadows Ln
Las Vegas . . . . (702) 870-6906
Jezzard Galleries
3650 S Decatur Blvd # 23-130
Las Vegas . . . .(702) 364-0242
Joy People
1931 Helen Ave
North Las V... . . . . (702) 646-5667
Kelley Framing & Art Gallery
300 Promenade Blvd # 2018
Las Vegas . . . .(702) 878-9099
Las Vegas Art Museum
6130 W Charleston Blvd
Las Vegas . . . . (702) 259-4458
Lassen Publishing
831 Pilot Rd # 5a
Las Vegas . . . . (702) 263-9200
Le Gallerie Luministe
3205 Pinehurst Dr # A
Las Vegas . . . . (702) 796-0007
Left Of Ctr Gallery
2207 W Gowan Rd
North Las V... . . . . (702) 647-7378
Legends Of Art Inc

6000 S Eastern Ave
Las Vegas . . . . (702) 736-7466
Mark Masuoka Gallery Inc
417 S Martin L King Blvd
Las Vegas . . . . (702) 366-0377
Martiz Gallery
6495 W Oquendo Rd
Las Vegas . . . . (702) 248-7088
MNJ Distribution
1330 S Commerce St
Las Vegas . . . . (702) 384-2061
Moapa Valley Artist's Gallery
387 S Moapa Valley Blvd
Overton . . . . (702) 397-8323
Moonstruck Gallery
6322 West Sahara Avenue
Las Vegas . . . . (702) 364-0531
Multi-Media Visual Art Inc
1055 E Flamingo Rd
Las Vegas . . . . (702) 734-7185
Nava-Hopi Gallery
1300 W Sunset Rd
Henderson . . . . (702) 458-2254
Nevada Institute For Contemporary Art
3455 E. Flamingo Rd
Las Vegas . . . . (702) 434-2666
Nubian Queens
2901 W Washington Ave # C111
Las Vegas . . . . (702) 459-0846
One Art USA
9230 W Sahara Ave
Las Vegas . . . . (702) 363-7355
One Art USA
8140 S Eastern Ave
Las Vegas . . . . (702) 897-7320
P S Galleries
3645 Las Vegas Blvd S
Las Vegas . . . . (702) 733-0705
Picture It
4874 W Lone Mountain Rd # C102
Las Vegas . . . . (702) 655-0543
Prized Possessions
4601 W Sahara Ave # H
Las Vegas . . . . (702) 220-4902
Purcell Studio
2000 Pinto Rd
Henderson . . . . (702) 564-9565
Regal Art Gallery
3315 E Russell Rd # K
Las Vegas . . . . (702) 436-4146
Richard Tam Enterprises
2140 W Charleston Blvd
Las Vegas . . . . (702) 382-5498
Ron Lee's World Of Clowns Inc
330 Carousel Pkwy
Henderson . . . .(702) 434-1700
Ryan Gallery & Picture Frames
2972 S Rainbow Blvd
Las Vegas . . . .(702) 368-0545
Searchlight Gallery
575 S Highway 95
Searchlight . . . . (702) 297-1540

Seven Rings Gallery
2650 S Maryland Pkwy # A1
Las Vegas . . . . (702) 732-2131
Studio West Custom Framing
8447 W Lake Mead Blvd
Las Vegas . . . . (702) 228-1901
Sunset Picture Framing
730 W Sunset Rd
Henderson . . . . (702) 558-7654
Thomas Charles Fine Art
4301 S Valley View Blvd
Las Vegas . . . . (702) 248-6056
Thomas Charles Gallery
3500 Las Vegas Blvd S
Las Vegas . . . . (702) 369-8000
Timeless Treasures
6125 W Tropicana Ave
Las Vegas . . . . (702) 222-3661
Tribal Art
4421 Lookout Peak Way
Las Vegas . . . . (702) 658-4229
Trinity Black Art Gallery
2657 Las Vegas Blvd N
North Las V... . . . . (702) 399-1125
Uncle Don's
1618 Las Vegas Blvd N
North Las V... . . . . (702) 642-7151
Unique Art Gallery
925 S Rainbow Blvd
Las Vegas . . . . (702) 870-2121
Valley Oriental
4255 Spring Mountain Rd # C106
Las Vegas . . . . (702) 365-9228
Veterans Art Museum
700 E Naples Dr
Las Vegas . . . . (702) 792-8387
Wallscapes
1717 S Decatur Blvd
Las Vegas . . . . (702) 259-7055
Winged Horse Gallerie
3750 S Valley View Blvd # 11
Las Vegas . . . . (702) 227-3445
Wyland Gallery Of Las Vegas
3200 Las Vegas Blvd S # 322
Las Vegas . . . . (702) 699-9970
Youngblood Motorsport Gallery
3685 S Highland Dr
Las Vegas . . . .(702) 876-5900

Art Instruction

Art For Kids
900 S Valley View Blvd
Las Vegas . . . . (702) 258-4088
Supplies 4 Less
13001 Las Vegas Blvd S
Las Vegas . . . . (702) 361-3600

Attractions

A. J. Hackett Bungy
810 Circus Circus Dr
Las Vegas . . . .(702) 385-4321

Adventure Canyon Log Flume
Buffalo Bill's Resort Stateline
Las Vegas
Adventuredome At Circus Circus
Circus Circus
2880 Las Vegas Blvd. South.
Las Vegas . . . . (702) 794-3939
All American Sportpark
121 E. Sunset Rd. (At Las Vegas Blvd.)
Las Vegas . . . . (702) 798-7777
Atlantis Fountain Show
Forum Shops At Caesars Palace
3500 Las Vegas Blvd S
Las Vegas . . . . (702) 893-4800
Big Shot
Stratosphere Hotel And Casino
2000 Las Vegas Blvd. S.
Las Vegas . . . . (702) 380-7777
Bonnie & Clyde's "Death Car"
Primm . . . . (702) 382-1212
Bonnie Springs / Old Nevada
1 Bonnie Springs Ranch Rd
Old Nevada . . . . (702) 875-4191
Buccaneer Bay Sea Battle
Treasure Island Hotel Front Entrance
3300 Las Vegas Blvd. South
Las Vegas . . . . (702) 650-7400
Buffalo Bills
Las Vegas . . . . (702) 382-1212
Caesars Palace
3570 Las Vegas Blvd. South
Las Vegas . . . . (702) 731-7333
Cinema Ride
Forum Shops At Caesars
3500 Las Vegas Blvd. S.
Las Vegas . . . . (702) 369-4008
Circus Circus
2880 Las Vegas Blvd. S
Las Vegas . . . . (702) 734-0410
City Of Las Vegas Fire Department
Las Vegas . . . . (702) 383-2888
Cranberry World West
1301 American Pacific Dr.
Las Vegas . . . . (702) 566-7160
Dansey's Indoor Race Track
Las Vegas . . . . (702) 453-7223
Desert Storm Paintball Games
Las Vegas . . . . (702) 595-2555
Desperado Roller Coaster
Buffalos Bill's Resort Casino
Las Vegas . . . . (702) 382-1212
Discovery Zone
2020 Olympic Ave
Henderson . . . . (702) 434-9950
Dolphin Habitat
Mirage Hotel
3400 Las Vegas Blvd S
Las Vegas . . . . (702) 791-7111
Dragon Battle
Excalibur Hotel
3850 Las Vegas Blvd. South
Las Vegas . . . . (702) 597-7777

directory

Ethel M Chocolate Factory And Cactus Garden
2 Cactus Garden Dr
Las Vegas . . . . (702) 433-2500

Famous Brands Marshmellow Factory
1180 Marshmallow Lane
Las Vegas . . . . (702) 564-3878

Fantasy Faire
Excaliiber
3850 S Las Vegas Bl
Las Vegas . . . . (702) 597-7777

Festival Fountain
Forum Shops
3500 Las Vegas Blvd S
Las Vegas . . . . (702) 893-4800

Flyaway Indoor Skydiving
200 Convention Center Drive
Las Vegas . . . . (702) 731-4768

Formula K Family Fun Park
2980 South Sandhill Rd
Las Vegas . . . . (702) 431-7223

Fountains Of Bellagio
3600 Las Vegas Blvd. South
Las Vegas . . . . (702) 693-7111

Funtazmic
4975 Polaris Av
Las Vegas . . . . (702) 795-4386

Futuristic Motion Theaters
Luxor Hotel
3900 Las Vegas Blvd. South
Las Vegas . . . . (702) 262-4000

Gameworks
Showcase Mall
3785 S Las Vegas Blvd
Las Vegas . . . . (702) 432-Game

Gilcrease Nature Sanctuary
8103 Racel Street
Las Vegas . . . . (702) 645-4224

Gold Coast Hotel & Casino
4000 W. Flamingo Rd
Las Vegas . . . . (702) 367-7111

Grand Slam Canyon Adventuredome
2880 Las Vegas Blvd. S
Circus Circus
Las Vegas . . . .(702) 734-0410

Henderson Bird Viewing Preserve
2400 Moser Drive
Henderson . . . . (702) 565-2063

Las Vegas Mini Gran Prix
1401 N. Rainbow Blvd
Las Vegas . . . .(702) 259-7000

Las Vegas Motor Speedway
Las Vegas . . . .(702) 644-4444

Luxor
Luxor Hotel & Casino
3900 Las Vegas Blvd. S
Las Vegas . . . .(702) 262-4555

M & M World
Showcase Mall
Las Vegas . . . .(702) 597-3122

Magic & Movie Hall Of Fame
Las Vegas . . . .(702) 737-1343

Magic Motion Machine
Excalibur Hotel
3850 Las Vegas Blvd. South
Las Vegas . . . . (702) 597-7777

Manhattan Express
New York-New York
Las Vegas . . . . (702) 740-6969

Masquerade Village
Rio Suite Hotel & Casino
Las Vegas . . . .(702) 252-7777

Mccarran Airport
5795 Paradise Rd
Las Vegas . . . . (702) 261-5153

Meadows Mall
4300 Meadows Ln
Las Vegas . . . .(702) 878-4849

MGM Grand Adventures Theme Park
3799 Las Vegas Blvd South
Las Vegas . . . . (702) 891-7979

Mini Gran Prix
Las Vegas . . . .(702) 259-7000

Motown Cafe
Las Vegas . . . .(702) 740-6440

Mountasia Family Fun Center
2050 Olympic Ave
Henderson . . . . (702) 898-7777

Mystic Falls
Sam's Town
5111 Boulder Hwy
Las Vegas . . . . (702) 456-7777

Nellis Air Force Base
Salt Lake Hwy
Las Vegas . . . . (702) 652-4018

Nevada Zoological Foundation
Las Vegas . . . .(702) 647-4685

New York New York
Las Vegas . . . .(702) 740-6969

Omnimax Theater
Caesar's Palace
3570 Las Vegas Blvd. S
Las Vegas . . . . (702) 731-7900

Planet Hollywood
Las Vegas . . . .(702) 791-9827

Planetarium
Cheyenne Campus Of The Community College
3200 E. Cheyenne Ave
Las Vegas . . . . (702) 651-5059

Powerhouse Indoor Climbing Center
Las Vegas . . . .(702) 254-5604

Primadonna Resorts
Las Vegas . . . .(800) 386-7867

Race For Atlantis
Forum Shops At Caesars Palace
3570 Las Vegas Blvd S
Las Vegas . . . . (702) 733-9000

Rocks And Ropes
Las Vegas . . . .(702) 434-3388

Ron Lee's World Of Clowns Factory & Tour
330 Carousel Pkwy
Las Vegas . . . . (702) 434-1700

Sahara Speedworld
The Sahara
Las Vegas . . . .(702) 737-2750

Santa Fe Hotel & Casino - Ice Skating Rink
Las Vegas . . . . (702) 658-4991
Saturn Of West Sahara
5325 W. Sahara Ave
Las Vegas . . . . (702) 362-0733
Scandia Family Fun Center
2900 Sirius Ave
Las Vegas . . . . (702) 364-0070
Secret Garden Of Siegfried & Roy
Mirage Hotel.
3400 Las Vegas Blvd S
Las Vegas . . . .(702) 791-7111
Showcase Mall
3785 Las Vegas Blvd S
Las Vegas . . . . (702) 597-3122
Southern Nevada Zoological-Botanical Park
1775 N Rancho Dr
Las Vegas . . . . (702) 648-5955
Sports Hall-Of-Fame
18 Fremont St
Las Vegas Club Hotel & Casino
Las Vegas . . . . (702) 385-1664
Star Trek: The Experience
Las Vegas Hilton
Las Vegas . . . .(702) 697-8700
Stratosphere
Las Vegas . . . .(702) 380-7777
Sunset Stampede
Sam's Town
5111 Boulder Hwy
Las Vegas . . . .(702) 456-7777
The Forum Shops At Caesars Palace
Las Vegas . . . . (702) 731-7990
The Fountains Of Bellagio
3600 Las Vegas Blvd. South
Las Vegas . . . . (702) 693-7111
The Menagerie Carousel
4300 Meadow Ln.
The Meadows Mall
Las Vegas . . . . (702) 878-4849
The Showcase
3785 Las Vegas Blvd. S.
Las Vegas . . . . (702) 597-3122
Tiger Habitat
3801 Las Vegas Blvd. S.
Tropicana
Las Vegas . . . . (702) 739-2222
Turbo Drop
Buffalo Bill's Resort
Las Vegas . . . .(702) 382-1212
Ultrazone, The Ultimate Laser Adventure
2555 S. Maryland Parkway
Las Vegas . . . . (702) 734-1577
United States Post Office
1001 E. Sunset Rd
Las Vegas . . . . (702) 361-9242
Vegas Chip Factory
2945 N. Martin Luther King Blvd.
Las Vegas . . . . (702) 727-6900
Volcano
Mirage Hotel
3400 Las Vegas Blvd S
Las Vegas . . . . (702) 791-7111

Wet'n Wild
2601 Las Vegas Blvd S
Las Vegas . . . . (702) 737-3819
White Tiger Habitat
The Mirage
3400 Las Vegas Blvd. S.
Las Vegas . . . . (702) 791-7111
Wildlife Habitat
Flamingo Hilton Hotel:
3555 Las Vegas Blvd
Las Vegas . . . . (702) 733-3111
Wildlife Walk
Tropicana
3801 S. Las Vegas Blvd
Las Vegas . . . . (702) 739-2222
World Of Coca-Cola
3785 S. Las Vegas Blvd.
Las Vegas

Automobile Renting

A A Auto Rentals
1613 E Sahara Ave
Las Vegas . . . . (702) 893-1333
A-Abbey Rent-A-Car
4990 Paradise Rd
Las Vegas . . . . (702) 795-7380
A-Fairway Rent-A-Car
2915 Industrial Rd
Las Vegas . . . . (702) 369-7216
AAA Cash Deposit Car Rental
3317 Las Vegas Blvd S
Las Vegas . . . . (702) 731-3600
Aax-Press Rent A Car
3767 Las Vegas Blvd S
Las Vegas . . . . (702) 795-4008
ABS Rent-A-Car
3100 W Sahara Ave # 110
Las Vegas . . . . (702) 368-4061
Agency Rent A Car
4251 Boulder Hwy
Las Vegas . . . . (702) 451-1507
Airport Rent-A-Car
3325 Las Vegas Blvd S
Las Vegas . . . . (702) 732-4232
Airport Rent-A-Car
4990 Paradise Rd # 109
Las Vegas . . . . (702) 795-0800
Alamo Rent A Car
4263 Boulder Hwy
Las Vegas . . . . (702) 435-1449
Alamo Rent A Car
6855 Bermuda Rd
Las Vegas . . . . (702) 263-8411
All State Car Rental
1815 E Sahara Ave
Las Vegas . . . . (702) 733-7717
Allstate Car & Truck Rental
5175 Rent Car Rd
Las Vegas . . . . (702) 736-6147
Allstate Car Rental
330 N Gibson Rd
Henderson . . . .(702) 565-7937

Allstate Car Rental
2901 Las Vegas Blvd S
Las Vegas . . . . (702) 794-9457
Allstate Car Rental
3000 Las Vegas Blvd S
Las Vegas . . . . (702) 732-6288
Allstate Car Rental
3667 Las Vegas Blvd S
Las Vegas . . . . (702) 791-0241
Allstate Car Rental
1 N Main St
Las Vegas . . . . (702) 382-2918
Allstate Car Rental
Base Exchange Bldg 340
Nellis Afb . . . . (702) 644-5567
Allstate Car Rental Sales
2525 S Bruce St
Las Vegas . . . . (702) 870-1500
Americar
5021 Swenson St
Las Vegas . . . . (702) 597-0427
Americar Rental Systems
4700 Paradise Rd
Las Vegas . . . . (702) 798-6100
Avis Rent A Car
5164 Rent Car Rd
Las Vegas . . . . (702) 261-5595
Avis Rent A Car
3645 Las Vegas Blvd S
Las Vegas . . . .(702) 736-1935
Avis Rent A Car
3000 Paradise Rd
Las Vegas . . . . (702) 734-8011
Avis Rent A Car
3570 Las Vegas Blvd S
Las Vegas . . . . (702) 731-7790
Brooks Rent A Car
3041 Las Vegas Blvd S
Las Vegas . . . . (702) 735-3344
Budget Rent A Car
3267 Las Vegas Blvd S
Las Vegas . . . . (702) 736-6107
Budget Rent A Car
2830 Las Vegas Blvd S
Las Vegas . . . . (702) 731-6776
Budget Rent A Car
4475 W Tropicana Ave
Las Vegas . . . .(702) 362-8668
Budget Rent A Car
3743 Las Vegas Blvd S
Las Vegas . . . .(702) 736-2144
Budget Rent A Car
3535 Las Vegas Blvd S
Las Vegas . . . . (702) 732-9108
Budget Rent A Car
5188 Paradise Rd
Las Vegas . . . . (702) 736-1212
Budget Rent A Car
1900 S Casino Dr
Laughlin . . . .(702) 299-0200
Budget Rent A Car
Flamingo Hilton
Laughlin . . . .(702) 299-9200
Classy Chassis Motor Co

3740 S Valley View Blvd
Las Vegas . . . . (702) 889-4900
Convertible Rentals
5021 Swenson St
Las Vegas . . . . (702) 597-0427
Cormier Leasing & Sales
Po Box 94863
Las Vegas . . . . (702) 795-0516
Corvette Rentals
5021 Swenson St
Las Vegas . . . . (702) 736-2592
Dollar Rent A Car
129 Fremont St
Las Vegas . . . . (702) 383-8552
Dollar Rent A Car
3713 Las Vegas Blvd S
Las Vegas . . . . (702) 791-6865
Dollar Rent A Car
3555 Las Vegas Blvd S
Las Vegas . . . . (702) 732-4180
Dollar Rent A Car
5301 Rent Car Rd
Las Vegas . . . . (702) 739-8408
Dollar Rent A Car
3900 Las Vegas Blvd S
Las Vegas . . . . (702) 262-4385
Dollar Rent A Car
3300 Las Vegas Blvd S
Las Vegas . . . . (702) 737-1081
Dollar Rent A Car
3400 Las Vegas Blvd S
Las Vegas . . . . (702) 791-7425
Dollar Rent A Car
2880 Las Vegas Blvd S
Las Vegas . . . . (702) 369-9302
Dollar Rent A Car
3850 Las Vegas Blvd S
Las Vegas . . . . (702) 736-1369
Dollar Rent A Car
3799 Las Vegas Blvd S
Las Vegas . . . .(702) 891-3012
Dollar Rent A Car
206 N 3rd St
Las Vegas . . . . (702) 474-0060
Enterprise Rent A Car
280 N Gibson Rd
Henderson . . . . (702) 558-4160
Enterprise Rent A Car
3740 Las Vegas Blvd S
Las Vegas . . . . (702) 734-3977
Enterprise Rent A Car
5185 W Sahara Ave
Las Vegas . . . . (702) 873-5470
Enterprise Rent A Car
2711 E Sahara Ave
Las Vegas . . . . (702) 431-0884
Enterprise Rent A Car
4645 W Tropicana Ave
Las Vegas . . . . (702) 597-2515
Enterprise Rent A Car
6900 W Sahara Ave
Las Vegas . . . . (702) 242-3277

Enterprise Rent A Car
2580 Duneville St # 108
Las Vegas . . . . (702) 368-3772

Enterprise Rent A Car
4950 Alta Dr
Las Vegas . . . . (702) 870-4144

Enterprise Rent A Car
3470 Boulder Hwy
Las Vegas . . . . (702) 457-0990

Enterprise Rent A Car
5800 W Sahara Ave
Las Vegas . . . . (702) 368-6972

Enterprise Rent A Car
2575 E Sahara Ave
Las Vegas . . . . (702) 641-1078

Enterprise Rent A Car
2333 S Decatur Blvd
Las Vegas . . . . (702) 362-2053

Enterprise Rent A Car
3200 S Rancho Dr
Las Vegas . . . . (702) 365-6662

Enterprise Rent A Car
5032 Palo Verde Rd
Las Vegas . . . . (702) 795-8842

Enterprise Rent A Car
2121 E Sahara Ave
Las Vegas . . . . (702) 735-2124

Enterprise Rent A Car
3400 S Jones Blvd # 14b
Las Vegas . . . . (702) 871-8508

Enterprise Rent A Car
3745 Boulder Hwy
Las Vegas . . . . (702) 457-0066

Enterprise Rent A Car
1900 S Casino Dr
Laughlin . . . . (702) 298-1822

Exchange Rent-A-Car
5021 Swenson St
Las Vegas . . . . (702) 597-0427

Fairway Rent-A-Car System
2915 Industrial Rd
Las Vegas . . . . (702) 369-8533

First Acceptance
8801 Las Vegas Blvd S
Las Vegas . . . . (702) 896-5774

First Leasing
2570 S Eastern Ave
Las Vegas . . . . (702) 641-7828

Funway Rentals
5021 Swenson St
Las Vegas . . . . (702) 798-7774

Group Tour Car Rental Svc
5101 Rent Car Rd
Las Vegas . . . . (702) 736-1234

Gsa Sato
5021 Swenson St
Las Vegas . . . . (702) 597-0682

Hertz Rent A Car
5300 Rent Car Rd
Las Vegas . . . . (702) 736-4900

Hertz Rent A Car
3145 Las Vegas Blvd S
Las Vegas . . . . (702) 735-4597

Ladki International Rent A Car
795 E Tropicana Ave
Las Vegas . . . . (702) 597-1501

Lease Mark
390 W Mesquite Blvd
Mesquite . . . . (702) 346-3460

Lloyd's International Rent Car
3951 Las Vegas Blvd S
Las Vegas . . . . (702) 736-2663

Luxury Classic Sports
3939 Las Vegas Blvd S
Las Vegas . . . . (702) 736-2610

Master Lease Plan
5030 Paradise Rd
Las Vegas . . . . (702) 739-1951

Montgomery Ward Car Rental
376 E Warm Springs Rd
Las Vegas . . . . (702) 896-5566

National Car Rental
5233 Rent Car Rd
Las Vegas . . . . (702) 261-5391

Nellis Rent-A-Car
3735 N Nellis Blvd
Las Vegas . . . . (702) 643-8400

Nevada Tourist Svc Ctr
3713 Las Vegas Blvd S
Las Vegas . . . . (702) 736-7671

Practical Rent A Car
3765 Las Vegas Blvd S # H
Las Vegas . . . . (702) 798-5253

Practical Systems Inc
1500 E Tropicana Ave # 123
Las Vegas . . . . (702) 798-0025

Preferred Rent-A-Car
700 E Naples Dr
Las Vegas . . . . (702) 894-9936

Rent-A-Vette
5021 Swenson St
Las Vegas . . . . (702) 736-8016

Rent-A-Wreck
2310 Las Vegas Blvd S
Las Vegas . . . . (702) 474-0037

Resort Rent A Car
5080 Paradise Rd
Las Vegas . . . . (702) 795-3800

S & C Leasing Corp
2800 W Sahara Ave
Las Vegas . . . . (702) 364-1003

Sahara Avenue Motor Cars
1875 E Sahara Ave
Las Vegas . . . . (702) 369-5555

Sav-Mor Rent-A-Car
5101 Rent Car Rd
Las Vegas . . . . (702) 736-1234

Savmor Rental Car
2535 Las Vegas Blvd S
Las Vegas . . . . (702) 737-2839

Sears Car & Truck Rental
6188 S Paradise Rd
Las Vegas . . . . (702) 736-8006

Sears Car & Truck Rental
3105 E Sahara Ave
Las Vegas . . . . (702) 457-2277

directory

Sears Car & Truck Rental
5188 Paradise Rd
Las Vegas . . . . (702) 736-8006
Select Leasing Neveda Inc
1500 E Tropicana Ave
Las Vegas . . . . (702) 795-7740
Snappy Car Rental
6135 W Sahara Ave
Las Vegas . . . . (702) 367-4999
Sports Car Rentals
5021 Swenson St
Las Vegas . . . . (702) 736-2592
Sunbelt Car Rental
3317 Las Vegas Blvd S
Las Vegas . . . . (702) 731-3600
Thrifty Car Rental
5750 W Sahara Ave
Las Vegas . . . . (702) 362-0315
Thrifty Car Rental
376 E Warm Springs Rd
Las Vegas . . . . (702) 896-7600
Unique Movie Cars
641 Middlegate Rd
Henderson . . . . (702) 566-6193
Us Rent A Car
4700 Paradise Rd
Las Vegas . . . . (702) 798-6100
Value Rent A Car
3025 Las Vegas Blvd S # 116
Las Vegas . . . . (702) 735-3758
Value Rent A Car
301 Fremont St
Las Vegas . . . . (702) 388-2142
World-Wide
5021 Swenson St
Las Vegas . . . . (702) 597-0427

Banks

American Bancorp Of Nevada
4425 Spring Mountain Rd
Las Vegas . . . . (702) 362-7222
American Bank Of Commerce
4425 Spring Mountain Rd
Las Vegas . . . . (702) 362-7222
Bank Of America
900 Nevada Hwy
Boulder City . . . . (702) 654-6000
Bank Of America
2798 N Green Valley Pkwy
Henderson . . . . (702) 654-1000
Bank Of America
4854 W Lone Mountain Rd
Las Vegas . . . . (702) 654-1000
Bank Of America
101 Convention Center Dr
Las Vegas . . . . (702) 654-1000
Bank Of America
1140 E Desert Inn Rd
Las Vegas . . . . (702) 654-1000
Bank Of America
3580 S Jones Blvd
Las Vegas . . . . (702) 654-1000

Bank Of America
835 N Martin L King Blvd
Las Vegas . . . . (702) 654-1000
Bank Of America
2500 E Desert Inn Rd
Las Vegas . . . . (702) 654-1000
Bank Of America
3325 E Russell Rd
Las Vegas . . . . (702) 654-1000
Bank Of America
3220 Las Vegas Blvd N
Las Vegas . . . . (702) 654-1000
Bank Of America
3150 N Rainbow Blvd
Las Vegas . . . . (702) 654-1000
Bank Of America
1801 S Rainbow Blvd
Las Vegas . . . . (702) 654-1000
Bank Of America
2595 Fremont St
Las Vegas . . . . (702) 654-1000
Bank Of America
4610 W Sahara Ave
Las Vegas . . . . (702) 654-1000
Bank Of America
300 S Decatur Blvd
Las Vegas . . . . (702) 654-1000
Bank Of America
6900 Westcliff Dr
Las Vegas . . . . (702) 654-1000
Bank Of America
3430 E Tropicana Ave
Las Vegas . . . . (702) 654-1000
Bank Of America
1077 E Sahara Ave
Las Vegas . . . . (702) 654-1000
Bank Of America
901 Rancho Ln
Las Vegas . . . . (702) 654-1000
Bank Of America
801 N Nellis Blvd
Las Vegas . . . . (702) 654-1000
Bank Of America
4795 S Maryland Pkwy
Las Vegas . . . . (702) 654-1000
Bank Of America
4850 W Flamingo Rd
Las Vegas . . . . (702) 654-1000
Bank Of America
4801 W Charleston Blvd
Las Vegas . . . . (702) 654-1000
Bank Of America
4111 E Charleston Blvd
Las Vegas . . . . (702) 654-1000
Bank Of America
3680 E Flamingo Rd
Las Vegas . . . . (702) 654-1000
Bank Of America
1975 S Casino Dr
Laughlin . . . . (702) 298-2250
Bank Of America
81 W Mesquite Blvd
Mesquite . . . . (702) 346-5271

directory

Bank Of America
2060 Las Vegas Blvd N
North Las V... . . . . (702) 654-1000

Bank Of America
140 N Moapa Valley Blvd
Overton . . . . (702) 397-2300

Bank Of America Nevada
300 S 4th St # 2
Las Vegas . . . . (702) 654-1000

Bankwest Of Nevada
2700 W Sahara Ave
Las Vegas . . . . (702) 248-4200

California Federal Bank
2891 N Green Valley Pkwy
Henderson . . . . (702) 458-1446

California Federal Bank
2920 S Rainbow Blvd # 130
Las Vegas . . . . (702) 367-4110

California Federal Bank
3990 S Maryland Pkwy
Las Vegas . . . . (702) 796-4200

California Federal Bank
398 S Decatur Blvd
Las Vegas . . . . (702) 870-9261

California Federal Bank
2820 W Charleston Blvd
Las Vegas . . . . (702) 367-2300

California Federal Bank
2920 S Rainbow Blvd
Las Vegas . . . . (702) 367-4110

Celebrity Bank Of Nevada
2800 W Sahara Ave # 1a
Las Vegas . . . . (702) 365-9999

Citibank
4110 S Maryland Pkwy
Las Vegas . . . . (702) 734-2484

Citibank
4065 S Jones Blvd
Las Vegas . . . . (702) 364-5664

Citibank
8725 W Sahara Ave
Las Vegas . . . . (702) 797-4444

Citibank
8701 W Sahara Ave
Las Vegas . . . . (702) 228-2500

Citibank Nevada
3900 Paradise Rd # 127
Las Vegas . . . . (702) 796-3030

Citibank Nevada
3900 Paradise Rd # 127
Las Vegas . . . . (702) 796-3000

Citibank Nevada Na
2215 N Rampart Blvd
Las Vegas . . . . (702) 363-8488

Commercial Bank Of Nevada
2820 W Charleston Blvd
Las Vegas . . . . (702) 258-9990

Community Bank Of Nevada
1400 S Rainbow Blvd
Las Vegas . . . . (702) 878-0700

Comstock Bank
333 N Rancho Dr # 810
Las Vegas . . . . (702) 631-1515

Federal Reserve Bank
1912 Civic Center Dr
North Las V... . . . . (702) 399-9959

Fernlee Trading Inc
6767 W Tropicana Ave # 202
Las Vegas . . . . (702) 248-1020

First Financial Investments
3800 Howard Hughes Pkwy
Las Vegas . . . . (702) 735-2017

First Interstate Bank
2501 S Rainbow Blvd
Las Vegas . . . . (702) 385-8000

First Republic Savings Bank
2510 S Maryland Pky
Las Vegas . . . . (702) 792-2200

First Security Bank
701 N Valle Verde Dr
Henderson . . . . (702) 251-1100

First Security Bank
4950 W Flamingo Rd
Las Vegas . . . . (702) 251-1100

First Security Bank
2820 W Charleston Blvd # B15
Las Vegas . . . . (702) 878-5987

First Security Bank
2925 S Rainbow Blvd
Las Vegas . . . . (702) 368-1969

First Security Bank
4813 S Eastern Ave
Las Vegas . . . . (702) 251-1100

First Security Bank
3340 W Sahara Ave
Las Vegas . . . . (702) 251-1100

First Security Bank
2980 W Sahara Ave
Las Vegas . . . . (702) 362-7222

First Security Bank
727 S 9th St
Las Vegas . . . . (702) 362-7222

First Security Bank
1690 E Flamingo Rd
Las Vegas . . . . (702) 362-7222

First Security Bank
520 W Mesquite Blvd
Mesquite . . . . (702) 346-6520

First Security Bank
4050 Losee Rd
North Las V... . . . . (702) 362-7222

First Security Bank Of Nevada
530 Las Vegas Blvd S
Las Vegas . . . . (702) 251-1100

First Security Trust Co
530 Las Vegas Blvd S
Las Vegas . . . . (702) 383-8526

First Suburban Corp
3014 S Rancho Dr
Las Vegas . . . . (702) 251-0990

Goleta National Bank
4170 S Decatur Blvd # D4
Las Vegas . . . . (702) 870-0870

Kirkwood Lending Ctr
6900 Westcliff Dr # 702
Las Vegas . . . . (702) 228-0941

directory

Las Vegas Business Bank
3885 S Maryland Pkwy
Las Vegas . . . . (702) 794-0070

Laughlin National Bank
3100 Needles Hwy # 100
Laughlin . . . . (702) 298-4300

Laughlin National Bank
1775 S Casino Dr
Laughlin . . . . (702) 298-0555

Mesquite State Bank
Po Box 2999
Mesquite . . . . (702) 346-6600

Milwaukee Investment Holding
2920 N Green Valley Pkwy
Henderson . . . . (702) 454-5522

Monicor Motgage Inc
3180 W Sahara Ave # C12b
Las Vegas . . . . (702) 253-0940

National Pacific Mortgage Corp
4530 S Eastern Ave
Las Vegas . . . . (702) 732-0151

Nevada Atm Svc
3200 Polaris Ave
Las Vegas . . . . (702) 365-9493

Nevada State Bank
4602 E Sunset Rd
Henderson . . . .(702) 456-3776

Nevada State Bank
830 S Boulder Hwy
Henderson . . . . (702) 566-8862

Nevada State Bank
8555 W Sahara Ave
Las Vegas . . . . (702) 254-7719

Nevada State Bank
6130 W Tropicana Ave
Las Vegas . . . . (702) 873-2834

Nevada State Bank
450 N Nellis Blvd
Las Vegas . . . . (702) 453-2067

Nevada State Bank
2450 S Maryland Pkwy
Las Vegas . . . . (702) 369-5609

Nevada State Bank
232 N Jones Blvd
Las Vegas . . . . (702) 258-2902

Nevada State Bank
216 Las Vegas Blvd S
Las Vegas . . . . (702) 383-4160

Nevada State Bank
2211 N Rampart Blvd
Las Vegas . . . . (702) 256-5003

Nevada State Bank
2017 N Nellis Blvd
Las Vegas . . . .(702) 438-2231

Nevada State Bank
4970 E Tropicana Ave
Las Vegas . . . .(702) 898-8730

Nevada State Bank
6100 Spring Mountain Rd
Las Vegas . . . . (702) 367-8390

Nevada State Bank
3480 W Sahara Ave
Las Vegas . . . . (702) 248-6417

Nevada State Bank
4440 N Rancho Dr
Las Vegas . . . . (702) 658-8441

Nevada State Bank
201 S 4th St
Las Vegas . . . . (702) 383-4111

Nevada State Bank
208 Las Vegas Blvd S
Las Vegas . . . . (702) 383-4160

Nevada State Bank
212 Las Vegas Blvd S
Las Vegas . . . . (702) 383-4262

Nevada State Bank
3850 E Flamingo Rd
Las Vegas . . . . (702) 458-4715

Nevada State Bank
3345 S Maryland Pky
Las Vegas . . . . (702) 737-7006

Nevada State Bank
350 N Sandhill Blvd
Mesquite . . . . (702) 346-3400

Nevada State Bank
1912 Civic Center Dr
North Las V... . . . . (702) 399-5626

Nevada State Bank
2255 Las Vegas Blvd N
North Las V... . . . . (702) 649-4496

Norwest Bank
1411 W Sunset Rd
Henderson . . . . (702) 765-2500

Norwest Bank
546 S Boulder Hwy
Henderson . . . . (702) 765-2600

Norwest Bank
2231 N Green Valley Pkwy
Henderson . . . . (702) 435-5542

Norwest Bank
8190 W Sahara Ave
Las Vegas . . . . (702) 365-3310

Norwest Bank
4016 S Rainbow Blvd
Las Vegas . . . . (702) 871-2420

Norwest Bank
103 S Rainbow Blvd
Las Vegas . . . . (702) 765-1875

Norwest Bank
3726 E Flamingo Rd
Las Vegas . . . . (702) 765-2575

Norwest Bank
3745 S Maryland Pkwy
Las Vegas . . . .(702) 765-2750

Norwest Bank
3340 E Tropicana Ave
Las Vegas . . . . (702) 365-3310

Norwest Bank
3900 Meadows Ln
Las Vegas . . . . (702) 765-2200

Norwest Bank
1700 E Charleston Blvd
Las Vegas . . . . (702) 765-1950

Norwest Bank
4800 W Charleston Blvd
Las Vegas . . . . (702) 365-3600

Norwest Bank
9325 W Sahara Ave
Las Vegas . . . . (702) 765-2000

Norwest Bank
3104 N Rainbow Blvd
Las Vegas . . . . (702) 656-2125

Norwest Bank
910 W Owens Ave
Las Vegas . . . . (702) 646-1281

Norwest Bank
2283 N Rampart Blvd
Las Vegas . . . . (702) 254-2038

Norwest Bank
9350 W Lake Mead Blvd
Las Vegas . . . . (702) 765-2150

Norwest Bank
2690 E Sunset Rd
Las Vegas . . . . (702) 765-1500

Norwest Bank
6145 Spring Mountain Rd
Las Vegas . . . . (702) 765-2350

Norwest Bank
201 Las Vegas Blvd S
Las Vegas . . . . (702) 365-3310

Norwest Bank
5140 E Bonanza Rd
Las Vegas . . . . (702) 765-1975

Norwest Bank
3333 E Tropicana Ave
Las Vegas . . . . (702) 871-2430

Norwest Bank
1775 N Decatur Blvd
Las Vegas . . . . (702) 871-2450

Norwest Bank
2625 E Desert Inn Rd
Las Vegas . . . . (702) 796-7575

Norwest Bank
21 Marion Dr
Las Vegas . . . . (702) 871-2090

Norwest Bank
100 S Valley View Blvd
Las Vegas . . . . (702) 259-8613

Norwest Bank
316 Bridger Ave # 104
Las Vegas . . . . (702) 871-2400

Norwest Bank
5811 W Sahara Ave
Las Vegas . . . . (702) 873-0458

Norwest Bank
9325 W Sahara Ave
Las Vegas . . . . (702) 256-5215

Norwest Bank
5085 E Bonanza Rd
Las Vegas . . . . (702) 453-2438

Norwest Bank
2887 S Maryland Pky
Las Vegas . . . . (702) 871-2000

Norwest Bank
6120 W Tropicana Ave
Las Vegas . . . . (702) 367-3088

Norwest Bank
2025 Civic Center Dr
North Las V... . . . . (702) 765-1700

Norwest Bank
2125 E Lake Mead Blvd
North Las V... . . . . (702) 871-2440

Norwest Bank Nevada
3300 W Sahara Ave
Las Vegas . . . . (702) 765-3009

Norwest Bank Nevada
2700 W Sahara Ave
Las Vegas . . . . (702) 871-2000

Pioneer Citizens Bank
4001 E Sunset Rd
Henderson . . . . (702) 454-1121

Pioneer Citizens Bank
4170 S Maryland Pkwy
Las Vegas . . . . (702) 731-2222

Pioneer Citizens Bank
4949 Spring Mountain Rd
Las Vegas . . . . (702) 873-4837

Pioneer Citizens Bank
8400 W Lake Mead Blvd
Las Vegas . . . . (702) 242-1279

Pioneer Citizens Bank
230 Las Vegas Blvd S
Las Vegas . . . . (702) 382-3440

Pioneer Citizens Bank
8260 W Sahara Ave
Las Vegas . . . . (702) 228-3102

Pioneer Citizens Bank
4170 S Maryland Pky
Las Vegas . . . . (702) 731-2222

Plaza Home Mortgage Bank
3763 Howard Hughes Pkwy
Las Vegas . . . . (702) 893-8431

Premier Cashlink
308 La Rue Ct
Las Vegas . . . . (702) 433-0433

Primerit Bank
3900 Meadows Ln
Las Vegas . . . . (702) 365-3310

Sierra West Bank
2340 Paseo Del Frado # 111d
Las Vegas . . . . (702) 364-4506

Silver State Bank
691 N Valle Verde Dr
Henderson . . . .(702) 433-8300

Sun Coast Acquisition Inc
300 S 4th St
Las Vegas . . . . (702) 388-1948

Sun State Bank
4343 E Sunset Rd
Henderson . . . .(702) 454-9177

Sun State Bank
3650 Pecos Mcleod
Las Vegas . . . .(702) 364-2440

Sun State Bank
3760 Pecos Mcleod
Las Vegas . . . . (702) 898-8255

Sun State Bank
4240 W Flamingo Rd
Las Vegas . . . . (702) 364-2440

Sun State Bank
9454 Del Webb Blvd
Las Vegas . . . . (702) 364-2440

directory

U S Bank
65 W Lake Mead Dr
Henderson . . . . (702) 565-8987
U S Bank
4550 E Sunset Rd
Henderson . . . . (702) 451-1020
U S Bank
3864 W Sahara Ave
Las Vegas . . . . (702) 227-3355
U S Bank
1955 N Nellis Blvd
Las Vegas . . . . (702) 459-8660
U S Bank
948 N Nellis Blvd
Las Vegas . . . . (702) 438-4690
U S Bank
5940 W Flamingo Rd
Las Vegas . . . . (702) 386-3780
U S Bank
2300 W Sahara Ave
Las Vegas . . . . (702) 386-3658
U S Bank
6175 W Sahara Ave
Las Vegas . . . . (702) 362-3990
U S Bank
9004 W Sahara Ave
Las Vegas . . . . (702) 254-8090
U S Bank
3681 S Maryland Pkwy
Las Vegas . . . . (702) 737-7127
U S Bank
2135 S Decatur Blvd
Las Vegas . . . . (702) 364-4888
U S Bank
801 E Charleston Blvd
Las Vegas . . . . (702) 387-1919
U S Bank
4320 E Tropicana Ave
Las Vegas . . . . (702) 434-2225
U S Bank
2200 E Lake Mead Blvd
North Las V... . . . . (702) 657-8224
US Savings Bank
5811 W Sahara Ave
Las Vegas . . . . (702) 222-9800
USAA Credit Card Bank
3773 Howard Hughes Pkwy
Las Vegas . . . . (702) 862-8891
Wells Fargo Bank
412 Nevada Hwy
Boulder City . . . . (702) 791-6277
Wells Fargo Bank
2762 N Green Valley Pkwy
Henderson . . . . (702) 385-8000
Wells Fargo Bank
2835 S Nellis Blvd
Las Vegas . . . . (702) 385-8000
Wells Fargo Bank
2501 S Rainbow Blvd
Las Vegas . . . . (702) 385-8000
Wells Fargo Bank
1700 S Main St
Las Vegas . . . . (702) 385-8000
Wells Fargo Bank

4595 W Charleston Blvd
Las Vegas . . . . (702) 385-8000
Wells Fargo Bank
300 Carson Ave
Las Vegas . . . . (702) 385-8000
Wells Fargo Bank
3255 E Sahara Ave
Las Vegas . . . . (702) 385-8000
Wells Fargo Bank
Paradise Rd
Las Vegas . . . . (702) 385-8000
Wells Fargo Bank
4540 Spencer St # B28
Las Vegas . . . . (702) 385-8208
Wells Fargo Bank
2989 Paradise Rd
Las Vegas . . . . (702) 385-8011
Western Financial Savings Bank
6655 W Sahara Ave
Las Vegas . . . . (702) 247-1442
WTC Corporate Svc
3753 Howard Hughes Pky # 200
Las Vegas . . . . (702) 892-3772
Zions Bank Public Financing
3345 S Maryland Pkwy
Las Vegas . . . . (702) 796-7080
Zions Credit Corp
201 S 4th St
Las Vegas . . . . (702) 383-4278
Zions Credit Corp
3345 S Maryland Pky
Las Vegas . . . . (702) 383-4278
Zions Investment Securities
3345 S Maryland Pky
Las Vegas . . . . (702) 792-4184
Zions Investment Securities
3480 W Sahara Ave
Las Vegas . . . . (702) 362-6622

Baseball Cards & Comics

Alternate Reality Comics
4800 S Maryland Pkwy # D
Las Vegas . . . . (702) 736-3673
Asylum Comics
4241 W Charleston Blvd
Las Vegas . . . . (702) 368-7740
Bat Cave
2290 E Flamingo Rd
Las Vegas . . . . (702) 696-0089
Big Entertainment
2000 Las Vegas Blvd S
Las Vegas . . . . (702) 471-0065
Blood Moon Social Club
5197 W Charleston Blvd
Las Vegas . . . . (702) 877-1813
Comic Zone
5020 E Tropicana Ave # A
Las Vegas . . . . (702) 435-2525
Comikaze Comics & Cards
6140 W Tropicana Ave
Las Vegas . . . . (702) 253-5506

Cosmic Comics
3330 E Tropicana Ave # W
Las Vegas . . . . (702) 451-6611

Dreamwell Comics
5706 W Charleston Blvd
Las Vegas . . . . (702) 870-1268

House Of Cards
900 Karen Ave
Las Vegas . . . . (702) 791-0959

Kool Kollectables
5197 W Charleston Blvd
Las Vegas . . . . (702) 877-5665

Outer Limits
2221 N Rampart Blvd
Las Vegas . . . . (702) 228-2221

Riddler Comics
3919 W Charleston Blvd
Las Vegas . . . . (702) 258-7783

Silver Cactus Comics
560 N Nellis Blvd # E8
Las Vegas . . . . (702) 438-4408

Smokey's Sports Cards Inc
3734 Las Vegas Blvd S
Las Vegas . . . . (702) 739-0003

White Knight
900 Karen Ave # D204
Las Vegas . . . . (702) 893-0701

Wizard's Playground
7380 S Eastern Ave # 122
Las Vegas . . . . (702) 260-4924

World Of Hero's
3650 S Decatur Blvd # 11
Las Vegas . . . . (702) 873-3103

Bicycle Rentals & Tours

Downhill Bicycle Tours Inc
7934 Cadenza Ln
Las Vegas . . . . (702) 897-8287

Postal Plus
133 N 4th St
Las Vegas . . . . (702) 383-3337

R & C Cycling Of Las Vegas
3310 S Nellis Blvd
Las Vegas . . . . (702) 451-9586

Bicycle Retailers

Bicycle Depot
2801 N Green Valley Pkwy # B
Henderson . . . . (702) 458-0888

Bicycle Depot
5665 W Sahara Ave
Las Vegas . . . . (702) 252-4316

Bicycle King
2470 E Tropicana Ave
Las Vegas . . . . (702) 451-2580

Bike Art
1672 Nevada Hwy
Boulder City . . . .(702) 293-4652

Bike Stuff
1268 Wyoming St
Boulder City . . . .(702) 293-2453

Bike Trail
6816 W Cheyenne Ave
Las Vegas . . . . (702) 656-2026

Bike World
1901 S Rainbow Blvd
Las Vegas . . . . (702) 254-1718

Bike World
2320 E Flamingo Rd
Las Vegas . . . . (702) 735-7551

Bikes USA
1539 N Eastern Ave
Las Vegas . . . . (702) 642-2453

Bmxperts
1000 Nevada Hwy
Boulder City . . . . (702) 294-2454

City Streets Bike Tours
Po Box 50262
Henderson . . . . (702) 596-2953

Cyclery N Cafe Coffee Bar
7016 W Charleston Blvd
Las Vegas . . . . (702) 228-9460

Etcs Mountain Bike Adventures
8221 W Charleston Blvd # 100
Las Vegas . . . . (702) 596-2953

First Choice Bicycle
1000 E Charleston Blvd
Las Vegas . . . . (702) 382-5775

House Of Bikes
6162 Spring Mountain Rd
Las Vegas . . . . (702) 871-0871

Just Mountain Bikes
745 W Sunset Rd
Henderson . . . . (702) 564-5501

Thrills On Wheels
6500 Vegas Dr # 1116
Las Vegas . . . . (702) 453-2824

Boat Rental & Charters

Action Water Sports
1949 N Boulder Hwy
Henderson . . . . (702) 564-7271

Action Watercraft Inc
Po Box 1814
Overton . . . . (702) 564-5452

Action Watercraft Rentals
444 N Water St
Henderson . . . . (702) 564-5452

Advanced Marine Service & Transport
Las Vegas . . . . (701) 565-1005

Boat Doc
Las Vegas . . . . (702) 452-1191

Boulder City Water Sports
1108 Nevada Hwy
Boulder City . . . . (702) 293-7526

Callville Bay Resort & Marina
Hc 30 Box 100
Las Vegas . . . . (702) 565-8958

East Side Sports
6055 E Lake Mead Blvd
Las Vegas . . . . (702) 452-5579

Extreme Marine
2310 E Lake Mead Blvd
North Las V... . . . . (702) 564-8111

Get It Wet Watercraft
Las Vegas . . . .(702) 294-7547
Golden Ski's & Tee's
2411 Western Ave
Las Vegas . . . . (702) 382-7493
Jet Away
5435 E Lake Mead Blvd
Las Vegas . . . . (702) 452-1215
Lake Mead Resort & Marina
322 Lakeshore Rd
Boulder City . . . . (702) 293-2484
River Rat Watersports
1955 S Casino Dr
Laughlin . . . . (702) 298-7547
River Runners Watersports
1950 S Casion Dr
Laughlin . . . . (702) 299-9102
Tom's Water Sports Charter
Las Vegas . . . . (702) 433-3263

Book Stores

Albion Book Co
2466 E Desert Inn Rd # G
Las Vegas . . . . (702) 792-9554
As Vegas Trivia
4660 W Charleston Blvd
Las Vegas . . . . (702) 431-7208
B Dalton Bookseller
1300 W Sunset Rd
Henderson . . . . (702) 434-1331
B Dalton Bookseller
3680 S Maryland Pkwy
Las Vegas . . . .(702) 735-0008
B Dalton Bookseller
4300 Meadows Ln
Las Vegas . . . .(702) 878-4405
Barnes & Noble Inc
567 Stephanie St
Henderson . . . .(702) 434-1533
Beehive Book
4180 S Sandhill Rd # B2
Las Vegas . . . .(702) 732-9110
Bell Book & Candle
1725 E Charleston Blvd
Las Vegas . . . . (702) 384-6807
Bob Coffin Books
1139 5th Pl
Las Vegas . . . .(702) 598-0982
Book Round-Up
858 S Boulder Hwy
Henderson . . . . (702) 565-0665
Book Shoppe
2232 S Nellis Blvd # G1
Las Vegas . . . . (702) 641-1155
Book Warehouse
9155 Las Vegas Blvd S
Las Vegas . . . . (702) 896-5344
Books Etc
280 S Moapa Valley Blvd
Overton . . . . (702) 397-8010
Bookstar
4730 Faircenter Pkwy
Las Vegas . . . . (702) 877-1872

Bookstar
3910 S Maryland Pkwy
Las Vegas . . . . (702) 732-7882
Borders Book Shop
2323 S Decatur Blvd
Las Vegas . . . . (702) 258-0999
Borders Books & Music
1445 W Sunset Rd
Henderson . . . .(702) 433-6222
Boulevard Books & Video
1147 Las Vegas Blvd S
Las Vegas . . . . (702) 383-8326
Crescent Book & Video Store
1402 D St
Las Vegas . . . . (702) 648-6275
Deseret Book
1905 N Green Valley Pkwy
Henderson . . . . (702) 896-6676
Deseret Book
560 N Nellis Blvd
Las Vegas . . . . (702) 453-5611
Deseret Book
336 S Decatur Blvd
Las Vegas . . . . (702) 877-2066
Desert Book
4350 Las Vegas Blvd N
Las Vegas . . . . (702) 643-7982
Dianetics Book Ctr
846 E Sahara Ave
Las Vegas . . . . (702) 731-5525
Family Book Stores
1230 S Decatur Blvd
Las Vegas . . . . (702) 870-9550
Final Call Books & Tapes
1402 D St
Las Vegas . . . . (702) 647-0414
Genesis Books
1815 W Charleston Blvd
Las Vegas . . . . (702) 386-0099
Get Booked
4640 Paradise Rd
Las Vegas . . . . (702) 737-7780
Great Wall Bookstore
4255 Spring Mountain Rd
Las Vegas . . . . (702) 876-8875
Latter Day Book & Craft
7450 W Cheyenne Ave
Las Vegas . . . .(702) 645-7300
Latter Day Book & Craft
4660 W Charleston Blvd
Las Vegas . . . . (702) 877-2880
Lemstone Books
4300 Meadows Ln
Las Vegas . . . . (702) 870-9996
Libreria Las Americas
1560 N Eastern Ave
Las Vegas . . . . (702) 399-0902
Native Son
1301 D St
Las Vegas . . . . (702) 647-0101
Readmore Magazine & Book Store
2560 S Maryland Pkwy
Las Vegas . . . . (702) 732-4453

Readmore Magazine & Book Store
6154 W Flamingo Rd
Las Vegas . . . . (702) 362-3762
Readmore Magazine & Book Store
2250 E Tropicana Ave
Las Vegas . . . . (702) 798-7863
Rebelbooks
4440 S Maryland Pkwy
Las Vegas . . . . (702) 796-4141
Sport Stat
1217 Torington Dr
Las Vegas . . . . (702) 877-6633
Star Of The Story
3151 N Rainbow Blvd # 181
Las Vegas . . . . (702) 240-0182
T & M Direct
1433 N Jones Blvd # 188
Las Vegas . . . . (702) 647-3202
Traveling Books & Maps
4001 S Decatur Blvd
Las Vegas . . . . (702) 871-8082
UNLV Bookstore
4505 S Maryland Pkwy
Las Vegas . . . . (702) 736-3955
Waldenbooks
4300 Meadows Ln
Las Vegas . . . . (702) 870-4914
Waldenbooks
3200 Las Vegas Blvd S
Las Vegas . . . . (702) 733-1049

Bowling Centers

Arizona Charlie's Hotel & Casino
Las Vegas . . . . (702) 258-5200
Boulder Bowl
504 California Ave
Boulder City . . . . (702) 293-2368
Gold Coast Hotel
4000 W. Flamingo Rd
Las Vegas . . . . (702) 367-4700
Lucky Strike
Las Vegas . . . . (702) 564-7118
Orleans Hotel
4500 W. Tropicana Ave.
Las Vegas . . . . (702) 365-7111
Primm Valley Resort
Las Vegas . . . . (702) 382-1212
Sam's Town Hotel
5111 Boulder Hwy
Las Vegas . . . . (702) 456-7777
Santa Fe Hotel
4949 N. Rancho Dr
Las Vegas . . . . (702) 658-4995
Showboat Hotel
2800 Fremont Street
Las Vegas . . . . (702) 385-9153
Silver Nugget
2140 N. Las Vegas Blvd
Las Vegas . . . . (702) 657-2750

Southern Nevada Bowling Assn
3111 S Valley View Blvd # O102
Las Vegas . . . . (702) 362-5550
Sunset Lanes
4451 E Sunset Rd
Henderson . . . . (702) 736-2695
Sunset Lanes
4565 E. Sunset Rd
Las Vegas . . . . (702) 736-2695
Terrible's Town Casino & Bowl
642 S. Boulder Hwy
Las Vegas . . . . (702) 564-7118
The Orleans Hotel
4500 W. Tropicana Ave
Las Vegas . . . . (702) 365-711

Campgrounds and RV Parks

American Campgrounds
3440 Las Vegas Blvd N
Las Vegas . . . . (702) 643-1222
Bond Trailer Lodge
284 E Tropicana Ave
Las Vegas . . . . (702) 736-1550
Boomtown Rv Park
3333 Blue Diamond Rd.
Las Vegas . . . . (702) 263-7777
Boulder Lakes Rv Resort
6201 Boulder Hwy
Las Vegas . . . . (702) 435-1157
Boulder Oaks Rv Resort
1010 Industrial Rd
Boulder City . . . . (702) 294-4425
California Hotel Casino & Rv
100 E Stewart Ave
Las Vegas . . . . (702) 388-2602
Canyon Trail Rv Park
1200 Industrial Rd
Boulder City . . . . (702) 293-1200
Circusland Rv Park
2880 Las Vegas Blvd S
Las Vegas . . . . (702) 794-3757
Cottonwood Cove Resort & Marina
Lake Mohave
P.O. Box 1000
Las Vegas . . . . (702) 297-1464
Covered Wagon Rv Park
6635 Boulder Hwy
Las Vegas . . . . (702) 384-4076
Desert Sands Rv Park & Motel
1940 N Boulder Hwy
Henderson . . . . (702) 565-1945
Fun N Sun Trailer Park
280 N Cooper Rd
Overton . . . . (702) 397-8894
Good Sam's Hitchin Post Camper Park
3640 Las Vegas Blvd North
Las Vegas . . . . (702) 644-1043
Holiday Travel Trailer
3890 S Nellis Blvd
Las Vegas . . . . (702) 451-8005

Indian Springs Trailer Park
372 Tonopah Hwy
Indian Springs . . . . (702) 879-3129

King's Row
3660 Boulder Hwy.,
Las Vegas . . . . (702) 649-7439

KOA Campgrounds
4315 Boulder Hwy.,
Las Vegas . . . . (702) 451-5527

Lakeshore Trailer Village
268 Lakeshore Rd
Boulder City . . . . (702) 293-2540

Midway Trailer Park
125 E Merlayne Dr
Henderson . . . . (702) 564-0905

Mount Charleston Rv Site
State Rd 157
Las Vegas . . . .(800) 283-2267

Nevada Palace Vip Travel Trailer Park
5325 Boulder Hwy
Las Vegas . . . . (702) 451-0232

Oasis Las Vegas Motor Coach
2711 W Windmill Ln
Las Vegas . . . . (702) 260-2020

Primadonna Hotel Rv Park
Jct 1-15 & 1-15 Bus Rt., Exit 120 E
Las Vegas . . . . (702) 382-1212

Riviera Travel Trailer
2200 Palm St
Las Vegas . . . . (702) 457-8700

Riviera Travel Trailer Park
2200 Palm Street
Las Vegas . . . . (702) 457-8700

Road Runner Rv Park
4711 Boulder Hwy
Las Vegas . . . . (702) 456-4711

Sam Boyd's California Hotel And Rv Park
1ST St. And Ogden Ave
Las Vegas . . . . (702) 388-2602

Sam's Town Rv Park - Boulder
5225 Boulder Hwy
Las Vegas . . . . (702) 454-8055

Sam's Town Rv Park - Nellis
4040 S. Nellis Blvd
Las Vegas . . . . (702) 454-8056

Silver Nugget Casino And Rv Park
2236 N. Las Vegas Blvd.,
Las Vegas . . . . (702) 649-7439

Sun City Mobile Home Park
1630 Las Vegas Blvd N
North Las V... . . . . (702) 642-7124

Sunrise Resort & Rv Park
4445 Boulder Hwy
Las Vegas . . . . (702) 458-7275

Thousand Trails Inc
4295 Boulder Hwy
Las Vegas . . . . (702) 451-7632

Child Care and Nursery Schools

A Small World Learning Ctr
10 N 28th St
Las Vegas . . . . (702) 386-1006

A To Z Child Care & Learning
5653 S Mojave Rd
Las Vegas . . . . (702) 433-1411

ABC Preschool & Day Care Ctr
1730 N Pecos Rd
Las Vegas . . . . (702) 642-5176

Adventures In Learning
3338 Oneida Way
Las Vegas . . . . (702) 893-3080

All Saints' Day School
4201 W Washington Ave
Las Vegas . . . . (702) 878-1205

Almost Home
7029 Oakland Cir
Las Vegas . . . . (702) 363-4219

Angel Care Child Care
549 N Lamb Blvd
Las Vegas . . . . (702) 459-2138

Angel Care Child Care
4320 E Bonanza Rd
Las Vegas . . . . (702) 459-9541

Around The Clock
3871 S Valley View Blvd # 16
Las Vegas . . . . (702) 365-1040

Babyland Infant Ctr
3825 Raymert Dr
Las Vegas . . . . (702) 451-1633

Black Mountain Christian Day
315 S Water St
Henderson . . . . (702) 564-2435

Bright Start Childrens Ctr
2750 Robindale Rd
Henderson . . . . (702) 361-5437

Bright Start Childrens Ctr
1551 E Warm Springs Rd
Las Vegas . . . . (702) 451-2660

Bright Start Childrens Ctr
6100 W Cheyenne Ave
Las Vegas . . . . (702) 658-5064

Bright Start Childrens Ctr
2121 Harbor Island Dr
Las Vegas . . . . (702) 255-5657

Bright Start Childrens Ctr
6200 Smoke Ranch Rd
Las Vegas . . . . (702) 658-5437

Bright Start Childrens Ctr
2785 S Rainbow Blvd
Las Vegas . . . . (702) 362-4453

Bright Start Childrens Ctr
8451 Boseck Dr
Las Vegas . . . . (702) 255-9252

Building Blocks Child Care
7570 Peace Way
Las Vegas . . . . (702) 873-7340

Calvary Church Pre-School
2929 Cedar Ave
Las Vegas . . . . (702) 382-6133

Captain Kidd's Treasure Island
3883 Mesa Vista Way
Las Vegas . . . . (702) 456-1133

Carol A Okin Family Care Home
9046 Trumpet Ct
Henderson . . . . (702) 896-6112

Carousel Christian Child Dev
800 N Bruce St
Las Vegas .... (702) 649-7160

Carrie Jones Family Day Care
5176 Pine Cone Pl
Las Vegas .... (702) 646-8893

Cathy's Home Child Care
605 N Crestline Dr
Las Vegas .... (702) 878-8825

Cecile Lockridge Family Child
1640 L St
Las Vegas .... (702) 638-7215

Celida Novo
1701 Diamond Oaks Ct
Las Vegas .... (702) 243-6409

Chadad Preschool
1254 Vista Dr
Las Vegas .... (702) 259-0777

Charissa Stastny Child Care
3925 Monja Cir
Las Vegas .... (702) 641-6614

Charleston Heights Day Care
1665 Lindell Rd
Las Vegas .... (702) 878-6261

Child Kingdom
3551 E Sunset Rd
Las Vegas .... (702) 451-9801

Children's First Challenge
1213 Balzar Ave
Las Vegas ....(702) 646-5135

Children's Garden
594 Blackridge Rd
Henderson ....(702) 564-2201

Children's Oasis School
720 Rancho Del Norte Dr
North Las V... ....(702) 649-5425

Children's Paradise
4220 Mcleod Dr
Las Vegas ....(702) 454-0440

Children's World Learning Ctr
705 N Valle Verde Dr
Henderson ....(702) 436-4707

Children's World Learning Ctr
1901 N Green Valley Pkwy
Henderson ....(702) 263-9326

Children's World Learning Ctr
2861 Business Park Ct
Las Vegas ....(702) 254-0311

Children's World Learning Ctr
2600 Lake Sahara Dr
Las Vegas ....(702) 254-9111

Childrens Center Of The Arts
2620 Regatta Dr
Las Vegas ....(702) 363-3520

Childrens Learning Ctr
5000 Edna Ave
Las Vegas ....(702) 873-6518

Childrens Learning Ctr
6565 Smoke Ranch Rd
Las Vegas ....(702) 648-6565

Childrens Oasis School
2750 Lake Sahara Dr
Las Vegas ....(702) 363-2124

Christ Lutheran Children's Ctr
111 N Torrey Pines Dr
Las Vegas .... (702) 878-1176

Cinderella Careskool
4270 S Maryland Pkwy
Las Vegas .... (702) 732-0230

Cindy Moniz Family Care Home
5183 Outline Ave
Las Vegas .... (702) 641-3870

Clark County Child Care Assn
Po Box 15372
Las Vegas .... (702) 734-0504

Community Care Of America
3254 Civic Center Dr
North Las V... .... (702) 657-1272

Community College-Southern Nv
3200 E Cheyenne Ave
North Las V... .... (702) 651-4518

Coral Smith Child Care Svc
6609 Chardonay Way
Las Vegas .... (702) 395-8881

Country Cousins
7980 S Eastern Ave
Las Vegas .... (702) 361-1725

Country School
4965 Bevvie Dr
Las Vegas .... (702) 646-4977

Creative Kids Learning Ctr
6531 Annie Oakley Dr
Henderson .... (702) 456-7008

Creative Kids Learning Ctr
501 Harris St
Henderson .... (702) 565-0007

Creative Kids Learning Ctr
5025 Bond St
Las Vegas .... (702) 871-0078

Creative Kids Learning Ctr
124 N Tenaya Way
Las Vegas .... (702) 363-1919

Creative Kids Learning Ctr
6565 Smoke Ranch Rd
Las Vegas .... (702) 648-6565

Creative Kids Learning Ctr
5125 S Torrey Pines Dr
Las Vegas .... (702) 364-2223

Creative Kids Learning Ctr
2575 S Fort Apache Rd
Las Vegas .... (702) 255-0443

Creative Kids Learning Ctr
5001 E Craig Rd
Las Vegas .... (702) 645-3734

Creative Kids Learning Ctr
6620 W Katie Ave
Las Vegas .... (702) 871-7311

Creative Kids Learning Ctr
3220 N Rainbow Blvd
Las Vegas .... (702) 645-0001

D Grondel Child Care Svc
3100 Bassler St
North Las V... .... (702) 649-8428

D J's Daycare Ctr
360 E Horizon Dr
Henderson .... (702) 566-4070

Dawna Crouch
1960 Continental Ave
Las Vegas . . . . (702) 459-7832

Debbie's Childcare
1971 Autumn Gold Ave
Las Vegas . . . . (702) 270-6794

Dillon Family Home Day Care
6808 White Sands Ave
Las Vegas . . . . (702) 233-0911

Dixon Child Care
4904 Crimson Glory Ln
Las Vegas . . . . (702) 645-2587

Exodus Christian Pre-School
407 Spencer St
Las Vegas . . . . (702) 385-0808

Fellowship Family Day Care
6210 W Cheyenne Ave
Las Vegas . . . . (702) 645-4339

Fielday School Northwest
3570 N Buffalo Dr
Las Vegas . . . . (702) 655-6565

First Christian Church Child
101 S Rancho Dr
Las Vegas . . . . (702) 384-4839

First Presbyterian Preschool
1515 W Charleston Blvd
Las Vegas . . . . (702) 382-9032

First Step Kids Care
4701 E Owens Ave
Las Vegas . . . . (702) 453-3736

Friendship Child Care
2249 W Washington Ave
Las Vegas . . . . (702) 646-7726

Grammy's Lil' Bits
600 Altamira Rd
Las Vegas . . . . (702) 363-2437

Grandma Dotti's Babysitting
3838 Raymert Dr # 7
Las Vegas . . . . (702) 456-1175

Grandma Thompson's Romp N Play
1804 Weldon Pl
Las Vegas . . . . (702) 735-0176

Grandma's House
4995 Irene Ave
Las Vegas . . . . (702) 452-5437

Green Frog Early Learning Ctr
4610 Monterrey Ave
Las Vegas . . . . (702) 458-2828

Green Valley Christian Ctr
711 N Valle Verde Dr
Henderson . . . . (702) 454-4056

Griffith United Methodist
1701 E Oakey Blvd
Las Vegas . . . . (702) 382-7836

Hallmark Academy West
3460 Arville St
Las Vegas . . . . (702) 367-8337

Hallmark Academy-East
4929 E Bonanza Rd
Las Vegas . . . . (702) 459-3332

Happy Days Child Care
3710 S Sandhill Rd
Las Vegas . . . . (702) 458-2875

Happy Days Child Care

2950 E Tropicana Ave
Las Vegas . . . . (702) 451-8952

Happy Days Child Care Pre-Sch
2301 Las Verdes St
Las Vegas . . . . (702) 871-0600

Happy House Nursery
5690 Rio Vista St
Las Vegas . . . . (702) 645-3044

Heidi Torres Child Care Svc
4129 Lucas Ave
Las Vegas . . . . (702) 433-1236

Helping Hands Child Care
3916 Sequoia Ave
Las Vegas . . . . (702) 438-8628

Hill & Dale Child Dev Ctr
3720 E Tropicana Ave
Las Vegas . . . . (702) 458-2243

Holy Family Day Care Ctr
451 E Twain Ave
Las Vegas . . . . (702) 735-4358

Imagination Plus Child Dev
5580 S Pecos Rd
Las Vegas . . . . (702) 451-5437

Imagination Plus Child Dev Ctr
3525 E Sunset Rd
Las Vegas . . . . (702) 433-6044

Imagination Plus Child Dev Ctr
1617 Alta Dr
Las Vegas . . . . (702) 384-5437

J P Kiddy Shack
616 Stewart Ave
Las Vegas . . . . (702) 382-4962

Jillene Brown
1152 Pleasant Brook St
Las Vegas . . . . (702) 431-2211

Joy School & Home Day Care
1008 Santa Helena Ave
Henderson . . . . (702) 564-8580

Juanita Ballard Child Care
3021 Nutwood St
Las Vegas . . . . (702) 658-3225

Julie A Platko Childcare
3552 Moraga Dr
Las Vegas . . . . (702) 253-5002

Just For Kids
6027 Peach Orchard Rd
Las Vegas . . . . (702) 431-5510

Kathy Reed Day Care Ctr
3621 Alliance St
Las Vegas . . . . (702) 656-5388

Kelly Jo Demont
1620 Sierra Hills Way
Las Vegas . . . . (702) 233-5121

Kiddie Korral Daycare
51 N Yucca St
Mesquite . . . . (702) 346-7873

Kids Care Connection
4535 W Sahara Ave
Las Vegas . . . . (702) 871-5555

Kids Connection
1085 Betty Ln
Las Vegas . . . . (702) 438-0017

Kids Cove Daycare & Preschool
4975 E Saint Louis Ave
Las Vegas . . . . (702) 431-2222

Kids Korral
5320 E Lake Mead Blvd
Las Vegas . . . . (702) 459-0091

Kids Quest
4111 Boulder Hwy
Las Vegas . . . . (702) 432-7569

Kids R Smart Learning Ctr
1001 N Tonopah Dr
Las Vegas . . . . (702) 647-5712

Kids Will Be Kids Preschool
5580 S Pecos Rd
Las Vegas . . . . (702) 451-5437

Kinder Care Learning Ctr
1655 E Warm Springs Rd
Las Vegas . . . . (702) 897-1544

Kinder Care Learning Ctr
3223 N Rainbow Blvd
Las Vegas . . . . (702) 645-9895

Kinder Care Learning Ctr
4845 Community Ln
Las Vegas . . . . (702) 456-5772

Kinder Care Learning Ctr
4301 Stewart Ave
Las Vegas . . . . (702) 453-6997

Kinder Care Learning Ctr
4912 Vegas Dr
Las Vegas . . . . (702) 648-1473

Kinder Care Learning Ctr
6204 W Charleston Blvd
Las Vegas . . . . (702) 878-9219

Kinder Care Learning Ctr
4050 S Torrey Pines Dr
Las Vegas . . . . (702) 367-0822

Klassy Kids Academy
6050 W Lone Mountain Rd
Las Vegas . . . . (702) 658-9902

Kritter Kare School
4316 N Decatur Blvd
Las Vegas . . . . (702) 655-2100

La Petite Academy
2401 Tech Center Ct
Las Vegas . . . . (702) 233-1077

La Petite Academy
5270 S Pecos Rd
Las Vegas . . . . (702) 454-7434

La Petite Academy
4554 E Charleston Blvd
Las Vegas . . . . (702) 459-1228

La Petite Academy
4270 S Rainbow Blvd
Las Vegas . . . . (702) 252-0155

Ladean Cox
6928 Montcliff Ave
Las Vegas . . . . (702) 368-0996

Larsen's Childcare-Infant Tdlr
5216 Del Rey Ave
Las Vegas . . . . (702) 878-8497

Las Vegas Day School
3198 S Jones Blvd
Las Vegas . . . . (702) 362-1180

Laurie Gallia Day Care Svc
5645 N Juliano Rd
Las Vegas . . . . (702) 645-6857

Learning Blocks Preschool
5540 Spring Mountain Rd
Las Vegas . . . . (702) 247-4767

Learning Tree
4640 E Desert Inn Rd
Las Vegas . . . . (702) 456-4986

Linda J Hirth Day Care Svc
837 Rainbow Rock St
Las Vegas . . . . (702) 260-9265

Lit'l Scholar Academy
3233 E Desert Inn Rd
Las Vegas . . . . (702) 732-4292

Lit'l Scholar Academy
8951 Hillpointe Rd
Las Vegas . . . . (702) 256-5300

Lit'l Scholar Academy
4980 Powell Ave
Las Vegas . . . . (702) 458-1414

Lit'l Scholar Academy
1300 E Sahara Ave
Las Vegas . . . . (702) 735-1122

Lit'l Scholar Academy
2301 W Charleston Blvd
Las Vegas . . . . (702) 870-0666

Lit'l Scholar Academy
1951 S Rainbow Blvd
Las Vegas . . . . (702) 254-5000

Little Grubbies
9037 Union Gap Rd
Las Vegas . . . . (702) 897-6420

Little Margie's
3707 Vegas Dr
Las Vegas . . . . (702) 646-1133

Little Red School House
1515 W Whipple Ave
Logandale . . . . (702) 398-3491

Little Roundup
3700 Vegas Dr
Las Vegas . . . . (702) 648-6655

Little Tyke Day Care
1023 San Eduardo Ave
Henderson . . . . (702) 566-0851

Little Wranglers
555 Page St
Las Vegas . . . . (702) 452-3100

Marcia's Child Care Ctr
2016 E Carey Ave
North Las V... . . . . (702) 649-4541

Meyer Daycare
1220 Barton Green Dr
Las Vegas . . . . (702) 228-4825

Mom Eaze
100 Moose Ln
Las Vegas . . . . (702) 228-3840

Montessori Academy Of Nevada
3338 Oneida Way
Las Vegas . . . . (702) 735-5070

Montessori Child Care Academy
6000 W Oakey Blvd
Las Vegas . . . . (702) 870-5117

Montessori Child Care Academy
6000 W Oakey Blvd
Las Vegas . . . . (702) 878-3744

Morrison Child Care
6645 Joe Michael Way
Las Vegas . . . . (702) 395-7960

Mother Goose College
2760 S Jones Blvd
Las Vegas . . . . (702) 362-5801

Mother Goose Nursery
2760 S Jones Blvd
Las Vegas . . . . (702) 362-5801

Mountain View Lutheran Church
920 S Decatur Blvd
Las Vegas . . . . (702) 878-7532

Mountain View Lutheran Preschl
9550 W Cheyenne Ave
Las Vegas . . . . (702) 233-9323

Mountain View Lutheran Preschl
920 S Decatur Blvd
Las Vegas . . . . (702) 878-6848

My Little Schoolhouse
3790 Redwood St
Las Vegas . . . . (702) 362-9255

Nana's Sitter Svc
3650 S Pointe Cir # 205
Laughlin . . . . (702) 299-7272

Nanny's & Granny's
6440 Coley Ave
Las Vegas . . . . (702) 364-4700

Narda Fichter Child Care
7025 Edwin Aldrin Cir
Las Vegas . . . . (702) 363-4612

Nellis Baptist Church Day Care
4300 Las Vegas Blvd N
Las Vegas . . . . (702) 643-8800

New Horizons Early Learning
6233 Bristol Way
Las Vegas . . . . (702) 880-3514

Nicholas Nursery
3320 E Lake Mead Blvd
North Las V... . . . . (702) 649-0766

Once Upon A Time Learning Ctr
5055 Duneville St
Las Vegas . . . .(702) 368-7757

Operation Independence
1966 Genoa Dr
Las Vegas . . . .(702) 647-1790

Parents Express Child Care
2860 E Flamingo Rd
Las Vegas . . . .(702) 453-8771

Patty Cake Patty Cake Daycare
4789 San Rafael Ave
Las Vegas . . . .(702) 434-1799

Primetime Preschool Ctr
4514 Meadows Ln
Las Vegas . . . .(702) 258-8858

Pumpkin Shell Day Care
1934 S Walnut Rd
Las Vegas . . . .(702) 641-8118

Rainbow Bridge
3301 W Charleston Blvd
Las Vegas . . . .(702) 878-0133

Reber's Pre-School & Child
1105 Orange Ave
Las Vegas . . . . (702) 646-5120

Robin D Evans Child Care
6188 Mount Mckinley Ave
Las Vegas . . . . (702) 453-0323

Rock Solid Christian Day Care
800 N Rancho Dr
Las Vegas . . . . (702) 648-1644

Roda's Rosebuds Preschool
5616 Royal Castle Ln
Las Vegas . . . . (702) 645-6139

Romp 'N Play Nursery
3412 S Decatur Blvd
Las Vegas . . . . (702) 873-9091

Romp 'N Play Nursery
1804 Weldon Pl
Las Vegas . . . . (702) 735-0176

Sarah's Wee Ones
2205 Lenwood Ave
North Las V... . . . . (702) 399-7242

See World
5100 Alta Dr
Las Vegas . . . . (702) 258-9055

Seton Academy
1592 E Hacienda Ave
Las Vegas . . . . (702) 736-4246

Shannon Murray Child Care
6513 Miragrande Dr
Las Vegas . . . . (702) 645-8755

Sitters R Us
820 S 6th St
Las Vegas . . . . (702) 380-1080

Sleepy Hollow Childcare-Presch
3150 S Decatur Blvd
Las Vegas . . . . (702) 873-2424

Small Wonders Child Care
4170 Lucas Ave
Las Vegas . . . . (702) 436-0836

Smart Start
1260 W Owens Ave
Las Vegas . . . . (702) 647-5700

St John Child Care Ctr
2301 Comstock Dr
North Las V... . . . . (702) 647-7393

Sunshine Co
1499 N Lamb Blvd
Las Vegas . . . . (702) 459-2023

Sunshine Sitters
823 Las Vegas Blvd S
Las Vegas . . . . (702) 385-9966

Supertots Child Care Ctr
2300 Canosa Ave
Las Vegas . . . . (702) 641-6627

Sussan Alighchi Family Home
1012 Matagorda Ln
Las Vegas . . . . (702) 242-9412

Sweet Pea Learning Ctr
1441 E Hacienda Ave
Las Vegas . . . . (702) 798-2772

Teacher's Apple
2253 E Desert Inn Rd
Las Vegas . . . . (702) 731-4650

Teddy Bear Junction
1905 E Warm Springs Rd
Las Vegas . . . . (702) 361-1795
Terry & Friends Family Daycare
3618 Elegant Saint Ct
Las Vegas . . . . (702) 651-6181
Tlc Child Care Ctr
6741 W Alexander Rd
Las Vegas . . . . (702) 645-3989
Toddle Towne
2775 S Jones Blvd
Las Vegas . . . . (702) 367-3021
Toddle Towne
4095 W Craig Rd
North Las V... . . . . (702) 646-4386
Tracey Mckinney
1721 Navajo Lake Way
Las Vegas . . . . (702) 363-6930
Trinity Life Pre-School
928 E Sahara Ave
Las Vegas . . . . (702) 732-2787
University United Methodist
4412 S Maryland Pky
Las Vegas . . . . (702) 733-7155
Variety Day Home
990 D St
Las Vegas . . . . (702) 647-4907
Vegas Valley Babysitting Svc
3111 S Valley View Blvd # 03
Las Vegas . . . . (702) 871-5161
Vegas Valley Child Care
5515 Mountain Vista St
Las Vegas . . . . (702) 451-9665
Vegas Valley Christian Preschl
5515 Mountain Vista St
Las Vegas . . . . (702) 451-9665
Wags Child Care Home
370 Citrus Cir
Henderson . . . . (702) 565-5400
Wassell's Home Daycare
5000 Edna Ave
Las Vegas . . . . (702) 876-7970
West Charleston Baptist Church
6701 W Charleston Blvd
Las Vegas . . . . (702) 878-5798
West Oakey Baptist Child Care
4400 W Oakey Blvd
Las Vegas . . . . (702) 870-7644
Wilma Morgan Care Home
4555 Tee Pee Ln
Las Vegas . . . . (702) 396-5339
Wimett Home Child Care
5517 Seattle Slew Dr
Las Vegas . . . . (702) 648-2824

Cinemas and Theaters

Boulder Station Cinemas
Boulder Station
4111 Boulder Hwy
Las Vegas . . . . (702) 221-2283
Boulder Theatre
1225 Arizona Street
Boulder City . . . .(702) 293-3145

Century 12 Theatres
2606 S Lamb Blvd
Las Vegas . . . . (702) 641-2500
Century Desert 16
2606 S Lamb Blvd
Las Vegas . . . . (702) 641-2500
Century Rancho Santa Fe Thtrs
6001 N Rainbow Blvd
Las Vegas . . . . (702) 645-5518
Cinedome 12
851 S. Boulder Hwy
Henderson . . . . (702) 566-1570
Cinedome 12
3200 S Decature Blvd
Las Vegas . . . .(702) 362-2550
Cinedome Theatres Of Las Vegas
3200 S Decatur Blvd
Las Vegas . . . . (702) 362-2133
Cinema 8
3025 E. Desert Inn Rd
Las Vegas . . . . (702) 734-2124
Cinema 8
3025 E Desert Inn Rd
Las Vegas . . . . (702) 734-2124
Green Valley Cinemas
4500 E. Sunset Rd
Henderson . . . . (702) 458-2880
Gold Coast Twin
Gold Coast Casino
4000 W. Flamingo Rd
Las Vegas . . . . (702) 367-7111
Mountain View Cinema
3400 S Jones Blvd
Las Vegas . . . . (702) 593-3331
Omnimax Theater At Caesars
3570 Las Vegas Blvd S
Las Vegas . . . . (702) 731-7900
Paradise Cinemas
3330 E Tropicana Ave
Las Vegas . . . . (702) 451-7373
Rainbow Promenade Theater
2321 N. Rainbow Blvd.
Las Vegas . . . . (702) 225-4828
Rancho-Sante Fe Theater
5101 N. Rqancho Dr
Las Vegas . . . . (702) 645-5518
Redrock 11 Theaters
5201 W. Charleston Blvd
Las Vegas . . . . (702) 878-9255
Redrock Theatres
5201 W Charleston Blvd
Las Vegas . . . . (702) 870-1423
Showcase Cinema
Showcase Mall
3785 Las Vegas Blvd. S
Las Vegas . . . .(702) 740-2468
Startime Cinema
1800 E Sahara Ave
Las Vegas . . . . (702) 792-7443
Sunrise 7 Theatres
727 N Nellis Blvd
Las Vegas . . . . (702) 438-3866

Sunrise Dollar 751 Cinema
751 N. Nellis Blvd
Las Vegas . . . . (702) 438-5321
Sunset Station Cinemas
1301 W. Sunset Rd
Henderson . . . .(702) 221-2283
Texas 12 Cinemas
2101 Texas Star Ln
Las Vegas . . . . (702) 221-2283
Torrey Pines Cinema
6344 W Sahara Ave
Las Vegas . . . . (702) 876-4334
Torrey Pines Discount Cinema
6344 W. Sahara
Las Vegas . . . .(702) 876-4334
Vegas 4 Drive In Theatre
4158 Smoke Ranch Rd
North Las V... . . . .(702) 646-3565
Vegas 4 Drive-In Theatre
4158 W. Carey Ave
Las Vegas . . . .(702) 646-3565

Clothing Stores - Childrens

Babyland
2037 Civic Center Dr
North Las V... . . . . (702) 399-0127
Buster Brown Kidswear
7400 Las Vegas Blvd S
Las Vegas . . . . (702) 269-1473
Carter's Childrenswear
7400 Las Vegas Blvd S
Las Vegas . . . .(702) 896-4532
Children's Boutique Co
3528 S Maryland Pkwy
Las Vegas . . . . (702) 794-0064
Children's Orchard
881 S Rainbow Blvd
Las Vegas . . . . (702) 877-2223
Cho Store
953 E Sahara Ave
Las Vegas . . . . (702) 369-6797
Cho's Kids
574 N Eastern Ave
Las Vegas . . . .(702) 380-8301
Dagermans Just For Kids
2510 E Sunset Rd # 1
Las Vegas . . . . (702) 798-5437
Gap Kids
1300 W Sunset Rd
Henderson . . . . (702) 434-3110
Gap Kids
3528 S Maryland Pkwy
Las Vegas . . . . (702) 734-7077
Gymboree
1300 W Sunset Rd
Henderson . . . . (702) 898-8010
Gymboree
3200 Las Vegas Blvd S
Las Vegas . . . . (702) 369-8909
Gymboree
4300 Meadows Ln # 124
Las Vegas . . . . (702) 880-4228

Gymboree
3680 S Maryland Pkwy
Las Vegas . . . . (702) 369-4055
Jaba Kid's Wear
2901 W Washington Ave # D114
Las Vegas . . . . (702) 453-7950
Jazzman's Kids World
556 N Eastern Ave # E
Las Vegas . . . . (702) 471-6716
Jelly Smeared Kisses
1717 S Decatur Blvd
Las Vegas . . . . (702) 258-9754
Kid Vegas
2000 Las Vegas Blvd S
Las Vegas . . . . (702) 388-4100
Kid's Kastle
3500 Las Vegas Blvd S
Las Vegas . . . . (702) 369-5437
Kids Kloset
6669 Smoke Ranch Rd
Las Vegas . . . . (702) 648-0243
Kids Kloset
4250 S Rainbow Blvd
Las Vegas . . . . (702) 368-1983
Kids Wear & Toys
5757 Wayne Newton Blvd
Las Vegas . . . . (702) 261-3444
Kidz World
2520 S Maryland Pkwy
Las Vegas . . . . (702) 732-8115
L D Fashions
574 N Eastern Ave
Las Vegas . . . . (702) 385-1559
Limited Too
1300 W Sunset Rd
Henderson . . . . (702) 451-8007
Magos
1560 N Eastern Ave
Las Vegas . . . . (702) 649-4010
Osh Kosh B'gosh
7400 Las Vegas Blvd S
Las Vegas . . . . (702) 897-1727
Penny Sax
2901 W Washington Ave
Las Vegas . . . . (702) 638-8638
Primary Years
7400 Las Vegas Blvd S
Las Vegas . . . . (702) 269-8610
So Fun Kids
7400 Las Vegas Blvd S
Las Vegas . . . . (702) 260-8809
Wee Ones
2248 S Nellis Blvd
Las Vegas . . . . (702) 431-9915
Brats
3200 Las Vegas Blvd S
Las Vegas . . . . (702) 735-2728
Children's Boutique Co
4300 Meadows Ln
Las Vegas . . . . (702) 878-7276
Genuine Kids
7400 Las Vegas Blvd S
Las Vegas . . . . (702) 263-0033

Jazzman's Kids World
556 N Eastern Ave
Las Vegas . . . . (702) 471-6716
Kid's Mart
1256 S Nellis Blvd
Las Vegas . . . . (702) 459-8116
Kid's Mart
4620 Meadows Ln
Las Vegas . . . . (702) 870-8883
Kiddy Town
2201 Civic Ctr
North Las V... . . . . (702) 399-0127
Kidz Wear
3799 Las Vegas Blvd S
Las Vegas . . . . (702) 739-7770
Little Angels
1717 S Decatur Blvd
Las Vegas . . . . (702) 259-4505
Sesame Street Retail Stores
3680 S Maryland Pky
Las Vegas . . . . (702) 794-2442
Storybook Heirlooms
7400 Las Vegas Blvd S
Las Vegas . . . . (702) 896-4663
Toy Store
5757 Wayne Newton Blvd
Las Vegas . . . . (702) 261-3444
Repeatables
3650 E Flamingo Rd
Las Vegas . . . . (702) 436-9601

Costume Rentals

Atelier
900 Karen Ave
Las Vegas . . . . (702) 732-2429
Halloween Experience
5525 S Valley View Blvd # 7
Las Vegas . . . . (702) 740-4224
Cal Themes Inc
5277 Cameron St
Las Vegas . . . . (702) 251-4461
Isabelle's Discount Party Ctr
4702 S Maryland Pky
Las Vegas . . . . (702) 736-0601
Party Land
3129 N Rainbow Blvd
Las Vegas . . . . (702) 645-9601
Pretty Party Place
2630 S Decatur Blvd
Las Vegas . . . . (702) 362-3631
Rising Inc
2712 S Highland Dr
Las Vegas . . . . (702) 796-0559
Star Costume & Theatrical
4601 W Sahara Ave
Las Vegas . . . . (702) 871-3395
American Costumes
390 W Sahara Ave
Las Vegas . . . . (702) 737-5683
Celebrity Costumes
26 Country Club Ln
Las Vegas . . . . (702) 732-3933

Dynamx
4301 Mountain View Blvd
Las Vegas . . . . (702) 259-3290
Emerson Costume & Dance Wear
15 N Mojave Rd
Las Vegas . . . . (702) 386-7999
Halloween Experience
1300 W Sunset Rd
Henderson . . . . (702) 740-4224
Outer Planets Theatrical Cstm
3347 Meade Ave
Las Vegas . . . . (702) 871-1202
Ram Design
417 Rosemary Ln
Las Vegas . . . . (702) 252-0015
Star Costume & Theatrical
4601 W Sahara Ave # 1
Las Vegas . . . . (702) 871-3395
Williams Costume Co
1226 S 3rd St
Las Vegas . . . . (702) 384-1384

Dance Studios - Instruction

Dance Fusion
1775 E Tropicana Ave
Las Vegas . . . . (702) 795-3332
A Step-N-Time Cultural Arts
1140 Almond Tree Ln # 310
Las Vegas . . . . (702) 369-6943
A-Z Dance Studio
900 Karen Ave # A116
Las Vegas . . . . (702) 369-2160
Academy Of Ballet
7235 Bermuda Rd
Las Vegas . . . . (702) 897-2728
Academy Of Nevada Dance
4850 Harrison Dr
Las Vegas . . . . (702) 898-6306
Alicia & James Carter Dance
620 S Decatur Blvd
Las Vegas . . . . (702) 877-1853
American Dance Studios Inc
2605 S Decatur Blvd
Las Vegas . . . . (702) 871-4501
Arthur Murray Dance Studio
4550 S Maryland Pkwy # N
Las Vegas . . . . (702) 798-4552
Backstage Dance Studio
3425 S Lamb Blvd
Las Vegas . . . . (702) 739-1446
Backstage Dance Studio
1942 E Sahara Ave
Las Vegas . . . . (702) 457-7310
Bunker Dance Ctr
2400 S Jones Blvd
Las Vegas . . . . (702) 870-7870
Carolyn Collette's Dance
3111 S Valley View Blvd # M104
Las Vegas . . . . (702) 871-1555
Christine Harper's Dance West
2081 N Jones Blvd
Las Vegas . . . . (702) 646-8040

Class Act-Preston's Dance
6250 Mountain Vista St # D2
Henderson . . . . (702) 451-3939
Cloggers Vegas Valley
2245 N Decatur Blvd # K
Las Vegas . . . . (702) 647-3501
Clogging
4468 El Tovar Rd
Las Vegas . . . . (702) 796-4357
Dance Charisma
6000 Spring Mountain Rd # 2
Las Vegas . . . . (702) 364-8700
Dance Etc Inc
525 Hotel Plz
Boulder City . . . . (702) 293-5001
Dance Vision USA
4270 Cameron St
Las Vegas . . . . (702) 365-6650
Desert Shores Dance Academy
2620 Regatta Dr # 118
Las Vegas . . . . (702) 363-3070
Fern Adair Conservatory
3265 E Patrick Ln
Las Vegas . . . . (702) 458-7575
Fred Astaire Dance Studio Inc
1801 E Tropicana Ave # 22
Las Vegas . . . . (702) 795-0041
Helene Gregory Talent Ctr
3755 E Desert Inn Rd
Las Vegas . . . . (702) 451-1666
Henry Le Tang Academy Of Dance
953 E Sahara Ave # B35
Las Vegas . . . . (702) 871-3999
Henry Le Tang Pro Dance
953 E Sahara Ave # B35
Las Vegas . . . . (702) 892-8499
Henry Letang Theatrical Studio
3700 E Desert Inn Rd # 4
Las Vegas . . . . (702) 898-6898
Icela's Studio
Po Box 34944
Las Vegas . . . . (702) 388-0948
Inez Mourning Studio One Dance
4601 W Sahara Ave # J
Las Vegas . . . . (702) 364-2077
Judy's Studio
7380 S Eastern Ave # 109d
Las Vegas . . . . (702) 896-3100
Kick Em Up Kids
2245 N Decatur Blvd # K
Las Vegas . . . . (702) 647-3501
Kids In Motion
4024 N Tenaya Way
Las Vegas . . . . (702) 645-5250
Kravenko School Of Dance
3400 S Jones Blvd # 11
Las Vegas . . . . (702) 876-2806
Lakes Dance School
2912 Lake East Dr
Las Vegas . . . . (702) 255-6110
Las Vegas Dance Studio
5155 Industrial Rd
Las Vegas . . . . (702) 736-0991

Las Vegas Dance Theatre Studio
3248 Civic Center Dr
North Las V... . . . . (702) 649-3932
Las Vegas Stars Dance Team
4700 Boston Ivy Ct
Las Vegas . . . . (702) 645-4840
London Dance Academy
2585 E Flamingo Rd
Las Vegas . . . . (702) 737-1202
Marliza's Magic Carpet Dancers
4133 W Charleston Blvd
Las Vegas . . . . (702) 870-5508
Merluzzi Dance & Gymnastic Ctr
1137 S Rainbow Blvd
Las Vegas . . . . (702) 254-6712
Mikel's Dance Adacemy
7034 W Charleston Blvd
Las Vegas . . . . (702) 256-4522
Rainbow Performing Arts Studio
21 N Mojave Rd # A
Las Vegas . . . . (702) 384-6268
Rainbow School Of Dance
21 N Mojave Rd
Las Vegas . . . . (702) 382-1223
Robert Allen Studios
3977 Vegas Valley Dr
Las Vegas . . . . (702) 431-8441
Sharon Lynn Academy Of Dance
3655 S Durango Dr
Las Vegas . . . . (702) 869-8580
Shining L
900 Karen Ave
Las Vegas . . . . (702) 734-8900
Silver Dolls Dancers
4601 W Sahara Ave
Las Vegas . . . . (702) 367-9811
Simba Studio
4229 Beth Ave
Las Vegas . . . . (702) 647-8808
Step By Step School-Ballroom
1801 E Tropicana Ave # 22
Las Vegas . . . . (702) 795-0041
Sunshine Generation Dance Co
2245 N Decatur Blvd
Las Vegas . . . . (702) 647-3501
Wonderland School Of Dance
3650 E Flamingo Rd
Las Vegas . . . . (702) 456-6668

Dentists - Childrens

A Childrens Dentist
2001 S Rainbow Blvd # C
Las Vegas . . . . (702) 255-0133
Jeffery B Kinner DDS
1811 S Rainbow Blvd # 101
Las Vegas . . . . (702) 254-4220
Mark C Peterson DDS
3600 Cambridge St
Las Vegas . . . . (702) 733-8341
Maryam Sina DDS
2551 N Green Vly Pkwy # 400a
Henderson . . . . (702) 458-6684

Myron L Caplan DDS
650 Shadow Ln # 3
Las Vegas . . . . (702) 387-1947

Pediatric Dental Care Assoc
1811 S Rainbow Blvd # 101
Las Vegas . . . . (702) 734-5333

Richard W Carr Jr DDS
2250 E Tropicana Ave # 19-505
. . . . (702) 798-5670

William F Waggoner DDS
1811 S Rainbow Blvd # 101
Las Vegas . . . . (702) 254-4220

Department Stores

99 Cent Store
1056 N Rancho Dr
Las Vegas . . . . (702) 638-8110

Bonanza Discount Ctr Inc
574 N Eastern Ave
Las Vegas . . . . (702) 388-0065

Broadway
4300 Meadows Ln
Las Vegas . . . . (702) 258-2100

Broadway
3634 S Maryland Pky
Las Vegas . . . . (702) 791-2100

Broadway Southwest Dept Stores
3634 S Maryland Pky
Las Vegas . . . . (702) 791-2161

Burlington Coat Factory
4750 S Eastern Ave
Las Vegas . . . . (702) 451-5581

Burlington Coat Factory
5959 W Sahara Ave
Las Vegas . . . . (702) 247-1268

County Seat
3680 S Maryland Pkwy
Las Vegas . . . . (702) 737-0228

Designer Brand Accessories
7400 Las Vegas Blvd S
Las Vegas . . . . (702) 896-2018

Dillard's Department Store
1320 W Sunset Rd
Henderson . . . .(702) 435-6300

Dillard's Department Store
3200 Las Vegas Blvd S
Las Vegas . . . .(702) 733-2008

Dillard's Department Store
4200 Meadows Ln
Las Vegas . . . . (702) 870-2039

Dillard's Department Store
3700 S Maryland Pkwy
Las Vegas . . . . (702) 734-2111

Disney Store
3500 Las Vegas Blvd S
Las Vegas . . . . (702) 732-9560

Disney Store
3680 S Maryland Pkwy
Las Vegas . . . . (702) 893-3390

Dollar Deals
6166 W Flamingo Rd
Las Vegas . . . . (702) 257-7507

Family Bargain Corp
141 N Nellis Blvd
Las Vegas . . . . (702) 459-8066

Family Bargain Corp
2364 E Bonanza Rd
Las Vegas . . . . (702) 366-1657

Family Bargain Corp
1740 E Charleston Blvd
Las Vegas . . . . (702) 388-1053

Family Bargain Corp
3262 Las Vegas Blvd N
Las Vegas . . . . (702) 644-0660

J C Penney Co
1312 W Sunset Rd
Henderson . . . . (702) 451-4545

J C Penney Co
771 S Rainbow Blvd
Las Vegas . . . . (702) 259-4898

J C Penney Co
3542 S Maryland Pkwy
Las Vegas . . . . (702) 735-5131

J C Penney Co
4400 Meadows Ln
Las Vegas . . . . (702) 870-9182

J C Penney Co
3542 S Maryland Pky
Las Vegas . . . . (702) 735-5131

Jay Jacobs
4300 Meadows Ln
Las Vegas . . . . (702) 877-1084

Just $1.00
4001 S Decatur Blvd
Las Vegas . . . . (702) 871-7520

Just 1-2-3
3876 W Sahara Ave
Las Vegas . . . . (702) 362-7388

Just 99 Cents Store
1401 N Decatur Blvd
Las Vegas . . . . (702) 647-9911

Just A Bargain
862 S Boulder Hwy
Henderson . . . . (702) 564-4998

Just A Bargain
6150 W Tropicana Ave
Las Vegas . . . . (702) 227-4341

Just A Bargain
2240 S Nellis Blvd
Las Vegas . . . . (702) 431-4750

K Mart
732 S Racetrack Rd
Henderson . . . . (702) 564-8860

K Mart
5050 E Bonanza Rd
Las Vegas . . . . (702) 459-2000

K Mart
4500 N Rancho Dr
Las Vegas . . . . (702) 658-5977

K Mart
3760 E Sunset Rd
Las Vegas . . . . (702) 458-8008

K Mart
3455 S Rainbow Blvd
Las Vegas . . . . (702) 367-8300

K Mart
2975 W Sahara Ave
Las Vegas . . . . (702) 457-1037

K Mart
3760 E Sunset Rd
Las Vegas . . . . (702) 459-2000

K Mart
2671 Las Vegas Blvd N
North Las V... . . . . (702) 642-2183

L A Street Clothing
714 Las Vegas Blvd N
Las Vegas . . . .(702) 384-5465

Macy's
3634 S Maryland Pkwy
Las Vegas . . . . (702) 791-2100

Macy's
3200 Las Vegas Blvd S
Las Vegas . . . . (702) 731-5111

Macy's
3200 Las Vegas Blvd S
Las Vegas . . . .(702) 733-6220

Macys Department Store
4100 Meadows Ln
Las Vegas . . . . (702) 258-2100

Marshalls
232 S Decatur Blvd
Las Vegas . . . . (702) 877-6107

Mervyn's
1316 W Sunset Rd
Henderson . . . . (702) 454-8881

Mervyn's
1155 E Twain Ave
Las Vegas . . . . (702) 737-1500

Mervyn's
4700 Meadows Ln
Las Vegas . . . . (702) 870-9000

Mervyn's
1300 S Nellis Blvd
Las Vegas . . . . (702) 453-8800

Montgomery Ward & Co
2875 E Charleston Blvd
Las Vegas . . . . (702) 385-6661

Montgomery Ward & Co
2120 S Decatur Blvd
Las Vegas . . . . (702) 251-7300

Neiman Marcus
3200 Las Vegas Blvd S
Las Vegas . . . . (702) 731-3636

Newberry's
2025 E Lake Mead Blvd
North Las V... . . . . (702) 649-3395

P & H Wear
574 N Eastern Ave
Las Vegas . . . . (702) 383-8277

Robinsons May
3200 Las Vegas Blvd S
Las Vegas . . . . (702) 737-8708

Ross Dress For Less
649 Stephanie St
Henderson . . . . (702) 458-1144

Ross Dress For Less
3021 N Rainbow Blvd
Las Vegas . . . . (702) 645-5530

Ross Dress For Less
121 N Nellis Blvd
Las Vegas . . . . (702) 438-9292

Ross Dress For Less
2420 E Desert Inn Rd
Las Vegas . . . . (702) 733-9001

Ross Dress For Less
516 S Decatur Blvd
Las Vegas . . . . (702) 878-3740

Saks Fifth Avenue
3200 Las Vegas Blvd S
Las Vegas . . . . (702) 733-8300

Sears Roebuck & Co
3450 S Maryland Pkwy
Las Vegas . . . . (702) 733-7333

Sears Roebuck & Co
4000 Meadows Ln
Las Vegas . . . . (702) 259-4242

Sears Roebuck & Co
3450 S Maryland Pky
Las Vegas . . . . (702) 894-4200

Service Merchandise
10 Sunset Way
Henderson . . . . (702) 451-2006

Service Merchandise
4701 Faircenter Pkwy
Las Vegas . . . . (702) 870-6332

Service Merchandise
1095 E Twain Ave
Las Vegas . . . . (702) 737-0008

Shoe Pavilion
9151 Las Vegas Blvd S
Las Vegas . . . . (702) 897-4655

T J Maxx
4640 W Sahara Ave
Las Vegas . . . . (702) 870-7161

T J Maxx
4000 S Maryland Pkwy
Las Vegas . . . . (702) 733-7730

T J Maxx
4486 N Rancho Dr
Las Vegas . . . . (702) 658-7713

T J Maxx
4100 E Lone Mountain Rd
North Las V... . . . .(702) 643-3224

Talbots Inc
3200 Las Vegas Blvd S
Las Vegas . . . . (702) 893-1706

Target
605 Stephanie St
Henderson . . . . (702) 451-5959

Target
3550 S Rainbow Blvd
Las Vegas . . . . (702) 253-5151

Target
801 S Rancho Dr
Las Vegas . . . . (702) 387-0580

Target
3210 N Tenaya Way
Las Vegas . . . . (702) 645-5440

Target
4001 S Maryland Pkwy
Las Vegas . . . . (702) 732-2218

Target
278 S Decatur Blvd
Las Vegas . . . . (702) 870-1981
Target
1200 S Nellis Blvd
Las Vegas . . . . (702) 438-8866
Wal-Mart
300 E Lake Mead Dr
Henderson . . . . (702) 564-3665
Wal-Mart
3041 N Rainbow Blvd
Las Vegas . . . . (702) 656-0199
Wal-Mart
3615 S Rainbow Blvd
Las Vegas . . . . (702) 367-9999
Wal-Mart
201 N Nellis Blvd
Las Vegas . . . . (702) 452-9998
Wal-Mart
3075 E Tropicana Ave # 1
Las Vegas . . . . (702) 451-8900

Diaper Service

ABC Diaper Svc
5115 Industrial Rd # 303
Las Vegas . . . . (702) 798-9222
Diaper Fresh Diaper Svc
3021 S Valley View Blvd # 107
Las Vegas . . . . (702) 876-2229

Dog and Cat Kennels

A Westside Feline Ctr
4301 W Sahara Ave
Las Vegas . . . . (702) 876-2338
A-Vip Kennels
6808 La Cienega St
Las Vegas . . . . (702) 361-8900
Animal Inn Kennels
3460 W Oquendo Rd
Las Vegas . . . . (702) 736-0036
Arkennels
1651 N Rancho Dr
Las Vegas . . . . (702) 648-0414
Cat's Cradle
3300 E Charleston Blvd
Las Vegas . . . . (702) 457-0370
Chaparral Animal Spa
2105 E Alexander Rd
North Las V... . . . . (702) 649-6383
Dewey Boarding Kennel
4800 W Dewey Dr
Las Vegas . . . . (702) 362-6048
Paws 'N Claws Animal Lodge
640 Eastgate Rd
Henderson . . . . (702) 565-7297
Tolgate Kennels
2670 Betty Ln
Las Vegas . . . . (702) 643-1015

Dolls and Doll Houses

A Doll's House
4225 E Sahara Ave
Las Vegas . . . . (702) 432-9665

Antique & Traditional Furn
3635 S Rainbow Blvd # 101
Las Vegas . . . . (702) 251-3447
Antiques & More
6115 W Tropicana Ave
Las Vegas . . . . (702) 739-8668
Barbie Dolls By Malia Hattie
821 N Lamb Blvd
Las Vegas . . . . (702) 438-8128
Imagination Unlimited
4934 E Tropicana Ave
Las Vegas . . . . (702) 434-5696
Lindoll Porcelain & Doll
4438 E Lake Mead Blvd
Las Vegas . . . . (702) 459-3309
Maudie's Antique Cottage
3310 E Charleston Blvd
Las Vegas . . . . (702) 457-4379
My Twinn
3200 Las Vegas Blvd S
Las Vegas . . . . (702) 734-7249
Reynolds Dolls & Gifts
552 Nevada Hwy
Boulder City . . . . (702) 294-2448

Golf

Angel Park Golf Club
100 S. Rampart Blvd
Las Vegas . . . . (702) 254-4653
Arnold Palmer Golf Academy
Po Box 2889
Mesquite . . . . (702) 346-7810
Badlands At Peccole Ranch
8600 W. Charleston Blvd. #1204
Las Vegas . . . . (702) 242-4653.
Badlands Golf Club
9119 Alta Dr
Las Vegas . . . . (702) 242-4653
Black Mountain Golf & Country
500 Greenway Rd
Henderson . . . . (702) 565-7933
Black Mountain Golf & Country Club
501 Country Club Dr
Las Vegas . . . . (702) 565-7933
Boulder City Municipal Golf Course
1 Clubhouse Dr
Boulder City . . . . (702) 293-9236
Callaway Golf Center
Las Vegas . . . . (702) 896-4100
Craig Ranch Golf Course
628 W Craig Rd
North Las V... . . . . (702) 642-9700
Desert Inn Golf Club
Las Vegas . . . . (702) 733-4290
Desert Pines (Municipal) Golf Course
Bonanza & Mojave (In Nature Park)
3415 E. Bonanza
Las Vegas . . . . (702) 436-7000
Desert Pines Golf Club
3415 E Bonanza Rd
Las Vegas . . . . (702) 388-4400

Desert Rose Golf Course
5483 Club House Dr
Las Vegas .... (702) 431-4653
Desert Rose Golf Course
5843 Club House Dr
East On Sahara 3 Blocks Past N
Las Vegas .... (702) 431-4653
Desert Willow
2010 Horizon Ridge Pwy
Las Vegas .... (702) 263-4653.
Eagle Crest Golf Course
2203 Thomas Ryan Blvd W
Las Vegas .... (702) 233-3096
Highland Falls Golf Club
Las Vegas .... (702) 254-7010
Las Vegas Golf Club
4300 W Washington Ave
Las Vegas .... (702) 646-3003
Las Vegas Golf Systems
4340 S Valley View Blvd
Las Vegas .... (702) 220-9225
Las Vegas Hilton Country Club
1911 E Desert Inn Rd
Las Vegas .... (702) 796-0016
Las Vegas Paiute Resort
10325 Nu Wav Kaiv Blvd
Las Vegas .... (702) 658-2660
Legacy Golf Club
130 Par Excellence Dr
Henderson .... (702) 897-2200
Los Prados Country Club
5150 Los Prados Circle
Las Vegas .... (702) 645-5696
Mirage Golf Club
3650 Las Vegas Blvd. S.
Las Vegas .... (702) 396-7111
Mt Charleston Golf Resort Inc
505 Kyle Canyon Rd
Las Vegas .... (702) 872-4653
North Las Vegas Golf Course
324 E. Brooks Ave.
Las Vegas .... (702) 649-7171
Oasis Golf Club
851 Oasis Blvd
Mesquite .... (702) 346-7820
Painted Desert Country Club
5555 Painted Mirage Rd
Las Vegas .... (702) 645-2568
Palm Palm Valley Golf Club
9201-B Del Webb Blvd.
Las Vegas .... (702) 363-4373
Primm Valley Golf Course
Las Vegas .... (702) 679-5553
Rhodes Ranch
Las Vegas .... (702) 740-4114
Rio Secco Golf Club
Las Vegas .... (702) 702-889-2400
Sahara Country Club
Las Vegas .... (702) 796-0013
Sheraton Desert Inn Country Club
3145 Las Vegas Blvd. S
Las Vegas .... (702) 733-4290

Summerlin Golf Course
9201 Del Webb Blvd
Las Vegas .... (702) 363-4373
Sun City Summerlin Golf Clubs
10201 Sun City Blvd
Las Vegas .... (702) 254-7010
Sunrise Country Club
Las Vegas .... (702) 456-2440
Tony's Pro Shop
1 Clubhouse Dr
Boulder City .... (702) 293-5654
Tournament Players Club
9851 Canyon Run Dr
Las Vegas .... (702) 256-2000
Wildhorse Country Club
1 Showboat Country Club Dr
Henderson .... (702) 434-9000
Gene Munk Pga
2414 La Estrella St
Henderson .... (702) 458-3389
Green Valley Golf Range Inc
1351 W Warm Springs Rd
Henderson .... (702) 434-4300
Las Vegas Golf Ctr
4813 Paradise Rd
Las Vegas .... (702) 650-9002
Star Golf Lounge
3000 Meade Ave
Las Vegas .... (702) 247-9683

Gymnastics

Desert Gymnastics
1924 Rock Springs Dr
Las Vegas .... (702) 341-5852
Go For It
4860 W Lone Mountain Rd
Las Vegas .... (702) 656-8333
Gym Cats Elite
440 Parkson Rd
Henderson .... (702) 566-1414
Gym Tyme Inc
276 S Decatur Blvd
Las Vegas .... (702) 870-5766
Gymboree Play Programs
918 S Valley View Blvd
Las Vegas .... (702) 877-0074
Las Vegas Flyers Gymnastics
1122 Vista Dr
Las Vegas .... (702) 877-2266
Spence Gymnastics & Dance
4860 W Lone Mountain Rd # A
Las Vegas .... (702) 658-9003

Hobby and Model Shops

B & R Railways
3450 S Procyon Ave # E
Las Vegas .... (702) 251-5787
Bill's Hobby Shop
1000 N Nellis Blvd # X
Las Vegas .... (702) 531-3282
Bronze Tablet
2595 Chandler Ave # 9
Las Vegas .... (702) 736-4657

Dansey's Indoor R-C & Hobbies
741 N Nellis Blvd
Las Vegas . . . . (702) 453-7223
Dave's Rc Specialties
4894 W Lone Mountain Rd # 205
Las Vegas . . . . (702) 631-6880
Flying Hawaiian Specialties
19 S Water St # D
Henderson . . . . (702) 565-8400
Great Train Store
2121 S Casino Dr
Laughlin . . . . (702) 298-6235
Hobbytown Usa
3121 N Rainbow Blvd
Las Vegas . . . . (702) 655-0693
Imagination Unlimited
3175 E Tropicana Ave # D1
Las Vegas . . . . (702) 434-7440
Imagination Unlimited
3262 Civic Center Dr # B
North Las V... . . . . (702) 649-3311
Klipper Karts
3111 S Valley View Blvd
Las Vegas . . . . (702) 873-1242
Nice Twice Hobbies & Sports
3111 S Valley View Blvd # A117
Las Vegas . . . . (702) 876-2280
PRC Trains Inc
3920 W Charleston Blvd
Las Vegas . . . . (702) 258-7768
R C Hobbies
4310 E Tropicana Ave
Las Vegas . . . . (702) 547-4401
Rad Trax
3650 S Decatur Blvd
Las Vegas . . . . (702) 253-7568
Slot Car City
4540 E Charleston Blvd
Las Vegas . . . . (702) 438-1760
Train Engineer
2550 Chandler Ave # 53
Las Vegas . . . . (702) 597-1754
Train Exchange
6008 Boulder Hwy
Las Vegas . . . . (702) 456-8766
Triple J Comics & Hobbies
4130 S Sandhill Rd
Las Vegas . . . . (702) 454-7166

Horseback Riding and Stables

2 R Riding Stables
1400 Desert Hills Dr
Las Vegas . . . . (702) 293-3434
Bonnie Springs
Hwy. 159 West Of Las Vegas
Las Vegas . . . . (702) 875-4191
Cowboy Trail Rides
1211 S. Eastern Ave.
Las Vegas . . . . (702) 387-2457
Equestrian Stables
7200 Pine St
Las Vegas . . . . (702) 458-9922

Ernest & Michelle Webb Stables
7145 Placid St
Las Vegas . . . . (702) 897-2005
Golden West Land & Cattle Corp
Po Box 19338
Las Vegas . . . . (702) 798-7788
Grove At Silk Purse Ranch
8101 Racel St
Las Vegas . . . . (702) 645-3223
Mount Charleston Riding Stable
Las Vegas . . . . (702) 872-7009
Mountain T Ranch
140 Kyle Canyon Rd
Las Vegas . . . . (702) 656-8025
Road Runner Ranch Inc
2855 Cherokee Rd
Sandy Valley . . . . (702) 723-5200
Shadowland Equestrian Ctr
6901 N Jones Blvd
Las Vegas . . . . (702) 655-1506
Silver State "Old West" Tours
Spring Mountain Ranch
Las Vegas . . . . (702) 798-6565

Hospitals and Emergency Clinics

Boulder City Hospital Inc
901 Adams Blvd
Boulder City . . . . (702) 293-4111
Desert Springs Hospital Inc
2075 E Flamingo Rd
Las Vegas . . . . (702) 733-8800
Fremont Medical Ctr
4415 W Flamingo Rd
Las Vegas . . . . (702) 871-5005
Galleria Urgent Care
600 Whitney Ranch Dr # A
Henderson . . . . (702) 454-8898
Green Valley Urgent Care
6301 Mountain Vista St # 100
Henderson . . . . (702) 451-3636
Health West Physicians
1090 E Desert Inn Rd # 100
Las Vegas . . . . (702) 733-2001
Isla Verde Medical Ctr
701 E Charleston Blvd
Las Vegas . . . . (702) 382-7699
Isla Verde Medical Ctr
1845 Civic Center Dr
North Las V... . . . . (702) 399-7655
Kumar Urgent Care Ctr-Nevada
6787 W Tropicana Ave
Las Vegas . . . . (702) 257-2400
Lake Mead Hospital Medical Ctr
1409 E Lake Mead Blvd
North Las V... . . . . (702) 649-7711
Legacy Urgent Care
105 N Pecos Rd # 111
Las Vegas . . . . (702) 263-4555
Mesquite Urgent Care & Med Ctr
250 W Mesquite Blvd # 122
Mesquite . . . . (702) 346-3030

directory

Neighborhood Medical Ctr
1725 E Warm Springs Rd
Las Vegas .... (702) 361-2300

Nellis Quick Care
61 N Nellis Blvd
Las Vegas .... (702) 644-8701

Nevada Medical Ctr Urgent Care
3880 S Jones Blvd
Las Vegas .... (702) 877-9500

Overton Urgent Care
461 N Moapa Valley Blvd
Overton .... (702) 397-6344

Rainbow Medical Ctr
731 N Nellis Blvd
Las Vegas .... (702) 438-4003

Rainbow Medical Ctr
4920 W Lone Mountain Rd
Las Vegas .... (702) 655-0550

Rainbow Medical Ctr
1341 S Rainbow Blvd # 101
Las Vegas .... (702) 255-4200

Rampart Medical Ctr
4215 Spring Mountain Rd
Las Vegas .... (702) 362-7877

Southwest Medical Assoc
888 S Rancho Dr # 215
Las Vegas .... (702) 877-8600

Summerlin Urgent Care
8440 W Lake Mead Blvd
Las Vegas .... (702) 254-4295

Sunrise Hospital & Medical Ctr
3186 S Maryland Pky
Las Vegas .... (702) 731-8056

UMC Quick Care Ctr
2760 Lake Sahara Dr # 108
Las Vegas .... (702) 254-4900

University Medical Ctr
1800 W Charleston Blvd
Las Vegas .... (702) 383-2000

University Medical Ctr
1769 E Russell Rd
Las Vegas .... (702) 261-3600

USAF Hospital
Nellis Air Force Base
Nellis AFB .... (702) 652-4895

Valley Hospital Medical Ctr
620 Shadow Ln
Las Vegas .... (702) 388-4000

Vegas Medical Center
3025 Las Vegas Blvd. S., Ste. 112
Across From The Stardust
Las Vegas .... (702) 892-8555

Westcliff Medical & Dental Ctr
6960 Westcliff Dr
Las Vegas .... (702) 363-0232

Hotels & Motels

Arizona Charlie's
740 S. Decatur Blvd
Las Vegas .... (702) 258-5200

Bally's
3645 Las Vegas Blvd S
Las Vegas .... (702) 739-4111

Barbary Coast
3595 Las Vegas Blvd S
Las Vegas .... (702) 737-7111

Binion's Horseshoe
128 Fremont Street
Las Vegas .... (702) 382-1600

Bonnie Springs Motel
1 Bonnie Springs Ranch Rd
Blue Diamond .... (702) 875-4400

Boulder Station
4111 Boulder Hwy
Las Vegas .... (702) 432-7777

Caesars Palace
3570 Las Vegas Blvd
Las Vegas .... (702) 731-7222

California Hotel
12 E Ogden Ave
Las Vegas .... (702) 385-1222

Circus Circus Hotel
2880 Las Vegas Blvd S
Las Vegas .... (702) 734-0410

Continental
4100 Paradise Rd.
Las Vegas .... (702) 737-5555

Del Mar Resort Motel
1411 Las Vegas Blvd S
Las Vegas .... (702) 384-5775

Desert Inn
3145 Las Vegas Blvd S
Las Vegas .... (702) 733-4444

El Cortez
600 E. Fremont Street
Las Vegas .... (702) 385-5200

Excalibur Hotel
3850 Las Vegas Blvd S
Las Vegas .... (702) 597-7777

Fiesta Casino Hotel
2400 Rancho Dr
Las Vegas .... (702) 631-7000

Fitgeralds/Holiday Inn
301 Fremont Street
Las Vegas .... (702) 388-2400

Flamingo Hilton Hotel
3555 Las Vegas Blvd. S
Las Vegas .... (702) 733-3111

Four Queens
202 Fremont Street
Las Vegas .... (702) 385-4011

Freemont Hotel
200 Fremont Street
Las Vegas .... (702) 385-3232

Gold Coast
4000 W. Flamingo Rd
Las Vegas .... (702) 367-7111

Gold Spike Hotel
400 E. Ogden Ave
Las Vegas .... (702) 384-8444

Golden Gate Hotel
1 Freemont Street
Las Vegas .... (702) 385-1906

Golden Nugget Hotel
129 Fremont Street
Las Vegas .... (702) 385-7111

Hard Rock Hotel
4455 Paradise Rd
Las Vegas . . . . (702) 693-5000

Harrah's
3475 Las Vegas Blvd. S
Las Vegas . . . . (702) 369-5000

Holiday Inn - Boardwalk
3750 Las Vegas Blvd S
Las Vegas . . . . (702) 735-2400

Imperial Palace Hotel
3535 Las Vegas Blvd S
Las Vegas . . . . (702) 731-3311

Jackie Gaughan's Plaza Hotel
1 Main Street
Las Vegas . . . . (702) 386-2110

Lady Luck Casino & Hotel
206 N. Third Street
Las Vegas . . . . (702) 477-3000

Las Vegas Club
18 Fremont Street
Las Vegas . . . . (702) 385-1664

Las Vegas Hilton
3000 Paradise Rd
Las Vegas . . . . (702) 732-5111

Las Vegas Holidays
1900 E Sahara Ave
Las Vegas . . . . (702) 457-8006

Luxor Hotel
3900 Las Vegas Blvd. S
Las Vegas . . . . (702) 262-4000

Main Street Station
200 N. Main Street
Las Vegas . . . . (702) 387-1896

Maxim Hotel
160 E. Flamingo Rd
Las Vegas . . . . (702) 731-4300

MGM Grand Hotel
3799 Las Vegas Blvd. S
Las Vegas . . . . (702) 891-1111

Mirage
3400 Las Vegas Blvd S
Las Vegas . . . . (702) 791-7111

Monte Carlo
3770 Las Vegas Blvd S
Las Vegas . . . . (702) 730-7000

Monte Carlo Resort Hotel
3770 Las Vegas Blvd S
Las Vegas . . . . (702) 730-7777

Nevada Palace
5255 Boulder Hwy
Las Vegas . . . . (702) 458-8810

New Frontier Hotel
3120 Las Vegas Blvd S
Las Vegas . . . . (702) 794-8200

New York New York
3790 Las Vegas Blvd S.
Las Vegas . . . . (702) 740-6969

Orleans Hotel & Casino
4500 W Tropicana Ave
Las Vegas . . . . (702) 365-7111

Palace Station
2411 W. Sahara Ave
Las Vegas . . . . (702) 367-2411

Quality Inn - Key Largo
377 E. Flamingo Rd
Las Vegas . . . . (702) 733-7777

Reserve Hotel
777 W. Lake Mead Dr
Las Vegas . . . . (702) 558-7000

Rio Suite Hotel
3700 W. Flamingo Rd
Las Vegas . . . . (702) 252-7777

Riviera Hotel
2901 Las Vegas Blvd S
Las Vegas . . . . (702) 734-5110

Royal Hotel
99 Convention Center Dr.
Las Vegas . . . . (702) 735-6117

Sahara Hotel
2535 Las Vegas Blvd S
Las Vegas . . . . (702) 737-2111

Sam's Town
5111 Boulder Hwy
Las Vegas . . . . (702) 456-7777

San Remo
115 E. Tropicana Ave
Las Vegas . . . . (702) 739-9000

Santa Fe Hotel
4949 N. Rancho Dr
Las Vegas . . . . (702) 658-4900

Showboat Hotel Casino
2800 Fremont St
Las Vegas . . . . (702) 383-9333

Silverton
3333 Blue Diamond Rd
Las Vegas . . . . (702) 263-7777

Stardust
3000 Las Vegas Blvd S
Las Vegas . . . . (702) 732-6111

Stratosphere
2000 Las Vegas Blvd S
Las Vegas . . . . (702) 380-7777

Sunset Station
1301 W. Sunset Rd
Las Vegas . . . . (702) 547-7777

Texas Station
2101 Texas Star Ln
Las Vegas . . . . (702) 631-1000

Town Palms
321 S Casino Center Blvd
Las Vegas . . . . (702) 382-1611

Treasure Island
3300 Las Vegas Blvd S
Las Vegas . . . . (702) 894-7111

Tropicana
3801 Las Vegas Blvd S
Las Vegas . . . . (702) 739-2222

Vacation Village
6711 Las Vegas Blvd S
Las Vegas . . . . (702) 897-1700

Western Hotel/Casino
899 Fremont Street
Las Vegas . . . . (702) 384-4620

Westward Hotel
2900 Las Vegas Blvd S
Las Vegas . . . . (702) 731-2900

directory

Libraries - Public

Blue Diamond Public Library
14 Cottonwood Dr
Blue Diamond . . . . (702) 875-4295
Boulder City Library
813 Arizona St
Boulder City . . . . (702) 293-1281
Clark Co Library-Mesquite Brch
121 W 1st St N
Mesquite . . . . (702) 346-5224
Clark County Library
200 W Virgin St
Bunkerville . . . . (702) 346-5238
Clark County Library
1401 E Flamingo Rd
Las Vegas . . . . (702) 733-7810
Family History Library
2555 St Joseph St
Logandale . . . . (702) 398-3266
Goodsprings Library
365 San Pedro St
Goodsprings . . . . (702) 874-1366
Green Valley Library
2797 N Green Valley Pkwy
Henderson . . . . (702) 435-1840
Henderson Library
1640 Price St
Henderson . . . . (702) 565-5816
Henderson Public Library
80 N Pecos Rd
Henderson . . . . (702) 263-7522
Henderson Public Library
280 S Water St
Henderson . . . . (702) 565-8402
Indian Springs Library
715 Gretta Lane
Indian Springs . . . . (702) 879-3845
Las Vegas Library
833 Las Vegas Blvd N
Las Vegas . . . . (702) 382-3493
Las Vegas-Clark County Library
1401 E Flamingo Rd
Las Vegas . . . . (702) 453-1180
Laughlin Library
2840 Needles Hwy
Laughlin . . . . (702) 298-1081
Moapa Town Library
1340 E Highway 168
Moapa . . . . (702) 864-2438
Moapa Valley Main Library
350 N Moapa Valley Blvd
Overton . . . . (702) 397-2690
Mt Charleston Public Library
1252 Aspen Ave
Las Vegas . . . . (702) 872-5585
Nevada Technical Library
2753 S Highland Dr
Las Vegas . . . . (702) 295-1274
Rainbow Library
3150 N Buffalo Dr
Las Vegas . . . . (702) 243-7323

Sahara West Library
9600 W Sahara Ave
Las Vegas . . . . (702) 228-1940
Sandy Valley Library
Quartz Ave
Sandy Valley . . . . (702) 723-5333
Spring Valley Library
4280 S Jones Blvd
Las Vegas . . . . (702) 368-4411
Sunrise Library
5400 Harris Ave
Las Vegas . . . . (702) 453-1104
Talking Book Library
1401 E Flamingo Rd
Las Vegas . . . . (702) 733-1925
West Charleston Library
6301 W Charleston Blvd
Las Vegas . . . . (702) 878-3682
West Las Vegas Library
951 W Lake Mead Blvd
Las Vegas . . . . (702) 647-2117
Whitney Library
5175 E Tropicana Ave
Las Vegas . . . . (702) 454-4575

Reservation Services

Assured Reservation Systems
2250 E Tropicana Ave
Las Vegas . . . . (702) 597-9710
Boulder Palms Luxury Suites
4350 Boulder Hwy
Las Vegas . . . . (702) 434-9900
City Wide Reservations
2929 E Desert Inn Rd
Las Vegas . . . . (702) 794-4599
DMC
1516 E Tropicana Ave # A13
Las Vegas . . . . (702) 315-5600
Holiday House Motel
2211 Las Vegas Blvd S
Las Vegas . . . . (702) 732-2468
Holiday Motel
2205 Las Vegas Blvd S
Las Vegas . . . . (702) 735-6464
Las Vegas Hotel Reservation
3172 N Rainbow Blvd # 404
Las Vegas . . . . (702) 656-6296
Las Vegas Reservation Network
4972 S Maryland Pkwy # 11
Las Vegas . . . . (702) 735-0211
National Reservations Bureau
1820 E Desert Inn Rd
Las Vegas . . . . (702) 794-4490
Nevada Destinations
1820 E Desert Inn Rd
Las Vegas . . . . (702) 794-2402
Ready Reservations
1800 E Sahara Ave
Las Vegas . . . . (702) 734-9115
Roomfinders Housing Svc
2595 Chandler Ave # 7
Las Vegas . . . . (702) 262-9083

USA Hosts Housing Svc
1055 E Tropicana Ave # 530
Las Vegas . . . . (702) 798-8309

Museums and Historical Places

African American Museum & Research Center
The Walker Foundation
705 W. Van Buren Ave.
Las Vegas . . . . (702) 647-2242

American Museum Of Historical Documents
Fashion Show Mall
Las Vegas

Bethany's Celebrity Doll & Wax Museum
3765 Las Vegas Blvd. South
Las Vegas . . . . (702) 798-3036

Boulder City-Hoover Dam Museum
444 Hotel Plz
Boulder City . . . . (702) 294-1988

Boulder City/Hoover Dam Museum
444 Hotel Plaza
Boulder City . . . . (702) 294-1988

Bruno's Indian & Turquiose Museum
1306 Nevada Highway
Boulder City . . . . (702) 293-4865

Children's Historical Museum
1636 E Charleston Blvd . . . .
Las Vegas . . . . (702) 383-6911

Clark County Heritage Museums
1830 S Boulder Hwy
Henderson . . . . (702) 455-7955

Debbie Reynolds Hollywood Movie Museum
305 Convention Center Dr.
Las Vegas . . . . (702) 733-2243

Desert Demonstration Gardens
Las Vegas . . . .(702) 258-3205

Gallery Of History
3200 S. Las Vegas Blvd.
Las Vegas . . . . (702) 731-2300

Green Valley Sculptures
Information Center
2501 N. Green Valley Pkwy
Las Vegas . . . .(702) 458-8855

Guinness World Book Of Records
2780 Las Vegas Blvd S
Las Vegas . . . . (702) 792-3766

Hard Rock Cafe
Las Vegas . . . .(702) 733-8400

Imperial Palace Auto Collection
3535 Las Vegas Blvd
Las Vegas . . . . (702) 731-3311

Judes Ranch
Las Vegas . . . .(702) 294-7172

Jurassic Chinasaur Exhibit
4255 Spring Mountain Rd
Las Vegas . . . .(702) 221-8448

King Tut Museum
Luxor
3900 S. Las Vegas Blvd
Las Vegas . . . .(702) 262-4000

Las Vegas Art Museum
9600 W. Sahara Ave.
Las Vegas . . . . (702) 360-8000

Las Vegas Natural History
900 Las Vegas Blvd N
Las Vegas . . . . (702) 384-3466

Las Vegas Valley Water District
3701 West Alta Drive
Las Vegas . . . . (702) 258-3205

Liberace Museum
1775 E Tropicana
Las Vegas . . . . (702) 798-5595

Lied Discovery Children's
833 Las Vegas Blvd N
Las Vegas . . . . (702) 382-3445

Lost City Museum
721 S Moapa Valley Blvd
Overton . . . . (702) 397-2193

Magic & Movie Hall Of Fame
3555 Las Vegas Blvd S
Las Vegas . . . . (702) 737-1343

Marjorie Barrick Museum Of Natural History
4505 S Maryland Pkwy (At Unlv)
Las Vegas . . . . (702) 895-3381

Mccarran Aviation Heritage Museum
Mccarran International Airport
Las Vegas . . . .(702) 261-5743

Museum Of Natural History
4505 S. Maryland Pkwy. - UNLV
Las Vegas . . . . (702) 895-3381

Nevada State Museum & Historical Society
700 Twin Lakes Drive
Las Vegas . . . . (702) 486-5205

Old Las Vegas Mormon Fort Historic Park
908 N. Las Vegas Blvd
Las Vegas . . . . (702) 486-3511

Vegas Vic
25 Fremont Street
Las Vegas . . . .

World Of Clowns
330 Carousel Pkwy.
Las Vegas . . . . (702) 434-1700

Music - Instruction

Al Day Accordian Instruction
4206 Fulton Pl
Las Vegas . . . . (702) 878-3058

Amadeus School Of Music
900 Karen Ave # A122
Las Vegas . . . . (702) 733-1820

Carrescia's Violin House
1305 Vegas Valley Dr
Las Vegas . . . . (702) 733-0482

Family Music Ctr
110 S Rainbow Blvd
Las Vegas . . . . (702) 360-4080

Frank Da Silva Piano Studio
2225 Carroll St
North Las V... . . . . (702) 399-6622

Grand Piano Studio
1631 E Sunset Rd
Las Vegas . . . . (702) 263-3066

Green Valley Piano Studio
1851 N Green Valley Pkwy
Henderson . . . . (702) 361-1507
Guitar Shack
3021 E Charleston Blvd
Las Vegas . . . . (702) 384-2363
In-Young Lee Piano Studio
3383 S Jones Blvd
Las Vegas . . . . (702) 247-9410
Jimmy Kay Banjo Bass & Guitar
4212 Via Olivero Ave
Las Vegas . . . . (702) 871-0024
Las Vegas Music Teachers Assn
5012 Churchill Ave
Las Vegas . . . . (702) 877-1743
Nevada School Of The Arts
315 S 7th St
Las Vegas . . . . (702) 386-2787
Piano Lessons-Mark Thomas
2312 N Green Valley Pkwy
Henderson . . . . (702) 898-1233
Today's Music
7770 W Sahara Ave
Las Vegas . . . . (702) 256-9400
Vince Martin Piano Instructor
6421 Aberdeen Ln
Las Vegas . . . . (702) 258-3528
Las Vegas Pianos & Organs
3004 S Rancho Dr
Las Vegas . . . . (702) 871-4418
Accent Music
3839 W Sahara Ave
Las Vegas . . . . (702) 362-0036
Berns Suzuki Studio
5221 S Eastern Ave
Las Vegas . . . . (702) 736-3585
Bonnie's Music Shoppe
1500 E Sahara Ave # A
Las Vegas . . . . (702) 732-0777
Family Music Ctr
2714 N Green Valley Pkwy
Henderson . . . . (702) 435-4080
Kessler & Sons Music
3047 E Charleston Blvd
Las Vegas . . . . (702) 385-2263
Kessler & Sons Music
1725 S Rainbow Blvd # 16
Las Vegas . . . . (702) 242-2263
Mahoney's Pro Music & Drum
608 S Maryland Pkwy
Las Vegas . . . . (702) 382-9147

Parks - City and State

Alexander Villas Park
3620 Lincoln Rd
Las Vegas
Allegro Park
1023 Seven Hills Dr
Henderson
An San Sister City Park
Ducharme Ave And Villa Monterey
Las Vegas

Arroyo Grande Sports Complex
298 Arroyo Grande Blvd
Henderson
Ash Meadows National Wildlife Refuge
Las Vegas . . . . (702) 372-5435
Beaver Dam State Park
Las Vegas
Beckley School Park
3223 S. Glenhurst Dr
Las Vegas
Blue Diamond Park
Blue Diamond
Boris Terrace Park
2200 E. Cartier Ave
N. Las Vegas
Boulder City Parks & Rec Dept
900 Arizona St
Boulder City . . . . (702) 293-9256
Brooks Tot Lot
1421 Brooks Ave
N. Las Vegas
Burkholder Jr. High
645 W. Victory Rd
Henderson
Cannon School Park
5850 Euclid Ave
Las Vegas
Cashman School Park
4622 W. Desert Inn Rd
Las Vegas
Cathedral Gorge State Park
Las Vegas
Charleston Heights Park
Maverick And Smoke Ranch Rd
Las Vegas
Chester Stupak Park
231 W. Boston Ave
Las Vegas
Cheyenne Ridge Park
3814 Scott Robinson Dr
N. Las Vegas
Children's Memorial Park
Gowan Rd And Torrey Pines Dr
Las Vegas
City Of Las Vegas Parks And Leisure
749 Veterans Memorial Dr
Las Vegas . . . . (702) 229-6297
City View Park
101 Cheyenne Ave
N. Las Vegas
Civic Center Park
200 Water Street
Henderson
Clark County Parks & Rec
1340 E Highway 168
Moapa . . . . (702) 864-2423
Clark County Parks-Recreation
500 S Grand Central Pkwy
Las Vegas . . . . (702) 455-2452
Coleman Park
Daybreak Rd And Carmen Blvd
Las Vegas

College Park
2613 Tonopah Ave
N. Las Vegas

Cragin Park
900 Hinsen Lane
Las Vegas

Davis Dam
Bullhead City . . . .(520) 754-3628

Davis Park
2796 Redwood St
Las Vegas

Dearing School Park
3046 S. Ferndale St
Las Vegas

Death Valley National Monument
Las Vegas . . . . (619) 786-2331

Desert Breeze
8425 Spring Mountain Rd
Las Vegas

Desert Inn Park
3570 Vista Del Monte Dr
Las Vegas

Dexter Park
Evergreen And Fulton Place
Las Vegas

Doolittle Park
W. Lake Mead Blvd And J Street
Las Vegas

Echo Canyon
Las Vegas

Ed Fountain Park
Vegas Drive And Decatur
Las Vegas

Eldorado Park
5900 Camino Eldorado Blvd
N. Las Vegas

Fitzgerald Tot Lot
H Street And Monroe Ave
Las Vegas

Floyd Lamb State Park
9200 Tule Springs Rd
Las Vegas . . . .(702) 486-5413

Fox Ridge Park
420 Valle Verde Dr
Henderson

Freedom Park
Mojave And E. Washington Ave
Las Vegas

Grand Canyon National Park
Las Vegas 602-638-7888

Grapevine Springs Park
5280 Palm Ave
Las Vegas

Great Basin
Las Vegas

Green Valley Park
370 N. Pecos Rd
Henderson

Hadland Park
2800 Stewart Ave
N. Las Vegas

Hebert Memorial Park
2701 Basswood Ave
N. Las Vegas

Heers Park
Smoke Ranch Rd And Zorro
Las Vegas

Henderson Parks & Recreation
240 Water Street
Henderson

Hidden Palms Park
8855 Hidden Palms Pksy
Las Vegas

Hoover Dam
Las Vegas . . . .(702) 293-8367

Huntridge Circle Park
Maryland Pkwy And Franklin Ave
Las Vegas

Jaycee Park
St. Louis And Eastern Ave
Las Vegas

Joe Kneip Park
2127 Mccarran Street
N. Las Vegas

Joe Shoong Park
1503 Wesley Street
Las Vegas

Lake Havasu/London Bridge
Bullhead City . . . .(520) 855-2784

Lake Mead National Recreation Area
Las Vegas . . . . (702) 293-8906

Las Vegas City Parks & Rec
749 Veterans Memorial Dr
Las Vegas . . . . (702) 229-6297

Las Vegas Parks & Leisure
821 Las Vegas Blvd N
Las Vegas . . . . (702) 229-6553

Las Vegas Recreation Div
749 Veterans Memorial Dr
Las Vegas . . . . (702) 229-6297

Laurelwood Park
4300 Newcastle Rd
Las Vegas

Lewis Family Park
1970 Tree Line Dr
Las Vegas

Lubertha Johnson Park
Balzar Ave And Concord Street
Las Vegas

Mary Dutton Park
Charleston Blvd And 10TH Street
Las Vegas

Maslow Park And Pool
4902 Lana Ave
Las Vegas

Mirabelli Park
6200 Elton Ave
Las Vegas

Moapa River Indian Reservation
Las Vegas

Mojave Ball Fields
Mojave Rd And Bonanza Rd
Las Vegas

Monte Vista Park
4910 Scott Robinson Dr
N. Las Vegas

Mount Charleston/Toiyabe National Forest
Las Vegas . . . . (702) 872-5500

Mountain View School Park
5436 E. Kell Ln
Las Vegas

Nellis Meadows
4949 E. Cheyenne Ave
Las Vegas

Nicholas E. Flores, Jr. Park
4133 Allen Ln
N. Las Vegas

North Las Vegas Parks & Recreation Dept
2200 Civic Center Dr.
N. Las Vegas . . . . (702) 633-1171

Old Las Vegas Mormon Fort
908 Las Vegas Blvd N
Las Vegas . . . . (702) 486-3511

Overton Park
Overton . . . . (702) 397-8787

Overton Town Park
Overton

Pahranagat National Wildlife Refuge
Las Vegas . . . . (702) 725-3417

Paradise Park
4770 S. Harrison Dr
Las Vegas

Paradise Park Community Ctr
4770 Harrison Dr
Las Vegas . . . . (702) 455-7513

Paradise School Park
851 E. Tropicana Ave
Las Vegas

Paradise Vista Park
5582 Stirrup Street
Las VegaS

Parkdale Park
3200 Ferndale Street
Las Vegas

Parks & Rec-Safekey Program
1951 Silver Springs Pkwy
Henderson . . . . (702) 435-3817

Parks & Recreation Dept
200 Virgin St
Bunkerville . . . . (702) 346-5260

Parks Division
4747 Vegas Dr
Las Vegas . . . . (702) 486-5126

Paul Meyer Park
4525 New Forest Dr
Las Vegas

Potosi Park
2790 Potosi St
Las Vegas

Prosperity Park
7101 Parasol Lane
Las Vegas

Pueblo Park
W Lake Mead Blvd And Pueblo Vista Dr
Las Vegas

Rainbow Family Park
Oakey Blvd And O'bannon Dr
Las Vegas

Red Rock Canyon
Las Vegas . . . .(702) 363-1921

Regional Park
4400 Horse Dr
N. Las Vegas

Richard Tam
Donna & Craig Streets
N. Las Vegas

Richard Walpole Rec. Area
1621 Yale Street
N. Las Vegas

River Mountain Park
1941 Appaloosa Rd
Henderson

Robert E. Lake School Park
2904 Meteoro Street
Las Vegas

Rotary Park
W. Charleston Blvd And Hinson Street
Las Vegas

Rotary Tot Lot
2600 Magnet Street
N. Las Vegas

Shadow Rock Park
2650 Los Feliz Street
Las Vegas

Silver Bowl Sports Complex
6800 E. Russell Rd
Las Vegas

Spring Mountain Ranch State
8000 West Blue Diamond
Blue Diamond . . . . (702) 875-4141

Spring Valley Park
4220 S. Ravenwood Dr
Las Vegas

Stewart Place Park
Marion Dr. And Chantilly Ave
Las Vegas

Sunrise Park Commun Ctr
2240 Linn Ln
Las Vegas . . . . (702) 455-7600

Sunset Park
2601 E Sunset Rd
Las Vegas . . . . (702) 455-8200

Tate School Park
2450 Lincoln Rd
Las Vegas

Thomas School Park
1560 E. Cherokee Ln
Las Vegas

Thurman White Middle School Park
1661 Galleria Dr
Henderson

Titanium Field
Lake Mead Dr And Water Street
Henderson

Toiyabe National Forest
Las Vegas . . . . (702) 873-8800

Tom Williams Park
1844 Belmont St.
N. Las Vegas

Tonopah Park
204 E. Tonopah Ave
N. Las Vegas

Ullom School Park
4869 Sun Valley Dr
Las Vegas
Valley View Park
2000 Bennett Street
N. Las Vegas
Valley-Fire State Park
Highway 169 Exit 75
Overton .... (702) 397-2088
Vegas Heights Tot Lot
Balzar Ave And Concord Street
Las Vegas
Walker Park
1509 June Ave
N. Las Vegas
Warm Springs Softball Complex
Eastern Ave At Warm Springs Rd
Las Vegas
Wayne Bunker Family Park
Tenaya Way And Alexander Rd
Las Vegas
West Charleston Lion Park
Essex Dr. And Fulton Place
Las Vegas
Whitney Park
5700 E. Missouri Ave
Las Vegas
Wildwood Park
Shadow Mountain And Wildwood
Las Vegas
Winchester Park
3130 S. Mcleod Dr
Las Vegas
Winterwood Park
5310 Consul Ave
Las Vegas
Woofter Family Park
Vegas Dr And Rock Springs Dr
Las Vegas
Youth Center Park
105 W. Basic Rd
Henderson

Pharmacies and Drug Stores

Payless Drug Store
716 S Boulder Hwy
Henderson .... (702) 565-7944
Payless Drug Store
2255 N Green Valley Pkwy
Henderson .... (702) 434-5010
Payless Drug Store
4230 S Rainbow Blvd
Las Vegas .... (702) 873-5874
Payless Drug Store
4530 E Charleston Blvd
Las Vegas .... (702) 452-6636
Payless Drug Store
3852 W Sahara Ave
Las Vegas .... (702) 871-6666
Payless Drug Store
4911 W Craig Rd
Las Vegas .... (702) 658-0810

Payless Drug Store
3651 S Maryland Pkwy
Las Vegas .... (702) 735-7191
Payless Drug Store
8530 W Lake Mead Blvd
Las Vegas .... (702) 255-9696
Payless Drug Store
3130 N Rainbow Blvd
Las Vegas .... (702) 658-4288
Payless Drug Store
3330 E Flamingo Rd
Las Vegas .... (702) 458-0044

Planetariums

Cheyenne Campus Planetarium
3200 E. Cheyenne Ave
Cheyenne Communinity College
Las Vegas .... (702) 651-5059

Shoppings Centers and Malls

Belz Factory Outlet World
7400 South Las Vegas Blvd.
Las Vegas .... (702) 896-5599
Boulevard Mall
3528 S Maryland Pkwy
Las Vegas .... (702) 735-8268
China Town Plaza Inc
4215 Spring Mountain Rd # B112
Las Vegas .... (702) 221-8448
Fashion Show Mall
3200 Las Vegas Blvd S
Las Vegas .... (702) 369-0704
Flamingo-Arville Plaza
4443 W Flamingo Rd
Las Vegas .... (702) 876-7467
Forum Shops At Caesars
3500 Las Vegas Blvd S
Las Vegas .... (702) 893-4800
Galleria At Sunset
Las Vegas
Las Vegas Factory Outlet Stores Of America
Las Vegas ....(702) 897-9090
Meadows Mall
4300 Meadows Ln
Las Vegas .... (702) 878-4849
New Orleans Square
900 Karen Ave
Las Vegas .... (702) 737-8551
Nucleus Plaza Inc
926 W Owens Ave
Las Vegas .... (702) 646-0220
Park Place
340 Lewis Ave
Las Vegas .... (702) 384-4488
Pecos Center
340 Lewis Ave
Las Vegas .... (702) 384-4488
Pecos Legacy Ctr
2562 Wigwam Pkwy
Henderson .... (702) 896-2613
Pecos Mc Leod Plaza
3050 E Desert Inn Rd
Las Vegas .... (702) 731-3133

directory

Plazas At First Western
2800 W Sahara Ave # 4a
Las Vegas . . . . (702) 362-2111
Plazas At First Western Square
2300 Paseo Del Prado
Las Vegas . . . . (702) 362-2111
Rainbow Express Village
1750 S Rainbow Blvd
Las Vegas . . . . (702) 870-1843
Sahara Pavilion
4760 W Sahara Ave
Las Vegas . . . . (702) 258-4330
Sahara Square
340 Lewis Ave
Las Vegas . . . . (702) 384-4488
Spring Mountain Business Park
3839 Spring Mountain Rd
Las Vegas . . . . (702) 368-0046
Sugarhouse Shopping Ctr
4161 S Eastern Ave
Las Vegas . . . . (702) 731-6526
Tower Shops At Stratosphere
Las Vegas . . . . (702) 388-1130.
Vegas Pointe Plaza
9155 Las Vegas Blvd. S.
Las Vegas . . . . (702) 897-9090.
Village Center Inc
1046 N Rancho Dr
Las Vegas . . . . (702) 648-8655
Village-East Plaza
5025 S Eastern Ave
Las Vegas . . . . (702) 736-7227

Skating

Crystal Palace
3901 N. Rancho Drive
Las Vegas . . . . (702) 645-4892
Crystal Palace
9295 W. Flamingo Rd
Las Vegas . . . . (702) 253-9832
Crystal Palace
1110 E. Lake Mead Dr
Las Vegas . . . . (702) 564-2790
Crystal Palace
4680 Boulder Hwy
Las Vegas . . . . (702) 458-7107
Las Vegas Ice Gardens
3896 Swenson St
Las Vegas . . . . (702) 731-1062
Mountasia Family Fun Center
2050 Olympic Ave
Henderson . . . . (702) 898-7777
Sahara Ice Palace
800 E Karen Ave
Las Vegas . . . . (702) 862-4262
Santa Fe Hotel Ice Arena
4949 N Rancho Dr
Las Vegas . . . . (702) 658-4993
Thrillseekers Unlimited
3172 N. Rainbow Blvd., Ste 321
Las Vegas . . . . (702) 699-5550

Sporting Goods Stores

A Quality Trampoline
4000 Boulder Hwy # 8
Las Vegas . . . . (702) 457-6564
Armando Salinas Sports Equpmnt
1560 N Eastern Ave # A20
Las Vegas . . . . (702) 798-6605
Bfk Sports Of Las Vegas Inc
3111 S Valley View Blvd
Las Vegas . . . . (702) 220-4340
Big 5 Sporting Goods
1140 S Decatur Blvd
Las Vegas . . . . (702) 878-6100
Big 5 Sporting Goods
4275 E Charleston Blvd
Las Vegas . . . . (702) 641-2224
Big 5 Sporting Goods
2797 S Maryland Pkwy
Las Vegas . . . . (702) 734-6664
Bowling Express
3375 Glen Ave
Las Vegas . . . . (702) 431-8590
Champs Sports
1300 W Sunset Rd
Henderson . . . . (702) 456-0903
Champs Sports
4300 Meadows Ln
Las Vegas . . . . (702) 258-5943
Champs Sports
3454 S Maryland Pkwy
Las Vegas . . . . (702) 369-0903
Copeland Sports
3860 S Maryland Pkwy
Las Vegas . . . . (702) 794-0119
Czech Sports
2675 E Patrick Ln # 8
Las Vegas . . . . (702) 383-6664
D & L Sports
1670 Santiago Dr
Henderson . . . . (702) 433-1828
Desert Rock Sports
8201 W Charleston Blvd # A
Las Vegas . . . . (702) 254-1143
Highroller Skate Shop
4343 N Rancho Dr # 240
Las Vegas . . . . (702) 395-7036
Holiday Hockey & Sport
4611 N Rancho Dr
Las Vegas . . . . (702) 645-4301
Horizon Turf Inc
4755 Procyon St
Las Vegas . . . . (702) 795-0330
J T's Golf
3475 S Jones Blvd
Las Vegas . . . . (702) 368-4331
Jadde Sports
Po Box 2820
Mesquite . . . . (702) 397-6480
Jock Shop
5785 W Sahara Ave
Las Vegas . . . . (702) 871-4910

Jumbo Sports
3071 N Rainbow Blvd
Las Vegas . . . . (702) 645-0410
M & G Sporting Goods Inc
3111 S Valley View Blvd # 105
Las Vegas . . . . (702) 362-3111
Mad Hatter
7400 Las Vegas Blvd S
Las Vegas . . . . (702) 897-5058
Mc Ghies Ski Chalet
4503 W Sahara Ave
Las Vegas . . . . (702) 252-8077
Oshman's Sporting Goods
4300 Meadows Ln
Las Vegas . . . . (702) 877-131
Peloton Sport Bicycles
911 N Buffalo Dr
Las Vegas . . . . (702) 363-1991
Penalty Box
6380 W Flamingo Rd
Las Vegas . . . . (702) 362-4884
Play It Again Sports
2250 E Tropicana Ave
Las Vegas . . . .(702) 261-9038
Play It Again Sports
2001 S Rainbow Blvd
Las Vegas . . . .(702) 228-1713
Powerhouse Rock Gym
8201 W Charleston Blvd # B
Las Vegas . . . .(702) 254-5604
Premier Image Corp
839 Pilot Rd
Las Vegas . . . .(702) 263-3500
Pro Image Inc
1300 W Sunset Rd
Henderson . . . .(702) 458-1202
Pro Image Inc
4300 Meadows Ln
Las Vegas . . . .(702) 878-2468
Pro Jersey
2120 S Decatur Blvd
Las Vegas . . . .(702) 251-7335
Roger Dunn Golf Shop
2261 N Green Valley Pkwy
Henderson . . . .(702) 456-4653
Rossi Golf Ctr
3000 Meade Ave
Las Vegas . . . .(702) 368-4653
Ski Chalet
3310 E Flamingo Rd
Las Vegas . . . .(702) 433-1120
Soccer Field
633 N Decatur Blvd
Las Vegas . . . .(702) 878-7860
Sporting Image
3645 Las Vegas Blvd S
Las Vegas . . . .(702) 699-7087
Sports Authority
1431 W Sunset Rd
Henderson . . . .(702) 433-2676
Sports Authority
3651 S Maryland Pkwy
Las Vegas . . . .(702) 796-5557

Sports Authority
2620 S Decatur Blvd
Las Vegas . . . . (702) 368-3335
Sports Fan Ctr
2437 Las Vegas Blvd S
Las Vegas . . . . (702) 893-4860
Sports-1 & Ski Slope
1062 N Rancho Dr
Las Vegas . . . . (702) 647-6000
Starter Outlet Store
7400 Las Vegas Blvd S
Las Vegas . . . . (702) 361-1355
Sub-Skates Etc
3736 E Flamingo Rd
Las Vegas . . . . (702) 435-1978
Team Canada
7380 S Eastern Ave # 109a
Las Vegas . . . . (702) 361-1300
Tobacco Road Sports
2103 Western Ave
Las Vegas . . . . (702) 382-8000
Turf Sporting Goods
3558 S Procyon Ave
Las Vegas . . . . (702) 873-2478
Vegas Golf Inc
3850 W Desert Inn Rd
Las Vegas . . . . (702) 873-8077
Warren Sports
1826 Paprika Way
Henderson . . . . (702) 435-7873

Sports Teams

Las Vegas Dust Devils . . . . (702) 739-8856
Las Vegas Flash . . . . (702) 262-9795
Las Vegas Stars Baseball
Cashman Field
Las Vegas . . . . (702) 386-7200
Las Vegas Sting . . . . (702) 739-8856
Las Vegas Thunder Hockey
Thomas & Mack Center On The Unlv Campus
P.O. Box 70065
Las Vegas . . . . (702) 798-7825

Swimming - Instruction

Bubble Swim School
2790 S Torrey Pines Dr
Las Vegas . . . . (702) 368-7946
Creative Kids Swim School
6620 W Katie Ave
Las Vegas . . . . (702) 871-8664
Desert Iguanas
7565 Holloran Ct
Las Vegas . . . . (702) 363-4850
Las Vegas Sandpiper Swim Team
2800 S Eastern Ave
Las Vegas . . . . (702) 737-7799
Skalak Swim School
6017 Fawn Ave
Las Vegas . . . . (702) 878-4532
Team Vegas Aquatics
3835 Raymert Dr
Las Vegas . . . . (702) 435-7946

Team Vegas Water Polo
7050 Ovation Way
Las Vegas .... (702) 896-2265

Swimming Pools - Public

Boulder City Swimming Pool
861 Avenue B
Boulder City .... (702) 293-9286
Clark County Pool
3280 N Moapa Valley Blvd
Logandale .... (702) 398-3126
Clark County Pool
375 W Thomas Ave
Overton .... (702) 397-8088
Doolittle Pool
1940 J St
Las Vegas .... (702) 229-6398
Henderson Bmi Swimming Pool
107 W Basic Rd
Henderson .... (702) 565-2168
Henderson Lorin Williams Pool
500 Palo Verde Dr
Henderson .... (702) 565-2123
Henderson Silver Springs Pool
1951 Silver Springs Pkwy
Henderson .... (702) 435-3819
Indian Springs Swimming Pool
Sky Rd
Indian Springs .... (702) 879-9930
Las Vegas Baker Pool
1100 E Saint Louis Ave
Las Vegas .... (702) 229-6395
Las Vegas Brinley Pool
2480 Maverick St
Las Vegas .... (702) 229-6784
Las Vegas Cragin Pool
900 Hinson St
Las Vegas .... (702) 229-6394
Las Vegas Garside Pool
400 S Torrey Pines Dr
Las Vegas .... (702) 229-6393
Las Vegas Hadland Pool
2800 Stewart Ave
Las Vegas .... (702) 229-6397
Las Vegas Municipal Pool
430 E Bonanza Rd
Las Vegas .... (702) 229-6309
Trails Pool
1920 Spring Gate Ln
Las Vegas .... (702) 229-4629

Transportation - Taxi Cabs

A Vegas Western Cab Co
5010 S Valley View Blvd
Las Vegas .... (702) 736-6121
A-North Las Vegas Cab
5010 S Valley View Blvd
Las Vegas .... (702) 643-1041
A-Virgin Valley Cab Co
312 W Mesquite Blvd # 111
Mesquite .... (702) 346-7461

ABC Union Cab Co
5010 S Valley View Blvd
Las Vegas .... (702) 736-8444
Ace Cab Co
5010 S Valley View Blvd
Las Vegas .... (702) 736-8383
Henderson Taxi
2030 Industrial Rd
Las Vegas .... (702) 384-2322
Nellis Cab Co
3215 Cinder Ln
Las Vegas .... (702) 367-6935
Western Cab Co
801 S Main St
Las Vegas .... (702) 382-7100
Whittlesea Blue Cab
1910 Industrial Rd
Las Vegas .... (702) 384-6111
Yellow Checker Star Cab Co
3950 W Tompkins Ave
Las Vegas .... (702) 873-2000

Tennis Courts

Aladdin Tennis Shop
3667 Las Vegas Blvd S # 12
Las Vegas .... (702) 736-0330
Angel Park
Westcliff and Durango Drives
Baker Park
1100 East St. Louis Ave.
Bally's
3645 Las Vegas Blvd. S. .... (702) 739-4598
Black Mountain
Henderson
Bob Baskin Park
South Rancho Dr. and West Okey Blvd.
Bruce Trent Park
West Vegas Dr. and Rampart Blvd.
Bunker Family Park
Las Vegas
Cheyenne Sports Complex
3500 E. Cheyenne Ave., N. Las Vegas
Clark County Parks & Leisure Activities
Las Vegas .... (702) 229-6297
Desert Inn
3145 Las Vegas Blvd. .... (702) 733-4577
Discovery Park
2011 Paseo Verde Pkwy., Henderson
Ethel Pearson Park
Washington Ave. and D Street
Flamingo Hilton Tennis Club
3555 Las Vegas Blvd S
Las Vegas .... (702) 733-3444
Frontier
3120 Las Vegas Blvd. .... (702) 794-8200
Gary Dexter Park
Evergreen and Fulton Place
Guinn Middle School
6480 Fairbanks Rd
Las Vegas .... (702) 455-8200
Hartke Park
1638 N. Bruce Street
N. Las Vegas

Hidden Palms
8855 Hidden Palms Pkwy
Las Vegas . . . . (702) 455-8200
Hills Park
Hillpoint Dr. and Rampart, Summerlin
James A. Gay III Park
Morgan and B Street
Joe Knelp Park
2127 Mccarran Street
N. Las Vegas
Las Vegas Racquet Club
3333 Raven Ave
Las Vegas . . . . (702) 361-2202
Las Vegas Sporting House
3025 Industrial Rd
Las Vegas . . . . (702) 733-8999
Laurelwood Park
4300 Newcastle Rd
Las Vegas . . . . (702) 455-7573
Lorenzi Park
3333 W. Washington Ave.
MGM Grand
3799 Las Vegas Blvd. . . . .(702) 891-3085
Morrell Park
500 Harris St., ...Henderson
Mountain View Park
1961 Wigwam Pkwy., Henderson
O'callaghan Park
201 Skyline Road, Henderson
Orr Middle School
1562 E. Katie Ave
Las Vegas . . . . (702) 799-5573
Paradise Park Community Center
4770 S. Harrison Dr
Las Vegas . . . . (702) 455-7513
Paseo Verde Park
Henderson
Paul Meyer Park
4525 New Forest Dr
Las Vegas . . . . (702) 455-7513
Pecos Legacy Park
150 Pecos Road, Henderson
Petitti Park
2505 N. Bruce Street
Las Vegas
River Mountain
1941 Appaloosa, Henderson
Riviera
2901 Las Vegas Blvd . . . .(702) 734-5110
Silver Springs Park
1950 Silver Springs Pkwy., Henderson
Sunrise Community Center
2240 Linn Ln
Las Vegas . . . . (702) 455-7600
Sunset Park
2575 E. Sunset Rd
Las Vegas . . . . (702) 455-8243
Sunset Tennis Club
Lorenzi Park
2601 E. Sunset Rd
Las Vegas . . . . (702) 260-9803
Terry's Hideaway
7909 Giles St
Las Vegas . . . . (702) 896-7384

Thurman White School Park
1661 Galleria, Henderson
Twin Lakes Racquet Club
3075 W Washington Ave
Las Vegas . . . . (702) 647-3434
Unlv
4505 S. Maryland Pkwy
Las Vegas . . . . (702) 895-3207
Von Tobel Park
Las Vegas
Wells Park
1608 Moser, Henderson
Whitney Community Center
5700 Missouri Ave
Las Vegas . . . . (702) 455-7573
Winchester Community Center
3130 S. Mcleod Dr
Las Vegas . . . . (702) 455-7340
Winterwood Park
5310 Consul Ave
Las Vegas . . . . (702) 455-7340

Tourist Information

A Las Vegas Welcome Ctr
3333 S Maryland Pkwy # 11
Las Vegas . . . . (702) 451-7648
All State Tours
999 E Tropicana Ave
Las Vegas . . . . (702) 798-5606
Boulder City Chamber Of Commercwe
. . . .(702) 293-2034
Clark County Cultural Affairs
. . . .(702) 455-8200
Clark County Tourism Ctr
Las Vegas Blvd 161 . . . . (702) 874-1360
Henderson Chamber Of Commerce
. . . .(702) 565-8951
Las Vegas Cultural Affairs
. . . .(702) 229-6713
Las Vegas Info
Po Box 2106
Las Vegas . . . . (702) 682-8002
Nevada Division Of State Parks
. . . .(702) 486-5126
Nevada State Tourists Ctr
3755 Las Vegas Blvd S
Las Vegas . . . . (702) 795-2600
Reservation Plus
2275 Renaissance Dr # A
Las Vegas . . . . (702) 795-3999
Sightseeing Tours Unlimited
612 S 3rd St
Las Vegas . . . . (702) 471-7155
Viva Services
2235 E Flamingo Rd
Las Vegas . . . . (702) 893-9401
What's Free Las Vegas
2235 E Flamingo Rd # 300c
Las Vegas . . . . (702) 866-6689
88 Tours Svc
3355 Spring Mountain Rd
Las Vegas . . . .(702) 876-9858

Tours

A Lake Mead Air
1301 Airport Rd
Boulder City . . . . (702) 293-1848

Adventure Airlines
500 Highway 146
Las Vegas . . . . (702) 631-7100

Adventure Photo Tours
Las Vegas . . . . (702) 889-8687

Air Canada Vacations
3900 Paradise Rd
Las Vegas . . . . (702) 732-2726

Air Vegas Inc
500 Highway 146
Las Vegas . . . . (702) 736-3599

American Pacific Tour
4608 Paradise Rd
Las Vegas . . . . (702) 796-9700

Apple Vacation
5538 S Eastern Ave
Las Vegas . . . . (702) 798-9997

Art & Dot Bradley's Escorted
731 W Sunset Rd
Henderson . . . . (702) 565-6566

ASAP-Las Vegas
3430 E Flamingo Rd
Las Vegas . . . . (702) 458-0090

Bill Mc Fee & Assoc
5538 S Eastern Ave
Las Vegas . . . . (702) 798-8000

Black Canyon Raft Tours
1297 Nevada Hwy
Boulder City . . . . (702) 293-3776

Blue River Safari's
1650 Casino Dr
Laughlin . . . . (702) 298-0910

Brazil Tours Of Las Vegas
444 E Naples Dr
Las Vegas . . . . (702) 733-6992

Cactus Jack's Wild West Tour
2217 Paradise Rd # A
Las Vegas . . . . (702) 731-9400

Cactus Jack's Wild West Tour Company
Las Vegas . . . . (702) 731-2425

California Holidays
700 E Naples Dr # 103
Las Vegas . . . . (702) 796-8687

Canadian Holidays
3900 Paradise Rd # 117
Las Vegas . . . . (702) 735-1566

Casino Hoppers Inc
2918 Gilmore Ave
North Las V... . . . . (702) 228-9763

CTN
425 S 6th St
Las Vegas . . . . (702) 385-9669

D & R Tours
3041 Las Vegas Blvd S
Las Vegas . . . . (702) 369-0133

Daehan Resort Co
953 E Sahara Ave
Las Vegas . . . . (702) 893-9313

Del Rio Beach Club
2900 S Casino Dr
Laughlin . . . . (702) 298-6828

Desert Princess
P.O. Box 62465
Hwy 95 At Lake Mead
Las Vegas . . . . (702) 293-6180

Destination Services
3900 Paradise Rd
Las Vegas . . . . (702) 732-4055

Double Lc Tours
344 Gana Ct
Henderson . . . . (702) 458-3160

Dream Chaser Wilderness Trips
821 N Lamb Blvd # 315
Las Vegas . . . . (702) 459-1400

Eagle Aviation Inc
2772 N Rancho Dr
Las Vegas . . . . (702) 876-1225

Edward & Edward Ltd Tours
765 N Nellis Blvd
Las Vegas . . . . (702) 452-1250

El Morocco Tickets/Tours
2975 Las Vegas Blvd S
Las Vegas . . . . (702) 731-6868

Escape The City Streets Hiking
Po Box 50262
Henderson . . . . (702) 596-2953

Express Tours
3500 W Naples Dr
Las Vegas . . . . (702) 739-8120

Express Usa Corp
4641 Paradise Rd
Las Vegas . . . . (702) 796-9599

Famous Tours Svc
1729 E Desert Inn Rd
Las Vegas . . . . (702) 732-8088

Fiesta West
5538 S Eastern Ave
Las Vegas . . . . (702) 795-7955

Flag Tours
4740 S Valley View Blvd
Las Vegas . . . . (702) 798-7077

Fuji's
5030 Paradise Rd
Las Vegas . . . . (702) 736-9191

Garth Tours Inc
833 S Rainbow Blvd
Las Vegas . . . . (702) 878-5501

Get It Wet Watercraft
661 W Lake Mead Dr.
Henderson . . . . (702) 564-1584

Gorham's Charters & Tours
6171 Forest Park Dr
Las Vegas . . . . (702) 438-7417

Grand Canyon Sightseeing
Las Vegas . . . . (702) 471-7155

Grand Canyon Tour Company
Las Vegas . . . . (702) 655-6060

Gray Line Tours
Las Vegas . . . . (702) 384-1234

Gray Line Tours Of Southern Nv
1550 Industrial Rd
Las Vegas . . . . (702) 384-1234

Guaranteed Tours
3734 Las Vegas Blvd S # 4
Las Vegas . . . . (702) 369-1000
Hers Service
1704 Silver Glen Ave
Las Vegas . . . . (702) 260-0267
Hiking Tours
8221 W. Charleston, Ste. 101
Las Vegas . . . . (702) 596-2953
His Tours
5030 Paradise Rd
Las Vegas . . . . (702) 798-3777
HLA Tourist Svc
708 Anatolia Ln
Las Vegas . . . . (702) 243-2786
Interstate Tours Inc
4740 S Valley View Blvd
Las Vegas . . . . (702) 293-2268
J C Casino Tours Inc
5030 Paradise Rd
Las Vegas . . . . (702) 597-5081
J-K Travel & Assoc
5030 Paradise Rd
Las Vegas . . . . (702) 736-0000
Japan International Inc
105 E Reno Ave
Las Vegas . . . . (702) 798-1180
Jeep Tours
2812 S Highland Dr
Las Vegas . . . . (702) 796-9355
JTB Intl
3743 Las Vegas Blvd S
Las Vegas . . . . (702) 262-0166
K-T Tours & Convention Svc
4020 E Lone Mountain Rd
North Las V... . . . .(702) 644-2233
Keytours
3305 Spring Mountain Rd
Las Vegas . . . . (702) 362-9355
King Express
537 E Sahara Ave # 219
Las Vegas . . . . (702) 696-9647
Lake Mead Cruises
707 Wells Rd
Boulder City . . . . (702) 293-6180
Las Vegas Adventure Tours
444 N Water St
Henderson . . . . (702) 564-5452
Las Vegas By Night
3875 Cambridge St # 814
Las Vegas . . . . (702) 369-9052
Las Vegas Connection
3355 Spring Mountain Rd
Las Vegas . . . . (702) 368-4487
Las Vegas Intl Student Ctr
2112 Paradise Rd
Las Vegas . . . . (702) 737-7374
Las Vegas Tour & Travel
Las Vegas . . . . (702) 739-8975
Las Vegas Vip Svc
3720 Howard Hughes Pkwy
Las Vegas . . . . (702) 794-3400

Latter Day Tours
5404 Alpine Pl
Las Vegas . . . . (702) 259-0341
Laughlin River Tours Inc
3080 Needles Hwy # 2700
Laughlin . . . . (702) 298-1047
Maverick Helicopter Tours
Las Vegas . . . . (702) 261-0007
Miyazuwa Inc
5030 Paradise Rd
Las Vegas . . . . (702) 798-7911
National Tour Co
1801 E Tropicana Ave
Las Vegas . . . . (702) 798-0605
New Image Tours
1655 E Sahara Ave # 1110
Las Vegas . . . . (702) 737-4787
New West Tour Svc
4444 W Russell Rd
Las Vegas . . . . (702) 876-7850
Orient Express Tours
900 E Desert Inn Rd
Las Vegas . . . . (702) 737-5242
Oriental Tours
4045 Spencer St # 121
Las Vegas . . . .(702) 693-6582
Outdoor Connection
3035 E Tropicana Ave # H63
Las Vegas . . . . (702) 220-9115
P S Holidays
5538 S Eastern Ave
Las Vegas . . . . (702) 798-7799
Pacific Aloha Tours-Hawaii
3489 Kensbrook St
Las Vegas . . . . (702) 732-4220
Papillon Grand Canyon Helicopters
Las Vegas . . . . (702) 736-7234
Philip Import & Export
4000 Schiff Dr
Las Vegas . . . . (702) 253-9836
Points West Tours
2470 Chandler Ave
Las Vegas . . . .(702) 891-8877
Prima Tours
953 E Sahara Ave
Las Vegas . . . . (702) 650-2424
R & B Las Vegas Tours
9030 W Sahara Ave
Las Vegas . . . . (702) 341-6965
Ra-Ma Tours
1133 Audrey Ave
Las Vegas . . . . (702) 739-7506
Red Rock Downhill Bicycle
5050 Tamarus St # 23-136
Las Vegas . . . . (702) 798-8452
Regent Tours Co
4699 Industrial Rd # 216
Las Vegas . . . . (702) 247-1300
Rep-Tur Las Vegas
3158 E Flamingo Rd # 204
Las Vegas . . . . (702) 436-1506
Santo Tours
1055 E Tropicana Ave # 100
Las Vegas . . . .(702) 798-0031

Scenic Airlines
2705 Airport Dr
North Las Vegas . . . . (702) 638-3200
Sheba Tours Inc
2901 N Rainbow Blvd # 1099
Las Vegas . . . . (702) 735-7005
Showtime Tours Of Las Vegas
4699 Industrial Rd
Las Vegas . . . .(702) 895-9976
Sightseeing Tours Unlimited
Las Vegas . . . . (702) 471-7155
Signature Vacations
5538 S Eastern Ave
Las Vegas . . . . (702) 798-5588
Silverwing Holidays
5538 S Eastern Ave
Las Vegas . . . . (702) 798-7587
Sky's The Limit Climbing Schl
Hc 33 Box 1
Las Vegas . . . . (702) 363-4533
Southwest Tours Inc
3640 La Junta Dr
Las Vegas . . . . (702) 458-7592
Sports & Adventure Tours
3557 S Valley View Blvd
Las Vegas . . . . (702) 364-8687
Sundance Helicopters And Tours
265 East Tropicana Avenue, Suite 130
Las Vegas . . . . (702) 736-0606
Sunquest Vacations
5538 S Eastern Ave
Las Vegas . . . .(702) 798-5585
Suntrips
835 E Desert Inn Rd
Las Vegas . . . . (702) 734-0700
Superior Tours
4740 S Valley View Blvd # 200
Las Vegas . . . . (702) 798-7311
Teddy Bear Express Inc
2235 E Flamingo Rd
Las Vegas . . . . (702) 737-6062
TNT Vacations
5538 S Eastern Ave
Las Vegas . . . . (702) 739-7722
Tomahawk Outfitters
Bunkerville . . . . (702) 346-5073
Topock Gorge Tours
2900 S Casino Dr
Laughlin . . . . (702) 298-6828
Tour Desk Inc
5030 Paradise Rd
Las Vegas . . . . (702) 597-0086
Tours Of Distinction
3430 E Flamingo Rd
Las Vegas . . . .(702) 454-3838
Trans Mapp Usa Inc
4220 S Maryland Pkwy # 400
Las Vegas . . . . (702) 735-8157
Trans Mappusa Inc
4220 S Maryland Pkwy
Las Vegas . . . . (702) 735-8158
Travel Hosts Inc
5030 Paradise Rd
Las Vegas . . . . (702) 798-4678

V F Enterprises
5030 Paradise Rd
Las Vegas . . . . (702) 739-7070
Vacation Tours
4600 Paradise Rd
Las Vegas . . . . (702) 737-9663
Vacation Tours
115 E Reno Ave
Las Vegas . . . . (702) 795-4777
Vegas Hawaii Tour
2408 Santa Clara Dr
Las Vegas . . . . (702) 796-7166
Viscount Air Tours Inc
1631 Cal Edison Dr # A6
Laughlin . . . . (702) 298-3000
Western Adventure Tours
Las Vegas
World Bus Tours Inc
3500 W Naples Dr
Las Vegas . . . . (702) 597-5545
World Class Tours
8108 Sapphire Bay Cir
Las Vegas . . . . (702) 360-4516

Toys

Airok Toys
2201 Civic Center Dr
North Las V... . . . . (702) 649-4074
Animal Crackers At The Forum
3500 Las Vegas Blvd S
Las Vegas . . . . (702) 796-0121
Beanie Exchange
3200 Las Vegas Blvd S # 600
Las Vegas . . . . (702) 733-8173
Discovery Toys Inc
231 Scotgrove St
Henderson . . . . (702) 434-2010
Disney Store
1300 W Sunset Rd
Henderson . . . . (702) 433-3666
Disney Store
3200 Las Vegas Blvd S
Las Vegas . . . . (702) 737-5400
Elf Shelf
6366 W Sahara Ave
Las Vegas . . . . (702) 258-6337
Jugeteria Delgado
1560 N Eastern Ave
Las Vegas . . . . (702) 399-6669
Kay Bee Toy & Hobby Shop
1300 W Sunset Rd
Henderson . . . . (702) 436-1778
Kay Bee Toy & Hobby Shop
3680 S Maryland Pkwy # 116
Las Vegas . . . . (702) 737-7715
Kay Bee Toy & Hobby Shop
3452 S Maryland Pkwy
Las Vegas . . . . (702) 737-5112
Kay Bee Toy & Hobby Shop
4300 Meadows Ln
Las Vegas . . . . (702) 878-0904

Kids Inc
Riviera Hotel
2901 Las Vegas Blvd S
Las Vegas . . . . (702) 733-6690

Mr Gwell Inc
5001 N Tomsik St
Las Vegas . . . . (702) 645-7457

Replay Used Toys & Things
6620 W Flamingo Rd
Las Vegas . . . . (702) 891-8697

Replay Used Toys & Things
4425 E Tropicana Ave
Las Vegas . . . . (702) 433-6802

Toy Liquidators
7400 Las Vegas Blvd S
Las Vegas . . . . (702) 361-8683

Toy Park
2201 Civic Center Dr
North Las Vegas . . . . (702) 657-6394

Toy Source
1717 S Decatur Blvd # E51
Las Vegas . . . . (702) 361-8953

Toys R Us
1425 W Sunset Rd
Henderson . . . . (702) 454-8697

Toys R Us
4550 Meadows Ln
Las Vegas . . . . (702) 877-9070

Toys R Us
4000 S Maryland Pkwy
Las Vegas . . . . (702) 732-3733

Whipper Snapperz
2555 S Jones Blvd # F1b
Las Vegas . . . . (702) 368-6810

Travel Agencies

Airport Travel Svc
5757 Wayne Newton Blvd # 2
Las Vegas . . . . (702) 261-5889

All State Ticketing
5030 Paradise Rd
Las Vegas . . . . (702) 597-5970

Ambassador Travel
3920 W Charleston Blvd
Las Vegas . . . . (702) 870-7000

Around The World Travel Inc
2003 Las Vegas Blvd S
Las Vegas . . . . (702) 731-1006

Casino Travel & Tours
3850 Las Vegas Blvd S
Las Vegas . . . . (702) 798-7020

Go Go Tours
1900 E Sahara Ave
Las Vegas . . . . (702) 457-2267

Las Vegas Tour & Travel
5191 Las Vegas Blvd S
Las Vegas . . . . (702) 739-8975

New Zealand Experience
2330 Paseo Del Prado
Las Vegas . . . . (702) 253-5494

Pacific International Travel
4608 Paradise Rd
Las Vegas . . . . (702) 796-9699

Where To Cruise Ctr
1722 E University Ave # 5
Las Vegas . . . . (702) 362-6722

Youth Organizations and Centers

4-H Club Office
1897 N Moapa Valley Blvd
Logandale . . . . (702) 397-2604

A-Train Records
2256 Losee Rd
Las Vegas . . . . (702) 642-4212

Baker Park Community School
1020 E Saint Louis Ave
Las Vegas . . . . (702) 733-6599

Boy Scouts Of America
1135 University Rd
Las Vegas . . . . (702) 736-4366

Boys & Girls Club
1011 Dumont Blvd
Las Vegas . . . . (702) 792-1388

Boys & Girls Clubs-Las Vegas
2801 Stewart Ave
Las Vegas . . . . (702) 388-2828

Boys & Girls Clubs-Las Vegas
2850 Lindell Rd
Las Vegas . . . . (702) 367-2582

Boys & Girls Clubs-Las Vegas
817 N St
Las Vegas . . . . (702) 646-8457

Boys & Girls Clubs-Las Vegas
2530 E Carey Ave
North Las V.... . . . . (702) 649-2656

Doolittle Community Ctr
1940 J St
Las Vegas . . . . (702) 229-6374

East Clark County Extension
250 Mesquite Blvd
Logandale . . . . (702) 346-7215

Girl Scouts
1206 6th
Boulder City . . . .(702) 293-2336

Girl Scouts
310 W Pacific Ave
Henderson . . . . (702) 565-9018

Girl Scouts
4 Shaver Dr
Las Vegas . . . . (702) 643-9144

Girl Scouts
2530 Stewart Ave
Las Vegas . . . . (702) 385-3677

Inner City Games
233 S 4th St
Las Vegas . . . . (702) 382-5447

Las Vegas Recreation Div
821 Las Vegas Blvd N
Las Vegas . . . . (702) 229-2256

Las Vegas Youth Swimming Assn
633 S 4th St
Las Vegas . . . . (702) 385-7946

Mc Dowell Youth Homes Inc
2680 Chandler Ave
Las Vegas . . . . (702) 795-1077

Mirabelli Community Ctr
6200 Elton Ave
Las Vegas . . . . (702) 229-6359
Nike House Residential Ctr
4775 Pioneer Ave
Las Vegas . . . . (702) 871-5448
North Las Vegas Recreation Ctr
1638 N Bruce St
North Las V... . . . . (702) 633-1600
Project Youth
1201 Miller Ave
Las Vegas . . . . (702) 647-5800
Rafeal Riviera Community Ctr
2900 Stewart Ave
Las Vegas . . . . (702) 229-4600
Silver State Girls Soccer
1200 S Jones Blvd
Las Vegas . . . . (702) 259-0699
Southern Nevada Jr Golf Assn
3430 E Flamingo Rd
Las Vegas . . . . (702) 433-0626
Stupak Community Ctr
300 W Boston Ave
Las Vegas . . . . (702) 229-2488
Vegas West Youth Soccer League
8344 Spinnaker Cove Dr
Las Vegas . . . . (702) 228-0344
YMCA
4141 Meadows Ln
Las Vegas . . . . (702) 877-9622

Zoos & Preserves

Gilcrease Bird Preserve
8103 Racel St
Las Vegas . . . . (702) 645-4224
Southern Nevada Zoological
1775 N Rancho Dr
Las Vegas . . . . (702) 648-5955

Symbols

(IHOP). 147
2 R Riding Stables 136
5 n Diner 144

A

A Lake Mead Air 12
A. J. Hackett Bungy 46
ABC Fiesta Jumping Balloons 175
Action Adventure Watercraft Rentals 138
Actors Repertory Theatre 25
Advanced Marine Service & Transport 138
Adventure Canyon 46
Adventure Canyon Log Flume 46
Adventure Photo Tours 139
Adventuredome At Circus Circus 46, 155
Aeroexo 12
Aerolineas Argentinas 11
African American Museum 26, 43
Air Canada 11
Air Nevada 12
Alan Bible Visitor Center 134
Alaska Airlines 11
Alexander Villas Park 115
Alexis Park 166
All American Sport Park 101, 108, 173
All In One Balloons & Entertainment 175
All Star Cafe 144
All You Can Eat Buffet 144
Allegro Park 115
America Cafe 144
American Airlines 11
American Campgrounds 170
American Dance Company 24
American Superstars 94
American Trans Air 11
American West Airlines 11
Amtrak 11
An San Sister City Park 115
Angel Park 110
Angel Park Golf Club 105
Anglers Guide Service 114
Apple Annies 175
Applebee's 144
Arcades 45
Archery 102
Arizona Charlie's 142, 166
Arroyo Grande Sports Complex 115
Art Affair 41
Art Encounter 41
Art Galleries & Museums 41
Art Museums 43
Artemus Ham Hall 25
Ash Meadows National Wildlife Refuge 128
Astro Jump of Las Vegas 175
Atari© Adventure Arcade 45
Atlantis Fountain Show 46
August Entertainment 176

B

B. Dalton Bookseller 96
Badlands at Peccole Ranch Golf Club 105
Baker Park 110, 115
Bally's 110, 142, 166
Barbary Coast 166
Barnes & Noble 96
Baseball 100

Beckley School Park 115
Belz Factory Outlet Mall 124
Best Western Mardi Gras Inn 166
Big Kitchen Buffet 142
Big Shot 47, 81
Big West Football and Basketball 100
Bike Rentals and Tours 102, 103
Bike Trails 103
Binion's Horseshoe 166
Black Angus Restaurant 145
Black Canyon Raft Tour 137
Black Mountain Golf & Country Club 105
Blue Diamond Bicycles 103
Blue Diamond Buffet 144
Blue Diamond Library 98
Blue Diamond Park 115
Blueberry Hill Family Restaurant 145
Boat Doc 138
Bob Baskin Park 110, 115
BoBo & Precious 176
Bond Trailer Lodge 170
Bonnie & Clyde's "Death Car" 47
Bonnie Springs / Old Nevada 47, 128
Bonnie Springs Ranch Restaurant 145
Bonnie Springs Trail Rides 136
Book Warehouse 97
BookStar 97
Bookstores 96
Borders Book Shop 97
Boris Terrace Park 116
Botanical Park 75, 175
Boulder City Art Gallery 41
Boulder City Library 98
Boulder City Municipal Golf Course 105
Boulder City Museum 26
Boulder City Water Sports 135
Boulder Lakes RV Resort and Country Club . . 170
Boulder Station 142, 160, 166
Boulder Station Buffett 162
Boulder Station Cinemas 94
Boulder Theatre 94
Boulevard Mall 124
Bounces Plus 176
Bowling Centers 103
British Airways 11
Broadway Cabaret 94
Brooks Tot Lot 116
Brown Bag Concerts 24
Bruce Trent Park 110, 116
Bruno's Indian & Turquoise Museum 28
Buccaneer Bay Sea Battle 48
Buffalo Bill's Resort 142, 166
Buffet of Champions 143
Buffets 142
Bunker Family Park 110
Burger King Restaurants 173
Burkholder Jr. High 116
Bus 11

C

Cactus Garden 51
Cactus Jack's Wild West Tour Company 139
Cadillac Grille 145
Caesars Magical Empire 88, 165
Caesar's Palace 92, 142, 164, 166
Cakes 4 Kids 176
Calico Farms Pony Rides 176

index

California Hotel 166
Callaway Golf Center 105
Callville Bay Resort & Marina 138
Calvin Bay Marina Lake Mead 138
Canada 3000 11
Canadian Airlines 11
Cannon School Park 116
Canyon Blaster 81
Canyon Trail RV Park 170
Captain's Buffet 143
Car Rental Companies 14
Caricatures 157, 175
Carluccio's Restaurant 145
Carnival Midway 156
Carnival Of Critters 176
Carnival World Buffet. 143
Carrara Galleries 42
Carrow's Restaurant 145
Cashman School Park 116
CAT: Citizens Area Transit. 20
Cattleman's Buffet 142
Celebrate Kids 173
Central Telephone Co. 8
Century Desert 94
Chapala Mexican Restaurant 145
Charles Vanda Master Series 24
Charleston Heights Arts Center 42
Charleston Heights Park 116
Charlie the Clown 176
Charter Services 12
Chester Stupak Park 116
Chevy's Mexican Restaurant 145
Cheyenne Ridge Park 116
Cheyenne Sports Complex . . . . 110 ,116
Children's Discovery Trail 133
Children's Memorial Park 116
Chili's Bar & Grill 145
China Airlines 11
Chuck E. Cheese's Pizza 146
Cinedome 12, 95
Cinema 8 95
Cinema Ride 49
Circus Circus Buffet. 142
Circus Circus Hotel 142, 155
Circusland RV Park 170
City of Las Vegas Fire Department 49
City of Las Vegas Parks and Leisure 116
City of Las Vegas Public Libraries 97
City Phone Numbers 8
City View Park 116
Civic Center Park 116
Clark County Heritage Museum 28
Clark County Parks & Recreation 102, 112
Classic Kids Parties. 176
Clowns. 157, 175
Clowns Plus 176
Coca-Cola 88
Coleman Park 116
College Park 117
Colorado River Rafting Trips 137
Comedy Magic 89
Competition Grand Prix 49
Condor German Airlines 11
Contemporary Arts Collective 42
Continental. 66
Continental Airlines 11
Cottonwood Cove Resort & Marina 138,170

Country Inn 146
Cowboy George's 176
Cowboy Trail Rides 136
Coyote Cafe. 146
Cragin Park 117
Craig Ranch Golf Course 105
Cranberry World 49
Crocodile Cafe 146
Cruise Lake Mead 138
Crystal Palace Roller Rink 108, 173
Curfew Laws 6
Cyber Station 45

D

Dance 24
Dancing Bear Desserts & Novelties 76
Dandy the Clown 176
Dansey's Indoor Race Track 50, 173
Davis Dam 128
Davis Park 117
Dearing School Park 117
Death Valley National Monument 128
Delta Airlines 11
Desert Breeze 117
Desert Demonstration Gardens 29
Desert Inn (Sheraton) Hotel. 92, 110, 142, 166
Desert Inn Golf Club 106
Desert Inn Park 117
Desert Pines (Municipal) Golf Course 106
Desert Princess 138
Desert Rose Golf Course. 106
Desert Sands RV Park and Motel 170
Desert Storm Paintball Games 50
Desperado 82
Dexter Park 117
DiMartino's Your Neighborhood Italian Eatery . . 146
Discovery Park 111, 117
Discovery Zone 51, 173
Dive! 146
Dixie Dooley. 89
Dixie Pony Rides 176
Dolphin Habitat 51, 74
Dona Maria's 146
Donna Beam Fine Arts Gallery 42
Donoho's Guide Service 114
Doolittle Park 117
Down River Outfitters 138
Downhill Bicycle Tours Inc. 103

E

Eagle Canyon Airlines 12
Ed Fountain Park 118
EFX 93
El Cortez 166
Eldorado Park 118
Emperor's Buffet 143
Enterprise Library 98
Entertainment 88
Entertainment 4 All 176
Escape The City Streets Mountain Bike Tours . . 103
Escape The City Streets! Hiking Tours 140
Ethel M Chocolate Factory 51
Ethel Pearson Park 111, 118
Excalibur Hotel 92, 142, 159, 166
Excalibur Motion Machines 81

F

Face Painting 175, 160
Fantasy Faire 159
Fashion Show Mall 124
Favorite Brands International
    Marshmallow Factory 53
Feast Around the World 144
Festival Buffet 142
Festival Fountains 54
Fiesta Casino Hotel 142, 166
Finnnair 11
Fish, Inc. 114
Fishing and Hunting. 113
Fishing Boats 203
Fishing Charters and Guides. 114
Fitgeralds/Holiday Inn 142, 167
Fitzgerald Tot Lot 118
Flamingo Branch Library 98
Flamingo Hilton Hotel 92, 110, 142, 166
Flamingo Hilton Wildlife Habitat 86
Floyd Lamb State Park 103, 114
Flyaway Indoor Skydiving 55
Football 100
Forever Plaid 92
Formula K Family Fun Park 56
Forum Shops At Caesar's Palace 56, 125
Fountains Of Bellagio 57
Four Queens 167
Fox Ridge Park 118
Freddie G's Deli & Diner 146
Freedom Park 118
Fremont Hotel 142, 167
Fremont Street Experience 58
French Market Buffet. 144
Frontier Airlines 11
Frontier Hotel 111,142, 167
Fun House Express 59
Furr's Cafeterias 146

G

Galleria at Sunset 125
Gallery of History 29
GameWorks. 45, 60, 146, 173
Gandhi India. 147
Garden Club Buffet 143
Garlic Cafe 147
Gary Dexter Park 111
Get It Wet Watercraft 139
Gilcrease Nature Sanctuary 61
Glass Artistry 42
Gold Coast Bowling Center 103, 174
Gold Coast Buffet 142
Gold Coast Hotel 167
Gold Coast Twin 95
Gold Strike Buffet 142
Golden Nugget Buffet 142
Golden Nugget Hotel. 167
Golf Courses 105
Good Sam's Hitchin Post Camper Park 170
Grand Buffet 143
Grand Canyon -
    Colorado River Rafting Trips 137
Grand Canyon Flights 12
Grand Canyon National Park. 129
Grand Canyon Sightseeing 139
Grand Canyon Tour Company 139

Grape Street Cafe 147
Grapevine Canyon 134
Grapevine Springs Park 118
Gray Line Tours 139
Green Shack 147
Green Valley Cinemas 95
Green Valley Library 98
Green Valley Park 118
Green Valley Sculptures 43
Greyhound 11
Guided Hikes 135
Guinn Middle School 111
Guinness World of Records Museum 30

H

Hadland Park 118
Happy Days Diner 147
Hard Rock Cafe 31, 61,147
Hard Rock Hotel 167
Harrah's Hotel Las Vegas 89, 142, 167
Hartke Park 111, 118
Haunted Graveyard Run 57
Hawaiian Airlines 11
Hebert Memorial Park 118
Heers Park 118
Henderson Bird Preserve 61
Henderson Civic Symphony 24
Henderson Library 98
Henderson Water Department 8
Hidden Palms Park 111, 118
High Roller 61, 81
Highland Falls Golf Club 106
Hiking 132
Hill Top House Supper Club 147
Hills Park 111, 118
Historic Railroad Trail 134
Hockey 99
Holiday Inn Boardwalk 89, 92, 142, 167
Holiday Travel Trailer Park 170
Hoover Dam. 27, 129
Hoover Dam Museum 26
Horseback Riding & Wagon Adventures. 136
Hotel Shuttles 21
Hotels. 166
Houdini Theatre 91
Hungry Hunter 147
Huntridge Circle Park 119

I

Imagine: A Theatrical Odyssey 93
IMAX Theater. 62, 163
Imperial Palace 92, 143, 167
Imperial Palace Auto Collection 31
Imperial Palace Hotel. 167
In Search of the Obelisk 162
Indoor Arena Football 100
International House of Pancakes 147

J

J R Pony Parties 174
Jackson Hole Mountain Guides 135
James A. Gay III Park 111, 118
Jamm's Restaurant 147
Japan Airlines 11
Jaycee Park. 111, 119
Jeremiah's Steak House 147

index

Joe Knelp Park 111, 118
Joe Shoong Park 118
Joe's Crab Shack 147
Jr.'s Guide Service 114
Judes Ranch 32
Jugglers 160, 175

K

Kanyon Air 12
Karen Jones Fishing Guide 114
Keuken Dutch 148
Kid's Parties 173
Kid's Quest Child Care Center 161
King Air 12
King Arthur's Tournament 92, 159
King Tut's Tomb 32, 163
King's Row 170
KLM Airlines 11
KOA Campgrounds 170
Korean Air 11
Kyle Ranch 32

L

La Barca 148
La Piazza Food Court 148
Lacasa Airlines 11
Lady Luck Buffet 143
Lady Luck Casino & Hotel 89, 167
Lake Havasu 129
Lake Mead Hatchery 62
Lake Mead National Recreation Area
. . . . 27, 114, 130, 134, 135
Lake Mead Resort Marina 139
Lake Mohave 128
Lake Powell Air Service 12
Lakeshore Trailer Village 170
Lance Burton 90
Las Vegas Airlines 12
Las Vegas Area Parks 115
Las Vegas Art Museum 43
Las Vegas Civic Ballet 24
Las Vegas Club Hotel & Casino 41, 167
Las Vegas Dust Devils 99
Las Vegas Entertainment Productions 176
Las Vegas Factory Stores of America 125
Las Vegas Flash 100
Las Vegas Golf Club 106
Las Vegas Hilton Country Club 106
Las Vegas Hilton Hotel 111, 143, 167
Las Vegas Ice Gardens 109
Las Vegas Little Theatre 26
Las Vegas Motor Speedway 100
Las Vegas Natural History Museum 33
Las Vegas Paiute Golf Course 106
Las Vegas Racquet Club 111
Las Vegas Ski & Snowboard Resort 109
Las Vegas Sporting House 111
Las Vegas Stars 100
Las Vegas Sting 100
Las Vegas Thunder 99
Las Vegas Tour & Travel 140
Las Vegas Valley Bicycle Club 103
Las Vegas Valley Water District 8
Las Vegas Youth Orchestra 24
Laurelwood Park 112, 119
Lee Canyon Ski Area 109

Legacy Golf Club 107
Legends in Concert 92
Lewis Family Park 119
Liberace Museum 34
Libraries 97
Lied Discovery Children's Museum 36, 174
Lightning Bolt 80
Lindo Michoacan Mexican Restaurant 148
Lion Habitat 62
Little Falls Spring 133
Little League 102
London Bridge 129
Lone Mountain Buffet 143
Lone Star Steakhouse & Saloon 148
Lord of the Dance 93
Lords & Ladies 176
Lorenzi Park 112, 119
Lorenzi Park Pond 114
Los Cabos 148
Lost City Museum of Archaeology 37
Lost Creek 133
Lucky the Clown Show 176
Lufthansa 11
Luxor Hotel & Casino 93, 143, 162, 167
Luxor Imax Theatre 62
Luxor Live 45

M

M & M's World 63
Macayo Vegas 148
Magic 88, 175
Magic and Movie Hall of Fame 35
Magicians 88, 175
Magicians & Clowns & Co. 177
Main Street Station 143, 167
Manhattan Express 82
Marabelli Community Center 119, 174
Margarita Grille 148
Marie Callendar's Restaurant & Bakery 148
Marjorie Barrick Museum of Natural History . . . 38
Marshmallow the Clown & Company 177
Mary Dutton Park 119
Maslow Park and Pool 119
Masquerade Show in the Sky 64
Maverick Helicopter Tours 140
Maxim Buffet 143
Maxim Hotel 89, 167
McCarran Aviation Heritage Museum 38
McCarran International Airport 12, 66
McDonald's 174
Meadows Mall 126
Menagerie Carousel 66
Merlin's Magic Motion Machines 158
Metro Pizza 148
Mexicana Airlines 11
MGM Grand Adventures Theme Park 66, 152
MGM Grand Hotel 45, 93, 112, 143, 152, 167
MGM Grand Youth Activity Center 152
Michael Flatley's Lord of the Dance 93
Midway Airlines 11
Midway Games 158
Midwest Express 12
Mini Gran Prix 66
Mirabelli Park 119
Mirage Hotel 89, 143, 167
Miss Ashley's Buffet 142
Moenkopi 133

Mojave Ball Fields 120
Molly's Buffet. 142
Monte Carlo 143, 168
Monte Carlo Buffet 143
Monte Vista Park 120
Moonstruck Gallery 42
More Magic 91
Morrell Park 112, 120
Motown Café 67
Mount Charleston 131, 133
Mount Charleston Golf Resort. 107
Mount Charleston Library 98
Mount Charleston Riding Stable 136
Mount Charleston RV Site 170
Mountain T Ranch 136
Mountain View Park. 112, 120
Mountain View School Park 120
Mountasia Family Fun Center &
   Roller Rink 67, 109, 174
Movie Theaters 94
Museums & Historical Sites. 26
Music 24
Mutiny Bay 45
My Paint Box 174
Mystére 94
Mystic Falls Park 68, 80

N

Nellis Air Force Base 69
Nellis Meadows 103, 120
Nevada. 6
Nevada Chamber Symphony 24
Nevada Dance Theatre 24
Nevada Institute for Contemporary Art 42
Nevada Palace. 168
Nevada Palace VIP Travel Trailer Park 170
Nevada Power Co. 8
Nevada School of the Arts 25
Nevada State Museum and Historical Society . . 39
Nevada Symphony Orchestra 25
New Frontier Hotel 168
New West Theatre 26
New York - New York 93, 168
Nicholas E. Flores, Jr. Park 120
North Las Vegas Golf Course 107
North Las Vegas Parks & Recreation Dept 120
North Las Vegas Public Library 98
Northwest Airlines 11

O

Oasis Buffet 143
O'Callaghan Park. 112, 120
Old Las Vegas Fort 41
Old Nevada 47, 128
Olive Garden Italian Restaurant. 149
Omelet House 149
Omelet House & More 149
Omnimax Theater 69, 164
Original Pancake House 149
Orleans Hotel & Bowling Center 104, 144, 168
Orr Middle School 112
O'Shea's Casino 35, 91
Outback Steakhouse 149
Outdoor Adventure 127
Outdoor Sculpture Museum 43
Overton Town Park 120

P

Pacific Archery. 102
Pacific State Airlines 12
Painted Desert Country Club 107
Palace Station 143, 168
Palatium Buffet 142
Palm Valley Golf Club 107
Panini 149
Papillon Grand Canyon Helicopters 140
Paradise Buffet 142
Paradise Garden Buffet 142
Paradise Park 120
Paradise Park Community Center 112
Paradise Vista Park 120
Parkdale Park 120
Party Performers 175
Pasta Mia 149
Pasta Shop & Ristorante 149
Paul Meyer Park 112, 121
Pecos Legacy Park 112, 121
Peking Market 149
Performing Arts 24
Peter Piper Pizza 149, 174
Petitti Park 112, 121
Petroglyph Canyon 134
Pharaoh's Feast 143
Pick Up Stix 150
Pink Pony Cafe 150
Pioneer Territory Wagon Tours 137
Pizza Hut 150
Pizza Palace 150
Pizzeria Uno. 150
Planet Hollywood 70, 150
Planetarium 70
Plaza Hotel 168
Pocket Change 45
Pony Express. 177
Pony Parties 177
Pony Path Ranch. 177
Pony Rides. 177
Pop Warner Football 102
Potosi Park 121
Powerhouse Indoor Climbing Center 70
Primadonna Hotel & Resort. 143, 168
PrimaDonna Hotel RV Park 170
Prime Cable of Las Vegas 8
Primm Valley Golf Course 107
Primm Valley Resort 104
Prosperity Park 121
Pueblo Park 121

Q

Quality Inn - Key Largo 168
Quantas Airways 12
Quark's Bar & Restaurant 150

R

Race for Atlantis. 70
Rad Trax. 71
Rainbow Company Theatre. 26
Rainbow Family Park 121
Rainbow Library 98
Rainbow Promenade Theater. 95
Rancho-Sante Fe Theater 95
Recreation 99
Red Lobster 150

Red Robin Grill and Spirits 150
Red Rock Canyon National
   Conservation Area 103, 131, 133, 135
Redrock 11 Theaters 95
Redstone 134
Regal Gallery 43
Regional Park. 121
Reno Air 12
Reserve Hotel 168
Rhodes Ranch Golf Course. 107
Ricardo's Mexican Restaurant 150
Richard Walpole Rec. Area 121
Richard Tam Park 121
Rick Thomas 91
Rim Runner 81
Rim Trail System 103
Rio Secco Golf Club 108
Rio Suite Hotel & Casino 143, 168
Ristorante de Fiori Buffet. 143
River Mountain Hiking Trail 134
River Mountain Park 121
Riviera Hotel 112, 143, 168
Riviera Travel Trailer Park 171
Road Runner RV Park 171
Roadhouse Grill 150
Robert E. Lake School Park 121
Rock Climbing 135
Rocks and Ropes 71
Roller Hockey 141
Romano's Macaroni Grill 151
Ron Lee's World of Clowns 41, 87
Rotary Park 121
Rotary Tot Lot 121
Round Table Pizza 151
Roundtable Buffet 142
Royal Hotel 168
RV Parks and Campgrounds 170

S

Sahara Hotel 71, 143, 168
Sahara Ice Palace 109
Sahara Speedworld 71
Sahara West Library 98
Sam Boyd's California Hotel and RV Park 171
Sam's Town Bowling Center. 104
Sam's Town Hotel 68, 143, 168
Sam's Town RV Park - Boulder 171
Sam's Town RV Park - Nellis 171
San Remo Hotel 90, 94, 143, 168
Sante Fe Bowling Center. 104
Santa Fe Hotel 168
Santa Fe Hotel Ice Arena. 109, 175
Saturn of West Sahara 72
Scandia Family Fun Center. 73
Scenic Airlines 12
Scenic Loop. 103
Searchlight Library. 98
Secret Garden of Siegfried & Roy 74
Shadow Rock Park 121
Shopping 124
Showboat Hotel 143, 169
Showboat Hotel Bowling Center 104
Showcase Cinema 95
Showcase Mall 74
Siegfried & Roy 89
Sierra Club 135
Sierra Winds. 25

Sightseeing Tours Unlimited 140
Silver Bowl Sports Complex 102, 121
Silver Nugget Bowling Center 104
Silver Nugget Casino and RV Park 171
Silver Springs Park 103, 112, 121
Silver State "Old West" Tours 137
Silverton Hotel 144, 169
Singapore Airlines 11
Sizzler. 151
Skating 108
Sky Screamer 75, 80
Skyline Buffet. 144
Skyline Casino 144
Sky's The Limit 135
Skyscreamer 75, 80, 153
Skywest-Delta Connection 12
Slot Car City 75
Snow Skiing. 109
Soccer 100
South Meadows Park 122
Southern Nevada Community
   Concert Association 25
Southern Nevada Musical Arts Society. 25
Southern Nevada Zoological-Botanical Park . . . 75
Southwest Airlines 12
Southwest Gas Corporation 8
Spectator Sports 99
Spellbound 89
Spence Tumble Bus 175
Sports and Recreation. 99
Sports Hall-of-Fame. 271
Spring Mountain Ranch. 132
Spring Mountain State Park 26
Spring Valley Library 99
Spring Valley Park 122
Star Trek: The Experience 76
Stardust Hotel 144, 168
State And National Parks 128
Sternwheeler 138
Steve Wyrick 89
Steve-N-Kids 177
Stewart Place Park 122
Stiltwalking 175
Stratosphere Buffet 144
Stratosphere Hotel and Casino 94, 168
Stratosphere Tower 78, 126
Streamers 177
Strings Italian Cafe 151
Strip Trolley 20
Studio Walk Arcade 153
Submarine Race 57
Sue-Z-Q-Rides & Expo 177
Summerlin Library and Performing Arts 99
Sunrise Children's Hospital 80
Sunrise Community Center 112
Sunrise Dollar 751 Cinema 95
Sunrise Library 99
Sunrise Park 112, 122
Sunrise RV Park 171
Sunset Lanes. 104
Sunset Park 102, 122
Sunset Park Pond 114
Sunset Stampede 68, 80
Sunset Station 144, 169
Sunset Station Cinemas 96
Sunset Tennis Club 113

Super Shots Arcade 26
Super Summer Theatre 26
Surf Buffet 142

T

Taca Airlines 12
Tate School Park 122
Tennis 110
Terrace Point Buffet 142
Terrible Mike's 151
Terrible's Town Casino & Bowl 104
Texas 12 Cinemas 96
Texas Station 144, 168
TGI Friday's 151
That's Magic 91
The Buffet 144
The Dream King 92
The Egg & I 146
The Feast 143
The Feast Buffet 142
The Great Buffet 143
The Greens Buffet 143
The Hush Puppy 147
The Mirage Buffet 143
The Orleans 168
The Walker Foundation 26, 43
Theaters............................ 25, 94
Thirstbusters 151
Thomas School Park 122
Thrill Rides........................... 80
Thrillseekers Unlimited 109, 135
Thunderbirds 69
Thurman White School Park 113, 122
Tiger Habitat 80
Titanium Field 122
Toiyabe National Forest................ 131
Tom Williams Park 122
Tom's Water Sports Charter 139
Tonopah Park 139
Tony Roma's 151
Torrey Pines Discount Cinema 96
Tours & Excursions 139
Tower Shops at Stratosphere 126
Train................................. 11
Trans World Airlines 12
Treasure Island 94, 144, 169
Treasure Island Buffet 144
Tristar Airlines 12
Tropicana Resort and Casino 91, 144, 169
Tule Springs.......................... 129
Turbo Drop.......................... 80, 82
Tuscany Grill 151

U

Ullom School Park 122
Ultrazone........................... 83, 175
United Airlines 12
United States Post Office 83
UNLV................................ 113
USAir 12
Utility Companies 8

V

Vacation Village 169

Valentine Vox 35, 91
Valley of Fire 132, 134
Valley View Park 122
Vegas 4 Drive-In Theatre................ 96
Vegas Chip Factory 83
Vegas Heights Tot Lot 123
Veterans Art Museum................... 43
Volcano 83

W

Wagon Wheel Buffet 144
Waldenbooks.......................... 97
Walker Park 123
Warehouse Buffet 144
Warm Springs Softball complex 123
Water Activities 137
Wayne Bunker Family Park 123
Weather.............................. 6
Wells Park 113, 123
West Charleston Library 99
West Charleston Lion Park 123
West Las Vegas Library 99
Western Hotel/Casino.................. 169
Western Pacific Airlines............... 12
Westward Ho Hotel 144, 169
Wet ën Wild 84
Whiskey Pete's 144, 169
White Rock Spring 133
White Tiger Habitat 85
Whitney Community Center............. 113
Whitney Library 99
Whitney Park 123
Wild West Buffet 142
Wildhorse Country Club 108, 113
Wildlife Habitat 86
Wildlife Walk 87
Wildwood Park 123
Willow Beach 137
Winchester Community Center.......... 113
Winchester Park...................... 123
Winterwood Park 113, 124
Wizard's Arcade...................... 159
Woofter Family Park 124
World of Clowns...................... 41, 87
World of Coca-Cola.................... 88
World Of The Unreal Magic Show 89
World's Fare Buffet 143

Y

YMCA 113
Youth Center Park 124
Youth Sports 102

Z

Zoo 75, 175

order form

For additional information about ordering, obtaining bulk order discounts or any information regarding *101 Things for Kids in New Orleans* or other upcoming titles please call or write:

Questions?
Journey Publications
2920 Kingman Street, Suite 202
Metairie, LA 70006
(504) 454-7702

To place an order for *101 Things For Kids in New Orleans* or *101 Things For Kids in Las Vegas*

Orders
Call 1-800-247-6553
24 hours a day — 7 days a week
Major credit cards acccepted

Or send a check or money order in the amount of $12.95 + $3.50 shipping for each title to:

Book Masters
P.O. Box 388
Ashland, OH 44805

Name: _____

Address: _____

City, State, Zip: _____

Credit Card Type: _____

Credit Card Number: _____

Expiration Date: _____

Ship To: _____

Address: _____

City, State, Zip: _____

Please indicate which book _____*101 Things For Kids in New Orleans*
_____*101 Things For Kids in Las Vegas*

QUESTIONS: **(504) 454-7702**

For additional information about ordering, obtaining bulk order discounts or any information regarding *101 Things for Kids in New Orleans* or other upcoming titles please call or write:

Questions?
Journey Publications
2920 Kingman Street, Suite 202
Metairie, LA 70006
(504) 454-7702

To place an order for ***101 Things For Kids in New Orleans*** or
101 Things For Kids in Las Vegas (after January 1, 1999)

Orders
Call 1-800-247-6553
24 hours a day — 7 days a week
Major credit cards acccepted

Or send a check or money order in the amount of $12.95 + $3.50 shipping for each title to:

Book Masters
P.O. Box 388
Ashland, OH 44805

Name: _____

Address: _____

City, State, Zip: _____

Credit Card Type: _____

Credit Card Number: _____

Expiration Date: _____

Ship To: _____

Address: _____

City, State, Zip: _____

Please indicate which book _____*101 Things For Kids in New Orleans*
_____*101 Things For Kids in Las Vegas*

QUESTIONS: **(504) 454-7702**

order form

For additional information about ordering, obtaining bulk order discounts or any information regarding *101 Things for Kids in New Orleans* or other upcoming titles please call or write:

Questions?
Journey Publications
2920 Kingman Street, Suite 202
Metairie, LA 70006
(504) 454-7702

To place an order for *101 Things For Kids in New Orleans* or *101 Things For Kids in Las Vegas*

Orders
Call 1-800-247-6553
24 hours a day — 7 days a week
Major credit cards accepted

Or send a check or money order in the amount of $12.95 + $3.50 shipping for each title to:

Book Masters
P.O. Box 388
Ashland, OH 44805

Name: _____

Address: _____

City, State, Zip: _____

Credit Card Type: _____

Credit Card Number: _____

Expiration Date: _____

Ship To: _____

Address: _____

City, State, Zip: _____

Please indicate which book _____*101 Things For Kids in New Orleans*
_____*101 Things For Kids in Las Vegas*

QUESTIONS: **(504) 454-7702**